The
Celtic Church

Origins and Growth

Rewarding Learning

COLOURPOINT
EDUCATIONAL

Anne Hughes

First Edition
Third Impression, 2014

© Anne Hughes and Colourpoint Books
   2008

Designed by: Colourpoint Books, Newtownards
Printed by: GPS Colour Graphics Ltd, Belfast

ISBN: 978 1 904242 92 5

Except where otherwise stated, the Scripture quotations contained herein are from The New International Version.

Cover picture: iStockphoto.com

COLOURPOINT
EDUCATIONAL

Colourpoint Educational
An imprint of Colourpoint Creative Ltd
Colourpoint House
Jubilee Business Park
21 Jubilee Road
Newtownards
County Down
Northern Ireland
BT23 4YH

Tel: 028 9182 6339
Fax: 028 9182 1900
E-mail: info@colourpoint.co.uk
Web site: www.colourpointeducational.com

The author

Anne Hughes

Anne Hughes has been a Religious Education teacher for seventeen years. She is Assistant Head of Department in Our Lady and Saint Patrick's College, Belfast. She has been involved in the examining of CCEA's A Level Religious Studies for fifteen years. She is married to Gerry and they live in Belfast with their three children Rónán, Éile and Tiarnán.

For Gerry, Rónán, Éile and Tiarnán. I dedicate this book to them.

Contents

Author Preface

This text has been specifically written to help both teachers and students meet the requirements of CCEA's GCE Religious Studies AS and A2 courses on the Origins and Development of the Celtic Church. The first section of the book addresses the AS course, 'The Origins of the Celtic Church in Ireland and the beginnings of its Missionary Outreach'. This section also specifically addresses CCEA's requirement to explore 'Other aspects of human experience'. Some advice has been given and a range of suggestions made in relation to this, throughout the text. The second section deals with the A2 course, 'The development and impact of the Celtic Church in the 5th, 6th and 7th centuries.'

This book is essentially a collation of the work of a wide range of theologians and historians (ecclesiastical and other), such as Kenney, Bieler, Chadwick, Duffy, O'Loughlin, Ó Cróinín and Thomas to name but a few. Every attempt has been made to acknowledge sources and opinions in both the main body of the text and in the endnotes. Students are advised to pay attention to endnotes when referring to the views of scholars in their own work.

I extend my thanks to a number of people whose support was invaluable in the writing of this book. Thanks to Donna Finlay (CCEA) and Colourpoint Books for giving me the opportunity to write this textbook. Thanks as well to Sheila Johnston and the editors at Colourpoint for the benefit of their expertise and professional advice: Julie Trouton, Michael Collins and Una McCann. I would also like to thank Dominic Kealey (Our Lady and Saint Patrick's College) for the encouragement he gave me in undertaking this project; Sister Bríghid Vallely for her valuable advice and Juliana Gilbride for her patience and reassurance during many hours of conversation throughout the writing of this book. I am also grateful to the staff of Newtownbreda Library for their hard work in tracking down many, and often difficult-to-source books, and to Monsignor Richard Mohan, Prior of Lough Derg, for his kind permission to include photographs of Lough Derg in this book. Thanks too, to Peter Kane (Our Lady and Saint Patrick's College, Belfast) for the benefit of his expertise in the Irish language.

I owe particular thanks to Cathal O'Connor (Saint Michael's Grammar School, Enniskillen), who has been very generous in the extensive gift of his time in the proofing of this book. He was unstinting in the commitment he gave to the reading of each chapter, and his positive and helpful suggestions have done much to improve the readability of the book. It would not have been possible to complete the book without his input and moral support. I am also very appreciative of Cathal's kind donation of photographs, which can be seen throughout the book.

I would also like to thank my students, past and present, whose work on the application of the taught course to 'other aspects of humans experience' has done much to inspire and inform my own ideas. I thank in particular Gemma Doherty, Elizabeth Bogue, Adam McMaster, Aishling Mageean, Sarah Hawkins and Paul Conlon for their kind permission to reproduce extracts of their work in this book.

Very special thanks to my family; my husband Gerry for his support and patience with a wife who was often distracted or preoccupied; to my children Rónán, Éile and not least Tiarnán, whose timely birth christened section 2 of the book! I am grateful for their tolerance (and sometimes not!) of a busy mum who seemed permanently attached to a computer.

Anne Hughes, August 2008

A note on how to use this book

This book is intended primarily as a pupil text. It should be used with teacher guidance. I have included a large number of viewpoints and opinions of scholars throughout the book. That is not to say that students would be expected to include all of these in any exam response offered. You should be selective of the views you include but also try to reflect a range of opinion. Avoid just 'listing' these in any answer. Use them to support or challenge arguments you are making.

A selection of tasks has been included throughout. These include individual, group and whole class work. Some of these are 'processing' tasks – suggesting some of the ways in which you might think about issues as a topic progresses. Other tasks are 'summative', where you are asked to show your knowledge and understanding at the end of a topic. These appear as essay titles in each chapter.

Suggestions have also been made as to how you might apply the taught course to other aspects of human experience. These are primarily intended to provide stimuli for you to come up with your own ideas. You should not take these suggestions to be a recommended 'answer' plan to the second part of Section B essays.

At the end of each chapter, I have included a summary of the main points, arguments and ideas in each topic and/or learning outcome. These can also be used to check your knowledge and understanding of topics covered, or as a revision checklist.

Chapter 1

The background to the mission of Patrick

LEARNING OUTCOMES

Knowledge, understanding and evaluation of:

— the social, political and religious background to the arrival of Patrick

— the arrival and presence of Christianity in Ireland before Patrick

— the historical sources for Christianity in Ireland before Patrick

— Palladius

INTRODUCTION

A study of the world which Patrick came from, and indeed the reality into which he came, is crucial for both an understanding of his writings and his mission.

The tension of the contrast between those two realities provide a backdrop to the mission and writings of Patrick, and indeed presented to him a challenge, which had to be surmounted if he were to succeed, or even survive in the fifth century society in which he found himself. Only when we fully understand his cultural and historical context, can we come to know and understand Patrick the man, Patrick the writer, and Patrick the missionary.

Patrick was essentially a citizen of the Roman Empire. Two thousand years ago the world was ruled by Rome and the Empire stretched from England to Africa and from Syria to Spain. The city of Rome was its heart. Almost one in four people on the earth lived in the Empire. This was the world that Patrick inhabited.

1. THE BRITAIN PATRICK CAME FROM – ITS SOCIAL, POLITICAL AND RELIGIOUS MAKE-UP

Roman Britain (c AD43–410) probably comprised England and Wales. There is little evidence to suggest that the far North of Britain had been Romanised.[1] Indeed, walls were built to surround and protect the Empire from the Celtic tribes, which remained unconquered by Rome. Hadrian's Wall was built around 230 from the Tyne to the Solway Firth, and the wall of Antoninus Pius (140s) extended from the Forth to the Clyde. Although attacks and incursions from the unconquered peoples were no doubt frequent, these were largely contained by garrisoned forts all connected by an elaborate system of roads.

So, what was life like for citizens of Britain when they became part of the Empire? Rome's contribution was unity and order, common identity, prosperity and peace, the great '*Pax Romana*'.

Towns

Firstly, it is important to point out that towns were growing up. Archaeological evidence suggests that spacious houses, baths and schools were all provided in the towns. The towns were walled to keep out beasts, criminals and barbarians, and to control traffic into and out of them.

Romans firmly believed that towns went with civilisation, and in order to civilise the masses, they often populated the towns with ex-soldiers who would be good role models for the untamed Britons. The excavated Roman town of Silchester gives testament to the splendid architectural and engineering abilities of the Romans. It is likely that the Britons were given money and engineers to help them design and build streets, roads, bridges and aqueducts, and of course, the quintessentially Roman arch. Charles Thomas argues, indeed, that in terms of the civilising effects of the Empire "innovations were primarily urban".[2]

Life on the rural farmsteads was probably less fundamentally altered by the invasion of the Romans. Thomas further argues that it was actually the south-eastern part of Britain which underwent the most "profound and effective Romanisation".[3] Patrick is thought to have come from an urban part of the area of Britain, which had been fairly effectively Romanised.

Law

All Roman citizens were subject to Roman law. Roman law was designed with the same intricacy as the towns, roads and aqueducts. Like these, it was designed to go on working for a long time and for this reason elaborate codes of law were created, which had fairness and clarity at their core.

Roman justice was central to the smooth running of the Empire. Its code of law governed many everyday practices regardless of what the native practices of these peoples had been. In 212 the Emperor Caracalla made all freemen resident in the Empire, Roman citizens. All freemen were now equal in law. Although there is little doubt that Roman society was stratified, any person who displayed loyalty to Rome, could effectively become a citizen. Living in the Empire, however, came at a price for its citizens; taxes were high.

The Latin language

The Romans brought with them their language. Most historians agree that the spoken language of Britain was a Celtic tongue, 'British'. Kenneth Jackson believes it was spoken "from Penzance to Edinburgh".[4] After invasion by the Empire, Roman Britain might well have been a bilingual province. Hamp, however, presents "evidence, in short, for a gradient of speech varieties which probably matched a spectrum of social groups and situations".[5]

Charles Thomas argues that while British was probably the spoken language, "only Latin was both spoken and written".[6] Rivet and Smith point out that there may have been the practice of writing British words in Latin characters.[7]

Nonetheless, Latin would have been the language in which government, law and religion would have been practised. While Patrick probably knew and spoke British, he would also have been familiar with Latin as the official language of the province of Britain. One or all of the above could account, at least in part, for the much debated style of Patrick's Latin.

Christianity

Roman Britain would have been influenced by the practice of religion brought by their invaders. John T McNeill argues "that we cannot know how or when Christianity first appeared in Britain".[8] Gildas[8a] seems sure that the practice of Christianity came to Britain during the time of the Emperor Tiberius in the early first century AD. Acts of the Apostles tells us "they that were scattered abroad went everywhere preaching the word" (Acts 8:4).

Reliable source material on the arrival and practice of the Christian faith in Britain is very scarce, but it is probable that it did arrive and grow within the environment of the many Roman settlements. Some argue that Rome's organised religion did have a profound impact on Britain.

Others, such as John Chandler, believe that the inhabitants of Roman Britain might well have been 'nominal Christians', who believed in principle and perhaps practised publicly when the need arose, but without any real consistency or sincerity.[9] This may be one reason for the religious apathy displayed by Patrick (*Confessio* 1). Most accept however that there was an established Church in Britain, from at least the time of Constantine onwards. Charles Thomas is sure there were a reasonable number of bishops in the fourth century British Church and that "by 313, the structure of Christianity throughout the Empire was uniform".[10]

In the towns at least, Christianity was quite well established with urban churches and fully developed dioceses in the fourth century. McNeill agrees that during times of stability in the Empire, there must have been positive growth for the Christian Church in Britain and he accepts the 'boast' of Tertullian that "in the regions of the Britons beyond Roman sway but subjected to Christ ... the name of Christ now reigns".[11] The growth of the Christian faith then, was one clear consequence of the Roman occupation of Britain.

The fall of the Empire

In spite of all this, critical to any understanding of the Britain Patrick came from, is the slow but sure disintegration of the Empire. Many reasons have been suggested for the collapse of the Empire. It may have been that the seeds of its destruction lay within itself, its might, sheer size, its slave-based economy, its increasingly burdensome taxation system, all contributing to its final demise.

Increased weakening gave rise to barbarian attacks all over the Empire. It became vitally important to defend Rome itself, so more and more troops were withdrawn from the frontiers of Britain. As Corish points out, "during Saint Patrick's lifetime the world seemed to be falling into ruin ... [The] greatest political organisation which had ever been known seemed to be broken beyond hope of recovery".[12]

What happened?

In 395 Emperor Theodosius died without leaving a viable successor and barbarian tribes began to decimate Italy; by the year 400 little could be done to check their advance.

- In 407, the Vandals sacked Gaul.

- However, it was the events of 410 which were to really rock the Empire. The hitherto unthinkable happened, when the Goths invaded Rome and pillaged the city for three days. This, for most of the inhabitants of the Empire, was a sign that the end of the world was surely near. This idea is echoed throughout the *Confessio* of Patrick. (See Chapter 2.)

- After this, the disintegration of the Empire in the West was rapid. By 410–11, Charles Thomas argues Britain had undergone "a series of events and political changes that rendered it outside the control of the Emperors of the West".[13] It seems that a significant number of troops had been withdrawn from Britain by 401 and again in 407.

- Gildas tells us of wars 'internal' and 'external', the latter possibly referring to the invasion of the Angles and the Saxons (Germanic peoples). The Irish raiders and invaders were no doubt also a threat. Gildas, an important source for this period in Britain's history, tells us that at this stage Britain had twenty-eight cities. It may have been that town life in some areas continued with little effect, but certainly unpaid soldiers and hitherto contented townspeople in other areas seem to have mutinied, and the agrarian economy was on the point of collapse.

Corish fittingly comments that "the world in which [Gildas] lived gives us ... a great deal of information about Saint Patrick".[14] Thomas Finan agrees: "out of such dark times did Patrick write. In a world breaking down, where an ancient civilisation was in decline ... where an already ancient Christianity was being overrun by the resurgent heathen".[15] Indeed, this backdrop is crucial to an understanding of his mission and writings. By 476 the great Roman Empire had effectively collapsed.

 TASK

Identify the main advantages and disadvantages that came with living in the Roman Empire.

2. THE IRELAND PATRICK CAME TO – ITS SOCIAL AND POLITICAL MAKE UP
Who were the Celts?

Most historians use the word 'Celt' to refer to an identifiable people who spoke a common group of six or so languages deemed to be 'Celtic', rather than an easily identifiable race as such. Nonetheless, some observers do identify some characteristics shared in common among Celtic tribal peoples. McNeill argues that the Celts were "essentially a single people" with racial characteristics in common, for example, "bodily stature, facial features, clothing and war gear, religion, habits and temperament".[16] Powell agrees: "the term Celt ... should not necessarily be restricted to mean Celtic-speaking, which is a concept of academic thought of quite modern times".[17] Although a powerful force in Europe from about 1000BC when the first Celtic expansion began, the Celts as a tribal force were largely subsumed into the growing Roman Empire. The conquest of Gaul during which the Celts were submerged occurred in 51BC. The conquest was led by Julius Caesar who felt that the Celts were "too much given to faction" to retain a strong identity within the Empire. Ireland, however, lying as it did outside the realm of the Empire, essentially remained one of the final outposts of Celtic culture.

We have little concrete information about the precise condition of the Ireland Patrick arrived in. Archaeological evidence can give us some insight but the written sources which we have available to us are chiefly from a later period. This is really the era of pre-history, although many scholars now assume that later written sources do reflect the practices that would have been current in Ireland in the fifth century.

Political and social structure

The population of Ireland at this time would have been certainly no more than half a million. Binchy's classification of Celtic society at this time is most useful. He defines it as "tribal, rural, hierarchical and familiar".[18] Each of these deserves to be dealt with in turn.

(a) Celtic society was **tribal** in that the country was decentralised, with no high king (there is no record of a high king in Ireland until as late as the eighth century).

- It was divided up into around 150 small kingdoms or *tuatha*,[19] which Ó Cróinín calls "a myriad of small tribal kingdoms, each separate and independent, and each ruled by its own king". The term given to this grade of king in the law tracts is *rí*.

- A distinction was made in Irish law between a minor king and an over-king. The over-king was probably the representative of a number of *tuatha* which had joined together to form an alliance or confederation, probably necessitated by the constant battling of one petty kingdom against another and the general strife characteristic of the period. Such a practice provided protection for vulnerable petty kingdoms.

- It is important to note that in terms of law the over-king really had no rights superior to that of the petty king. Individual *tuatha* retained their independent status in law, although they were obliged to pay tribute to the over-king. The only *tuatha* exempt from tribute were those whose own kings shared the dynasty of the over-king. Francis Byrne points out that "all sub-king[s] ... acknowledged their inferior status by receiving gifts (*tuarastal* or 'wages') from the over-king".[20]

- In royal families, each member of the king's *deirbfhine* (up to four generations of family on the male line) could be elected as king. Sometimes a *tánaise ríg*, which was really an heir apparent, could be chosen in a reigning king's lifetime to avoid dispute over succession.

- The role of the king was primarily to lead his people in times of war and to represent them in times of peace.

- Although he sometimes settled disputes in his kingdom, he was not a judge and could not legislate in the sense of making laws. He was essentially a figurehead. He was bound, in an almost sacred sense, to his people. Some seventh century documents refer to the king "as the embodiment of his people's luck and prosperity".[21]

- Inauguration rites of kings often took place in sacred places where the ceremony involved a ritualistic 'mating' with the pagan goddess. Indeed, Liam de Paor points out that the "inauguration of the king of Tara was a symbolic mating

(feis) with the goddess"(Medb).[22] He goes on to argue that "prehistoric kingship
... was intimately connected with pagan beliefs and customs".[23]

(b) Celtic society was also **rural** in the sense that there were no towns and cities.

• Most dwellings were isolated farmsteads dotted sporadically across a country,
  which was heavily forested.

• There was a complete absence of any communication network. For the ordinary
  commoner, travel between homestead and homestead would have been difficult,
  across mountain, bog or through forest.

• The most common dwelling was probably a ring fort or *ráth*. These were usually
  enclosed by earthen banks, surrounded by a ditch and were approximately
  30–40 metres in diameter. These dwellings were usually made with wattle and
  daub, but stone may have been used in the southwest where wood would have
  been scarce. Some 30,000 or so remains of these have been found throughout
  Ireland. Some also contained a *souterain* or underground passage. These may have
  been for the cool storage of food, or as safe hiding places in the face of an enemy
  attack.

• The *Crannóg* or lake dwelling was also common. These were artificial islands in
  the centre of a bog or lake, constructed from layers of peat and brushwood built
  on a foundation of logs. The *crannóg* dwellings were a kind of wickerwork house,
  round, oval or rectangular in shape, which were surrounded by a barrier of
  vertical logs. These dwellings may have been perceived as being safer, but they
  were no safeguard against the damp.

• There is little doubt that kings and noblemen had grander dwellings. Indeed,
  Brehon Law (see p16) required that the king's house should be doubly
  ramparted. These were sometimes referred to as a *dún* (fortress) and may have
  been surrounded by two or more earthen banks with a ditch separating them.
  These tended to be built in more easily defensible locations, perhaps on a cliff-
  top or mountainside. In this sense they were hill forts rather than simple ring
  forts. In the southwest, where stone would have been more commonly used,
  some of the walls surrounding these hill forts were up to thirteen feet thick
  enclosing an area of up to ninety metres in diameter. Again the isolation of
  these individual dwellings, as they have been found or excavated, is testament
  to the rural nature of early Celtic society.

(c) Celtic society was fairly rigidly stratified or **hierarchical** in nature. It is possible
  to uncover four tiers of social structure.[24]

• At the top of the hierarchy is the king, followed by nobles. The interesting thing
  about the stratification of Celtic society was that social mobility was possible.
  This is illustrated in the old Irish maxim *"Is ferr fer a chiniud"* which really
  meant that a man was better than his birth.[25] Rank was determined by one's

```
                    KING
                  NOBLES
               (nemed means
             privileged) two grades:
            druids, Brehons, poets;
          'Base nemed' physicians,
       blacksmiths, harpists, carpenters
                 FREEMAN
        majority of the adult male population,
    Two categories of farmer: the ócaire and the bóaire.
    These were 'small' and 'strong' farmers respectively
                 THE UNFREE
   dóer, one who has no honour price because he has no land– two types:
  Those who can leave their master by giving two thirds of their produce
              Those who cannot – serfs (slaves)
```

birth but also one's wealth. It was possible to rise and fall in status and learning was also a qualification for rank. The noble classes comprised the druids, the Brehons and the poets.

- Beneath the nobles in status were the freemen. Francis Byrne points out that "all freemen were landowning."[26] The *bóaire* seems to have been the highest grade of landowning freeman. Wealth was measured in terms of ownership of land (*cumal*) and cattle (the *bóaire* would have had land to the value of 63 milch cows). The home of the *bóaire* is described in the *Crith Gablach* (a legal poem from the seventh century):

"All the furniture of his house is in its proper place … work tools for every season … a fire always alive, a candle on the candlestick without fail … he owns seven houses: a kiln, a barn, a mill, a house of twenty-seven feet, an outhouse of seventeen feet, a pig-sty, a pen for calves, a sheep pen. He and his wife have four suits of clothes." [27]

The *ócaire* were smaller farmers with a lower honour price. Those who had a trade were also considered free, for example, smiths and harpers were free as were physicians.

- The unfree classes largely comprised the slaves, captured on various raids as Patrick himself was. The unfree class were not only the slaves, but also those without land or trade; these would have included the labourer, herdsman, those who squatted on waste ground and of course, the outlaw or fugitive. These people did not have the legal rights of the free, and the fugitive or *fudir* were particularly unwelcome in any *tuath*.

- It is important to note that in Celtic Ireland at this time, one did not have any rights outside one's own *tuath* and was not free to travel, unless special permission had been granted. This will become important later when a study of Patrick's writings will illustrate how his mission was affected by this practice. Soldiers were usually on guard at the areas which marked the boundary of each *tuath*. Some people were however allowed freedom of the 'highways'. The *áes dána* (people of poetry) were members of the learned class, which was made up of poets, historians, craftsmen of particular skill, historians, physicians, the harpist and the lawyer. All of these could travel freely, as could the druid. The *Táin Bó* (The Cattle Raid of Cooley) tells us that: "Each of Ulster's heroic warriors, had his day … to take care of every man who came that way with poetry, and to fight any others."[28]

- As Byrne points out, "a man's status was expressed in very material terms by his *eneclann* or 'honour-price'".[29] A man could only make a bargain or a contract to the value of his honour price and any damages owed to him were assessed on the basis on that honour price, according to Brehon law. The highest grade of nobleman had twenty *sét(s)* as his honour price, which was the maximum he could pledge and which he had to be able to pay if necessity demanded.[30] It is important to note that the conditions of inter-relationships between the various social groups in Ireland at this time was dictated by the complex Brehon law, which will be dealt with on p16.

(d) Finally, Ireland was a **familiar** society essentially based on membership of the family group.

- The individual did not have legal rights as such and his or her rights were determined by membership of the family group.
- A family was responsible for the misdeeds and crimes of its members and was also duty bound to vengeance for the abuse of the rights of anyone within the family group.
- In the case of the murder of a family member, the clan were duty bound to seek blood vengeance. In reality, a payment of blood money or *éraic* from the slayer was often given and accepted. If the individual concerned did not pay the *éraic*, again his family were liable.
- Brehon law outlines the structure of the family group. It was this group who essentially owned the *fintiu* or family land.
- In the law tracts *deirbfhine* seems to refer to four generations who shared a common great-grandfather.
- Land tended to be shared equally among brothers on inheritance, and although women could not directly inherit land, they were entitled to a life stake in their father's land.
- The killing of a member of one's own family was considered to be the worst of crimes. No legal vengeance or compensation could possibly eradicate this as a crime.

Customs and laws in Celtic society

The Brehon Laws were a fairly comprehensive body of law tracts, which somehow seem to have ensured some sort of cultural unity in decentralised and rural Ireland. They also give us remarkable insight into the cultural practices of the Celtic people of Ireland in the time period with which we are concerned. They seem to have covered almost every aspect of daily life and laid down the precepts of what was deemed to be acceptable and appropriate behaviour. Kathleen Hughes identifies kin (family) and status as two basic principles on which Brehon law is based.[31] These principles have been dealt with earlier. However, the Brehon laws also illustrate the complexity of interpersonal relationships in early Celtic society. Ó Cróinín points out that there were, "no crimes against society as such … only injuries done by individuals to other individuals".[32] The Brehon laws cover a vastly diverse range of topics. We see in the fines imposed for everything from bee stings (graded according to the part of body affected), to the articles of clothing considered appropriate for a child to have. It would be inappropriate to go through all and each of the precepts laid down by Brehon law here, so we will select a few of the more relevant.

Sureties or guarantees

The law was based on an elaborate system of sureties or guarantees, which were essentially sets of obligations to another person, which were guaranteed by a third party to ensure the implementation of a legal contract. However a man could not go surety for a person of higher rank than himself, as he would not have enough property to fulfil the guarantee should there be a default. In *Confessio* 52 we see the surety system in practice when Patrick's surety arrangements, which he must have made with local kings, were implemented after a period of fourteen days.

Sick maintenance

The Celts had a system of sick maintenance whereby not only was the victim eligible for compensation, according to his own honour-price and the seriousness of the injury, but account was also taken of the part of the body on which the wound was inflicted (eg facial injuries were considered more serious and therefore elicited a greater payment). In addition, when one man injured another he also had to undertake the convalescence of the victim either in his own home or by providing a safe house for his recovery. The perpetrator also had to provide a substitute labourer to carry out the work of the injured party.

Fasting

Fasting was another important Celtic practice. Fasting was essentially a means of asserting one's rights. The custom entailed protest outside the door of a wrongdoer, abstaining from all food and drink until the wrong was acknowledged and compensation given. If the wrongdoer did not acknowledge the one who fasted then he lost all character and recognition. We are told, "he that does not give a pledge to the fasting is an evader of all: he who disregards … should not be paid …".[33]

Fosterage

This was a custom that was widely practised. This was the system whereby children were given to other families to be reared and perhaps given a skill or a trade. It was probably a means of forging alliances between the immediate and the wider kinship group and seems to have been very tightly regulated by Brehon law. The education of a girl seems to have been more expensive than that of a boy because more time and effort would be required with her instruction, which would ultimately be of less benefit to the fosterer.[34] No doubt strong bonds were forged by the system of fosterage. Scherman goes as far as to suggest, "the bonds of sympathy and affection that grew from this relationship were often stronger than the ties of the blood family and lasted a lifetime; the foster child in return for his early care was responsible for his adoptive parents in old age, poverty or illness".[35]

Hospitality

This was an attractive feature of Brehon law. A man was not entitled to claim hospitality from those of lower rank than himself. Brehon law laid down in fairly minute detail the extent of hospitality to which one was entitled, in accordance with his social status. The free small farmer when travelling in his own *tuath* could claim hospitality for himself and one other person; the food he was to be given was milk and curds and corn bread but no butter was to be given. The higher the status of the person, the more hospitality they were entitled to. To fail to give hospitality to one who was entitled by law to receive it was to lose all honour. Some, however, were not entitled to hospitality, for example, men who stole and those who had not paid the sick maintenance or had refused hospitality to another.

Marriage

It would seem that women were fairly well protected by law. As we have already seen, they could not inherit land directly but did have a life stake in the family land. Although some law tracts prohibit the consideration of testimony given by women, they can give evidence in marital matters. A woman who becomes pregnant as a result of a sexual liaison with a man who was not her husband and where the affair was an illicit one was also protected in law.[36] In *Confessio* 49 Patrick illustrates the fact that women could give away their own personal possessions, such as jewellery, to the Church. By the seventh century men and women seem to have been able to keep control of their own personal property within marriage and on divorce received back what had personally been theirs prior to the marriage. The grounds for divorce were wide but again women seem to have been afforded some protection in law. Initially, it would seem that men had greater grounds for divorce than women; for example in the case of her infidelity, or if she caused or sought an abortion or if she did not carry out her work in terms of spinning, weaving or dyeing with due care and attention. Her housekeeping abilities were also held in esteem and judged harshly by her husband should they be lacking in any way. Divorce of a woman was permissible for any domestic inadequacy. Women seem to have about fourteen grounds for divorce, which take account of her need for protection physically, and psychologically.[37] These seem to have included, for example, her husband's failure to meet her sexual needs, for physical abuse where it was not issued in correction and where it left a lasting scar.

A study of Brehon law seems to indicate the aim of the Brehon lawyer was to cover almost every eventuality and circumstance, to ensure all freemen were clear about their rights and obligations to others, and thereby to avoid the general mayhem which might otherwise have arisen in a barbaric and decentralised society such as Ireland was at this time.

 PRACTICE ESSAY TITLE

(a) **Give an account of the political and social characteristics of Celtic society before the arrival of Patrick. (35)**

    In your answer you could refer to some of the following:
- The decentralised nature of Celtic society (*tuatha*)
- The role of the king
- Dwellings
- Importance of family
- Brehon Law and customs

Try this one later.

(b) **Explore the view that conditions in Ireland were the main difficulty that Patrick faced. Justify your answer. (15)**

The religious conditions in Ireland before the arrival of Patrick

Early Celtic society was also pagan, and the Celts, whilst pagan, were a very religious people. In fact, as Davies observes, "there was no aspect of life which was not in some way touched by the intricate webs of ritual and belief that gave meaning to the Celtic world".[38] Any detailed study of the pagan religious practices of the Celts is severely hindered by the lack of any written source material contemporaneous to the period. Archaeology has been of some assistance in uncovering some of the ritualistic practices of the pagan Celts, although it tells us less about the actual nature of that belief. Burial sites, such as the passage tombs at Knowth and Dowth are useful to us, as of course is the remarkable site at Newgrange. (Both of these aspects of Celtic paganism will be dealt with later in this chapter.)

We also have information from some sources external to Ireland but often these deal with a period earlier than the one we are concerned with and give insight into the beliefs of Celtic peoples populating Europe prior to the rise of the Roman Empire. Nonetheless, it is likely that the Celtic peoples inhabiting Ireland retained some of the deities and cultic practices of their Celtic forbearers in Europe.

Sun worship

It seems safe to assume that their faith somehow incorporated worship of the sun. Patrick himself refers to this in *Confessio* 60 and the site at Newgrange also attests to it, as well as to the ritual surrounding death and burial. Newgrange comprises a circle of roughly cut standing stones, partly surrounding a mound about 250 feet in diameter. Behind this lies a sixty-foot passageway leading into a hill, with the sidewalls decorated with geometric carvings. This passageway finally ends in a cross-shaped area with a round chamber and a highly vaulted roof with three smaller side chambers. It is believed these chambers may have been repositories for the ashes of the dead. On

Newgrange in County Meath is one of the finest monuments to Ireland's pagan heritage.

(Photo courtesy of Cathal O'Connor)

the shortest day of the year, the rays of the sun as it rises penetrate the passageway to fill the circular chamber with the first light of the dawn. To this end, a slit, six feet above the entrance, has been carved and the passage has been constructed so that it ascends to the inner chamber. This must have been quite a feat of construction in its day. It is difficult to believe that the careful architectural execution of this site was merely to facilitate the burial of the dead. The ritual marking of sunrise on the shortest day of the year would have had particular significance for an agricultural people who could then accurately calculate the start of the planting season.

Death and burial

Passage graves themselves were also of religious significance. They were, as Timothy Joyce identifies, one of the Celtic "thin places".[39] The pagan Celts had a very strong sense of the other world, which they believed was especially close to them in "thin places", which were sacred to them. Burial sites were sacred "thin places" as

The Abbey Well in Ballyshannon, County Donegal is one example of many ancient wells throughout Ireland. *(Photo courtesy of Cathal O'Connor)*

were wells, which were perceived to be entrances to the other world, places which connected the underworld to the world above. These places were especially sacred during 'thin times' such as the feast of Samhain which marked the Celtic New Year on 1 November or thereabouts. It was believed that at this time, between the end of the old year and the start of the new, the spirits roved freely in the world.[40] Celtic belief in the other world found substance in the soul's journey to Tír na nÓg after death. This was the land of eternal youth and meant that for the Celts, death was not something to be feared.

The gods

Over 400 gods can be identified with the Celtic peoples. McNeill argues that these are probably in many cases local names given to essentially the same god.[41] Like many other pagan peoples, the Celts had particular gods to deal with almost all aspects of human concern. They had gods who shared the characteristics of the animal species, particularly the stag, the bull, the bear and the horse. They had a tendency, as Joyce says, to "find the divine in all of created nature", and so had gods to ensure the fertility of the earth as well as of humans.[42]

An Dagda was a title meaning 'the Good' and represented, as Scherman points out, "an older generalised pantheon".[43] He was good, not necessarily in the moral sense but in the sense of being 'good for everything'; all powerful. It was believed that when in battle, *Dagda* had all the powers combined that other gods had only individually. He was so invincible that it took eight men to carry his club; he fed them all from his magic cauldron, which refilled endlessly, and his sexual unions with goddesses meant his people were protected from hostile gods.

Lug was another important Celtic god and seems to have been worshipped across Europe as well as in Ireland. His feast day was kept on 1 August, at *Lughnasa*, the harvest festival. *Lug* appears to have been the favoured god of this heroic age, who could defeat an army single-handedly, cure the sick, work spells and was deadly with a spear and a sling.[44]

Manannán, the son of *Lir*, was a great sea-god, who travelled the oceans in his chariot.

Liam de Paor points out that "goddesses appear in every part of Ireland ... as divinities of natural forces of motherhood, fertility, growth and destruction".[45] Here the importance of triunities (groups of three) to the Celts is clear, in that female deities were often triple in character. They tended to, in their triune shape, appear in the form of crows or ravens who presided over battle. So, while some goddesses are deities associated with fertility such as Brigit, Anu and Dana; others were agents of death. Scherman points out that Brigit presided over childbirth, while threefold goddesses presided over battle.[46] Badh and Macha were crow goddesses whose food was the heads of warriors slain in battle. They might have appeared in the form of an animal to execute torture on a lone fighter. Maebh was both a goddess of fertility and war. Animals had superstitious significance; birds in particular were often messengers from another world: the swan a symbol of purity; the wren, the crane and the raven signs of bad fortune or upcoming evil events.

Sanctuaries and places of worship

Celtic respect for and love of nature is illustrated in the fact that their place of worship was not the temple of the Roman Empire but the oak grove, the woodland, the river bank or the mound (which was the home of the *sid* or fairy folk). These were all the sanctuaries of the pagan Celts. Davies argues that, "we see among the Celts an interpenetration of religion and landscape ... the transcendent did not speak ... outside and beyond its natural environment".[47] Trees and water had a particular religious significance. The spirits were thought to preside over rivers and lakes; for example the River Boyne is named after the goddess *Bo* and water everywhere was associated with fertility and life.

In fact, particular trees were thought to be sacred, such as the rowan and the yew, from which druids' wands were made. The oak is thought to be the particular sacred tree of the Continental Celts and possibly those who inhabited Ireland as well, given the propensity to build later Christian monasteries and churches in oak groves (*doire*).

Ritual stones are as close as the pagan Celts came to temple buildings and these in themselves depict various beliefs held by the Celts. One stone appearing in the later Patrician legends, in the Plain of Prostrations in County Cavan, required the king and his people to prostrate themselves before it and offer sacrifice. The Turoe stone, probably dating from the third century BC, is another symbol of the fertility rites that often took place at such sites. The carvings on some of these stones show the religious symbolism attached to the human head, as with the Janus figures (carvings of two-headed people) found at Boa Island in County Fermanagh. The head was thought to embody wisdom, fertility, prophecy and healing. The same stone carving also depicts what may well be the horned being, usually symbolic of Satan. The serpent is also commonly carved. It may have been the attendant of the horned god, and is generally taken to be a phallic symbol.

Feasts and festivals

Although any ritualistic worship of the pagan Celts is lost in obscurity, they did, it is clear, set aside certain feasts and festivals during which they venerated the various gods. *Samhain* as we have already seen, marked the beginning of the Celtic New Year and on its eve the spirits of the other world came out of the earth to challenge and to sometimes destroy humans.

Bealtaine took place on 1 May when cattle were driven between two fires to protect them against disease. *Lug* was honoured at the feast of *Lughnasa* on 1 August, and finally *Imbolc* marked the beginning of the period of lactation of ewes.

Janus figures on Boa Island, County Fermanagh. *(Photo courtesy of Cathal O'Connor)*

The priests

The *druids* were the priests of the pagan Celtic religion. They officiated at feasts and festivals, practised magic, facilitated the offering of sacrifice, foretold the future and designed horoscopes. They were recruited from the aristocratic class and could only be admitted to the druidic order after many years of study in druidical schools. It is important to remember that they were not only priests but also advisors, both personal and political and seem to have been at the very centre of Celtic life. They taught moral philosophy and science. They also officiated at marriage ceremonies and funeral rites. Joyce believes they provided "a structured office to embody the spiritual, mystical, earthly and cultural values of a people otherwise only united by language and origin".[48] They are often referred to as *magi* and are portrayed as the enemy of Christian leaders from Saint Paul to Saint Patrick. It was really the arrival of Christianity that sounded the death knell for the supremacy of the druids in Celtic Ireland.

TASK

Identify the main differences between the world that Patrick came from and the Ireland that Patrick came to.

You should include reference to social, political and religious differences between Roman Britain and Celtic Ireland.

This will help you to understand the mission and the writings of Patrick that are covered in Chapter 2.

TIP! There are some key words you should use when writing about this topic; for example: **tribal, rural, hierarchical, familiar, centralised, civilised, decentralised, barbarous**

	Roman Britain	Celtic Ireland
Political structure		
Religious beliefs and practices		
Communication and social structure		
Laws customs and values	all Freemen equal in law	status and rights graded according to 'honour price'

3. CHRISTIANITY IN IRELAND BEFORE PATRICK – THE HISTORICAL SOURCES FOR ITS EXISTENCE

Is it accurate to assume that Ireland was totally pagan before the arrival of Patrick? The answer in short, is no. There is a range of evidence to suggest that Christianity had already reached Ireland before the mission of Patrick and although piecemeal, the emerging picture is fairly conclusive. The Ireland that Patrick came to was not exclusively pagan.

Linguistic evidence

James Kenney points out that linguistic evidence is important in uncovering the nature and extent of Christianity in Ireland before Patrick. He believes the evidence to be of Latin origin, although probably derived from British speech, and was in all likelihood learned by the Irish from British Christians.[49]

Zimmer argues that this points to the fact that there may have been a gradual conversion of Ireland in the fourth century by British missionaries.[50]

The words which have survived in archaic Irish and are *Cáisc,* which translates as 'Easter' and *Cruimther,* which means 'priest'. These indicate some rudimentary practice of the faith, but the absence of any further word for, for example, 'diocese' or 'bishop', indicates a lack of any real development of a Christian Church as such. Greene believes these words couldn't really be later than the mid-fourth century.[51]

There also seem to have been other primitive words, for example, *ires* meaning 'faith', *cresen* meaning 'Christian', and *domnach* meaning 'church'.

Binchy argues that these were "sufficient to provide a 'skeleton service' of Christian terminology", prior to Patrick's arrival.[52]

Saints

There is a fairly strong tradition of a number of saints in Ireland who appear to be pre-Patrician in origin. Little is known of them since their Lives, in the hagiographical[53] sense, were not written until approximately the twelfth century.

These are Saint Ciaran, thought to be born about AD375 and associated with County Cork; Saint Ailbe born perhaps around AD360 who reportedly travelled Ireland converting people before finally settling in Emly, County Tipperary. Saint Ibar was reportedly active around County Wexford and Saint Declan who is said to have founded an oratory in Ardmore in County Waterford.

Although the details of these saints lives must be treated with caution, it is interesting to note that they were apparently active in the south rather that the north of the country, which was the later missionary territory of Patrick.

Although Thompson argues that these saints were British by birth and formed the basis of the Patrician mission to Ireland, the weight of scholarship seems to support the view that Patrick was active in the *north* of the country and that he perceived it to be pagan rather than Christian territory.[54]

The tradition is strong suggesting that all of these saints belong to a period earlier than Patrick's mission to Ireland, although the concrete evidence for their ministry is scant.

Heresy

Historians such as Kenney believe there to be some association between the heretic Pelagius[55] and Ireland. He bases his assumption on evidence from the writings of Saint Jerome, who in the prologue to his *Commentary on Jeremiah* refers to Pelagius as *"pultibus Scottorum praegravatus"*, which translates as 'stuffed with the porridge of the Scots'.

There is little doubt that the terms Scotti and Scots were taken to refer to the Irish at the time, but it is the view of most scholars, (McNeill, for example) that Jerome "thought of Britain and Ireland alike as remote and barbarous nations" and that in this particular instance, the term 'Scot' was "merely a term of abuse" rather than a statement of Pelagius' national origin.[56]

It seems certain that the Pelagian heresy had contaminated the Church in Britain and to this end Germanus seems to have been sent to the Church in Britain early in the fifth century.57 The mission of Palladius to Ireland, which is discussed later, seems to have been, in part, to prevent the contamination of the infant Irish Church.58 It would have to be assumed that any trace of heresy in the Irish Church at the time, came from British Christians who had contact with it, or as a result of heresy from a later period.

Palladius

The most convincing evidence for pre-Patrician Christianity comes from a source outside Ireland and is therefore irrefutable. The source is Prosper of Aquitaine, a resident of Marseilles, who was an opponent of Pelagius and seems to have obtained the position of papal chancery around 444.[59] Prosper tells us in his *Chronicles* in 431 *"To the Irish believing in Christ, Palladius, having being ordained by Pope Celestine, is sent as the first bishop"*.[60]

Clearly there is a sufficient number of Christians in Ireland to warrant the appointment of a Bishop, and the community is important enough for a bishop to be sent from the Church on the Continent rather than from Britain. The significance of all the early Christian references to Palladius will be discussed in more detail later. Clearly the mission was ongoing in 434 when Prosper again mentions it.

The writings of Patrick himself

The final suggestion of pre-Patrician Christianity comes from the pen of Patrick himself. In *Confessio* 51 he writes that he had gone to places "where no one else had ever penetrated, in order to order to baptise, or to ordain clergy, or to confirm the people".

This seems to imply that he himself may have been aware of the existence of a mission other than his own, in another part of the country perhaps. Certainly he appears to feel that the sacraments have been administered to Christians elsewhere in Ireland, but that the area within which he labours is pagan and he is the first to minister to them.

References external to Ireland

Jerome writing, at the latest, in the opening decades of the fifth century also seems to allude to the practice of Christianity in Ireland: *"and the Irish peoples and all the barbarian nations round to the very ocean, have come to know Moses and the prophets"*.[61] Saint Augustine agrees in a passage dating, in de Paor's opinion, from the very early fifth century: *"Have you not seen that by now there are no peoples to whom the Gospel has not been preached … even in the islands which are set in the middle of the sea; even they are full of Christians"*.[62]

All of the evidence leads Liam de Paor to conclude that "the numbers of Christians in Ireland had increased in recent times – perhaps even in the fourth century".[63] Thomas agrees that "between 360 and 430, the Church may and probably did gain a real foothold in Ireland".[64]

4. THE STORY OF THE ARRIVAL OF CHRISTIANITY IN IRELAND BEFORE PATRICK

What then, was the source of the Christian faith in Ireland? There is evidence a-plenty for contact with the Roman Empire, and although Ireland had not been Romanised, it was not completely isolated and it is likely that the many sources of contact with the Empire may have been instrumental in the entry of the faith into Ireland. The Celts were a seafaring people. Charles Thomas argues that "Ireland, if far enough from Britain to be a separate country, is nonetheless too close to have experienced a separate history".[65]

Colonies

Thomas also argues that by the fourth century there were probably groups from Roman Britain residing in Ireland, perhaps trading as merchants and involved actively in Irish life to some extent.[66] In addition, perhaps as early as the third century, there seem to have been groups of Irish living in Britain in colonies which doubtless kept up a contact with home, imparting perhaps certain aspects of the Christian faith they had grasped.

It is the view of Richard Warner that there may have been some British refugees who fled the initial Roman expansion into Britain. That may well be true, but it seems more likely that there were some who fled to Ireland at the time of the collapse of the Empire, even perhaps as Thomas suggests, some deserting soldiers.[67] We know for certain of the Dál Riatan settlement in Scotland, who by the time of Colmcille, still retained close contacts with their kin in Ireland.

There were also Irish colonies in Cornwall and in Wales. These settlements are referred to in the tenth century *Glossary of Cormac mac Cuileannáin* which refers to Irish strongholds in the "lands of the Cornish Britons".[68] These seem to descend from a branch of the *Erainn* from east Cork. There seems to be evidence that these colonists maintained contact with the homeland until well into the eighth century. It would be difficult to prove that these settlers were Christianised to any great extent but we do have a reference to an Irish bishop of York as a signatory on a report sent to Pope Silvester I regarding the Synod of Arles in 314.[69] Kenney offers evidence to suggest that there are also clear traces of the presence of Cornish Christians in Ireland.[70]

Trade

There is also the clear possibility that there was organised and regular trade both between Ireland and Britain and between Ireland and the Continent. Both Tacitus and Ptolemy in the first and second centuries respectively, display clear knowledge of at least the eastern and southern coasts of Ireland; Ptolemy was able to name the rivers Boyne and Barrow.

Warner believes that these estuaries in particular, were good access points for traders as they were "places where landing is safe, and access to the interior straightforward".[71] The Irish imported wine and oil – as finds in the south of the country, particularly in the region of Cork, attest to – and it is also thought that pottery and metalwork (which were the primary industries of the Empire) were also imported. The Irish probably also had plenty to export, such as the classic wolfhound, cattle and precious metals. Recent findings of coins seem proof positive of the ongoing trade relationship between Ireland and the Continent, especially those found in the region of the Boyne valley. The coins date from the fourth century, and include *solidi*. Claire O'Kelly is of the view that these were deposited by Roman British traders as an offering to local Celtic deities so that they could perhaps impress the Irish enough to gain a foothold in a trade relationship with them.[72] This practice was not unheard of in trade relations with countries as far flung as India. Certainly trade seems to have been frequent enough for some basic knowledge of the Christian faith to have filtered through.

Scholars

Francois Henry also believes that development in Celtic artistic technique would also point to contact with the Empire, indicating a relationship closer than that of mere trading acquaintances.[73]

James Carney argues that the same degree of intercourse is also evident in writing; archaic Irish poetry exhibits the use of very early Latin loan words which "show a non-Christian Ireland, having very close contacts with and knowledge of the Roman Empire".[74] James Kenney too, argues that the seventh century *Hisperica Famina* was produced by descendants of learned men from Gaul who had fled the barbarian invasion there and came to Ireland in the fifth century. The twelfth century *Leiden Glossary* gives testament to such an exodus: *"all the learned men on this side of the sea took flight, and in transmarine parts, namely in Ireland … brought a very great increase in learning to the inhabitants of those regions"*. In fact, Patrick himself makes reference to these 'rhetoricians' in *Confessio* 13. It seems more plausible to believe that the basic tenets of the Christian faith were passed on by such scholarly exchanges, more so than by the activities of the merchant.

The slave trade

Ongoing slave raids by the Irish on Britain and possibly the Continent were perhaps another source of the Christian faith in Ireland. Captured slaves may have been among those living in reasonable numbers in Ireland in the fourth century. There were a series of fairly significant incursions of this nature between the third and the fifth century and it is probable that many captives were Christian, as Patrick himself was. Some argue that the Christian community to which Palladius was sent was in fact a community of captured slaves, although this is unlikely. Some of these did, no doubt, have opportunity to influence their owners, although it is unlikely that they preached to them directly.

The story of the arrival of Christianity into Ireland is very unclear, but of its existence on the island before the arrival of Patrick there can be little doubt.

 PRACTICE ESSAY TITLE

Discuss the evidence for the arrival of Christianity in Ireland before Patrick's mission to the Irish. (35)

Your answer should include reference to some of the following:

- Linguistic studies
- Pre-Patrician saints
- Heresy
- Palladius
- Patrick's writings
- Commercial and slave trade
- Scholarly fugitives
- Ongoing contact with colonies
- The views of scholars

5. THE SIGNIFICANCE OF PALLADIUS
Palladius at a glance

Date	Source	What do we know?
429	Prosper's *Chronicles*	Palladius convinces Pope Celestine to send Germanus to Britain to fight Pelagian heresy
431	Prosper's *Chronicles*	Palladius sent to Ireland as a bishop to a community of believers
434	Prosper's *Contra Collatorem*	Work in Ireland is ongoing; mission seems to extend to include evangelisation; also engages in fight against heresy in Britain
7th century	Muirchú's *Life of Patrick*	Mission ends in failure. Palladius dies within a year of commencing mission
7th century	Tírechán's *Brief Account*	Palladius was also known as Patricius

The sources on Palladius in detail

The most significant piece of evidence to suggest the existence of Christianity in Ireland before Patrick was the appointment of Palladius as the first bishop. Although Irish sources on Palladius are scarce, all early Christian references to him are of the utmost significance.

1) We first hear of Palladius in 429. In Prosper's *Chronicles* we are told:

"The Pelagian ... corrupts the churches of Britain by the propagation of his doctrine. But at the instigation of the deacon Palladius, Pope Celestine sends Germanus, bishop of Auxerre, in his stead, who overthrows the heretics and guides the Britons to the catholic faith."

- This reference is indeed significant for the light it throws on the person of Palladius. He clearly is a figure of some standing and influence in the Church and obviously has the ear of Pope Celestine, who acts on his advice. He is also a "pillar of orthodoxy", actively involved in the fight against the Pelagian heresy, which damaged the church at the time.[75]

- It would seem then that he is a character unlikely to be daunted by difficulty and opposition. He seems to be aware of and concerned with issues facing the Church in places other than the papal residency – fairly unusual for a time when the church was heavily involved in defending itself on the home front.

- It is also important to note at this stage that his own mission to Ireland was an offshoot of the mission of Germanus to Britain. Indeed, it is the contention of McNeill that prior to 429, Palladius had acquired a sound knowledge of the condition of the Christian Church in Britain and Ireland.[76]

2) Palladius is mentioned again by Prosper in 431, this time in direct reference to Ireland itself.

"To the Irish believing in Christ, Palladius, having been ordained by Pope Celestine, is sent as the first bishop." (*Ad Scotos in Christum credentes ordinates a papa Caelestino Palladius primus episcopus mittitur.*)

- Historically this reference to an event taking place in Ireland is crucial. It marks the beginning of Ireland's written history and we leave pre-historic Ireland behind. It comes from a source outside Ireland so its reliability is difficult to question.

- The implications of this reference are huge. Firstly, it is important to point out that the mission was not an evangelising one at this time. Rather Palladius was being sent to minister to already believing Christians. This proves conclusively that there were quite significant numbers of Christians in Ireland at this time. Numbers were significant enough to concern the Church on the Continent with regard to their lack of leadership, particularly in light of the Pelagian

heresy which seems to have gained a real foothold in the church in Britain.
As Charles-Edwards suggests, "his task was partly to safeguard the orthodoxy
of existing Irish Christians".[77] The view of some scholars, that these were
probably captured slaves, can be questioned on the grounds that it was not the
widespread practice of the Church at the time to send a bishop unless one was
requested. If this is true, then this group is much more likely to have been 'free'
Christians, who had the freedom to liaise either with Germanus in Britain or
directly with the Papacy.

- That this appointment was considered an important one in the history of the
church is attested to by the fact that Prosper, in writing of the achievements
of Pope Celestine, does not elsewhere mention the appointment of any other
bishop to any see or diocese. It is also very clear that Palladius and not Patrick
was the first bishop to the Irish. Interestingly, a bishop was sent direct from
the papacy rather than by the neighbouring British Church. This might have
been because of the weak condition of the British Church as a result of both
barbarian invasions and Pelagianism.

- The reference to the Irish as 'Scotti' has prompted James Carney to question that
Palladius was ever, in fact, in Ireland. He assumes that this was a geographical
reference to Scotland rather than to the inhabitants of Ireland, and cites a
number of churches of a 'Saint Paldy' whom he believes to be Palladius.[78]

3) In contradiction to Carney, Prosper again refers to the mission of Palladius in 434
in his *Contra Collatorem*:

> "… and by ordaining a bishop for the Irish, whilst he strove to keep the Roman island
> catholic, he also made the barbarous island Christian."

- It seems beyond dispute that the mission of Palladius was to Ireland and not to
Scotland; although Carney continues to argue that the barbarous island refers to
Scotland, the area beyond Hadrian's Wall, which had not yet been Romanised.

- The weight of scholarly opinion seems to associate Palladius with the east of the
country in the area around Leinster. We would have to assume that he sailed
from Nantes and possibly arrived on the east coast of Ireland. Tradition links his
arrival to the port of Arklow. This is also the area that Warner argues had traces
of the closest links with the Roman Empire. Binchy too, concurs that "it was
in the east and the south-east of the country that Christianity first put down
its roots".[79] Patrick Corish argues that fragments of topographical evidence are
attached to the name of Palladius in Leinster.[80] The *Annals of the Four Masters*
also tell us that he landed in Leinster[81]:

> "In the second year of Laoghaire [430] … Pope Celestine the First sent Palladius to
> Ireland to propagate the faith among the Irish and he landed in the country of Leinster."

- The second reference in Prosper implies that the mission of Palladius was still ongoing at the time and interestingly no mention is made of the beginning of Patrick's mission. O'Rahilly optimistically believes Palladius to have laboured in Ireland for about thirty years until his death in 461. Hanson also feels it is curious that Prosper did not allude to the death or failure of Palladius had it occurred in 432 as Muirchú later suggests, although John Ryan is convinced that he was indeed dead within the year.[82] This reference also seems to imply that the nature of Palladius' mission had changed somewhat to incorporate some evangelisation as well as the fighting of heresy. Bieler on the other hand is convinced enough by the validity of Prosper to argue that he must have been fairly active in Ireland up to two or three years after his arrival.[83]

- There ends any Roman reference to the mission of Palladius. Prosper and others remain strangely silent about him thereafter.

4) We have no further Irish references to him until the seventh century, when Muirchú in his *Life of Patrick* tells us that:

"Palladius had been consecrated and sent to be established in this island of wintry cold in order to convert it … Palladius was denied success for these wild and obdurate people did not readily accept his doctrine and he himself did not wish to spend a long time in a foreign country, but to return to him who had sent him … having begun his journey, he ended his life in the confines of the Britons."

- Most, with the exception perhaps of Ryan, dismiss the claims of Muirchú as an attempt to associate Patrick as closely as possible with the origins of Christianity in Ireland and to discredit any achievement of Palladius, as is typical of any hagiographer.

- It may well be that there was no further concrete evidence of the work of Palladius, though it is questionable if this should be a valid reason to assume that his work was short-lived or indeed a failure. It is natural that the memory of Patrick would become more indelible given the survival of two texts written by him.

- Many believe Palladius' work to have been carried on by the figures of Auxilius and Secundinus, also strongly associated with the Leinster area. Sites at Kilashee (the cell of Auxilius) and Dunshaughlin (the fort of Secundinus) preserve the memory of these, whom it seems certain were early fifth century missionaries. Given this evidence, they cannot easily be associated with the mission of Patrick, which was largely northern in its sphere.

5) Tírechán in his *Brief Account* might also shed some light on the elusiveness of Palladius after 434, when he says: *"Palladius also called Patricius"*.

- This reference prompts O'Rahilly to argue that the name Palladius never took hold in the Irish language and that he was known as Patricius there. This accounts for the lack of reference to the work of the missionary Palladius. Instead his work became attributed to and intertwined with the work of the later Patrick the Briton.[84]

- It may well be that the reference in *Confessio* 51, dealt with earlier (see p26) could indicate some awareness on Patrick's part of the Palladian mission, although some argue had the mission of Palladius been in any way significant, the humble Patrick would surely have mentioned it.

- The mission of Palladius is shrouded in mystery and it seems appropriate to end our discussion with the observation of Ó Cróinín that, "despite the fact that Palladius disappeared almost without trace from the historical record, in Ireland and in his native Auxerre, his formative influence on the earliest Irish Christianity cannot be denied".[85]

 PRACTICE ESSAY TITLE

Explain the significance of early Christian references to Palladius. (35)

Your answer may include reference to the following:
- The content of the three references from Prosper
- The significance of this information in giving insight into the person of Palladius; pre-Patrician Christianity; relations between Ireland and Rome
- The views of scholars on the mission of Palladius
- The reliability and significance of Tírechán and Muirchú

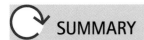

SUMMARY

Patrick, as a citizen of the Roman Empire, was civilised, Christian, and was familiar with Latin. He also lived through the Empire's collapse.

The Ireland that Patrick came to was largely pagan. It was decentralised, barbaric, tribal, rural, hierarchical and familiar.

Evidence suggests that Christianity had already reached parts of Ireland before the arrival of Patrick. It may have arrived via slave and commercial trade, contact with colonies of settlers, fleeing learned literati.

Palladius and not Patrick was first bishop to the Irish. Palladius was a prominent and important figure in the Church.

Endnotes

1 There is little consensus as to when the Empire in Britain finally and totally collapsed but for the purposes of this study circa 410 can be accepted.

2 Thomas, C, *Christianity in Roman Britain to AD500*, Batsford, London, 1981, p140

3 *ibid*

4 Jackson, KH, 'The British languages and their evolution', ed D Daiches & A Thorlby, *Literature and Western Civilisation: 11, the Medieval World*, London, 1973, pp113–126

5 Hamp, EP, *Social Gradience in British Spoken Latin*, Brittania 6, 1975, pp150–162

6 Thomas, *Christianity in Roman Britain, op cit*, p62

7 Rivet & Smith, CC, *The Place names of Roman Britain*, London, 1979, pp14–18

8 McNeill, JT, *The Celtic Churches, A History, AD200 to 1200*, University of Chicago Press, Chicago & London, 1974, p16

8a Gildas was a sixth century churchman who wrote *On the Ruin and Conquest of Britain*.

9 Chandler, JH, *The nature of Christianity in Roman Britain* (lecture Dorchester 1978)

10 Thomas, *Christianity in Roman Britain, op cit*, p155

11 McNeill, *The Celtic Churches, op cit*, p8

12 Corish, PJ, *The World St Patrick Came From*, Far East March 1961, pp2–5

13 Thomas, *Christianity in Roman Britain, op cit*, p240

14 Corish, *The World Patrick came from, op cit*, p2

15 Finan, T, 'Hiberno-Latin Christian Literature' in *An Introduction to Celtic Christianity*, ed JP Mackey, T&T Clark Ltd, 1995, p67

16 McNeill, *The Celtic Churches, op cit*, p6r

17 Powell, TGE, *The Celts*, New York, 1958, p17

18 Binchy, 'Secular Institutions' in *Early Irish Society*, ed M Dillon, Dublin 1954, p54; Binchy uses the word 'familiar' in its oldest sense to mean family based.

19 A *tuath* refers to a tribe or a people and the territory that they inhabit.

20 Byrne, FJ, 'Early Irish Society (1st–9thCentury)' in *The Course of Irish History*, ed Moody & Martin, Mercier Press, Dublin 1967,1984, p55

21 Wallace-Hadrill, JM, *Early Germanic Kingship in England and on the Continent*, Oxford 1971, p57

22 De Paor, L, *Saint Patrick's World*, Four Courts Press Dublin, 1996, p28

23 *ibid*

24 This structure is that suggested by Fergus Kelly in his analysis of early Irish law tracts; Kelly, F, *A guide to early Irish Law*, Dublin Institute for Advanced Studies, 1991

25 Byrne, 'Early Irish Society' in *The Course of Irish History, op cit*, p51

26 *ibid*

27 Binchy, DA, (ed), *Crith Gablach*, 1941, p7ff Nos 14–15

28 Kinsella, T, (ed & trans), *The Tain*, London OUP 1969

29 Byrne, 'Early Irish Society' in *The Course of Irish History, op cit*, p52

30 A sét was a milch cow, or young heifer and was the basic form of currency in Celtic Ireland at this time.

31 Hughes, K, *Early Christian Ireland: Introduction to the Sources*, Hodder & Stoughton, 1972, p49

32 Ó Cróinín, D, *Early Medieval Ireland AD400–1200*, Longman, London, 1995, p114

33 Joyce, PW, *A Social History of Ancient Ireland*, Dublin, 1924, p56

34 Hughes, *Early Christian Ireland, op cit*, p60

35 Scherman, K, *The Flowering of Ireland, Saints, Scholars and Kings*, Victor Gollancz Ltd, London, 1981, p34

36 Thurneyson, R, *Die Falshen Urteilsspruche Caratnia's*, 1925, p302–376

37 For a range of examples see Kelly, F, *A guide to early Irish Law*, Dublin,1988, p74ff

38 Davies, O, & Bowie, F, *Celtic Christian Spirituality* SPCK, 1995, p5

39 Joyce, TJ, *Celtic Christianity: A Sacred Tradition, a Vision of Hope*, Orbis Books, New York, 1998, p10

40 *ibid*

41 McNeill, *The Celtic Churches, op cit*, p7

42 Joyce, *Celtic Christianity, op cit*, p11

43 Scherman, *The Flowering of Ireland, Saints, Scholars and Kings, op cit*, p51

44 *ibid*

45 De Paor, *Saint Patrick's World, op cit*, p29

46 Scherman, *The Flowering of Ireland, op cit*, p53

47 Davies and Bowie, *Celtic Christian Spirituality, op cit*, p6

48 Joyce, *Celtic Christianity, op cit*, p12

49 Kenney, JF, *The Sources for the Early History of Ireland: Ecclesiastical, an introduction and guide*, Columbia University Press, 1929, p160

50 Zimmer, H, '*Die Keltische Kirche*' trans by A Meyer, *The Celtic Church in Britain and Ireland 1902*

51 Greene, D, *Some linguistic evidence relating to the British Church*, ed MW Barley & Hanson RPC, 1968, p80

52 Binchy, DA, *Patrick and His Biographers: Ancient and modern in Studia Hibernica No.2*, Colaiste Phadraig, 1962, p166

53 A hagiography is a type of religious writing emphasising the holiness of the saint by giving examples of their prayer and miracles.

54 Thompson, EA, *Who was Saint Patrick?*, Suffolk Woodbridge, 1985

55 Pelagius was a controversial figure of the 4th and early 5th century who believed that we are not given salvation as a result of God's grace or goodness but rather by our own actions. As such he denies one of the basic teachings of the Church and was therefore a heretic.

56 McNeill, *The Celtic Churches, op cit*, p29

57 Bede seems to imply that the British Church felt ill-equipped to deal with the heresy and sent to the Church in Gaul for assistance.

58 See the reference of Prosper *Contra Collatorem* 434

59 More detail on Prosper can be found in Kenney *The Sources for the Early History of Ireland*, 1929, p164–166

60 As quoted in Kenney, p165

61 Saint Jerome, letters no. 130

62 St Augustine, 2nd sermon on Psalm 101 in Dekkers DE & Fraiont J, 1956

63 De Paor, *Saint Patrick's World, op cit*, p38

64 Thomas, *Christianity in Roman Britain to AD 500, op cit*, p300

65 *ibid*, p295

66 *ibid*

67 *ibid*

68 Coplestone-Crow, B, *The dual nature of the Irish colonisation of Dyfed in the Dark Ages 1981-82* in Studia Celtica, pp1–24

69 Munier, C, (ed), *Conciliae Galliae AD314–506*, 1963, p4

70 Kenney, *The Sources for the Early History of Ireland, op cit*, p352

71 Warner, ER, *Some observations on the context & importation of exotic material in Ireland 1st century B.C. to 2nd century AD*, Proc Royal Irish Academy, *1976, p284,*

72 Carson, RAG, & O'Kelly, *A Catalogue of the Roman coins from Newgrange Co. Meath*, Proc Royal Irish Academy, 1977, pp35–55

73 Henry, F, 'Irish enamels of the Dark Ages' in *Dark-Age Britain*, ed DB Harden, London, *1956*, p76

74 Carney, J, *Three Old Irish Accentual Poems*, 1971, pp73–80,

75 Ó Cróinín, *Early medieval Ireland, op cit*, p21

76 McNeill, JT, *The Celtic Churches, op cit*, p31

77 Charles-Edwards, TM, 'Palladius, Prosper and Leo the Great' in *Saint Patrick AD493–1993*, ed D Dumville, The Boydell Press, 1993, p8

78 Carney, J, *The Problem of Saint Patrick*, Dublin Institute for Advanced Studies, 1961, pp49–52

79 Binchy, DA, *Patrick and His Biographers: Ancient and modern, op cit*, p165

80 Corish, PJ, *The Irish Catholic Experience: An Historical Survey*, Dublin, 1985

81 As quoted in de Paor, L, *Saint Patrick's World*, p126

82 Hanson, RPC, *St Patrick – His origins and career*, Oxford, 1968, pp52–54; Ryan, J, *The Traditional view* in *Saint Patrick*, 1958, pp10–23

83 Bieler, L, 'Saint Patrick and the coming of Christianity' in *A History of Irish Catholicism*, vol 1 ed P Corish, 1967

84 The issue of the Two Patricks Theory will be dealt with in greater detail at A2 Level.

85 Ó Cróinín, *Early Medieval Ireland, op cit*, p23

The work of Patrick

INTRODUCTION

Saint Patrick, regarded by many as the Apostle of Ireland, left two surviving writings conclusively accepted as his own: his *Confessio* and his *Letter to Coroticus*.

These emerge essentially from the era of pre-history, described in Chapter 1, and are identified by Máire de Paor as "the darkest of the Dark Ages". They are the only personal documents to survive from either the British or the Irish Church in that period.[1]

The *Confessio* is the longer and the more personal of the two, although in the view of the majority of scholars, certainly Bieler and Conneely, it was written after the *Letter*. Liam de Paor would however disagree, arguing that the similarity of wording in passages and phrases is so striking, that they must have been written close in time, with the *Confessio* written first and its phrases and references then borrowed for the *Letter*. Nonetheless, it is the *Confessio* which will be examined first here. In the words of Patrick himself, it is very much his "spiritual legacy" to us, his believers and children (C14).

The authenticity of both texts have never seriously been doubted by any historian, leading Ó Raifeartaigh to claim that "the two compositions ... breathe such a transparent truth and simplicity, combine such utter humility with such perfect confidence in divine guidance ... speak to us so directly, so vividly, unaffectedly and sincerely ... it is beyond human imagination for them to emanate from the pen of a medieval forger".[2]

By reading his writings, we can really come to listen to Patrick on his own terms. He speaks, in the words of David Howlett, "articulately, authoritatively, compellingly across fifteen centuries, with a power he believed to be not his own but God's."[3]

A commentary on both the *Confessio* and *Letter to Coroticus* is provided below. A copy of each is required to read alongside the notes and explanations offered.[4] The commentaries are designed to help you gain a fuller understanding of Patrick's writings. **Please note:** *Confessio* is abbreviated to 'C' and *Letter to Coroticus* to 'L'.

1. A COMMENTARY ON THE *CONFESSIO* OF PATRICK

C1 The humble Patrick

Here we see the self-deprecation and humility of Patrick. It is important to point out that this was a conventional literary style of the day, particularly that of the churchmen of Gaul at the time.

Referring to the self as "sinner" was considered to be good literary breeding and echoed the style of Paul and Augustine. Nonetheless, the vast majority of modern scholars suggest that the self-abasement and humility expressed by Patrick goes well beyond mere literary convention.

It is not surprising to learn that Patrick came from a clerical background as clerical marriage in the church was permitted and practised at the time and indeed up until around the eleventh century.

Indeed, it becomes a recurring theme in the document and is very much at the heart of his spirituality. Patrick is very aware of his own 'littleness' in the face of God's greatness, "of the vast abyss between himself and the total Otherness of the all-Holy God."[5]

In the *Letter*, we learn that Patrick's father, Calpurnius, was a decurion (ie a person responsible for the collection of taxes in a local council area). Decurions were liable for any shortfall in tax collected.

A way to avoid this may have been to undertake Holy Orders. Was this true in the case of Calpurnius?

We have no way of knowing, but it may account for Patrick's lack of religious fervour.

Patrick's reference to his father's estate certainly implies a financially secure and materially comfortable background, which is confirmed in the *Letter to Coroticus* in the reference to the servants which were employed in the family home (L10). This experience of being taken captive as a sixteen year old boy must have severely traumatised Patrick and indeed has a spiritual significance for him. Even at the end of the document he still sees himself as an orphan and exile, destitute in Ireland.

In terms of professed lack of religious fervour, Bieler argues however that Patrick was "neither better nor worse than his surroundings – exactly what would have been expected of a young lad of good family in a nominally Christian, but thoroughly secularised society."[6]

C2 The beginning of conversion

Patrick begins the narrative of his conversion experience. He sees the hand of God at work in his anguish and it was in his isolation and loneliness that he first comes to knowledge of God and his 'pilgrimage of faith' begins. Máire de Paor points out that the two contrasting stories – the story of Patrick, the nobleman's son and the story of Patrick the slave – echo the theme of the Parable of the Prodigal Son. Thus, Patrick, the lost son of Calpurnius, is now comforted by his heavenly Father. She further points out the echo of Mary's Magnificat (Luke 1: 46–56) which also expresses the essence of the spirituality of the *Confessio*, a celebration of God's favour bestowed on his lowly ones.[7] Patrick admits his youth and ignorance here, "*and God took notice of my humble state and pitied my youth and ignorance*". Patrick clearly perceives the role of suffering in God's plan for himself as it was for the disciples of old.

C3 Why write?

Patrick makes explicit here, for the first time, one reason for writing the *Confessio*. It is two-fold at this point: to thank, and to preach and **declare** and make known. We see his compulsion to write, moved by something strong and powerful within. "*And that is why I cannot keep silent about the great acts of goodness and great grace which the Lord generously gave me in the land of my captivity.*" He sees the writing of this document as a repayment for all that God has done for and in him, and it fills him with joy and jubilation. He perceives his enslavement as an act of God both to punish and transform him. In the words of de Paor, he has been "stripped back of all that stands between him and God."[8] For Patrick, suffering is redemptive.

C4 Profession of faith

Hanson argues that this is surely a reproduction of another document, the *Rule of Faith*. The written style is not consistent with the rest of the *Confessio*. While Hanson believes it formed part of Patrick's clerical education, and is therefore the *Rule of Faith* of the British Church,[9] other scholars, such as Bieler, are more inclined to argue for a Continental training for Patrick and believe it to originate in the Church of Gaul. Oulton argues that it features a Gallican tradition "within which Patrick stands ... revealed by his credal statements".[10] Conneely points out that while Patrick does not specifically address the Pelagian heresy, he refutes it here and in so doing gives testament to his own orthodoxy.[11]

C5

Biblical references here are to Psalm 50:15 as well as to Tobit 12:7.

C6 For brethren and kin

Hanson believes *"brethren"* refers to fellow Christians and *"kin"* (relations), to refer to his extended family group.[12] He needs his relatives and friends to understand why he must be parted from them, for the sake of the kingdom.

C7 and 8 Judgement Day

The references are to 2 Timothy 1:8; Psalm 5:6; Wisdom 1:11; Matthew 12:36. These echo the **theme of judgement** and eschatology which run throughout the *Confessio*, synonymous with someone who feels themselves to be living and working in the last times.

> Eschatology is concerned with the final events in the history of the world. It is clear throughout the Confession that Patrick has a sense that the end of the world is near.

"So that is why I ought with fear and trembling to dread ... that day on which nobody will be able to steal away." The truth of his *Confessio* is forcefully supported by use of Scripture. This is particularly important to him in his quest to refute allegations made against him, which he later deals with. The Scripture references used are: Ephesians 6:5; Romans 14:10, 12 and 2 Corinthians 5:10.

Confessio 9–13 form the crux of Patrick's Apologia concerning his lack of education and in the view of Nerney, closely parallels that of Paul in 2 Corinthians.[13]

C9 and 10

Patrick has told us he was *"despised by many"*. He now makes it clear that those to whom he compares himself unfavourably within the Church, are those who are more educated than he. It is this lack of education that is the cause of Patrick's own sense of personal inadequacy. *"That is why I am now ashamed and afraid of revealing my unskilfulness."*

Growing up in Roman Britain, Patrick most certainly would have availed of the education system open to young boys of his social class and background.

When Patrick was captured as a boy of sixteen years, his education was undoubtedly interrupted. He specifies here that his education is most lacking in the areas of law, literature and speech. Hanson identifies the latter as the practice of rhetoric.[14] He presents the three-fold nature of Roman education as follows:

• the *'ludus* which was attended until age twelve and where reading, writing and basic mathematics would have been taught.	• *ludus grammaticus* from twelve until approximately sixteen years, when grammar and literature were studied.	• the school *rhetor* where the art of fluent argument, both oral and written, would have been studied.

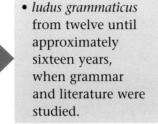

It was clearly this final stage, which Patrick was unable to experience. It provided the art of perfecting eloquent argument that was then practised in the law courts. This in turn necessitated the knowledge of law, to which Patrick refers. Bieler argues that although Patrick would have acquired such knowledge in his later clerical training, sophisticated rhetorical Latin "remained for him a foreign language, into which he had to 'translate'".[15]

It seems to Patrick that this is the reason that many try to oppose his mission (C46).

Many modern scholars dispute Patrick's much stated inadequacy with regard to his professed lack of learning. Howlett points out a most sophisticated use of Scripture, not only for quotation purposes but also for *"the structure of his thought, and the manner of implying more than he seems to say"* and presents the use of scriptural allusion and the artistry inherent in Patrick's writings.[16] Conneely also points out his extensive use of the writings of the Fathers of the Church.[17] And Nora Chadwick similarly argues that *"the author of the Patrician documents, although a provincial, was no isolated rustic, but was a partaker in the cultural thought of Western Europe in his own day".*[18]

There is also perhaps a reference in this chapter to Patrick's use of inculturation (adapting the Gospel to the culture being evangelised), translating his words into *"a foreign tongue"*, which probably refers to the Gaelic language that he had learned in preparation for his mission. It may also imply the translation of the faith into a culture that was foreign to Patrick. This leads Máire de Paor to conclude that this "cultural adaptation was an important component of his integrity as a missionary".[19]

C11

Patrick seems to be replying to an inference made by his clerical colleagues that God chooses the learned and the wise, and rejects the rustic and uneducated. Patrick echoes the Pauline theme of God made great in weakness, and seems to also allude to Saint Augustine that *"non enim electi sunt quia boni fuerunt qui boni non essent nisi electi essent"*[20]: "persons are not called because they are good but so that they can be good". Patrick believes that he has been chosen because of his rusticity so that God could be made great in him. He may also be referring to his 'rustic work', that of bringing the Gospel to countrified places, areas beyond the civilised Empire, of which his peers are probably critical. Howlett seems to be convinced that Patrick is referring to "his life and work, hard work among a rural people", which, because of its nature, his peers did not support.[21]

C12 A return to conversion

Patrick contrasts the period of his life before God intervened in it, with the transformation of himself after that intervention. His early life centres on negativity, a lack of knowledge and understanding which has resulted now in Patrick's exaltation. These are two distinct phases of Patrick's life which illustrate again Patrick's own powerlessness in contrast to God's greatness. In drawing out the contrast between the two, Patrick is showing a deep consciousness of the extent of the grace of God at work in his own life. There seem to be echoes of Psalm 119:67, "*Before I was humbled I went astray, but now I keep your word*", and also Psalm 69:14 "*rescue me from sinking in the mire*". The specific reference to the stone may have come from 1 Peter 2:4–8.[22] Again we hear the echo of the Magnificat; He who is mighty raising the lowly. This is really a Biblical allusion and gives insight into the sophistication of the mind of the author.[23]

C13 Justification of divine calling

Patrick draws out the comparison between himself and those to whom he feels inferior: the masters of rhetoric whom Hanson identifies as British clergy. Patrick is confident that God has called him in preference to those who are learned. Patrick feels that one reason for the opposition of the British clergy to his mission is his inferior education, yet it is he who has triumphed over them serving God in constancy and faith. Although he is inadequate in learning, he has been granted a large measure and quality of faith, which is needed to serve the Irish for the rest of his days. He is very aware of his responsibility towards the Irish. The idea of serving without complaint in spite of difficulty is also found in 1 Thessalonians and 2 Corinthians. Patrick applies the Christian convictions of Paul to his own mission.

C14 and 15 Leaving a legacy

Patrick again makes explicit one of his reasons for writing: to leave a legacy to his brethren and children. The brethren are taken to refer to fellow clerics while children are undoubtedly his Irish converts. The very essence of his life's purpose is to "*promulgate the name of God everywhere fearlessly*". This is the legacy he wishes to leave the Irish, that they too will carry on this mission of everywhere "*expounding the name of God*". He alludes to the success of his mission, claiming to baptise "*so many thousands*". Hanson agrees we have no reason to doubt him. It also echoes chapter 1 of the *Confessio* when Patrick was enslaved with so many thousands, but he has now brought so many thousands to Christ; all are slaves in Christ. The section ends on a note of awe and wonder in all that God has so unexpectedly, to Patrick, achieved in him and through him.

C16 Conversion narrative

Patrick returns to his conversion narrative. Again it is at the lowest point of Patrick's life that God makes himself known. There is a huge contrast between the comfort of his father's villa and the *"woods and the mountains"* that are now his home. He has exchanged his noble identity and his free-born status for that of a slave for whom the isolation and loneliness would have been intolerable. Yet Patrick sees the hand of God at work; this was a crucial point in the redemptive suffering experienced by Patrick, and an important step on his pilgrimage of faith.

The Holy Spirit is the source of all that is now to happen to Patrick. It is God's gift to him and Patrick becomes passive and obedient under the Spirit's influence. Prayer is in the heart of his life from here on in.

The story is written retrospectively and is a narration of the spiritual experience. He gives us no real clue as to the location of the *"woods"* or *"mountains"* on which he finds himself.

C17–19 comprises the escape story

C17 The dream

Patrick begins the narration of his escape. These are the first two of Patrick's experiences of God's direct communication to him in the form of a dream. There are a further five dreams narrated in which God communicates with Patrick. The message is clear: Patrick will return to his own country, Britain. This may be a hint as to the possible location of Patrick's place of captivity. There is greater discussion of this issue in part two of this book. However, the reference to a port 200 miles away, need not have been the nearest port but perhaps the safest one for an escaping slave to use. Máire de Paor points out that the "motif of prayer and fasting underpins this whole section of his *Confessio*".[24]

C18 The power of prayer

The ship had already been set afloat or somehow detached from its moorings. Patrick has the means by which to travel with them. There is debate amongst scholars as to the identity of these men. Traditionally, they have been taken to be traders exporting Irish wolfhounds and they may have finally agreed to take Patrick because as a shepherd boy he may have been of some use in the handling of the dogs, or perhaps his multi-lingualism was of use. However, more recent scholarship interprets their initial reluctance to take Patrick as distrust of him; fear that he might somehow betray them. These might have been the real fears of Irish plunderers and raiders, particularly upon hearing Patrick's British accent. It would also account for their insistence that Patrick give them a pledge or guarantee, a sign of the bond of friendship that he could extend to them in the old pagan Celtic practice of nipple-sucking. They appeared to accept his refusal and accepted instead his word as his bond, on his own terms rather than on their pagan terms. Patrick's faith contrasts sharply with their paganism. Patrick's increasing openness to the Spirit is also clear, as is his ability to see the hand of God at work in every aspect of his life.

The reference to his return to the little hut in which he was staying may well be a reference to assistance given by an Irish Christian to the escaping slave. As a slave he had no rights of hospitality and would have been given none by the native Irish. The port of departure in this case, could have been somewhere in the south-east of the country in the vicinity of Waterford or Wexford where traditionally the earliest Christian communities existed.

C19 Destination

The journey takes three days sailing which makes it less likely to be a British destination. This has attracted many prominent scholars such as Bury to the possibility that Patrick's destination was in fact Gaul. Bieler concurs that they landed "obviously on the continent of Europe".[25] The journey through the wilderness for twenty-eight days, Bury takes to be Gaul after the barbarian invasions of 407.[26] Hanson denies the plausibility of this, as it would be in direct conflict with what Patrick himself has said, *"you will soon go to your own country"*. Hanson chooses to identify the place of arrival as a particularly densely forested part of Britain and translates Patrick's reference to *"wild honey"* as 'honey of the woodland'.[27]

Professor Powell points out the importance of the three day journey in the Pauline scheme of signs and revelations and argues that the shipwreck of Paul in which he feared his own loss of life (Acts 27:10), is mirrored here.[28]

Just as Paul's ship was forced to dock at Malta, Patrick's ship too was forced to make a landing, having been blown off course by quite some miles. This is supported in C61 when Patrick points out that he had only just escaped from Ireland with difficulty. Máire de Paor agrees that the text depicting the Pauline shipwreck is a similar journey narrative, as is the reference in Jonah to his three day stay inside the belly of a whale (Jon 1:17).[29] This story could then be another biblical allusion. Just as Jonah of old was rescued by divine intervention, so too were Patrick and his companions. Joseph Duffy too, is aware of the rich biblical symbolism of this passage, and believes that Patrick deliberately draws out the comparison with Moses and the Exodus.[30]

Patrick ends the story with one of his few direct references to pagan practices when he refuses the honey sacrifice, which had perhaps been offered, or could be offered, to a pagan god. The *Book of Leviticus* also tells us that honey was not an appropriate

The work of Patrick

sacrifice to God (Lev 2:11–12). It is Patrick's firm belief that God had provided for them and that without his intervention, death would have been certain.

C20 Temptation and testing

Patrick interrupts his narrative of events to recount a strange testing experience he has had. Patrick is trying to describe his own total helplessness in the face of the attack by Satan. He calls upon Elijah to help and it was the Risen Christ who came to his aid. Central to understanding this is the Jewish expectation that Elijah would return to herald the coming of the Messiah (Christ.) The meaning of the terminology has been much debated by scholars. It is one of three occasions in the *Confessio* when Patrick makes reference to the sun. The word 'Helias' is translated as 'Elijah', while 'Helios' is the 'sun'. Nonetheless, the gist is probably the triumph again of Christ as the *"true sun"*, which he returns to again in C60. There is a clear parallel between the Christ, the True Son and the pagan sun god. Máire de Paor also points out the play on words between 'Helios' (Elijah) and 'Eloi', the name for God used by Jesus on the cross in his desolation. Was it experienced as a share in the desolation of Christ on the cross? If so, it was also accompanied by a share in his Resurrection. Máire de Paor certainly sees this as the crux of his conversion experience, which again was experienced through suffering.[31]

C21 A second escape

This is one of Patrick's chronological leaps as described by Hanson.[32]

He believes it to be a reference ahead to a different time of captivity experienced by Patrick when he was a bishop to the Irish. Bury disagrees and takes this two month period to refer to the total time Patrick spent with the crew of the ship on which he escaped. Bieler tends to agree with Hanson and sees it as one the *"twelve dangers"* that Patrick refers to as occurring later in his mission to the Irish (C35).[33]

C22

This resumes the narrative of the escape story.

Confessio 23–25 deals with the call narrative

C23 The dream

Patrick is at home with his family in Britain again. We are not told what happened to him between his escape and now, which is clearly a few years later. Patrick experiences another dream or vision, which is the narrative of Patrick's call to the Irish. Patrick did not immediately respond to this dream. He makes it clear that it was the continued promptings of the Holy Spirit to which he finally responds.

45

However, in the vision, which Máire de Paor takes to correspond to Daniel's vision of a figure coming from on high. He hears *"the voice"* of those beside the forest of Foclut, which is near the western sea, calling him. The *"western sea"* is a reference to the Atlantic rather than the Irish Sea. Some scholars, Hanson among them, associate the voice with the voice of those among whom Patrick had been enslaved. This is because of the reference: "We ask you Holy Boy to come and walk among us again", in which the use of the word "again" could suggest a return to a place previously visited. These scholars therefore place his captivity in the West of Ireland. Others argue that Patrick was merely referring to those at the furthermost corner of Ireland of which he was aware, calling him to come to them. He appears to have been overwhelmed by the vision and delayed responding for many years.

C24 and 25 The role of the Holy Spirit

These emphasise the persistent intervention of the Holy Spirit in Patrick's ongoing call narrative. The Spirit prays within Patrick that he may resolve the conflict between the requests of his kin that he not return to the people who had enslaved him and the call of the Irish. Patrick refers, in other places, to his longing to see his family and homeland and also to the fact that he is bound by the Spirit to remain in Ireland. The conflict was not an easy one for him to resolve. Just as he has been called to conversion, he too must call the Irish to conversion. It is all part of God's plan. Patrick's return to the Irish is his response to three separate mystical experiences and through these mystical experiences Patrick has come into a 'relationship' with the three persons of the Trinity.

 PRACTICE ESSAY TITLE

Explore the view that both prayer and the Holy Spirit were important in Patrick's life. Justify your answer. (15)

> You might refer to, for example:
> • Patrick's early life
> • His period of slavery
> • The escape story
> • The vocation narrative
> • Times of trial and testing

C26 Opposition to Patrick

Although the meaning of the word *"seniors"* ('elders' in some translations), is not clear, Hanson takes it that Patrick is referring to those in positions of authority in the British Church. Bieler takes the lack of clarity to be out of charity. It would seem that Patrick had been in Ireland for quite some time and that his mission was a difficult one. Initial support and encouragement was given to Patrick which later gave way to an undermining of him. Numerous allegations against him are alluded to throughout the *Confessio* and it is not clear which are current here.

C27 and 28 The boyhood sin

Patrick, earlier in life, seems to have confessed a sin to his confessor or spiritual director. There is no clarity as to the nature of the sin. Patrick makes it clear that he has already completed the punishment for the sin and that it had been pardoned by his friend. The confession may have taken place before Patrick's ordination as a deacon, when perhaps his conscience was troubled by his less than religious youth. De Paor feels that it may have been the sin of idolatry of some kind which took place in less than an hour one day. This is possible, given the disintegrating state of the Empire and the resurgence of pagan practices which would have been part of that. In particular, sun worship seems to have recurred in the fifth century, and was addressed by Pope Leo. Although all purely conjecture, this explanation also fits with Patrick's three-time expression of the defeat of the sun by the True Son Christ. The sin however seems to have been a mere smokescreen for the wider accusations made against him and peppered throughout the *Confessio*. It seems that thirty years after Patrick had made the confession, the sin was brought up as evidence against him, or at least as a pretext for other allegations (see C46).

C29 Divine assurance

This is another obscure description of a dream wherein he saw an image of his own face accompanied by a derogatory message attached to it but with an accompanying divine voice, expressing displeasure at such denigration of Patrick. Patrick's confidence seems to be restored by the experience. This is Patrick's last recorded dream and assures Patrick that he is innocent in the sight of God.

C30 and 31 Thanksgiving

For all of this, Patrick once again renders thanks to God. In particular, he thanks God for saving his 'enterprise', which would surely have been ruined had his critics been successful. There is perhaps a reference to Patrick's vindication in his comment that *"my faith was approved in the sight of God and man"*. Patrick becomes more confident in his declaration, having received divine encouragement. He is now bold in his promulgation of truth. *"That is why I give thanks to Him who supported me in everything."*

 TASK

Go through the text of the *Confessio* and the commentary and make a list of all that Patrick feels he must thank God for.

C32 and 33 Betrayal by a friend

Patrick returns to the attack made on him. His friend appears to have spoken on his behalf in the period during which he was being considered for the episcopate to the Irish. On this occasion his friend seems to have supported him. Some time later, when Patrick had been in Ireland for a considerable time, his friend betrayed him, perhaps openly at a tribunal from which Patrick was absent, by publicly revealing the sin that Patrick had confessed to him. It would seem that when objections were made against Patrick, his friend took the side of his detractors, providing evidence against Patrick to support their position. Patrick's hurt at this betrayal emanates from the pages of the *Confessio*. It was one more occasion of suffering for him. For him it was not only a personal betrayal but also a betrayal of his divine calling and mission. Interestingly, Patrick still refers to this man as his *"dearest friend"*; he not only forgives him but grieves for him. *"I am sorry for my close friend."* It is here we come into most explicit contact with Patrick's Christ-like forgiveness.

Patrick calls a halt to his recollection. He has totally absorbed the incident into his own suffering and out of this is able to extend forgiveness. *"I have said enough."*

C34 Recurring thanksgiving

Patrick continues his long litany of thanksgiving to God. His gratitude to God as expressed here is indeed the very essence of the whole *Confessio*. The context of his thanksgiving is a reflection on all that has been achieved *"in the last days"*, *"before the end of the world"*. Patrick reiterates his firm belief that his work in evangelising the Irish corresponds with the final period of history and now that salvation has been brought to all, the world will end.[34]

C35 Dangers and difficulties

Patrick gives little detail on what the twelve perils were which put his life in danger and of the plots and other difficulties that he cannot put into words. In terms of the *"twelve perils"*, these may have indeed come from those in Ireland who had most to lose by the introduction of a new faith, namely the druids. He does not relate individually these twelve occasions in which his life was in danger. We have already seen to some extent some of the *"traps and things"* that he *"cannot describe in words"*, but assume there were more *"traps"* than those set by his fellow clergy in Britain. The reference to himself as an *"orphan"* shows the remaining trauma Patrick felt even now in his old age from the experience of his capture at sixteen years. As Hanson points out, he *"never completely ceased to regard himself, as a helpless, friendless victim of the rapine"*.[35] *"In the last days I should venture to undertake this task ... declare his Gospel as a testimony to all nations before the end of the world" (C34).*

PRACTICE ESSAY TITLE

a) Give an account of the challenges faced by Patrick in his mission to the Irish. (35) (You will need to read to the end of this commentary and refer back to Chapter 1 to help you with your answer.)

  You may include reference to, for example:
  - The decentralised nature of Celtic Society
  - The pagan faith/opposition from the druids
  - The customs and culture of the Irish
  - His lack of legal status and rights
  - His personal sense of inadequacy
  - Opposition from Britain

b) Explore the view that Patrick's period of slavery prepared him for his mission. Justify your answer. (15)

  You may include reference to some of the following:
  - It was a period of conversion
  - He began his prayer relationship with God
  - He came to know the Irish language and customs
  - It strengthened his character
  - It made him more sensitive to the plight of victims

C36 Cost and gift

The scripture references here are Mt 13:54 and Ps 38:5. Patrick emphasises the total self-sacrifice entailed in his response to his vocation, both the loss of family and homeland. His homeland of Roman Britain gave him the status of being a Roman citizen. As Bieler points out, this was for Patrick, very much a "double exile; from his own family and also from Roman civilisation", adding that "'Roman and Christian' on the one hand, and 'heathens and barbarians' on the other, were for Patrick interchangeable terms".[36] Máire de Paor sees these as the "twin pillars on which the whole *Confessio* hinges"; that is, cost and gift, and that the "gift *of knowing and loving God*" was great in comparison to the cost of country and family. [37]

C37 Insults and persecution

Having previously experienced criticism from his elders, Patrick now refuses to defer to them, not only on the matter of receiving gifts – which would have been bestowed on him as part of native Celtic culture – but also in the matter of their, on this occasion, well-meaning opposition to his Irish mission. This time, they seem to be concerned for his well-being in that he had to *"endure insults from unbelievers"* and *"persecutions even as far as being put into irons"*. Even the more friendly of his elders seem forced to express some opposition to his mission because of the clear danger in which he is putting himself. Patrick emphasises his desire for martyrdom, his desire for suffering rather than for reward; suffering, even to the point of death, would be a fitting reward for Patrick, a *"kindly grant"* from God.

C38 Administering the sacraments

The focus of Patrick's mission is the pagan population. He sees his work as corresponding to that of Peter and Paul in their mission to the Gentiles. The scripture references used by him here are Acts 13:47; Romans 1:2; Jer 16:19. Hanson takes the reference to *"confirmation"* to include admittance to the Eucharist and the reference to being *"reborn"* as clearly meaning baptism.[38] Administration of the sacraments of Christian initiation are so dear to Patrick that he refers to them around fourteen times in his writings. We also see clearly here Patrick's concern with training and ordaining a native clergy, referred to again in C40; 50; 51.

C39 Judgement Day

The theme of impending judgement occurs again but this time on that *"last day"* all, including his Irish converts who now constitute the *"believers from the whole world"*, will also sit at the table of *"Abraham, Isaac and Jacob"*.

 TASK

Think about and discuss why Patrick would have been preoccupied with the idea of Judgement Day.

C40 Defence of vocation

Patrick claims his authority for working as a bishop to the Irish to be the same authority as Christ gave to the twelve and draws extensively on scriptural support for that authority. This has prompted Bieler to comment that *"Patrick sees himself as the thirteenth apostle living and working in Ireland in the eleventh hour"*.[39] He is continuing the conversion of the peoples as foretold by the prophets.

C41 Christian perfection

Our main interest here is in Patrick's reference to *"the sons and daughters of Irish underkings who have become monks and virgins for Christ"*. He has clearly gained some support from local ruling authorities. But it is his interest in the ascetic life that is most striking. There is no evidence to suggest that Patrick established monasteries but he did encourage the ascetic life. We see his joy in his conversion of the pagan Irish. In particular, his joy is clear at the personal decision of these men and women to voluntarily, in their own homes, practise such virtue. The white martyrdom of the early Church was increasing in popularity as opportunity for red martyrdom decreased.

C42 Self-denial

Patrick singles out one member of the Irish nobility for high praise, but he expresses equal pride in, and concern for, those of lower social status who make similar choices. Patrick conveys to us that there was quite a price to be paid in fifth century pagan Ireland by those women deciding to undertake such a lifestyle. Herren points out that the spiritual role of virgins in the Church was to be one of strengthening, both their own faith and that of others whose faith was encouraged by the witness of such suffering. The suffering of women, he points out, often won great sympathy and united the community of observing Christians in their opposition to the perpetrators.[40] The *"widows"* probably refer to those whose husbands have died but have taken a personal decision not to remarry, as was becoming popular in the Church at the time and was indeed encouraged by Saint Ambrose.[41] Patrick also seems to refer to married Christians who have voluntarily decided to abstain from sexual relations. Although Hanson translates *"those of our race"* to be British Christians settled in Ireland, Howlett disagrees and takes the translation to be 'from our begetting', meaning those whom Patrick had baptised. *"Imitation"* refers to very strict imitation of the example of Christ. Máire de Paor is of the opinion that Patrick encouraged this type of 'proto-monasticism' among his converts in Ireland, which consisted of "celibacy, prayer and involvement with the local Christian community" and which was very like that model of Church depicted in the Acts of the Apostles.[42] This chapter highlights more than any other, the appeal of the Christian message to rich and poor alike, as well as to both genders.

C43 A visit to Gaul

Patrick's expression of a desire to visit Gaul has led many scholars to assume that he wished to return to visit the friends he had made there during his period of clerical training. It does seem to imply that he had at one time visited Gaul. He refers to two different categories of people in Gaul, *"brothers"* and *"holy ones"* which may refer to ordinary Christians and monks respectively. He certainly appears to look to the Christians of Gaul rather than those of Britain for inspiration. The deciding factor, as always, is for Patrick, the will of God rather than his own desire. He is *"bound by the Spirit"* and must be obedient to the Spirit.

He also fears the undermining of his work in his absence; perhaps he will not be permitted to return. Herren believes his fear of leaving arises out of concern for his *"virgins for Christ"* who had to be especially protected, more so than the rest of his community.[43] Máire de Paor disputes this as a "sole reason" for staying and argues that although his particular concern for his female converts is abundantly attested to (C42, 49 and L15, 19), his concern here is for all of his people.[44]

Patrick's determination to remain in Ireland for the rest of his life is clear and leads Hanson to conclude that he had not then, at this stage, made any attempt to ordain native bishops.[45]

C44 Temptation and faithfulness

Patrick gives testament to the fact that he has not led a *"perfect"* life as others have, but in spite of the temptations of Satan he has remained strong and his faith increased. Patrick is ever mindful of the power of temptation, constantly pushing him towards the spiritual death of sin. Again there is the implied need for particular watchfulness as he approaches *"the last times"*.

C45 Determined

Patrick returns to his conviction that he is laughed at and ridiculed and in spite of that, will continue single-mindedly with his purpose of making known the *"signs and wonders of God"*.

C46 Thanksgiving

The long narration of Patrick's thanksgiving to God continues. He seems to imply that he was not always aware of what God could achieve through him, particularly by bestowing on him the sacrament of ordination. He had hesitated in his response because he considered his own inadequacy rather than the power of God made great in weakness. In particular, his educational shortcomings, once more haunt him. His indecisiveness was compounded by the opposition of others to the mission. He concedes that on this occasion, their opposition was not from malice, but concern for his own safety and well-being as well as uncertainty as to how appropriate such a mission would be. The Church does not seem to have, up to this point, partaken in such an organised mission to convert pagans. He thus distinguishes these critics from others who have been more malicious in their condemnation of him and his mission, and brought *"grave accusations against my arduous episcopate"* (C26).

C47 Encouragement

His purpose in writing is more explicitly stated. He addresses two groups: his brothers and his fellow servants in Christ. This may be a collective way of addressing the entire Christian community, in whichever way they are choosing to live out their Christian calling. The particular audience Patrick addresses changes frequently throughout the *Confessio*. His purpose is stated as being *"to strengthen and reinforce your faith"* and to indeed encourage his readers to strive for Christian perfection, the same perfection he alludes to throughout the *Confessio*.

C48–54 Defence

These chapters are largely taken up with defence of himself against a charge that appears to have been levelled against him regarding dishonesty, misappropriation of funds or, in short, of making his mission to the Irish personally lucrative for himself.

C48 Protection of his converts

Patrick lays out his pastoral testimony, showing his continuing concern for the well-being of his converts. His words *"in case I should arouse persecution against them"* echo Matthew 18:6.[46] He does not want any slight or suspicion to be cast on his converts or the Church because of an action of his, so he seeks always to safeguard himself and thereby them.

C49 Refusal of gifts

Patrick claims that though he is unlearned, he is not unwise. Through the Holy Spirit he has received the gift of wisdom and so has been very careful in all his dealings with the Irish. Any payment or gift given to Patrick by the Irish would have been a gift 'in kind' as no coined currency was in circulation. These may have been a kind of 'tribute' payment to Patrick, and he is anxious to explain why these gifts were refused, a refusal that must have offended them. Patrick wishes to protect himself against any charge of simony being levelled against him.

Patrick's mention of the word *"altar"* is the only direct reference in his writings to the celebration of the Eucharist. It seems that the ceremony referred to in C38 was a single ceremony incorporating all three Sacraments of Initiation. The Eucharist, although not directly mentioned, must be assumed to be part of this, as Patrick's converts here have received it.

C50 Success

The reference to *"so many thousands"* is not just a statement of the success of Patrick's mission but also an echo of the *"many thousands"* taken in the raid in which Patrick was captured. Bieler underlines Patrick's concern to reiterate his absolute integrity in the administration of the sacraments.[47] In his defence he appeals both to those he baptised and the clergy whom he ordained. He refutes any accusation of avarice or financial gain. He throws down a challenge to his accusers to produce the evidence against him, challenging the clergy he ordained to also speak up.

C51 Other Christian communities

Instead he says he spent on their behalf. Nerney points out the Pauline parallel, echoing 2 Corinthians 12:15, when Paul defends himself against a similar set of accusations.[48] More interesting, in this chapter is the implied awareness of other areas in Ireland where the sacraments had indeed been previously administered by someone other than himself. There has been some suggestion that this might be an indirect reference to the mission of Palladius. This may well be the case, but it remains a suggestion rather than established fact.

C52–53 Justification of expenditure

Patrick is the only known bishop in Ireland at this time and as it was still a largely pagan country, churchmen had not yet been fitted into the social system and were not legislated for until at least late in the sixth century. A person had no rights outside the *tuath* and a stranger such as Patrick was afforded no protection under Brehon law. In order to preach in a kingdom, permission would have to be sought from the local king and some sort of protection money would have been payable for safe passage. Patrick appears to have acquired a retinue – the sons of kings who accompany him – perhaps for his own protection. He also seems to have made arrangements for safe passage on this occasion but a misunderstanding arose, which has resulted in his imprisonment. He is perhaps attempting to justify his expenditure to the British Church in these two chapters.

In C53, his reference to *"those who administered justice"*, probably refers to the Brehons. The price of *"fifteen men"* is probably an estimation of the compensation payable for death or injury. Máire de Paor feels that it is not coincidence that it was fifteen men who are said to have judged Israel in the *Book of Judges*. There occurs again the echo of 2 Cor 12:15. The payment to the Brehons may also have been for their assistance in, perhaps, translating the Word of God into the native tongue or for his instruction in native law. Máire de Paor further argues that he may also have had to spend money acquiring a site on which to build a new church, giving payment to both the Brehons and the newly Christianised druids. If this is true, it is not surprising that such unusual methods of evangelisation would cause surprise, unease, or even alarm on the part of the established Church. Patrick makes it clear that he has no regret regarding either the nature or amount of his expenditure.

C54

Reiterates the truth of his words by referencing 2 Cor 1:23; Gal 1:20; Thess 2:5; Heb 10:23; Titus 1:12.

TASK

Write summary notes on all the allegations which seem to have been made against Patrick by his fellow clerics in Britain. You will need to find references to support your answers.

You may include, for example:
- Patrick was not well enough educated to hold the office of Bishop
- He could not have been divinely chosen for the mission to the Irish

C55 Ever dangerous

Some further insight is provided into the nature of the difficulties experienced in Ireland on a daily basis. Patrick appears certain that suffering and death will be his *"portion"*, but feels no fear because he has placed himself in God's hands.

Conclusion

Confessio 56–62 form the conclusion of the document.

C56 Chosen by God

He begins his conclusion by reiterating the God-given nature of his vocation and restating his desire to place himself in the hands of God.

C57 Desire for martyrdom

His reference to his intention to repay God for all his goodness to him comes from Psalm 116, but de Paor interprets Patrick's making of a return to God for all his goodness as "the overarching theme of the *Confessio*".[49]

The reference to the desire *"to drink of his cup"* is to the request of James and John in Mark 10:35–41. He expresses his heartfelt desire for martyrdom and in referring to others who have suffered this fate, Hanson feels that Patrick may be making a reference to those martyred specifically in Ireland, perhaps Palladius.[50] It could also be a reference to his own converts butchered by Coroticus (see p64).

C58 Encouragement for the Irish

He prays for the Irish people whom he has converted, recognising them as God's people, for perseverance to the end, and once again for his own opportunity of martyrdom.

C59 Christ the true Son

Patrick believes that if the cup of martyrdom is granted to him, he will have gained his very soul and will reign from and through and in Christ forever. Christ was often depicted in early Christian art as the true rising sun and Patrick seems to be familiar with this portrayal but, on reading the next chapter, he does seem to be specifically addressing a pagan Celtic cult of sun worship which we otherwise know little about.

His repudiation of sun worship is so violent that it would seem that he has become all too familiar with it among the practices of the pagan Celts amongst whom he lived. He introduces here the idea, which he will develop in C60, of Christ as the true and reigning sun.

C60 Condemnation of sun worship

This is Patrick's third reference to the sun in his *Confessio*, and concludes his forceful condemnation of the practice of sun worship. He emphatically states Christ to be the *"true sun"*. He may be anxious to confirm his own orthodox faith, and to support the exhortation of Pope Leo the Great who had become concerned with an apparent resurgence of the cult.[51] He is in a sense proclaiming that Ireland has now been transformed "with the passing away of sun worship and its replacement by faith–life with the true Sun Christ".[52] As in the conclusion of the *Letter to Coroticus*, he ends on an invocation of the Trinity.

C61 The promise of the Gospel

His very reasons for being, as well as for writing are restated once more. As always with Patrick, the Gospel is at the heart of all he does and says.

C62 Final chapter

Patrick ends his *Confessio*, which has been essentially a glancing back along the road that he has travelled, as he began it, with a statement of such striking humility, *"and this is my Confession before I die"*. It is complete. All that is good, and all that Patrick has achieved, is from God, and is not of himself in any way.

 TASK

Go through the commentary and make a note of all the views of scholars mentioned. They will be useful to incorporate into any essay. You can read further by looking up the endnotes at the end of this chapter.

2. THE THEMES WITHIN PATRICK'S *CONFESSIO*

There are many themes within Patrick's *Confessio*. Each fresh reading and study probably unearths another emerging theme. The intention here is not to provide a comprehensive list of the themes within the document, but rather to try to explore some of the themes in order to facilitate greater understanding of that work. What follows, therefore, is by no means a prescriptive or exhaustive discussion, and it is more likely than not that other themes are present in abundance.[53]

Admission of worldly and sinful youth

Patrick introduces this theme in the opening chapter of the *Confessio* but refers back to it on many occasions. He came from a materially comfortable background, and despite its clerical nature, *"My father Calpurnius was a deacon and the son of the presbyter Potitus"*, Patrick points out that:

"I did not know the true God ... we had turned away from God; we neither kept his commandments nor obeyed our priests who used to warn us about our salvation."

Thomas O'Loughlin explains Patrick's lukewarm religious fervour by the practice of baptism later in life, either in the senior years of childhood or indeed in adulthood. Although children were brought up in a Christian environment, they were not baptised until they were ready to give personal commitment and to put past sins behind them. Baptism was perceived to be a serious commitment and, he argues, the practice of infant baptism only becomes prevalent in the Church after Augustine pointed out its necessity in the fifth century.[54]

Meanwhile, some argue that Patrick's awareness of his own sinfulness as a boy grew as a result of his later religious fervour, whilst others, for example, Conneely, urge us to take Patrick on his word on his sinful youth, *"for an entire argument is built on it"*.[55]

Certainly, it seems to have been a sufficient preoccupation for him to have mentioned it frequently and consistently throughout the document. He refers to his youthful sinfulness and ignorance in a variety of contexts. (C2; C5; C9; C10; C12; C44)

In C27 he refers to a particular boyhood sin which weighed heavily on his conscience and tells us that it was committed at a time when:

"I had not yet overcome my sinful ways ... I did not believe in the living God, but remained in death end unbelief" and was *"... in anxiety and of troubled mind."*

Conversion

Arising from this awareness of youthful sinfulness and unworthiness is the theme of conversion. In short, he was converted from a state of unbelief to being a servant of God (C1, C2, C27, C28, C33), which took place during the time of his captivity.

In C1 he points out that *"we deserved it"*; God's action in Patrick's captivity was then both punitive and redemptive. Indeed, redemption or salvation, and thus conversion occur for Patrick through deserved suffering.

It was at this time that *"the spirit was stirred within"* Patrick. The first step in this conversion experience is God's humbling of Patrick through *"hunger and nakedness"* (C27) in captivity. Then he goes on to *"open my unbelieving mind"*.[56] Finally, he totally transforms Patrick:

"He who is mighty came and in his mercy He not only pulled me out but lifted me up and placed me at the top of the wall."

In terms of this conversion narrative Conneely very much believes the *Confessio* to be essentially a 'Confessio of Grace'. Máire de Paor argues that Patrick has a "keen appreciation of the role of suffering in God's plan for salvation, and its necessity for discipleship".[57]

It was in utter humiliation and powerlessness that Patrick found God, and he continues to find him in such circumstances. In the testing experiences which Patrick describes, he seems to have come to the realisation that Christ had to suffer such things in order to come into his glory and so, therefore, should Patrick. In the rejection and betrayal by his friends and colleagues (C9; C13; C26; C27; C45), he was *"purified by the Lord"* (C28), as well as in the dangers and difficulties presented to him in the execution of his Irish mission (C35; C37; C51; C55).

Through these experiences, Patrick's transformation takes place and God achieves great things through him. Patrick wonders at the God *"who roused me, fool that I am, from among those who are considered wise"* (C13) and again, in C55, *"I see that even in this world I have been exalted beyond measure by the Lord"*.

 PRACTICE ESSAY TITLE

Explore the role that suffering played in the religious life and mission of Patrick. (15) Use the commentary to help you.

Praise and thanksgiving

It is in part, because of God's transformation and conversion of Patrick that the theme of praise and thanksgiving erupts powerfully from the *Confessio*. Patrick perceives that he has much to be grateful for because he sees the hand of God at work in every aspect of his life. He is first thankful for his conversion experience and would not exchange a single part of the horrors of his suffering, because through it he has been brought close to God (C1; C2; 27; C36).

In C3 he is explicit in giving thanks for *"the great grace which the Lord generously gave me in the land of my captivity"*, echoed again in C33.

- He is thankful for his God-given vocation (C13; C35; C46), and for the success which God bestowed on that mission, which Patrick sees as divine justification for it:

"I am very much in debt to God who gave me so much grace that through me so many people should be born again in God" (C38) and that those *"who up to now always worshipped idols and unclean things have lately become a people of the Lord and are called children of God"* (C41).

- He is also grateful that God intervened so many times on his behalf during many of his trials and tribulations. In C30 he specifies that God *"supported me in everything"*. He is also thankful for God's support in keeping him *"faithful in everything"* (C34) and for God's frequent intervention, which *"freed me from slavery; how he rescued me twelve times when my life was in danger"* (C35) by warning Patrick in advance through dreams and visions.

- God preserved Patrick in all his troubles and taught him to *"trust him unreservedly"* and for this Patrick *"gives thanks to him tirelessly"* (C34).

Defence

A strong defensive theme runs throughout the *Confessio*.

Patrick strongly defends the divine nature of his vocation to the Irish. In particular he sees the Holy Spirit as the source of his vocation, of whose action he gradually becomes aware, working within him: *"the Spirit was burning within me"* (C16).

He makes it clear that the call of the Irish came in the form of visions and experiences of divine origin in which he came into contact with the Holy Spirit. Patrick certainly sees dreams and visions as God's primary way of communicating His will to him. Part of one of these dreams was his experience of the Spirit praying within him (C25). It was through the persistence of the Spirit that Patrick finally came to comprehend that it was indeed God's will for him to go to the Irish, *"after very many years"* (C23).

The defence of his vocation being *"of the Spirit"* is attested to again in C43, where in spite of his desire to visit family and friends, he felt *"tied by the Spirit"* to remain in Ireland. Even when he himself hesitated (C45), and was compromised by the doubts of his fellow clerics, God once more attests to him in a vision, *"we have disapproved [of] the face of the chosen one deprived of his good name"* (C29).

Although he recognises that some among the ranks of the clergy do not believe such a person as Patrick to be worthy of the episcopate, he corrects their erroneous idea of God's grace, by disputing that God only calls the wise and the good to the episcopate, not sinners or the uneducated such as he. God has created 'rusticity' too. God's choice of Patrick is evidenced by the success which God granted to his mission, and in his protection of Patrick (C16; C17; C26; C33; C34; C35; C37; C52).

Lack of learning was therefore no obstacle to the episcopate.

Finally, he defends himself against the implied allegation that he had somehow made his mission lucrative for himself. He justifies and explains his expenditure, both to the British Church and to his Irish converts (C52; C53) and reassures the British clerics that he had not gained in any way from his converts (C49; C50; C51).

 TASK

Using the commentary, explore the themes of Faith and Prayer in Patrick's *Confessio.*

Success

As part of his defence, Patrick lays out clearly the evidence of the success of his mission, as proof of its divine approval. The success lies not just in the sheer number of his converts, *"the many thousands of them whom I have baptised in the Lord"* (C14; C38), but also in the wholeheartedness with which they have turned to God (C41; C42).

Final judgement

Finally, Patrick's awareness of the nearness of judgement day means that the theme of eschatology runs clearly throughout the *Confessio* from beginning to end.

The shadow of *"the last times"* is cast over the work from as early as C7 and C8:

"On the day of judgement men will render account for every careless word they utter … I therefore ought to dread with fear and trembling the sentence of that day when no one will be able to escape or hide …".

Thomas O'Loughlin points to Patrick's strong sense of being on the 'edge' of things; the edge of the world; the edge of society; the edge of all time.[58]

The context for his belief that the end was near was probably within his own life experience: the collapse of the great Roman Empire and the fall of the city of Rome itself.[59] At the time these were taken to be a portent that the end of the world was near.

Christians believe that it was God's promise that before the end, the Gospel would be preached to all people, to those at the very end of the known universe, which indeed was the geographical location of Ireland at the time. Hence, we have Patrick's testimony that *"the good news has been preached in distant parts in places beyond which nobody lives"* (C34). See also C38; C51.

Also in C34 he thanks God for the gift of undertaking *"in these latter days, this holy and wonderful work"*. It is indeed a great privilege felt by Patrick to have such a role in the final stages of salvation history. His own role in relation to the final stages of salvation history is outlined in C39 and C40, in Christ's missionary commands to the twelve: *"and then the end will come; and in the last days it shall be…"*.

The whole purpose of the mission of the apostles has now been fulfilled and there is little point in delaying the end of all history. Patrick clearly believes that history shall now enter its end phase because the Irish are now *"called children of God"*; they are now prepared.

His work marks the completion of the entire apostolic task and he clearly "presents himself as having a singular place in bringing about the consummation of creation".[60]

 PRACTICE ESSAY TITLE

a) Give an account of the themes of Patrick's *Confessio*. (35)

   Use the notes above to help you. Make sure you have a range of references to the text to support your answer.

b) Comment on the claim that the *Confessio* was written by a man who was disliked by many. Justify your answer. (15)

   Use the *Confessio* and the commentary to help you.

3. THE PURPOSE OF PATRICK'S *CONFESSIO*

Introduction – confession as a type of religious literature

When discussing Patrick's purpose in writing the *Confessio*, we need to establish the type of literature to which this belongs. In a sense the purpose of the *Confessio* is defined in its title, a title which Patrick himself gives it in the final chapter of his work. A confession is in the view of Dronke:

"the way in which a man, while telling about himself, telling … about the circumstances of his life, and confessing his own sinfulness, sees God as the indwelling presence in his life, the guiding force of his destiny and is moved to proclaim this to the world and again and again to give thanks for it."[61]

An autobiography

It is not autobiographical in the strict sense of what that implies, for it does not present to us the facts of Patrick's life in detail nor indeed chronologically. Neither would it be correct to say that it is *not* autobiographical, for it is Patrick's telling of his own story.

Patrick however is selective in his presentation of factual information, and tells us only of those details which are necessary or significant in his presentation of the much bigger picture. The bigger picture for Patrick was always the 'faith-life' as it is lived within the circumstances in which he finds himself.[62] Conneely argues that because it is a genre of religious writing, the title itself implies that it was primarily addressed to God.

A defence

Some rightly see the *Confessio* as an *apologia,* a defence or an explanation. Patrick's *Confessio* is certainly that. Indeed, one of his central purposes in writing seems to be to refute certain allegations made about him, which he does primarily in C48–54.

He also writes to defend himself against assumptions made about his ability and suitability for both the episcopate and the mission to the Irish. This defensive purpose, which permeates the whole text, is alluded to in the very first chapter (see also commentary on p59).

It is important to note however that if we accept that the *Letter* was written before the *Confessio,* then its outspoken condemnation may have caused renewed attacks to be made on the character and reputation of Patrick, to which Patrick then replies in the *Confessio.*

 TASK

Discuss in class the ways in which Patrick's Confessio shares the characteristics of this type of Literature.

Explicit purposes

Ultimately, Patrick's *Confessio* evolves into so much more than a mere defence. Patrick gives us a clear reason for writing in C3 and again in C33. This again reflects a religious confessional reason. We see his compulsion to write. So deep is his awareness of the saving and transforming power of God in his own life, that his retelling of it almost erupts from his pen, and it becomes imperative that he writes of it.

He writes therefore to declare and make known God's action in his life and to somehow, by the writing of this document offer a repayment for all that God has done in and through him. This idea of the *Confessio* as repayment is laid out in C3; C11; C12; C57. He wants to highlight the success of his mission and attribute this to God.

In this sense the purpose of the *Confessio* is primarily a religious one. He echoes this again in C14 when we get a sense of his repayment in the exaltation of God's name through the writing of the document:

"the gift of God and his eternal consolation must be made known, regardless of danger … I must fearlessly and confidently spread the name of God everywhere …".

He returns to this purpose at the very end of the document: *"I testify in truth and exaltation of heart…"* (C61). In the view of Máire de Paor "to make known the gift of God is the essence of Patrick's whole life endeavour." [63]

To give thanks

Because of Patrick's intention to declare and make known the greatness of God, the *Confessio* in its purpose also becomes "a magnificent canticle of gratitude to God."[64]

He writes to make his own song of praise and gratitude to God who involved himself in every aspect of Patrick's life. Patrick believes he has much to be thankful for. The thanksgiving purpose is attested to in abundance within the body of the text: C3; C30; C34; C45.

The purpose of the *Confessio* as thanksgiving has already been dealt with earlier (see page 57–58).

To meet the spiritual needs of his converts

A further purpose of Patrick's *Confessio* is to address the spiritual needs of his own community of converts and his own family and friends, and to this end he addresses them specifically several times in the text (C6; C14; C47).

The *"aspiration of my life"* referred to in C6 is to make his repayment to God for all his goodness to him as he attests in C3; C11; C12; C57.

He wants his relatives and friends to know that despite his love for them, which he alludes to in C23; C36; C43, he is bound by the Father and the Spirit to leave them forever.

In C14 he makes explicit his purpose to leave a spiritual legacy to his converts and his brothers; the legacy he wishes to leave is the gift of faith to which his whole confession attests. In this sense his *Confessio* is his last will and testament to his converts.

We see here his clear pastoral devotion to the welfare of his flock. It echoes his commitment to serve them as expressed in C13.

Elsewhere, in C47, he urges his converts to carry on his mission and to strive for Christian perfection. It would be the attainment of this perfection which would make them Patrick's pride and joy. For Patrick, Christian perfection was attained by the ascetic ideal (C41; C42).

Conclusion

Patrick's *Confessio* was written retrospectively and is a contemplation of the events of his life, his joys, his failures and his faith as it was experienced and lived out. It was a statement and a declaration of himself and an attempt to offer to the reader, his fellow clerics, his family and friends, his converts and indeed God himself, the very essence of all that Patrick was and could become.

 PRACTICE ESSAY TITLE

a) **Explain Patrick's reasons for writing the** *Confessio.* **(35)**

   Use the notes above and the *Confessio.* Remember to reference well.

b) **To what extent was Patrick's mission affected by conditions in Ireland? Justify your answer. (15)**

   Use Chapter 1, the commentary, the *Confessio* and the overview of Patrick's mission as provided to help you.
   Think about whether conditions in Ireland were the only thing to have an effect on the work of Patrick.

4. PATRICK'S *LETTER TO COROTICUS*
Introduction – Patrick's *Letter to Coroticus* written in response to the attack of Coroticus on Patrick's Christian community

In the opinion of most scholars, Patrick's *Letter* predates the *Confessio.* It is also generally accepted that Patrick had worked in Ireland for some considerable time before the incident occurred that precipitated the *Letter.* (L3 refers to a presbyter he had known since childhood.) Coroticus, a Welsh prince, had conducted a raid on Ireland, and had captured or killed many of Patrick's newly-baptised Christians. We also know that the *Letter,* which is still extant, is the second letter he wrote to Coroticus and his men. The first had met with derision (L3).

From the beginning of the Church there was a denunciation of those in the Christian community who led a life of immorality. Paul in 1 Cor 5:11, prescribes that Christians should *"not eat a meal with such a one".* The penalty issued was exclusion from the community and the imposition of penance until such time as the sinner was able to repent of their immorality. The writings of the Church Fathers imply that a sinner who commits a serious offence could only be re-admitted to the Church community after completion of public penance. If they persisted in grave sin, their exclusion from the community was more permanent.[65] Excommunication or exclusion could be both imposed and lifted by a bishop. Although Patrick does not specifically use the word excommunicate in the *Letter*, it is clear that is what is involved in this decree.

L1. Patrick as bishop

Although similar to the *Confessio* in its expression of humility, the formality of the *Letter* is seen in its opening chapter. Patrick is emphasising that he is a bishop and as such has full authority from God. He states plainly from the outset that whomever he might send this letter with, it does indeed bear the weight of his full personal authority as bishop. Although he writes with reluctance in such harsh terms, the gravity of the incident and his love of God and his converts necessitates this degree of harshness. It is with regret that Patrick so strongly denounces those responsible for the killings and abductions. He is aware that there are those in Britain who despise and belittle him and his work.

 TASK

Why was it important for Patrick to remind his readers that he was bishop to the Irish?

L2. The denunciation

Patrick reiterates the authority with which he writes and that authority is his own, because he is a bishop. The words used are solemn and formal. The audience to whom he addresses them, at this point, are the soldiers of Coroticus. Patrick seems sure of the identity of the attacker and protests to the soldiers almost immediately. Most scholars agree that the attack on Patrick's converts took place on the north-eastern coast, accessible to raiders from Britain. Coroticus and his men no longer deserve the civilised status bestowed on them – as a result of being citizens of the Roman Empire – because of the barbarity and evil of their actions. The Picts (painted ones, the unromanised inhabitants of Scotland) and Irish were the considered barbarians of the day. If Coroticus was king of Dumbarton, as some scholars suggest, he may well have had business dealings with these people. They have become even more tainted with the blood of innocent Christians; the innocence of the confirmed Christian victims contrasts with the behaviour of their slayers.

L3. Christian status

Patrick recounts the incident itself. It is important to Patrick that all those whom he addresses, recognise that this act was perpetrated against a *Christian people.*

L4. Grief

Patrick laments and grieves for all involved, those killed, those captured and the perpetrators themselves who are the captives of Satan. The punishment meted out to them will be eternal in hell. That is a matter of sorrow rather than satisfaction for Patrick.

L5–9 deals with the issue of excommunication

Here begins the formal decree of excommunication. For Patrick, because of the offences they have committed, Coroticus and his men have *"broken the bonds of ecclesiastical communion with the Church"*.[66] They are now *"strangers"* rather than fellow citizens. The full consequences of what that excommunication will mean for them is explained in L7. This chapter has within it the shadow of judgement day, which reflects Patrick's understanding that the end of the world is near.

L6. Authority of Patrick

Patrick again reiterates his authority. He may have been accused of 'speaking out of turn' as Coroticus and his men were not resident in the diocese of Patrick, but to Patrick's mind all bishops of the Church have a God-given authority. Joseph Duffy believes this to mean that "Patrick had the passive if not active backing of the local bishop".[67] Patrick's insistence is that his power is one which comes from on high; it is a divine authority. The plural use of the word *"priests"* in L6 suggests that he was not alone in his condemnation of the action of Coroticus and his men.

L7. Alienation from the whole Church

This chapter clarifies the nature of excommunication. It is addressed to the wider Christian community who may come into contact with these people. They are not to socialise or to dine with these men. The men themselves are to undertake rigorous penance and then are to undo what they can of their actions by freeing those they have enslaved. This is the established system of penance in the Church at the time as advocated by Paul in 1 Cor 5:11. Patrick is perhaps addressing any clergy who by their association implicitly condone the actions of Coroticus. He has reminded them of the dignity of their own office in L6, and in L7 makes it clear that the supreme dignity of the office which they hold has practical implications for their behaviour. It is perhaps this reminder which instils in the British clergy hostility against Patrick. At the very least the excommunication carried out by a bishop, not of Britain but of Ireland, must have been deeply embarrassing for the clerics of the British Church.

 TASK

Why might the content and tone of this Letter have caused his fellow countrymen to dislike and criticise Patrick?

L8. Scriptural authority

Patrick uses the full weight of scriptural authority for his action.

L9. The sin of avarice

For Patrick, reverence for God and reverence for the children of God are one and the same thing. In essence, Coroticus and his men have excommunicated themselves from the Church by their behaviour. Patrick clearly identifies avarice as the root cause of Coroticus' sin and sets about declaring his own abhorrence of such a sin.

L10. A personal attack

Patrick interprets the massacre carried out by Coroticus and his men as a sign of the contempt in which he is held by his own countrymen. He cannot resist sketching in the details of his background, illustrating the wealth of his family estate, "*the men and women servants of my father's house*", but also pointing out that he had chosen to trade all of it to assume the status of slave in Ireland. His father was of high rank indeed, a decurion, holding public office in Roman Britain. He believes that he should be listened to because he is bound by the Spirit to speak out.

> As an ex-slave and an individual without family ties, Patrick could be afforded no protection under Irish law.

L11. Christian dignity

For Patrick, the crime of Coroticus upon the Irish is made all the worse because it has been carried out by one Christian against another. It is clear from this chapter that Coroticus and his men are at least nominally Christian. Patrick feels compelled to remind them of the new status of his Irish converts, that by a process of "divine adoption", they have the highest dignity and "have the same God as Father".[68] This Christian dignity supercedes all, be it culture, race, or social class. The message is clear: they have murdered their brothers and sisters in Christ.

TASK

Why is it important for Patrick to point out that the Irish victims were Christian and not pagan? Recall what you learned in Chapter 1.

L12. The despair of the shepherd

Again it is clear in this chapter that Patrick feels the massacre to be a personal attack upon himself. He felt compelled to express his horror; he sees the Irish as "*sheep savaged, defenceless prey*". Conneely sees within this the cry of the "anguished shepherd whose flock has been ravished,"[69] rather than the stiff decree of excommunication issued earlier in the *Letter*. The vastness of the massacre overwhelms him: *"I cannot count their number."*

L13. Solidarity with the victims

This chapter calls on the whole Church to join in grief for the suffering of these members. No good Christian could be an accomplice to such a crime. No committed Christian could bring themselves to benefit in any way from the exploitation of another. The Church should grieve with those who suffer, not feast with the wrongdoer. Coroticus and his men will be held equally guilty for leading their associates into sin by offering them fruits of their plunder.

L14. Roman Christians in Gaul

As in the *Confessio*, Patrick makes reference to the Roman Christians of Gaul, offering further evidence for his close association with them (see also C32; C43). He compares the attitude of the Christians of Gaul with those of the British Christians in the same circumstances, both of whom, he emphasises are Roman Christians. The contrast is startling. While the Christians of Roman Gaul seek to save and buy back captured Christians, British Christians stand idly by and do nothing to help those captured. Again, it is easy to see why such a comparison would not endear him to his fellow clerics in Britain.

The reference to the gold coin, the solidus, is insightful and its relevance will be discussed later. (See the discussion on the dating of Patrick, p187.) The solidus was a coin which had been minted by Constantine (270–337), but by the year 410, it was no longer being minted in large quantities. It was probably out of circulation by the second half of the fifth century.

Patrick has particular concern for the female captives, fearing that they have perhaps been sold into prostitution. Patrick is all too aware that the sexual mores of paganism were very different from those of Christianity, and rightly feared for the safety of his captured converts in this regard.[70]

He makes it clear once more that there will be damnation not only for the perpetrator but the collaborator also.

L15. Grief for those killed

This chapter is concerned with those who were killed in the raid. The greed of Coroticus and his men knows no bounds; their pillage and plunder has led them into murder. The theme is the Church's solidarity with the victim. But Patrick grieves equally for those not yet killed because all are victims, all are martyrs. He seems to be referring to the same sinful pagan practices as in the previous chapter, *"where sin prevails openly ... into distant countries."* Patrick reminds his readers that because the Irish are now Christian, they are also free-born and share the status of the British Christians. This reminder is needed lest any of the listeners, in an inflated sense of their own superiority, feel that the killings were a fate fit for pagan barbarians.

L16. A racial attack

Patrick's grieving and mourning continues. His sense of helplessness in the face of such atrocity is clear. However, more noteworthy than his grief and sorrow is his complete solidarity with the victim. This chapter is addressed to the Irish themselves, all of the baptised community who are victims of this loss. He identifies completely with them. He means what he says: he has sold his own free-born status and become one with his converts. He seems to identify this as a racial attack. He reiterates: *"perhaps they do not believe we have received one baptism."*

L17 and 18. The reward of martyrdom

Continuing to address the Irish, this time he speaks to those who were murdered. His grief is tempered with joy in that those killed are now martyrs of the Church and so will reign forever from their world in paradise. Furthermore, those who perpetrated this wrong against them will be as *"ash under your feet."* The martyrs will reign with the saints because their death occurred so soon after baptism. No sin of any kind could have tainted them.

L19. Concern for women

His concern for the female captives continues. Máire de Paor believes that from the vocabulary and the structure used by Patrick, the men are the Christians who were killed and the women were taken as captives, to be distributed *"as prizes."* Hanson disputes this interpretation.[71] Patrick makes it clear that the fate of Coroticus and his men is to be *"lorded over"* for all eternity by those whom they regard to be *"barbarian Irish"*.

L20.

Again, Patrick verifies his own decree by referring to the source of its authority, a source which is divine, prophetic and apostolic authority. Patrick is making it clear that these words are not just his own but the guarantee of God himself. As in the *Confessio*, scripture affirms the testament of Patrick. He links the fate of his own martyrs with that of the apostles. The feasting with Abraham, Isaac and Jacob contrasts with the fate of those who collaborate with Coroticus by dining with him in L7. Patrick contrasts the reward of the martyrs with the fate of the perpetrators.

L21. A call to repentance

Patrick feels that his *Letter* should or will be read out before several different audiences. Joseph Duffy accepts the translation of *"all the tribes"* as being 'all the communities', "in order to convey that Patrick's letter was canonical and church-related, rather then a secular document."[72] Máire de Paor contrasts the Prologue with the Epilogue: in the former Patrick the sinner addresses Coroticus and his men, in the Epilogue he asks the sinners to repent.[73] Patrick's intention is to bring healing to the hurt caused to the Church. He encourages Coroticus and his men back to the Church. The door does not remain firmly shut upon them forever more, but they must begin to make the steps of the return journey. His desire is for the reconciliation of the sinner, and he ends somewhat clumsily, in the view of Hanson, by calling down upon Coroticus the peace of the three persons of the Trinity.

5. THE THEMES AND PURPOSE OF PATRICK'S *LETTER TO COROTICUS*

The purpose of Patrick's *Letter* is fairly explicit in the body of the text and the themes within it are also quite clearly expressed. A joint reading of the summary below together with the commentary provided should make them sufficiently clear.

The Themes

Denunciation

The first theme in the *Letter* is Patrick's denunciation of the crimes of Coroticus. He spells out clearly the nature of the crime (L3; L15) and expresses his judgement of Coroticus and his men as well as those who associate with them (L2; L4; L12; L18).

Patrick's judgement of the perpetrators of this massacre is harsh and unrelenting because the act itself was harsh and unrelenting. He refers to them, among other things, as:

"Fellow citizens of the devils; … fierce wolves; … murderers of father and brother; … ravenous wolves; … dogs; sorcerers and murderers".

Although he does not denounce the slave trade explicitly, his abhorrence of it is very clear in the concern he expresses for his captives (L14; L15; L21). In L10, his particular concern for those enslaved finds context in his own slavery.

Excommunication

The excommunication of Coroticus and his men forms the crux of the *Letter*. He begins the process in L5 and lays down the full import of what is entailed in L7; L13 and L19. He claims the authority of Scripture and God, and invokes a process already in use in the Church at the time (see p64). In this sense the excommunication is fully canonical. In addition to the formal decree issued by this *Letter*, Patrick makes it clear that it is Coroticus and his men who by their actions estranged themselves from God and from the Christian community.

Solidarity with the victim

A strong theme of solidarity with the victim emerges from the *Letter*. Patrick's expression of solidarity begins in L4: *"I do not know for whom I am to grieve"* and in L15 he has clear awareness of the scriptural command, *"to weep with those that weep"*. He makes it clear that the Church will stand side by side with the victim. His lamentation continues into L16 and his identification with the victim is clear in his cry, *"we have been treated as outsiders … it is a matter of contempt that we are Irish."* This lamentation evokes the image of the massacre of the Holy Innocents by Herod.[74]

Christian unity

Patrick also emphasises the unity of all Christians throughout his *Letter* (L2; L8; L11; L14; L15; L16).

He underlines the dignity of all Christians by virtue of their baptism. This dignity and identity will eclipse all notions of culture or race or gender. It is a matter of revulsion for Patrick that this crime should be perpetrated on one Christian by another, and in grappling with this issue, he echoes the words of Paul in Eph 4:5–6.

Patrick emphasises the idea of Christian unity by virtue of baptism and expresses his sorrow at disunity among the Christian brethren, *"one builds up and another tears down"* (L12). In L14 he holds up the example of the Gaulish Christians as a model of good practice in Christian fraternity.

Collaborative Guilt

A smaller but nonetheless important theme is 'guilt by collaboration'. Patrick also addresses those who associate with Coroticus – those who share food and drink with him (L7; L12; L13; L14). There is also an implicit reprimand to the British clergy and the wider Christian community who, by their failure to admonish Coroticus, have tacitly complied with his crime. The duty of the Christian is to speak out loudly clearly. Patrick is explicit in these passages that those who associate with the wrongdoer will also be judged as guilty.

The sin of avarice

Patrick has a particular abhorrence of the sin of avarice, which he believes lies at the heart of the actions of Coroticus. He launches a discourse against the evil of avarice in L8, and in L13, but he speaks particularly vehemently against the accumulation of wealth which has been begotten unjustly or by the exploitation of others. He declares that it *"will be vomited from his belly"* and warns, *"woe to those who fill themselves with what is not theirs"*. He cites the commandment *"not to covet thy neighbour's goods,"* alongside *"do not murder"*. For Patrick, greed lies at the root of so much evil, even murder.

Repentance

Patrick ends on the theme of repentance (L21). His anger does not continue unabated and has indeed been tempered by grief for those *"whom the devil has deeply ensnared"*(L4).

It is important that Patrick condemns the sin and has done so very forcefully throughout the *Letter*, but in the final analysis he separates the sin from the sinner. Although ending on a note of hope, Patrick stills places the onus upon Coroticus and his men; forgiveness can be extended to them only if they return to God. Penance and indeed reparation are still needed.

Nonetheless, as with any good pastor, his ultimate desire is to heal the hurt which has been inflicted by the sin of Coroticus – hurt to his Irish converts, hurt to himself as their shepherd, and hurt to Coroticus himself in his ensnarement by evil.

 PRACTICE ESSAY TITLE

a) **Give an account of the teaching contained in Patrick's *Letter to Coroticus*. (35)**

    Your answer might include reference to some of the following:
- Denunciation of wrongdoing
- The sin of covetousness and avarice
- Guilt by collaboration
- Importance of solidarity with the victim
- Christian unity and fraternity
- The seriousness of the sin of murder
- The hope of repentance

b) **Comment on the claim that Patrick was a good shepherd to his flock. Justify your answer. (15)**

    Your answer might include reference to some of the following:
- His desire to leave a legacy to his converts in the *Confessio*
- His concern for the plight of his female converts (*Confessio*)
- His grief for his mourning Irish converts (*Letter*)
- His outspokenness on behalf of his converts

The purpose

In light of the discussion above, the purpose of Patrick's *Letter* can be summarised as follows:

1. Patrick's purpose is clear from the opening chapter of the *Letter*: he wants to assert his authority as bishop. His words are formal: *"declare myself to be bishop"*. He reiterates this purpose again in L6: *"I am not exceeding my rights"* and emphasises the divine power Christ bestows on his priests *"to bind and loose."*

2. An explicit purpose was to denounce the action of Coroticus and his men and to formally excommunicate them from the Church.

3. He hopes to put pressure on the British clergy to speak out against Coroticus.

4. He also wishes to show solidarity with his Irish converts and to openly grieve with and for them.

5. He hopes to secure the release of the captives and the return of the spoils. (L3; L21; L7).

6. He wishes to challenge racism and appeal for Christian unity.

7. He writes to call Coroticus to repentance (L21). (See p72)

 TASK

Discuss in class the view that the purpose of the Letter is clearer than that of the *Confessio*.

6. THE MISSION OF PATRICK – AN OVERVIEW

Divine Origins

The mission of Patrick arose from a divine call, to which he attests throughout the *Confessio* (C23). God primarily communicated with Patrick through dreams and visions (C17; C20; C21; C23; C24; C25; C29).

His mission was the work of God (C15; C34; L10; L11). This is reflected not only in the call narratives but in the success which God bestowed upon his work. His own role within that was as Christ's legate, ambassador and apostle (C56; L5; C16; 34; 40). It can be argued that he sees Christ's missionary commands to the twelve as reflecting his own missionary purpose.

The completion of this apostolic directive has led Bieler to proclaim that, "he is in fact the last of the apostles bringing the faith to Ireland in the eleventh hour".[75] Hanson believes that Patrick sees his mission as corresponding to the final phase of salvation history – the completion of all Creation when all peoples will come to know God "after which then the world would end".[76] (L5; L9; C34; C38; C58)

Evangelisation

Patrick's mission was primarily to the pagan population (L1; C41; C48), whom he describes as barbarian (L10; C1). He perceived his mission as the salvation of souls (C28; C40; C41; C49). Several times he makes known his distaste for the pagan Celtic faith (C18; C20; C41; C60).

Salvation through the sacraments

Salvation was given to the Irish people through the administration of the sacraments of initiation (L2; C38; C51). Hanson contends that this "took the form of a single comprehensive ceremony including baptism ... for which they put on new white clothes and in which the bishop laid hands on them and anointed them with chrism and then Eucharist in which they communed in both kinds".[77] As a result of this the Irish were now *"the people of the Lord and the sons of God"* (C41).

Successful

Patrick's mission was successful. The Irish have now become, *"the people of the Lord and sons of God"* (C41) and Patrick's *"brethren and fellow servants of Christ"* (C47). In the *Letter* too, he is convinced that the Irish Church has been *"increasing excellently and most actively"* (L12), and *"the number of converts cannot be counted"* (L12; L16). In the *Confessio* he speaks of *"a great multitude and throng"* (C41), and *"so many thousands"* (C14; C50). Patrick also knew the importance of winning over the local rulers in particular (C42).

Ordination of clergy

Patrick's mission involved the ordination of a native clergy (C38; C40; C50; C51; L3). He does not mention the ordination of bishops. In the *Letter* in particular, Hanson argues that Patrick "insisted upon the authority of his order" and indeed the authority of all priests to whom there has been given "supreme divine, lofty power".[78] (L6)

Encouragement of Christian perfection

Patrick's mission involved the encouraging the virtue of Christian perfection. Bieler argues that this virtue was "especially close to Patrick's heart".[79] He refers to converts who became *"monks and virgins for Christ"* (L12; C41; C49). For Patrick, Christian perfection was achieved in the living of the ascetic life.

Difficult and dangerous

Patrick's mission was both difficult and dangerous. Some of the difficulties arose from the conditions in which Patrick lived and worked in Ireland. (See Chapter 1 and the task below). Bieler points out that "he would have had to overcome the natural distrust of strangers ... and prejudice against a new faith on the part of those who had a vested interest in the existing order of things".[80] Some of these difficulties were a result of the criticism he may have received from his fellow clerics in Britain, ie their distrust of his financial management (C48, 49, 50) and his suitability for the episcopacy (C26–32 and C9; 10; 13). It is clear from these passages that Patrick is indeed answerable to the Church in Britain and that they probably, in part at least, financed his mission. His somewhat unconventional means of evangelisation (see C49–50; C59–60) leads Kathleen Hughes to conclude that, "an ill-educated, itinerant bishop, travelling with a paid retinue of young nobles, distributing largesse to petty kings, may well have been regarded with misgiving by unimaginative churchmen in Gaul and Britain". She also points out that the peculiar conditions in Ireland necessitated "unconventional measures of evangelisation". (See below.)

Other difficulties may have been due to the ongoing slave trade. Patrick himself seems to fear re-capture (C35; C55) and his own converts fell victim to the raid of Coroticus.

Further difficulties are of a personal nature (C36, 43, 58, 62): his freedom, his status, his family and friends, as well as his own low self-esteem.

Inclusive

Patrick's mission was also an inclusive one. Joseph Duffy points out that Patrick "had a shrewd sensitivity to the political realities in which he found himself".[81] This cultural sensitivity is apparent on a number of occasions in Patrick's writings and led Patrick to employ the method of inculturation (C9; C52; C53; C60), rather than being countercultural. Duffy concludes: "he was concerned to respect fully native law and custom, unless they were contrary to the Christian Gospel, and to use them for his own ends".[82] Where Irish culture did run counter to Gospel values, especially in terms of the paganism Patrick encountered, he was vociferous in his condemnation of it (C18; C19; C41).

Patrick's mission was also gender inclusive. He is acutely aware of the particular vulnerability of women in the fifth century, reflected not only in his concern for the plight of female slaves in the *Letter to Coroticus*, but also throughout the *Confessio*. He is open and sensitive to the particular issues which affect women (C42; L7; L14; L15; L21) – slavery and prostitution among them. Noel Dermot O'Donoghue argues that Patrick certainly has no "neurotic fear and contempt for the feminine ... in this sense he is a complete man".[83] Aside from these apparent sensitivities, it is the faith of his female converts which he singles out for particular praise (C42), leading Helena Concannon to conclude that Patrick sees women "as active workers in the missionary field".[84]

In this way, Patrick's mission broke down many of the social conventions of his day and it is this perhaps which led to some of the attacks on his character, which he addresses in the *Confessio*.

TASK

From your knowledge of the background to the mission of Patrick, and both the Letter and the *Confessio*, discuss how Patrick's mission was affected by conditions in Ireland.

7. PATRICK'S CHARACTER AND MIND – A PORTRAIT OF PATRICK

A vulnerable man

It is within his own writings that we are clearly presented with the character and mind of Patrick. From a cursory glance at these texts, one is struck by the sheer vulnerability of the man that is Patrick. Throughout both texts, we have a strong sense of a person who is totally alone. He never truly recovered from the trauma of the wrench from family and homeland, and echoes of his sense of abandonment occur throughout his writings (C55; L1). His adult experiences continued to contribute to his sense of aloneness. His vulnerability leaps from the pages; for example, the contempt with which he feels himself to be held by his fellow countrymen, the sorrow and heartbreak with which he recalls the treachery of his close friend, and the intensity of the grief at the loss of his neophytes in the *Letter*. Patrick's narration of these experiences show, according to Seamus Mulholland, "the human face of the spiritual life: uncertainty, pain, hardship, ruined plans, exiled hopes … the spirituality of broken humanity". Patrick was a man "who was driven to breaking point by too much laughter and too little self-esteem".[85]

Humility

Yet in spite of this, Patrick is no victim. Even though he may be self-deprecating, he has a huge sense of pride that God chose him in preference to his better educated peers. It is in this realisation that lies Patrick's total and utter humility – his sense of God made great in his weakness. His success then is attributed to God rather than himself (C12; C13; C15; C31; C33; C55; C62).

Ken Thompson's statue of 'Patrick the Pilgrim' at the entrance to Lough Derg is an insightful portrayal of the young Patrick. *(Photo courtesy of Cathal O'Connor, with the kind permission of Monsignor Richard Mohan, Prior of Lough Derg)*

Courageous

Out of this humility comes Patrick's courage. All that is good in him comes from God. All of the authority of his office as bishop is God-given. It is this knowledge that gives him the strength and the courage to reprimand Coroticus, to demand the return of the captives and the booty, to implicitly rebuke the British clergy, and to vociferously speak up in his own defence in the *Confessio*. He was so confident in God's care and protection of him that he has the perseverance to remain with the Irish in spite of danger and difficulty. It is in the most trying of circumstances that we see Patrick's courage and determination.

Pastor and shepherd

Patrick also emerges from his writings as a shepherd and pastor of his flock. Indeed, it is this imagery that he himself uses in the *Letter to Coroticus* (L12). Hanson identifies in the *Letter* a cry of pain of the good shepherd whose flock has been torn asunder.[86] Duffy agrees that because Patrick was such a caring pastor, the *Letter* burns with "inconsolable heartache and deeply felt rage".[87] He is also the good shepherd not afraid of pastures new in his attempt to spread the *"name of God everywhere confidently and fearlessly"*. His pastoral concern for his flock is such that he is anxious that no action of his should reflect negatively on them (C48). Like any pastor, Patrick's concern is always for the vulnerable and oppressed. Máire de Paor points out that "his respect, reverence and concern for the Irish women … more specifically for the female slave is remarkable".[88] Such was his pastoral care of the Irish that he was compelled never to leave them, however much he missed his family and friends, instead choosing to work tirelessly in the interests of his beloved flock.

Prayerful

Patrick also emerges from his writings as deeply spiritual and prayerful. He has a deep consciousness of the Spirit within him and the importance of his persistence in prayer: *"as many as one hundred prayers a day."* The depth of his spirituality was such that he frequently felt *"the Spirit praying within me"*.

Practical

Patrick was also a man of considerable practical talent, as identified by Francis Shaw, who speaks of Patrick's "exceptional talent for organisation and government … and a natural practical capacity for organisation".[89] He realised the importance of ordaining a native clergy and with busying himself with day to day financial issues, and even of safeguarding himself in all financial dealings. He set about his evangelisation of the Irish purposefully, making sure to have gained the support of local nobles and kings, knowing the importance of *"leaving a legacy for my brethren and sons" (C14)*.

Charitable

One of Patrick's most striking characteristics is his 'Christlike charity'. His ability to respond to the Irish treatment despite their poor treatment of him, with "a Christlike vengeance, returning evil with good,"[90] is particularly noteworthy. His forgiveness knows no bounds, from his self-sacrificing mission to the Irish, his grief for the friend who betrayed him, and his call to Coroticus to repent of his actions. It is Patrick's charity which makes him "one of the great humanitarians, bishops, evangelists and human beings of the early Church".[91]

Exam tip!

Good responses are always well referenced to relevant texts!

 PRACTICE ESSAY TITLE

a) Give an account of Patrick's mission to the Irish. (35)

Use the notes above to help you.

b) Comment on the view that we come to know the person of Patrick in his writings. Justify your answer. (15)

 OTHER ASPECTS OF HUMAN EXPERIENCE

Section B of the AS exam paper requires an exploration of the ways in which the taught course can relate to other aspects of human experience. These aspects are identified on the specification and include: social; political; environmental; business; scientific; and artistic issues. Candidates may explore connections to alternative religions, spiritual and moral teachings, values, beliefs and practices.

The connections which candidates make can have historical and/or contemporary contexts.

By definition it is not possible or indeed desirable to provide a prescriptive, exhaustive 'list' of other aspects of human experience to which the taught course can be applied. By its very nature, this element of the exam is 'open' to whatever meaningful connections candidates can themselves make. What is offered below therefore, is intended merely to provide stimulus for further ideas or discussion on how *some* aspects of the taught course might be applied to *some* other aspects of experience.

Exam tip!

The connections you make should move beyond the taught course while still clearly and explicitly arising from it. They should give you an opportunity for exploration, discussion, and critical analysis, rather than being limited to simple comparative statements. (See the exemplar material provided overleaf.)

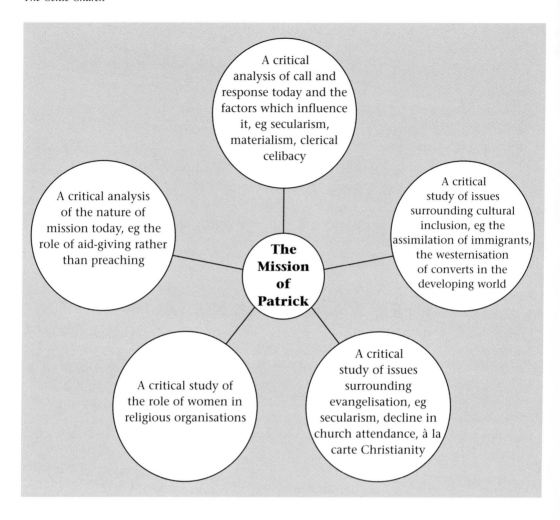

A critical analysis of call and response today and the factors which influence it, eg secularism, materialism, clerical celibacy

A critical analysis of the nature of mission today, eg the role of aid-giving rather than preaching

The Mission of Patrick

A critical study of issues surrounding cultural inclusion, eg the assimilation of immigrants, the westernisation of converts in the developing world

A critical study of the role of women in religious organisations

A critical study of issues surrounding evangelisation, eg secularism, decline in church attendance, à la carte Christianity

 TASK

Discuss how you might explore or develop these connections to other aspects of human experience. Can you add to them?

Find out about ...

- Challenges facing missionaries today (use publications of missionary organisations, eg Far East magazine)
- Views and issues surrounding the ordination of women in the Christian Church (interview priests and ministers; invite them to come to your class)
- The origins and reasons for clerical celibacy and a range of views within the Christian Church
- Practices and attitudes within other world faiths

Helpful examples of how connections might be made

1) Religious call and response

Although Patrick is clear that his mission is God-given, *"I did not go to Ireland of my own accord"*, and that he responded with hesitancy to the call "after so many years" ... the same hesitancy and reluctance is evident in terms of response to the call to mission today.

Today, there is a huge shortage of priests in Ireland. There are many reasons for this. Indeed, it is no coincidence that Patrick tells us of his own affluent background coupled with a sense of alienation from the Church. Historically, the response to the call to priesthood and religious life ebbs and flows with periods of economic boom and bust.

Others may identify a loss of trust and respect precipitated by accusations of paedophilia made and upheld against the clergy to be a reason for the decline. Often people identify the celibacy imposed on clergy of the Catholic Church as an area of difficulty for many. Pope Benedict argues that priests are needed who are totally dedicated to their mission and who could serve others by embracing the gift of celibacy. Some others warn against reducing every issue to one concerning sex, while others argue that a married clergy could much enrich the Church, especially in terms of, for example, family ministry. Some feel that celibacy was a much later 'man-made' add-on and it greatly impoverished the ministry of the Catholic Church. Nonetheless, Patrick makes it clear that his own mission was carried out *"at the cost of family and homeland"*.

2) A critical analysis of the nature of mission today

Patrick's mission primarily involved evangelisation, a telling *"of the great benefits and graces which the Lord conferred on me in the land of my captivity,"* and *"to spread God's name everywhere confidently and fearlessly"*. Is mission today still primarily about teaching the faith? There are those who would say it is more about praxis than orthodoxy, about aid and relief rather than evangelisation. However, statistically, it is clear that Church attendance has fallen. Some research suggests that it has fallen from 82% in 1982 to around 50% by 2004. Michael Paul Gallagher believes that apathy, alienation and secularism are the biggest challenges faced by the Church today. Pope John Paul II and Pope Benedict both see the culture of individualism and relativism as the biggest obstacles faced by the Church today. These value systems primarily involve the total reliance on the individual as a source of authority and deny the validity of any absolute religious authority. An apparent growth in 'à la carte Christianity', a 'cherry-picking' at the Church's teaching perhaps illustrates a need to return to simple evangelisation. Clarity on the Church's teachings and Gospel values such as those preached by Patrick is what is needed today.

3) A critical study of the role of women in religious organisations today

Patrick's mission was very much gender inclusive. He refers with pride to a *"blessed lady of high rank and noble birth"*. Although Patrick did attach particular value to the contribution made by his female converts, particularly the *"virgins of Christ"* and the *"widows"*, he did not ordain them. For many in the Christian Church today the issue of gender inclusivity is a crucial and difficult one. It has been estimated that around 80% of pastoral workers within the Church are women, yet no positions of authority are held by them. Many would argue that the Anglican Church on the other hand has been much enriched by the ordained ministry of women. Patrick may have seen women as *"active workers in the missionary field"* as Concannon argues, but in contrast today, many argue that the Church is a hierarchically male-dominated institution, which alienates women. While Patrick showed tremendous sensitivity on issues which primarily concern women, around the areas of sexuality and exploitation – lamenting the abuse of the *"poor baptised women, allotted as prizes"* – the Catholic Church does not show the same sensitivity to issues primarily concerning women, such as contraception. It is this perceived lack of sensitivity, as well as the 'glass ceiling' in terms of equality in ordained ministry, that causes the alienation of many women from the Church. Catholic theologian Mercedes Guitterez warns against this perception of the Church as a kind of 'corporate ladder', which she argues is primarily a secular idea. Nonetheless, the challenge of Patrick's mission for the Church today in terms of gender inclusivity is clear.

A brief commentary on the excerpts above

- The student does make connections to other aspects of human experience, eg cultural, social and economic issues.
- The connections are made clearly and explicitly arise from the area of study (which should be well referenced) yet also move beyond it.
- The work alludes to historical and contemporary values and practices.
- It considers alternative religious practices.
- Provides critical analysis and incorporates the views of scholars.
- The connections are well developed rather than being simply comparative.

Exam Tip!

Keep up to date with current affairs. Read newspapers and Church publications for the latest on current events as well as on issues which are being debated within the churches and religious groups. Use the internet. It is a good idea to keep a file of resources and ideas that you can use later.

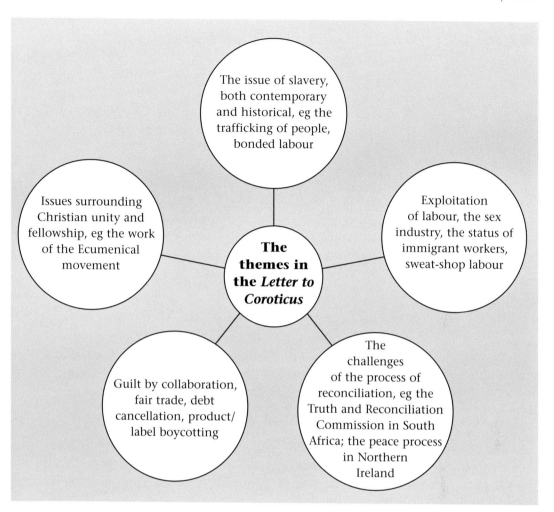

 RESEARCH TASK

Go through internet sites to find out about some of the issues above.

In particular, trawl newspaper archives for relevant articles and keep them in a folder.

Brainstorm the specific connections you can make between what you have found and the *Letter, Confessio* and Mission of Patrick.

Find out about social justice issues which concern organisations such as Trocaire and Christian Aid and their response to them.

You should be able to see ways in which you can make meaningful connections.

The following excerpts provide helpful examples of how some connections might be made.

Contemporary slavery

One of the most prominent themes in the *Letter to Coroticus* is slavery. As Duffy points out, it is an issue close to Patrick's heart, "in light of his personal experience Patrick remained sensitive to the plight of slaves".

The issue resonates in the 21st century as the slave market remains active. Although the face of slavery might have changed, and despite its illegality, it still operates today but under a different guise. For example, plantation workers in Latin America are caught up in a cycle of bonded labour which is passed from generation to generation because of debt and the extortionate interest accumulated on it. The slavery Patrick found so abhorrent in the fifth century is still an issue in the 21st century.

Fair Trade

Exploitation is explored by Patrick in his *Letter*. He makes it clear that Christians should beware of ill-gotten financial gain – wealth which has been *"amassed unjustly"* at the expense of others. This is relevant today in terms of the Fair Trade argument embraced by celebrities such as Chris Martin.

In terms of the coffee industry, there are 25 million coffee producers throughout the world. Many sell at a heavy loss while branded coffee sells at a hefty profit. This could be considered as *"wealth amassed unjustly"*. Nestle's annual profit margin is estimated at 26% on instant coffee. Patrick's warning still rings true: *"woe to those who fill themselves with what is not theirs"*.

Collaborative Guilt

Patrick proclaims that those who do not denounce evil are guilty because of their association with the wrongdoer, *"Which of the saints would not shudder at the thought of making merry or feasting with such men?"*

We, by our actions, often tacitly support the exploitation of others. A huge number of popular labels today are produced by exploitation and oppression. Countless reports show overseas workers ... to be underpaid, malnourished, physically and emotionally abused. Do we as Christians denounce such evil or give it our tacit support by buying the products? Patrick warns us all: *"not only those who do evil but those who agree with them are damned"*.

There is plenty of food for thought for the 21st century consumer.

 TASKS

In groups, comment on the above excerpts.

- What do you see as the strengths and weaknesses of each piece?
- Which aspects of human experience do the pieces of work relate to? (Check the introduction to this section and the specification.)
- Can you think of other connections that could be made between the *Letter to Coroticus* and other aspects of experience?

Below are some less successful attempts to make connections to other aspects of human experience.

An analysis of mission in the world today

Mother Teresa is a good example of a missionary today. When she was born on 26 August, 1910 in Skopje, she was called Agnes. She was the youngest of the family. Her father died when Agnes was about eight years old. As a child Agnes was fascinated by stories of the lives of missionaries and their work, and by the age of 12 she was convinced she should be a missionary. She left home at the age of 18 to join the Loreto sisters as a missionary. She never again saw her mother or sister.

Agnes went to Rathfarnham in Ireland to learn English – the language that the Sisters of Loreto used to teach school children in India. She arrived in India in 1929 and chose the name Teresa as her religious name, after Saint Therese of Liseuex – the patron saint of missionaries. She worked as a teacher at the Loreto convent school in eastern Calcutta.

Although Teresa enjoyed teaching at the school, she was very shocked and disturbed by the poverty she saw in Calcutta. On 10 September, 1946, Teresa had 'the call within the call'. "I was to leave the convent and help the poor while living among them. It was an order. To fail would have been to break the faith."

Teresa wrote in her diary that her first year was very difficult. She had no income and had to beg for food and supplies. Teresa did have doubt, and did feel loneliness and there was the temptation to go back to the comfort of convent life.

Teresa received permission from the Pope to form a new order, the Missionaries of Charity. Its mission was to care for, in her own words, "the hungry, the naked, the homeless, the crippled, the blind, … all those people who feel unwanted, unloved, uncared for …". It began as a small order with 13 members; today it has more than 4,000 nuns worldwide caring for refugees, the blind, disabled, aged, alcoholics, the poor and homeless. By 1996, she was operating 517 missions in more than 100 countries. Over the years, Mother Teresa's Missionaries of Charity grew from twelve to thousands, serving the "poorest of the poor" in 450 centres around the world. After a time of illness Mother Teresa died in September 1997.

A critical analysis of mission today

Many missionaries today respond to the call to mission just as Patrick did. The Kiltegan Fathers leave Ireland to go to many countries where people need them. Patrick's mission was both difficult and dangerous. Mission today can also be difficult and dangerous. Many missionaries today face the same difficulties as Patrick did. They too have to go to countries where the language and culture is different. Some face threats to their safety or even their lives, for example Father Kieran Creagh, who was shot while carrying out his mission.

Oscar Romero is another example of someone who was prepared to sacrifice his life for his mission. He was killed as he celebrated Mass.

 TASK

Read again the extracts above as well as those on pages 81–82.

- Note down the main similarities or differences between them and the extracts above.
- Read the commentary provided on page 82 on the previous examples. Now critically assess the extracts above. For example, the students do make connections to other aspects of human experience but...
- What suggestions would you make to these students as to how they could improve their work? (Remember that the task to make connections to other aspects of experience will always be an AO2 skill.)

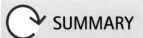

SUMMARY

Patrick the missionary came to Ireland in the fifth century. He left two surviving documents, the *Letter to Coroticus* and the *Confessio*.

It is possible to determine emerging themes and to establish his reason for writing.

The writings give us an important insight into the work of Patrick, the challenges he faced and how he perceived his role in the mission to the Irish.

The texts are better understood in the context of the background to the mission of Patrick in Chapter 1.

Certain personal qualities and characteristics emerge from the texts.

The texts have relevance to other aspects of human experience as outlined in the specification.

Endnotes

1 De Paor, M, *Patrick the Pilgrim Apostle of Ireland,* Veritas Publications, Dublin, 1998, p6

2 O Rafeartaigh, T, 'Misplacings in the text of Patrick's Confessio' in *The Maynooth Review X,* 1984.

3 Howlett, DR, *The Book of Letters of Saint Patrick the Bishop,* Four Courts Press, Dublin, 1993

4 There are many translations of Patrick's writings available; three suggestions are those of Joseph Duffy, Daniel Conneely, and Liam de Paor (details may be found in the bibliography). The reader is also asked to note that the ideas presented in the commentaries offered here are a collation of the commentaries of Bieler, Hanson, Conneely and Máire de Paor.

5 De Paor, *Patrick the pilgrim Apostle of Ireland, op cit,* p10

6 Bieler, L, *The Life and Legend of Saint Patrick, problems of modern scholarship,* Dublin, 1948, p53

7 De Paor, *Patrick the pilgrim Apostle of Ireland, op cit,* pp38–39

8 *ibid,* p40

9 Hanson, RPC, *The Life and Writings of the Historical Saint Patrick,* Seabury Press, New York, 1983, p79

10 Oulton, JEL, *The Credal Statements of Saint Patrick,* Dublin/OUP London, 1940, preface

11 Conneely, D, *The Letters of Saint Patrick,* An Saigart, Maynooth, 1993

12 Hanson, *The Life and Writings of the Historical Saint Patrick, op cit,* p81

13 Nerney, DS, 'A Study of Patrick's writings' in *Irish Ecclesiastical* Record 111, p110

14 Hanson, The *Life and Writings of Patrick, op cit,* p21

15 Bieler, *The Life and Legend of Saint Patrick, op cit,* p55

16 Howlett, DR, *Ex Saliva Scripturae Meae* 1989 and *The Book of Letters of Saint Patrick the Bishop* 1993

17 Conneely, D, *The Letters of Saint Patrick, op cit,* 1993

18 Chadwick, *The Age of the Saints of the Early Celtic Church,* Llanerch Publishers, Wales, 1960, pp28–29

19 De Paor, *Patrick the Pilgrim Apostle of Ireland, op cit,* p60

20 Joann, tract 86. 2.1

21 Howlett, D, *Ex Saliva Scripturae Meae,* p99

22 Dronke also sees the connection between the stone and its placing at the top of the wall in the second century Shepherd of Hermes.

23 For more details on the use of scriptural allusion in the writings of Patrick, Howlett, Máire de Paor and Daniel Conneely are recommended.

24 De Paor, *Patrick the Pilgrim Apostle of Ireland, op cit,* p85

25 Bieler, *The Life and Legend of Saint Patrick, op cit,* p60

26 Bury, JB, *Life of Saint Patrick,* Macmillan London, 1905

27 Hanson, RPC, *The Life and Writings of the Historical Saint Patrick, op cit,* p89

28 Powell, D, *The textual Integrity of Patrick's Confession,* 1969, p399

29 De Paor, *Patrick the Pilgrim Apostle of Ireland, op cit,* p88

30 Duffy, J, *Patrick in his own words,* p40, Veritas, Dublin, 2000, p40

31 De Paor, *Patrick the Pilgrim Apostle of Ireland, op cit,* pp105–113

32 Hanson, *The Life and Writings of Saint Patrick, op cit,* p93

33 Bieler, *The Life and Legend of Patrick, op cit,* p62

34 Hanson, *The Life and Writings of Saint Patrick, op cit,* p105

35 *ibid,* p107

36 Bieler, *The Life and Legend of Patrick, op cit,* p72

37 De Paor, *Patrick the Pilgrim Apostle of Ireland, op cit,* p155

38 Hanson, *The Life and Writings of Saint Patrick, op cit,* p108

39 Bieler, *The Life and Legend of Saint Patrick, op cit,* p71

40 Herren, M, *Mission and Monasticism in the Confession of St Patrick,* p84

41 Saint Ambrose, *Exhortation to Widows* 377/378

42 De Paor, *Patrick the Pilgrim Apostle of Ireland, op cit,* p125

43 Herren, *Mission and Monasticism in the Confession of Patrick, op cit,* p82

44 De Paor, *Patrick the Pilgrim Apostle of Ireland, op cit,* p131

45 Hanson, *The Life and Writings of Patrick, op cit,* p113

46 "If any of you puts a stumbling block before any of these little ones who believe in me, it would be better for you if a great millstone were fastened around your neck and you were drowned in the depths of the sea." Mt 18:6

47 Bieler, *The Life and Legend of Patrick, op cit,* p77

48 Nerney, D, 'A Study of Patrick's Sources' in *Irish Ecclesiastical Record* 1949, p499ff

49 De Paor, *Patrick the Pilgrim Apostle of Ireland, op cit,* p48

50 Hanson, *The Life and Writings of Patrick, op cit,* p121

51 Migne, J, *Patrologia Latina Sermon XXVII* 4

52 Conneely, D, *The Letters of Saint Patrick,* p125

53 These themes are again a collation of the research and labour of many Patrician scholars, most of whom are referred to in the body of the text, but would certainly include Joseph Duffy, Máire de Paor, Thomas O'Loughlin, and Daniel Conneely.

54 O'Loughlin, T, *Saint Patrick the man and his works,* Triangle SPCK London, 1999, pp22–23

55 Conneely, *The Letters of Saint Patrick, op cit,* p111

56 This is Conneely's translation; *ibid* p112

57 De Paor, *Patrick the Pilgrim Apostle of Ireland, op cit,* p40

58 O'Loughlin, *Saint Patrick the man and his works, op cit,* pp36–47

59 See Chapter 1 for a synopsis of the events current in Patrick's lifetime.

60 O'Loughlin, T, *Saint Patrick the man and his works, op cit,* p46

61 Dronke, P, *St Patrick's Reading,* Cambridge Medieval Celtic Studies 1, 1981, p26

62 The term 'faith-life' is one favoured by Daniel Conneely in his examination of the theology of Patrick's *Confessio* in *The Letters of Saint Patrick.*

63 De Paor, *Saint Patrick Pilgrim Apostle, op cit,* p65

64 Quoted in a foreword by Thomas A Finnegan in M de Paor, p1

65 Decrees of the Councils of Nicea, Arles and Elvira.

66 Conneely, *The Letters of Patrick, op cit,* p180

67 Duffy, *Patrick in his own words, op cit,* p84

68 De Paor, *Patrick the Pilgrim Apostle, op cit,* p182

69 Conneely, *The Letters of Saint Patrick, op cit,* p181

70 The Penitential of Finnian, written in the sixth century, attempts to outlaw the abuse of female slaves for sexual purposes.

71 Hanson, *The Life and Writings of Patrick, op cit,* p75

72 Duffy, *Patrick in his own words, op cit,* p85

73 De Paor, *Patrick the Pilgrim Apostle, op cit,* p191

74 *ibid,* p186

75 Bieler, *The Life and Legend of Patrick, op cit,* p71

76 Hanson, *The Life and Writings of Patrick, op cit,* p63

77 *ibid* pp 62–63

78 *ibid,* p65

79 Bieler, *The Life and Legend of Patrick, op cit*

80 *ibid*

81 Duffy, *Patrick in his own words, op cit,* p6

82 *ibid,* p44

83 O'Donoghue, DN, *Aristocracy of Soul: Patrick of Ireland,* Wilmington, Delaware, 1987, p22

84 Concannon, H, *Saint Patrick, his life and mission,* Dublin 1931

85 Mulholland, S, *The Confession of Patrick, a spirituality of broken humanity* in The Furrow, March 1992

86 Hanson, *The Life and Writings of Patrick, op cit,* p40

87 Duffy, *Patrick in his own words, op cit,* p6

88 De Paor, *Patrick the Pilgrim Apostle, op cit,* p204

89 Shaw, F, *The Real Saint Patrick,* CTS, Dublin, 1931, P9

90 *ibid*

91 Mulholland, *The Confession of Patrick, op cit,* p164

The beginnings of monasticism

Chapter 3

LEARNING OUTCOMES

Knowledge, understanding and evaluation of:

— the origins of monasticism in Ireland

— Monastic founders

— the role, nature and distinctive features of Celtic monasticism

1. THE ORIGINS OF MONASTICISM – AN INTRODUCTION

Monasticism is a religious practice which involves the rejection of worldly pursuits, a single-minded seeking of God, a devotion to the spiritual life and a pursuit of Christian perfection.

It is lived either in isolation or in community. In the modern Church it is usually referred to as 'the religious life'.

The teaching of Jesus

The origins of Christian monasticism are very much to be found in the specific teaching of Jesus himself:

"If anyone wants to follow me, he must renounce himself, take up his cross and follow me."[1]

In the case of the Rich Young Man, Christ specifies such renunciation and detachment as the pathway for those who seek Christian perfection:

"If thou will be perfect, go sell what thou has and give to the poor …".[2]

This implies a life totally filled with love and obedience to God. Basically, this involves a denial of all selfish tendencies and inclinations, an embracing of suffering and a desire to imitate Jesus in every way. John Ryan identifies this as a complete detachment from the self, and to an extent which is not demanded equally of all Christians.

In other instances, Jesus emphasises the necessity to leave mother, father, wife and children (Mt 10:37ff). He also infers Christian perfection can be attained through the wholehearted love and obedience of the disciple. He speaks of love of God with the whole heart, soul, mind and strength as well as love of one's neighbour.

The teachings of St Paul

St Paul often refers to the battle between the desire of the spirit and the weakness of the flesh,[3] and believes that in order to attain Christian perfection the body and the needs of the flesh must be brought into submission. He tells us:

> *"I chastise my body and bring it into subjection"* (1 Cor 9:27).

This is about more than just self-denial, and involves the repression of the self and all that the self desires. The term that best expresses this idea of Paul's, is 'asceticism'.

> Asceticism comes from the Greek term *askésis* meaning practice or training. It is the practice of renouncing worldly pleasures, eg the enjoyment of food, sexual intimacy, and close contact with family and friends. Instead it focuses on chastity, fasting, and abstinence, in the belief that purifying the body helps to purify the soul.

Early Christian practice

- The Acts of the Apostles tell us that the giving up of material possessions was common in the first Christian Community in Jerusalem (Acts 2:44–45). The text implies that they shared their goods in common and led a life of virginity. They lived this lifestyle in the confines of their own homes, but it is the view of John Ryan that these ascetics formed "a group apart".[4]

- St Ignatius of Antioch in writing to St Polycarp (c AD107), also speaks of such a group, which forms quite an important part of the early Christian Church.

- Chastity seems to have been a practice valued by the early Church Fathers. Those who lived a life of chastity were perceived as living a life of martyrdom.

- Clement of Alexandria calls the Christian ascetics the "elect among the elect" and it seems they sat in places of honour in liturgical services.

- Origen illustrates how seriously this celibate asceticism was taken when he says: *"We swear that we will punish or ill-treat our flesh and bring it into subjection, that we may be able to give life to the Spirit"*.

The characteristics of the ascetic life in the early Church seem to be:

- Poverty
- Fasting (Wednesday and Friday)
- Prayer
- Care for others (poor, sick and orphaned)
- Chastity

It became increasingly difficult for these ascetics to live such a life in the company of their family and friends, so from the third century their lifestyle became regulated by strict rules. By the fourth century these ascetics were forming groups, living under one roof and being regulated by a written rule.

The Desert Fathers – Egyptian monasticism

It seems to have become increasingly difficult for the ascetic to remain steadfast and focused on the pursuit of holiness while still living in the heart of the community. The desire to find a way in which one could 'go the extra mile' in terms of pursuing Christian perfection, became more pronounced. This was after the persecution of Christians had come to an end with Constantine's succession to power. There was a new drive to abandon the world and its distractions more completely. Thus began the period of the 'Desert Fathers'.

Saint Anthony

- Born in AD251 to wealthy parents
- Lived the ascetic life privately near his home
- Known for his holiness and mortification, living on a diet of bread, water and salt and keeping vigil
- In AD285 he withdrew to greater solitude, crossing the Nile into the mountains, living in isolation for 20 years
- His fame spread and he began to teach those who followed him
- They formed a group, living in separate huts, praying, eating, reading and working together
- As more and more hermits and visitors arrived, Anthony fled once more, living the rest of his life in solitude until his death, reported to have been in AD356.

Eremitical

The practices of Anthony mark the beginning of the **eremitical** lifestyle. The eremitical or semi-eremitical monastic life involved hermits living in isolation in forests, mountains or deserts, giving their life totally to prayer or penance and perhaps meeting with other hermits occasionally to pray or read Scripture together. Great emphasis was placed on learning Scripture by heart. Each ascetic was left to their own devices. There was no common rule or authority structure.

Cenobitical

Saint Pachomius

- He was a soldier in Constantine's army.
- While at war he was inspired by the lifestyle of some Christians whom he met and so was baptised.
- He joined a group of hermits but later formed a settlement of his own.
- His main contribution was the idea that all who joined him should be under his authority, live under one roof and keep to a rule.
- He is said to have had 100 monks under his authority.
- A version of his Rule was translated by St Jerome in AD404 and tells us much about this early monastic life.

This marked the beginning of **cenobitical** monastic lifestyle. Cenobitical monasticism emphasises community life, regulated by a common rule lived out in groups within a monastic compound. The main features of this movement, which was monastic in the strict sense, were:

- Monastic buildings (perhaps 30–40): church, meeting place, library, kitchen/food store, individual small cells
- Formal authority structure where a superior ruled over a number of houses called a tribe
- Common dress in a linen tunic and barefoot (or with sandals when travelling)
- Common prayer at dawn, mid-day, sundown and mid-night
- Two fast days per week. One/two daily meals
- Study and learning of Scripture
- Manual work in silence
- Penalties inflicted on those who broke rules

Note!
It will be important to bear these features in mind when we later discuss Celtic monasticism.

Saint Basil

- Influential in spreading monasticism into Greek-speaking lands
- Strongly emphasised the importance of community life
- Taught that cenobitical life was superior to eremitical
- Limited the size of each monastery to 30 or 40 brothers
- Introduced education for boys in the monasteries
- Believed monasteries should extend their duties to care for the poor and sick

Monasticism in the West

Saint Martin

- Trained as a soldier
- Inspired by the eremitical life
- Established a monastery at Ligugé in Gaul
- In AD371 Martin was made bishop of Tours and founded the monastery in the remote Marmoutier.
- These monasteries were considered schools of ascetical training
- Led by example more than written rule

John Cassian

- Had spent some time with the monks of Anthony in Egypt
- Was an ordained priest
- Established a monastery, and another for women at Marseilles
- Under his influence monasticism became popular in Gaul

Saint Honoratus

- Came from a wealthy background but renounced his wealth
- Established a monastery on the island of Lérins
- Monastery was built upon the Egyptian model – individual cells but with communal prayer
- Monastery had no written rule but was renowned for the strict discipline of its abbots

 TASK

Complete a potted history of the Christian monastic movement using the information you have been given. Your summary should not exceed 250 words.

2. THE INTRODUCTION OF MONASTICISM INTO IRELAND

The exact origins of this movement in Ireland are unclear. Various routes of entry have been suggested and it is certain that it came into the Irish Church through more than one channel.

Through Patrick himself

As we have already seen, Patrick seems to have encouraged the monastic life and indeed encouraged the pursuit of Christian perfection among his followers as evidenced in the text,[5] and as argued by Máire de Paor. [6] However, it is important to note that although he encouraged a desire for Christian perfection and ascetic practices, we have to agree with Hanson that Patrick did not found any monasteries. Patrick's converts were more likely to be individuals practising ascetic virtues within their own homes.[7] Ryan argues that these converts "were certainly regarded by Patrick as the fairest fruits of his missionary labours." [8]

Some scholars argue that Patrick did spend a period of time in training on the Continent, more specifically in the region of Gaul. This seems to be evidenced by Tírechán's *Brief Account* and supported by Patrick's own desire to visit Gaul again in C43. Scholars such as Oulton[9] and Bieler[10] accept Patrick's Gallic training. Ryan agrees, adding that Patrick was inspired by tales of the sanctity of Martin which he undoubtedly heard whilst there.[11] He further argues that Patrick spent some time studying under Honoratus at Lérins and if we accept Muirchú's account of his study under Germanus, would undoubtedly also have been familiar with Germanus' foundation at Yonne. Certainly tradition suggests some Patrician associations with the monastery at Lérins.

Regardless of one's position on this matter, we have to note Patrick's role in the introduction of the monastic/ascetic ideal into Ireland.

From the East

Nora Chadwick is of the view that the monks of the desert monasteries carried on "'active correspondence' with the wider world".[12] She believes that they involved themselves in the theological disputes of the day and cites, for example, the Letters of Cassian as evidence. They certainly possessed books and encouraged study – in fact reading was insisted upon by the Rule of Pachomius.[13] Indeed, Athanasius did write a *Life of Saint Anthony* and Chadwick argues that *Cassian's Dialogues* made the lives of the desert hermits known in the Western world.

Chadwick further claims that there was "a strong intellectual influence operating on our islands from the East Mediterranean … there can be little doubt that it was mainly through books that knowledge came to Ireland from the Eastern Church".[14] She believes writings were perhaps indirectly passed via Spain, and that these connections are preserved in our place names, particularly in the use of the word 'desert'/dysart, which "reflect obvious links with the East".[15] The Irish tendency to search out the island sanctuary reflects the spirit of the hermitages of the East.[16] George T Stokes concurs that "from the earliest times the anchorite system formed an essential part of Celtic monasticism".[17]

Francois Henry also points out an Eastern influence on Celtic art and manuscripts, which are closely related to Syrian manuscripts.[18]

From North Britain

About a generation before the mission of Patrick, Ninnian had set up a monastery called Candida Casa at Whithorn in Galloway. He dedicated the church there to Saint Martin of Tours who had greatly inspired him. John Ryan dates this establishment to the first decade of the fifth century.[19] It became a training school for the monastic life and from the early sixth century seems to have been the training ground of some Irish monastic founders. Enda of Aran, St Tigernach of Clones, St Eoghan of Ardstraw and St Finnian of Moville are all said to have trained here. Most of these, with perhaps the exception of Enda, went on to also become bishops, which underlines the important legacy of the school at Candida Casa. Influence was always strong between Ireland and the Church in Britain, so it stands to reason that the Irish should also have acquired the drive towards monasticism from there.

From Wales

- Saint Cadoc, a very prominent saint in the British Church, is said to have visited Ireland in a quest for learning. However, if his dates are fifth century this is hardly likely. Ryan dates him slightly later as a contemporary of Gildas. This makes a visit to Ireland a little more plausible. His monastic foundation at Llangarvan seems to have been a place of some repute in the third decade of the sixth century.

- Illtud had a foundation at Caldey Island which may have been influenced by that of Lérins. The *Life of Samson* tells us that Illtud *"was most accomplished in the Scriptures and in learning of every kind"*.[20] His monastery is important to us because he trained St Samson of Dol, St Cadoc and later St Gildas.

- Saint Samson is reported to have visited Ireland.

- Cadoc, a peer of Samson, is said to have had a close connection with Finnian of Clonard. Their relationship was one "of master and disciple".[21] He was also the 'soul friend' of Gildas who was to have a profound effect on Irish monasticism.

- One of several visits that Gildas may have made to Ireland is reported as having occurred in 565. Gildas was ardent about the ascetic life and highly critical of the abuses and worldly lifestyle he witnessed among some of the clerics and

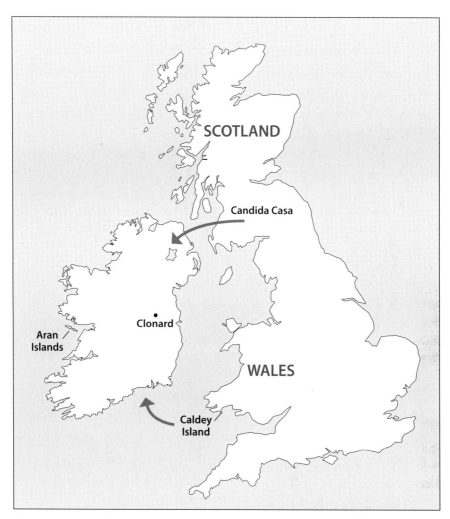

The introduction of monasticism into Ireland from North Britain and Wales

bishops of his day. Ryan is of the view that Gildas fervently preached his ideals to the Irish, and that he was the most able and highly respected teacher of the Irish in the sixth century. Indeed, "it is to him more than any other that the distinct monastic form assumed by the Church in Ireland is chiefly due".[22]

- Irishmen may also have numbered among the disciples of Saint David, such as Aedan of Ferns, Finnian of Clonard, Finbarr of Cork, and Brendan of Clonfert.

These connections are supported by the *Catalogues of the Irish Saints* which specifies a liturgy in use in Ireland, which was given by David and Gildas.

Nora Chadwick points out that while Patrick's influence is primarily Northern, the monastic movement certainly seems to have come into the country from the south.[23]

Conclusion

- Asceticism was practised in the Christian Church from an early time.
- Monasticism in a proper sense was introduced by the Desert Fathers.
- Some historians, such as Chadwick, argue that there was written correspondence between these settlements and the Continent, which Irish Christians were able to access.
- Asceticism spread into the West, and the Gallic foundations were important and influential.
- Some scholars argue that Patrick spent time studying at some of the foundations on the Continent; at the very least he would have been aware of the practices and the reputation of Martin and Honoratus, and certainly he seems to have encouraged ascetic practices. The origins of Celtic monasticism therefore come indirectly from the Continent.
- From the Continent, it spread to north Britain (Candida Casa) which, in turn, exercised a direct influence on Wales and on the Irish Celtic monastic founders.

 PRACTICE ESSAY TITLE

Give an account of the origins of Celtic monasticism in Ireland. (35)

Use the conclusion above as your answer plan and the notes in section 1 and 2.

Tip! The question is asking about the introduction of monasticism into **Ireland**, so that should form the bulk of your answer.

3. THE MONASTIC FOUNDERS

For Nora Chadwick the 'age of the saints' in the Celtic Church runs from the late fifth to the early seventh century.[24] The word 'saint' was not used in the same sense as in the modern Church and was often applied to holy men and women. In this particular period it was used to refer to the great founders and abbots of the Celtic Church.

Enda

It is with Enda and perhaps Finnian of Clonard that a new era begins in the history of the Celtic Church.

Enda is one of the great founding fathers of Celtic monasticism. It is probable that he was born in the middle of the fifth century and came from Meath. He was the only son of Conall, king of Oriel, and was, according to tradition, a warrior. He had succeeded to his father's throne and was considering marriage to a girl resident in his sister Fanchea's convent. Fanchea, critical of Enda's lifestyle, persuaded him to study for the priesthood.

Enda made his way to Ninnian's foundation, Candida Casa, in Galloway. Upon his return he asked his brother-in-law, King Aengus of Cashel, to grant him the land of Aran Island, County Galway. Aengus offered him the more fertile land of the Golden Vale but Enda insisted on the remote, lonely and unproductive land of Aran, which as we shall see was more in keeping with his idea of monastic life. Enda was dedicated to the virtue of asceticism through manual work. He made his foundation at Aran about the year 480. The island lies across the entrance to Galway Bay. It rises to three hundred foot cliffs on the north-west side. On the north-east shore, lie fields of bare rock.

Enda's foundation at Aran was noted for its severity. His monks were to be self-sufficient, fed and clothed by their own labour. Tradition has it that Enda forbade the use of tools or implements of any kind in the tilling of the rocky land of Aran. His monks were to use only their bare hands; indeed he himself is reported to have dug the great ditches around his monastery with his bare hands.

John Ryan tells us that it is with Enda that monasticism in the strict sense began in Ireland.[25] He copied much of what he had learned at Candida Casa, although his foundation at Aran took on an ascetical characteristic of its own. It was very much as a school of asceticism that Aran gained repute, although study was important. Many came to learn from Enda and it is said they built their churches all over the island. Some estimate that there were around ten daughter houses, although Enda remained abbot and head of this little monastic village.

Among the more famous of Enda's disciples were Finnian of Clonard, Ciaran of Clonmacnois and Kevin of Glendalough. Colmcille is reported to have called Aran "the sun of the West".

Enda died in AD530 and is reportedly buried on Aran.

Finnian of Clonard

Finnian is the second great monastic father of the Celtic Church, although many would argue that his foundation eclipsed that of Aran. John Ryan argues that Enda and Finnian "represent different trends in the monastic movement: Enda the dedicated practice of the virtues of penance, fasting, vigils, prayers, manual work; Finnian the same virtues but with greater emphasis on intellectual rather than manual work".[26]

Finnian was a native of Leinster, and like Enda, born into a noble class. He spent time studying under Enda, as well as studying under Fortchern. He also received spiritual direction from the recluse Coemhan.

He had contact with both David and Cadoc of Wales. He founded Clonard around 520 and although the settlement at Clonard is older than that of Cadoc, Finnian seems to have modelled his foundation on the Cadoc model. He also derived inspiration from the monastery at Lérins.

Finnian was a bishop as well as an abbot but seems to have kept the office of bishop very much to the background. This was perhaps due to the influence of Gildas with whom he appears to have corresponded on matters of monastic discipline. Finnian's legacy is reflected in the later inclination of bishops in the Irish Church to live a monastic, or at least an ascetic lifestyle.

There is no doubting Enda's influence on Finnian in terms of austerity. A scribe is thought to have written concerning Finnian: *"Senach beheld Finnian's meagreness … so great that his ribs could be counted. Senach saw the worm coming out of Finnian's side, and this was the cause, from the cold girdle of iron which he wore around him as penance for his body, and which cut to his bone."*[27]

Despite his ascetic practices, it was as a great teacher that Finnian became renowned. His school was said to be open to anyone who wanted to learn. It was in this regard that Finnian became known as the 'teacher of the saints of Ireland,' teaching among others, Ciaran of Clonmacnois, Colmcille of Iona, Sinnell of Cleenish Island, and Brendan of Clonfert. The importance of study was much emphasised by Finnian. Not only did Finnian educate these esteemed persons but he also encouraged them to go out and found monasteries of their own. His disciples became known as the 'Twelve Apostles of Ireland'. In this way his legacy and influence continued after his death. Ryan believes that "he set the Irish Church of his day on a course which lasted to the beginning of the twelfth century".[28]

Finnian died in 549.

Ciaran of Clonmacnois

Ciaran was born, possibly around 316. His family originated in Meath but had moved to Connacht. His family belonged to the *nemed* class as his father was a chariot-maker, and he was tutored under the deacon Justus.[29] In the *Life of Ciaran*, we are told that his father was "a rich man".

He studied under Finnian of Clonard, who in turn apparently advised him to study with Enda. A legend surrounding Ciaran tells us that Finnian gave over the care of the king's daughter to Ciaran when she was sent to Clonard to be educated. Ciaran was so pious in all that he did that he never once looked at her face and for the entire period of her education saw nothing but her feet. Tradition tells us that it was Enda who encouraged him to go out and found his own monastery. He settled first on an island in Loch Ríb, but vacated it to the possession of a wandering ascetic who reportedly was looking for somewhere to settle.

He travelled to the midlands of Ireland and there met a young exile prince of the

Uí Néill kings of the north of Ireland. The young prince helped Ciaran build a small church of wood. Ciaran prayed for him in return and prophesied that the young man would become king. The prophecy was fulfilled and Clonmacnois was thereafter supported by the Uí Néill kings of Ireland.

Ciaran showed a remarkable aptitude for practical organisation and Clonmacnois quickly flourished. Although the land was wet and poor and the monks had much heavy work to do, the site on the Shannon was an excellent one – it was one of the greatest highways of the country at the time. In addition, one of the main roads in Ireland at the time ran nearby. His foundation was as central as Enda's was remote. However, Ciaran's reign as its abbot was only to last seven short months. He died around AD549, reportedly of the yellow plague, aged not more than 33 years.[30]

Ciaran's legacy however, was to be Clonmacnois itself, which was to become one of the greatest monastic schools of Ireland, claiming authority over a range of churches spanning almost half of Ireland.

On the reputation of Ciaran's sanctity, it was believed that Ciaran would bring to heaven all those buried within the churchyard at Clonmacnois. Kings therefore continued to endow it and it increased in power and stature. Its churchyard contained the relics of many Irish kings and its library produced many of the annals (historical records) of the period.

Brendan of Clonfert

Brendan was born in 484 in Fenit, County Kerry. His father was Findlug and his mother was Cara. Some sources suggest that when he was only one year old, Brendan was fostered by Bishop Erc who handed him over to the care of Saint Ita of Killeedy. There he remained for five years, after which he returned to Erc. When Brendan was ready, Erc sent him to be educated at the great monasteries of Enda, Finnian and Jarlath.

Brendan returned to Erc to be ordained priest. He is said to have made monastic foundations on the Shannon and Loch Corrib. Brendan received a grant of land from the local king of Ardfert and with a small group of followers established a monastery there in either 554 or 559, according to the annals.

Clonfert, his foundation, became known as one of the great monastic schools. He also founded a convent at Annaghdown for his sister. Brendan however felt himself called to greater exile. In preparation, he withdrew alone to the top of Brandon Mountain.

Upon his return, Brendan gathered the monks that were to accompany him and they set about building a vessel: *"ribbed and sided with wood, strengthened with iron and ox hides … the sails with skins of animals … enough food for 40 days, water for goatskins and wine for mass"*.[31]

They stopped at Aran to receive the blessing of Enda and three days later sailed into the unknown. For Brendan no doubt, this voyage was not intended to be so momentous, but it was to be a step on a pilgrimage in the search of sanctity. He returned after seven years and continued his work as abbot, founding several more houses in Connacht and Munster. In his later life he is reported to have visited Gildas in Wales.

He died in Ireland at the convent of his sister at Annaghdown in 577 and is buried at Clonfert.

Brigit of Kildare

Most of the information we have on Brigit comes from her hagiographer Cogitosus.

Her father was a nobleman, Dubthach of Leinster, while her mother, Brocessa, was a slave girl. She was born about 450. The *Life of Brigit* says that she had some kind of early education, perhaps with a pagan druid, but was also skilled in the duties taught by her mother. She seems to have gone to assist her mother at some stage in the carrying out of her duties. She returned to her father's house and Dubthach decided it was time for Brigit to marry. Cogitosus tells us that her intended husband was to be *"a man of chaste life, a poet"*.

Brigit refused, declaring that she wished to be a 'Virgin for Christ'. She, and reportedly seven other girls, took their vows before Bishop Mel. They asked for a piece of land at the Curragh in Kildare, which translated means 'the Church of the Oak' (*Cill Dara*). Despite the king's initial refusal, Brigit got her land and built there a church and a convent. Many were attracted to her foundation by her piety and generosity to the poor.

She saw the need to have a bishop to administer the sacraments to her nuns and to help with the administration. The bishop Conleth ruled the monastery with her and thus was born the first double monastery in Ireland. Monks and nuns lived in separate quarters, but worshipped together in the same church. She is said to have been visited at Kildare by both Finnian and Brendan and her foundation was certainly a place of renown throughout Ireland and beyond. Brigit died around AD525.

Comgall of Bangor

Comgall was born in the territory of the Dál Riata in AD517. His father is said to have been a soldier. He studied under Fintan of Clonenagh and Finnian of Clonard. Later in life it is claimed that he associated with Colmcille and Ciaran of Clonmacnois. He also spent some time on an island retreat in Fermanagh before the establishment of his own monastery.

In 555 he founded the monastery of Bangor on the shores of Belfast Lough. It is thought that he visited Scotland where he founded the monastery of Tiree.

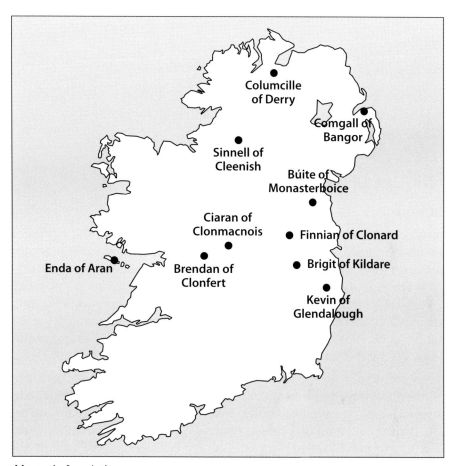

Monastic foundations

It is reported that for many years Comgall refused ordination, believing himself to be unworthy. Although expecting severe austerity of himself, Comgall was less exacting on his monks. It was the love of learning rather than severe asceticism that was the hallmark of his foundation, and so the school at Bangor became a place of great classical learning. An early hymn describes the Rule at Bangor:

"The good rule of Bangor, right and divine, strict, holy and careful – the best of rules, just and wonderful."

Comgall also educated Columbanus who went on to lecture at the monastic school in Bangor for some years. As John Ryan says, the monastery at Bangor was to remain "a religious centre of the very highest repute". Indeed, St Bernard, writing in the twelfth century, calls it "a place truly sacred, the nursery of the saints which brought forth fruit most abundantly for the glory of God ... saints poured from it like an inundation to distant lands".[32]

Comgall died at Bangor around AD603.

TASK

Complete a fact-file on the monastic founders.

Take care to include as much factual information as possible and include particular contributions of each, eg Enda was known for his asceticism.

Use the internet to help you.

4. THE NATURE OF CELTIC MONASTICISM

Introduction

Like monasticism elsewhere, Celtic monasticism was based on the virtues of asceticism and austerity. During this period in the church's history, it was perceived as 'green martyrdom': an abandonment of all that the monk holds dear for the love of God, and the practice of penance and repentance through fasting and work. As we have seen, these practices were undertaken to varying degrees depending on the monastic founder. Practices therefore differed from house to house and because of a lack of source material it is difficult to be precise about the exact nature of the daily routine followed by the Celtic monks.

We have various sources, which can lend an insight into some monastic practices current at the time. These sources include: hagiographical writings, particularly that of Adomnán and Jonas; and monastic rules, specifically the Rule of Columbanus, which is the earliest surviving monastic rule in existence, as well as those rules written in the eighth century but maybe reflecting sixth century practices (eg the Rule of Ailbe).

A monastic rule is a set of guidelines for the monastic life, outlining the principles of the life, the virtues that a good monk would be expected to follow, the hours and type of prayer, work, study and meals; the authority structure of the monastery and penalties for the breach of any of the rules.

The nature of Celtic monasticism

Poverty

This has been a feature of monastic practice since its origins. Columbanus' Rule tells us that for the monks:

"It is wrong for them not only to have what they do not need, but also to wish for such things … as they will have an abundance in the world to come, they ought to be satisfied in this world with the minimum that suffices to stave off extreme want."

Jonas' *Life of Columbanus* makes it clear that the monk is not to possess anything of his own, call anything his own or indeed treat anything as though it were his own; the penalty for such behaviour seems to be some form of exile from the community and the completion of heavy penance. All property was owned in common by the community and any monk who damaged such property was to make amends for it in labour.

The same simplicity and poverty was to be reflected in the dress of the monks. They would have worn a *tunica* or inner garment, and a *casula*, which was an outer woollen garment, and a *capa* or hood. Jonas' *Life of Columbanus* tells us that the monks were allowed to wear gloves when carrying out their work.

Chastity

This centred on the idea that a chaste love should fill both the heart and the mind. Columbanus' Rule tells that:

"The chastity of the monk will be judged by his thoughts … what value is it to be a virgin in body if one is not a virgin also in spirit."

The virtue of chastity was perhaps all the more important to the Celtic monks because of the still-remembered practice of paganism within which sexual immorality was not uncommon. Failure to lead a chaste life was regarded as the pathway to spiritual ruin. John Ryan tells us of a story wherein, *"such was the vigilance exercised by one abbess that one of the young nuns died without ever having learnt that there was any difference between the sexes!"*[33]

Obedience

The entire first chapter of the Rule of Columbanus deals with obedience:

"At the first word of a senior all must rise and go and do what they are commanded, for obedience is shown to God … if anyone does not rise at once to obey he is to be judged guilty of disobedience. If anyone murmurs he too is to be considered disobedient. Unto what point is obedience to be shown? Unto death … nothing, no matter how hard or exacting, is to be refused by the obedient."

It seems from various accounts in Adomnán's *Life of Colmcille* that obedience was also expected from Colmcille's monks, and indeed in Colman Elo's monastery one monk, who had been nicknamed 'the obedient', died when Colman was away. So obedient was he that the body remained in a preserved state until the return of Colman, who ordered the obedient monk to get up and he did so at once.[34]

The virtue of obedience was to be practised in imitation of Christ's obedience unto the Father and in order to foster a spirit of humility in the brethren.

Community

Life in the community was a central feature of monastic life. As we have already seen, all possessions were owned in common, and once a monk left his family his duty was to the monastic community, which was essentially his new family. As witnessed in the careers of the monastic founders, it was common to establish a monastery far from the native territory of the founder, and monks were encouraged to enter a monastery far from their home. Where this was not possible, according to the Community Rule of Columbanus, the monk could not be written to, spoken to, seen or heard from, without permission from the abbot.

It was important then that goodwill and charity were practised among the brethren. Adomnán's *Life* tells us of Colmcille's dying words to his community:

"Love each other with a genuine love and live together in peace."

Columbanus had to address the matter with his monks when he warns that:

"Nothing is sweeter to human nature than to discuss other people's business and to settle other people's affairs, to talk irresponsibly and to give a bad time to the absent. No matter how wise a man is if he says much, he says much that were better left unsaid."

Elsewhere in his Community Rule, he warns that:

"Great care must be taken that no vengeful or envious feelings must be harboured against a brother."

Asceticism

Mortification and asceticism in the life of the Celtic monk was practised in a variety of ways. Walker tells us that for Columbanus the life of the monk was a heroic and unremitting warfare to conquer his own self-will and sensuality.[35] Columbanus sums this up in the final chapter of his Monks' Rule:

"Let the monk live ... under the discipline of one father and in the company of many. Let him not do what he wishes, let him eat what he is bidden ... be subject to him whom he does not like. Let him come weary to his bed and let him be forced to rise when his sleep is not yet finished. Let him keep silence when he has suffered wrong."

Food and Fasting

Columbanus' Rule is our main source for the diet of the monk. His Rule states:

"The food of the monk should be poor in quality and taken in the evening ... the purpose in taking food is to sustain the body ... proper foods for this purpose are vegetables, flour mixed with water and a little loaf of bread. Food therefore should be taken in moderation ... the indulgence allowed to the body must be poor in quality and meagre in quantity."

- The ninth hour (3 pm) seems to have been the main meal time. In Columbanus' monastery, it seems that one meal a day was allowed. In Iona, Bede tells us that two meals a day, dinner and supper were served.

- Apart from the stipulation of Columbanus, which suggests a vegetarian diet, other monasteries occasionally served meat and those on island locations such as Skellig and Iona undoubtedly had fish. Indeed, Adomnán tells us that they supplemented the diet with oxen, sheep, seals and fish.

- Strangely, the monasteries were less rigorous about the consumption of liquids, and beer seems to have been allowed even in Columbanus' monasteries. However, the penalty for inebriation was often a long period (40 days in some monasteries) on bread and water. Later in the reforming spirit of the eighth century, St Máel-ruain reportedly says, *"The liquor that causes the forgetfulness of God shall not be drunk here"*, to which Duiblitir replied, *"well, my monks shall drink it and they will be in heaven along with yours"*.[36]

- Fasting was incorporated into the daily routine of the monk. Additionally, Wednesday and Friday were fast days and there was intense fasting during the Holy seasons of the Church year such as Lent and Advent. Columbanus states:

  "We are bound therefore to fast everyday."

- Account was taken of the elderly and infirm, and special exemption was given should a guest arrive at the monastery.

Prayer

- Prayer was both private and communal. Columbanus advises that monks should pray within their own cells, when entering and leaving a house, and before beginning and after stopping work. Gougaud also identifies the practice of praying *crosfigell* with extended arms, esteemed in Ireland because it denoted the crucifixion.[37]

- There was also communal prayer at set hours in the monastery, although there is little to suggest that these hours would have been the same everywhere. St Brendan had five periods of prayer: vespers, vigils, third, sixth and the ninth hour. These corresponded to the hour of Jesus' trial before Pilate, the hour of his Crucifixion and the hour of his death. Divine Office was central to the communal prayer of the monks. Night prayer was frequent; Columbanus stipulated that twenty-four psalms would be recited on summer nights and thirty-six in winter.

- Prayer was generally accompanied by a number of genuflections and prostrations to intensify the asceticism.

- The sign of the cross was used frequently on leaving the monastery, for example before using tools, utensils and cutlery.

Silence

Columbanus devotes a whole chapter to the rule of silence. The monk should only speak when necessary and only then with caution and wisdom. Silence was insisted upon, particularly in the refectory at meal times.

Sleep

Sleep deprivation was a means of mortification. At Iona, Adomnán tells us that the monks had beds made of pallets of straw. Colmcille himself had a stone for a pillow. Night time vigils were frequent and sleep was interrupted by frequent rising to prayer.

Work

Work was part of the ascetic exercise of the monk and Columbanus is clear that he is never to be idle. The monks were quite self-sufficient; by working they were able to provide their own food and generally maintain the monastic buildings. Adomnán tells us that the monks were engaged in ploughing, sowing, reaping, the milking of cows, working at the mill and kiln. Despite the existence of a horse and cart at Iona, there are also reports of monks carrying heavy loads on their backs.

Discipline

Penalties for breaches of discipline are laid down in Columbanus' Community Rule. In the opening sentence he says:

"A diversity of faults should be cured by the application of a diversity of penance.

The most common punishment is a fixed number of blows. For example, he who has not said grace at the table should receive six blows, as will he who speaks when eating. He who tells idle tales about another is condemned to silence or fifty blows. Coming late or noisily to prayer also necessitates fifty blows."

 TASK

Think about and discuss the view that too much was expected of the Celtic monk.

Roles within the monastery

- The monastery was governed by the 'Abbot', meaning 'father'. An abbot could select his own successor, as seems to have been the case with Iona and Clonmacnois. If possible, the position of abbot was passed down among members of the same family. Absolute authority was to be given to the abbot, although he also had great love for his children. Colmcille concerns himself with comforting his brethren as his death approaches, and Columbanus forces himself to take a certain tone lest he be overcome with emotion when he is forced to leave his monks at Luxeuil.

- 'Minister' was the name given to the person who assisted the abbot with practical aspects of his duties. He was similar to a private secretary. Colmcille's minister was Diarmait and Columbanus' was Domoal.

- 'Seniores' were elder brethren, accomplished in the practice of monastic virtue. Their role was to guide, direct and inspire the younger monks. The *Book of Lismore* tells us that this group had a house to themselves. They were to be obeyed by the junior monks.

- Larger monasteries required a 'Guest-master' who oversaw the needs of guests at the monastery. At times the guest-master may have been the only person to come into contact with the outside world so he needed to be an excellent ambassador for the monastery as well as a person of great tact and diplomacy.

- The 'Vice-abbot' held an important position in the larger settlements, and his role was to oversee the land and material resources of the monastery.

- The 'Cellarer' looked after the kitchen and its supplies.

Monastic sites

Monastic sites were carefully chosen. As we have seen, the founders often chose a site that was far from their native home. The locations generally have the following characteristics:

- Isolated foundations such as Skellig Michael, which could only be reached with difficulty by the population on the mainland. The monastery is cut into a triangle of rock, which lies eight miles out to sea from the west coast of the Waterville Peninsula in Kerry. The seas here are often rough. Similarly, we have Inishmurray, four miles off the coast of Sligo. Clearly, these monks wished to maintain their isolation.

- To a lesser degree we find some monasteries built on mountain tops, like that of Mount Brandon. Usually these were founded by hermits and ascetics.

- More influential monasteries were deliberately built on accessible sites, eg Bangor, near the southern coast of Belfast Lough, or Devenish on Lough Erne. It is important to note that at this time rivers and the sea were not viewed as barriers, but as highways. Some monasteries were built close to important road hubs; for example, Glendalough, and Clonmacnois, which appears to have been built at the junction of a road and a navigable river. Ann Hamlin argues that the site at Clonmacnois is "one of the most interesting monastic sites in Ireland."[38] Pádraig Ó Riain argues that the monasteries were deliberately sited at the boundaries of kingdoms.[39]

- Sometimes monasteries were built in places which formerly had pagan associations, eg Brigit's monastery at Kildare, Finnian's monastery at Moville.

- Some were built near royal forts, eg Derry and Clogher.

It is important to remember that the site of a monastery may well tell us something about its role and function.

 TASK

Think about and discuss the reasons why monasteries may have been founded at these locations.

Monastic buildings

The Celtic monks did not live in a single dwelling, but in a cluster of monastic buildings enclosed by a ditch. Within the enclosure the following buildings would have been found:

- **A church**, the central building, simple and rectangular in shape, usually made of oak. If a community grew too large for the church to house everyone, they tended to build smaller adjacent oratories surrounding the main church, rather than build a bigger church.
- **The refectory** or communal dining room
- **The library/scriptorium** for the pursuit of study and copying of texts
- **The guesthouse,** sometimes separate from the inner compound
- **Kitchen**
- Individual **cells** in which the monks slept, sometimes two or three to a cell.

While stone-built monasteries were the exception in Ireland, this reconstruction is an example of what the structure would have looked like. With its round tower, this structure would be from a later period. *(Reconstruction: Cathal O'Connor)*

Devenish Island outside Enniskillen, County Fermanagh, is a good example of the ancient monasteries that once existed throughout Ireland. *(Photo: Cathal O'Connor)*

Learning and study

According to Adomnán's *Life of Colmcille,* the monks began their day with prayer and then immediately went on to manual labour or study. Study was to be an integral part of the monastic life, and to this end monasteries had libraries and/or scriptoriums. Learning took the following forms:

- The study and copying of Scripture. This involved the learning by heart of Scripture, particularly the psalms, as well as biblical exegesis, including a knowledge of the hidden and allegorical meaning of the text. Surviving from this period is the Cathach,[40] traditionally taken to have come from the pen of Colmcille.
- This in turn necessitated the learning of the Latin language.
- A study of the Church Fathers.
- Secular learning, eg astronomy, Virgil, Horace and other pagan writers, the writing of poetry particularly nature poetry, grammar, mathematics.
- Art and illuminations, metal work.
- The writing of monastic rules and penitentials as well as annals.

It was this era that earned Ireland its reputation as the land of saints and scholars.

PRACTICE ESSAY TITLE

Give an account of the nature of Celtic monasticism. (35)

Your answer should include reference to the some of the following:
- Poverty, chastity, obedience
- Asceticism (fasting, silence, sleep, discipline, prayer)
- Buildings
- Learning
- Structure
- Some positions held within the monastic structure

Remember that good answers are well referenced so try to give some examples from monastic rules or other source material in your answer.

You will be given some suggestions for critical assessment later in the chapter.

5. THE IMPORTANCE OF THE MONASTERIES

A spiritual role

Primarily the monasteries had a religious purpose or function. The monastic lifestyle was perceived as the most perfect way of following Christ, and so monasticism was a way of achieving sanctity.

To this end then, the monasteries had an important role in the spiritual care of people. This was exercised primarily through the administration of penance or more specifically in the role of the *anamchara*. He was an individual of the penitent's choice who was essentially a soul friend and spiritual director, as well as a confessor. Penances were often carried out in the monasteries and Adomnán tells us of penitents visiting Iona who were then sent to the island of Hinba. (There will be more about this monastic function in the next chapter.)

Facilitators of learning

The monastic schools were open to the laity as well as to novices of the monastic life. It was customary in Ireland for children to be fostered from about the age of seven until puberty. Kathleen Hughes points out that "fosterage is one of the social functions which the monasteries carried out".

In fact, St Ita is called the 'foster mother of the saints of Ireland'. All of the Lives tell us that monastic education was particularly favoured by princes and kings. Young boys learned the Latin language and Scripture, as well as maths, geometry and the classics.The Venerable Bede admires the quality of learning in the Celtic monasteries and tells us that they gave the gift of learning freely.[41]

Preservers and transmitters of culture

As we have already seen, the monks were skilled copyists and because of them a wealth of literature has been preserved. The most notable works are perhaps the *Cathach*, the *Book of Durrow* and the *Lindesfarne Gospels,* as well as the slightly later *Book of Kells*. Adomnán tells us that Colmcille insists that when copying, a work must be diligently checked against the original and that brothers should avail of one another's assistance when checking. At times the scribe did more than just copy, and included his own reactions to what he was writing or indeed feeling on the day. In the *Armagh Gospels*, Kathleen Hughes points out that in the story of the betrayal of Jesus by Judas Iscariot, one scribe could not resist inserting the word 'wretch!' In other texts scribes complain in the margins of the text about the quality of the ink and the tiredness of their hand. Thus we get a wonderful insight into the thoughts and reactions of these monks who speak to us from the sixth and seventh centuries.

In addition to religious literature, the monasteries took over some of the functions of the *filid*, producing a wealth of poetry and saga. It was also at this time in the monasteries that the annals were produced, which were essentially the history books of the day. "Thus Ireland has kept an unusually rich early literature and lore, and the imaginative ideas of church writers were stimulated by secular tradition", Kathleen Hughes tells us.[42]

The monasteries were patrons of the arts, and their metal workers – as well as producing religious objects such as the Ardagh Chalice – also made brooches and belt fastenings, mostly for the noble classes.

Places of sanctuary

The grounds of monastic enclosures were protected by Brehon law from violence. In a warfaring society, as Celtic Ireland continued to be even after Christianisation, this function as a neutral buffer zone was important. Sometimes criminals also sought sanctuary in the monastic enclosure and they were encouraged to reform by the completion of lengthy penances.

It was not unusual for people to bring valuables, for example, stocks of corn to the monastery for safe-keeping in times of strife. In this sense then, monasteries may well have acted as a kind of bank.

Providers of hospitality

The monasteries very much reflected the culture of the society to which they belonged and in welcoming the laity and various guests, the monasteries experienced a fusion of secular and Christian values. As we have already seen, larger monasteries had guest houses attached and Adomnán's *Life* paints a wonderful picture of the treatment of guests who arrived at Iona:

"Prepare the guest-house straight away and draw water to wash the guests feet", and in another place, *"Go quickly and bring at once the pilgrims who have arrived from a far away district … the saint greeted them with a kiss"*.

Hardinge believes that "hospitality was an inflexible rule of all Celtic settlements". The Rule of Ailbe, written later but probably reflecting older practices, recommends: *"a clean house for guests and a big fire, washing and bathing for them, and a couch without sorrow"*.[43] Celtic settlements on the Continent often provided hospitality for pilgrims travelling to Rome.

The nucleus of a town or village

As discussed, the monasteries did not comprise one building but rather a collection of buildings situated within a compound. As numbers grew or needs increased, they tended to add more buildings. While the monks were largely self-sufficient, from time to time it was likely that specialist skills would be required. For that reason there may have been a variety of people living within the monastic compound at any given time. Not all were bound to the same degree by the monastic rule. Charles-Edwards identifies an' inncr core" consisting of those who had taken monastic vows, as well as those who were not strictly bound by them.[44] Hughcs and Hamlin agree that not all within the compound lived the ascetic life. Entire families often donated their land to the monastery and thus we see the formation of the *manaig* – a group of lay monks who were married, and farmed the monastic land. Hughes and Hamlin add that some people may have been born into the monastic life in this way, and therefore "a monastery must be seen 'as an estate directed to a religious purpose'".[45]

It is clear then, that the monasteries were places of employment. Charles-Edwards concludes that they were an "ecclesiastical civitas [which] served the role performed elsewhere by walled towns".[46]

 TASK

Think about and discuss in groups or as a class:

"On the surface monasteries appear unattractive, yet they attracted hundreds during this period of Ireland's history."

What were their attractive features? Give examples to support your points.

Make notes on your discussion. You will need to be clear on the attractive features of monasticism for the exam!

6. THE DISTINCTIVE FEATURES OF CELTIC MONASTICISM

⊗ TASKS

1) Read again the section on the origins of monasticism and the nature of Celtic monasticism. Can you identify the features borrowed from monasticism elsewhere?

2) Discuss the view that there was nothing completely new or innovative in Irish monasticism.

   Check your work. You should have included some of the following: chastity, poverty, obedience, community, learning, asceticism.

Asceticism

Although asceticism was practised to varying degrees by the Desert Fathers, most scholars agree that the degree to which the Irish monks subjected themselves to ascetic practices was greater then elsewhere. This is evidenced by the replacement of the harsh Rule of Columbanus with the more moderate Benedictine one. As we have already seen, the practice of praying *crosfigell* was common, the discipline of misdemeanour was harsh, and fasts were severe. Gougaud also highlights the practice of "plunging into a stream or pond and remaining there petrified with cold for a greater or lesser time".[47] Gougaud adds that while these types of practices were found elsewhere, they were never practised as habitually as they were in the Celtic Church.[48]

John Ryan argues that it was the union of such asceticism with a zeal for study which was unique. He believes it was the succession of the monks into roles previously occupied by the druids and the *filid* which made study so important.[49] Nonetheless, it is unusual to see these two features combined in such a way.

Apostolic and anchoritical

John Ryan refers to the tendency to combine two apparently conflicting practices within Celtic monasticism.[50] While the Celtic monk always had a desire for solitude and to seek the peace of the quiet place, he was also driven to meet the spiritual needs of the local community in which he found himself.[51] (Refer to page 113.) For the monks a priority was apostolic outreach, even when the very desire of his soul was to be 'far from the madding crowd'.

Peregrinatio

In many cases this apostolic outreach went beyond ministering to the local community and led to many Celtic monks embarking on a life of pilgrimage. Liam and Máire de Paor acknowledge that this was an important regard in which Celtic monasticism differed from the Egyptian prototype – the seeking of self-mortification by exiling oneself forever and living among strangers. Celtic monasticism was "from its beginnings ... a missionary movement".[52] They travelled to Britain[53] and to the Continent,[54] and while there was a range of motives for their action, they busied themselves with the spiritual needs of the communities among whom they found themselves, and in most cases they were never to return to Ireland.

Organisation and government

The structure of the Celtic Church itself became monastic. As the monasteries became 'ecclesiastical estates', they acquired secular as well as religious functions (see pages 112–114). Kings frequently endowed them and they often received donations of land from local families. Abbots who governed these estates ruled over what were sometimes huge expanses of church land. In this way they became the most important administrators, if not leaders of the Celtic Church in this period. This movement is unparalleled elsewhere. In addition, affiliations between monasteries were frequent when those owing allegiance to a common founder formed *Paruchiae*, which were larger than the dioceses established in the first generation of the Christian Church.[55]

Women

Celtic monasticism was also unique in the prominence it afforded to women. Many monastic foundations were founded for and by women, the most notable being of course Kildare. Ita and Monnine were also prominent female saints and they had a formative role in the spiritual lives of many other monastic founders, such as Brendan of Clonfert. The early martyrologies of the Celtic Church name over 200 women saints. Little is known of many of these early female foundations because in terms of secular law, women, while having a 'life stake' in property, could not inherit it. Upon the death of the woman, the foundation reverted to the donor's family and often became a male foundation instead.

Skene remarks that according to the *Catalogue of the Saints of Ireland*, the first Christians "... rejected not the service and society of women."[56] Gougaud notes a complaint made by three bishops of the province of Tours that the Celtic peregrini of Brittany "... with the assistance of women to whom you give the name conhospitae ... distribute the Eucharist, take the chalice and administer the Blood of Christ to the people".[57] Therefore it seems that the gender inclusivity of the early Celtic monasteries did not always meet with the approval of Church leaders elsewhere.

So, although largely derivative, Celtic monasticism did evolve in a unique fashion, and in the main, while not being entirely innovative, did choose to emphasise some monastic traits more than others and combine them in a way that was not seen elsewhere.

PRACTICE ESSAY TITLE

1) Describe the distinctive features of Celtic monasticism. (35)

   Use the information provided to help you. Give plenty of examples to support your answer.

2) Explore the view that care of the local community was the most important function of the Celtic monasteries. Justify your answer. (15)

 SUMMARY

Asceticism was practised by the earliest Christians and self-denial was encouraged in the teachings of Jesus.

⬇

Ascetics evolved into a group apart (Desert Fathers) and in turn spread the practice into the West where Martin of Tours and Honoratus had important foundations.

⬇

Patrick may have been familiar with these foundations on the Continent and as settlements were made in Britain, such as Candida Casa, Llangarvan and Caldey Island in Wales, they had a direct influence on the origins of monasticism in Ireland.

⬇

Ireland's own monastic founders, such as Enda and Finnian, studied at Candida Casa and Wales respectively, and in turn educated others, for example Comgall and Ciaran.

⬇

Although Celtic monasticism centred on poverty, chastity, obedience, community, asceticism, and learning, it also developed its own unique character.

OTHER ASPECTS OF HUMAN EXPERIENCE

The examples in the diagram below are suggestions for some connections between monastic spirituality and other aspects of human experience. You should try to think of other connections which might be made.

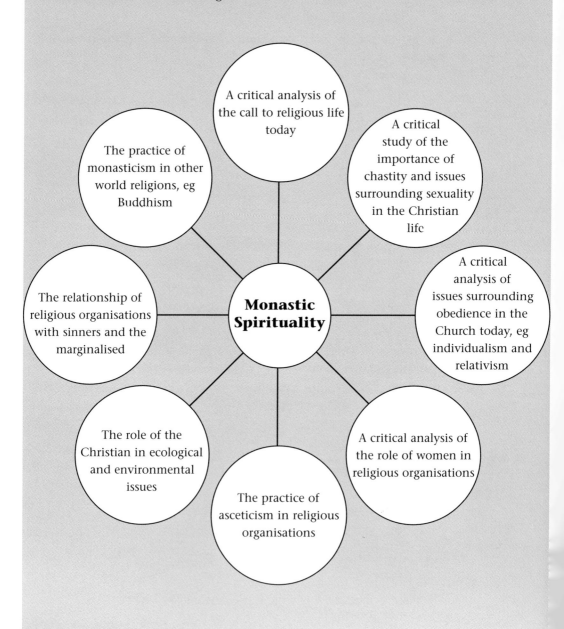

TASKS

1) Find out about the different ways in which people can practise asceticism today. You might consider a pilgrimage to Lough Derg or Croagh Patrick in Ireland. Use the internet to help you. Think about the purpose of such practices.

2) Find out about monastic practices in other world religions.

3) What do you think is the role of monasteries and religious orders in the Church and in the world today? Consider the view that monasticism is an outdated concept.

Some helpful examples of how connections might be made

An analysis of issues surrounding obedience in the Church today

The Celtic monks believed that "nothing must be refused in their obedience to be Christ's true disciples.....it will not be pleasing to the Lord." For many Christians, obedience poses a difficulty. Obedience to the Church's teaching in the contemporary world is becoming increasingly difficult. People baulk at the idea of authority in the Church, or indeed that there should be such an authority. Some suggest that there can be no absolute moral code. Groves argues that "people do not see the Church as having a real relevance in their everyday lives and therefore do not recognise its authority in everyday matters." The Celtic monks had no such difficulty. People rail against the idea that governments should try to interfere too much in the lives of people, or influence human behaviour in any way. Today, the morality of relativism is common; people make subjective decisions about what is right for them – there is no absolute moral code. 'Truth' is relative to one's own perception; individuals are answerable only to themselves. The issue was addressed in two Papal letters: 'The Splendour of Truth (1993) and 'The Gospel of Life' (1995). Pope Benedict too, recognises that relativism comes from a growing secularism across Europe. He believes that in such an environment the Church's role should be to make clear its teaching over and over again. Indeed, some sociologists argue that where religious organisations try to accommodate many different views and beliefs, or indeed try to 'water down' their own teachings, they actually become less popular. It seems that in some sense people need to feel that religious organisations do clearly try to direct and influence choices. Benedict says that on the other hand, "relativism ... does not recognise anything as being certain ... its highest goals are one's own ego and desire." The Celtic monks had a huge sense of a Divine Will that had to be obeyed – which we have lost. Columbanus reminds us, "by strict obedience shall the monk show his love of God." In addition, the monks had a wonderful sense of the community being more important than the individual.

The importance of chastity and issues surrounding sexuality

In relation to chastity, Columbanus argues that "a monk's chastity is indeed judged by his thoughts". Chastity was not just about sexual relations, it was about the purity of one's mind. Today we live in a society where sex is seen as a commodity, and people are objectified sexually. It is estimated that an average of seventy-five per cent of prime time television includes content of a sexual nature. Extra-marital sex is referred to, two out of three times every hour in soap operas. The UK sex industry is worth an estimated one billion pounds. The desire for freedom and for individual fulfilment had led to widespread sexual promiscuity, to a dramatic increase in sexually transmitted diseases, and to many unwanted pregnancies. Although Michael Maher points out that standards in Celtic monasteries "are severe particularly in the area of sexual morality", the sense of purity of the Celtic monks seems to have been lost. For many monks today, the vow of chastity gives freedom to give themselves totally to the pastoral care of others. Yet for many today, it is an outdated concept and problematic to the future of the priesthood in the Catholic Church.

The importance of caring for the weak and marginalised

The Celtic monks had inspirational solidarity with the marginalised. Brigit of Kildare for example had a truly preferential option for the poor. She vowed to the king of Leinster, "If I had all your wealth, I would take it and give it away to all Christ's poor." As a result, Brigit's monastery at Kildare became known as the City of the Poor. Aidan of Lindesfarne also expressed his solidarity with the poor when he gave away the king's gift of a horse to the first beggar he met. At the king's displeasure Aidan said, "Surely this son of a mare is not more important to you than that son of man." Some monasteries today reach out to the marginalised as part of their charism; for example, the Redemptorist monks at Clonard take it in turns to wait for the "hopeless and the helpless".

The Church, to its utter shame, has not always shared this solidarity with the poor and the marginalised. Leonardo Boff argues that "the Church became an abstract speculation removed from the original spirit of the Gospel message and out of touch with real life". The Church has been criticised for siding with the vested interest and in its history it has even been involved in supporting colonisation and the removal of land from the peasantry, in its commitment to obeying the law of the land. Richard Woods reminds us that 'justice and charity were the main hinges of Celtic social action'. Liberation theology today emphasises solidarity with the poor and argues that all Christians must work for social and economic justice, even if it means becoming politically involved. Bishop Casadaliga reminds us that "as long as there are poor people in the world and as long as there is a God who cares for the poor, there will be a need for a theology of Liberation." The spirit of Liberation Theology is evident in Celtic monastic spirituality in many ways, from care of the poor and the sinner, to welcoming the stranger. In the monasteries, hospitality was extremely generous as any stranger was sincerely welcomed and well looked after. The guest house was usually open to all who called. Welcome of the stranger has a special place in our society as is reflected in the problems faced by many asylum seekers and migrant workers. In 2004, 19% of asylum seekers were allowed to find refuge in Britain, while 78% were turned away. The Celtic monks in their openness to all, but especially to those who were weakest, turned no one away.

A brief commentary on the excerpts above

- The students do make connections with other aspects of human experience, eg cultural, social and economic issues.
- The connections are made clearly, and explicitly arise from the area of study.
- The connections are well referenced and make use of supportive evidence and examples.
- There has been reference to historical and contemporary values and practices.
- Alternative religious practices have been considered.
- Critical analysis and independent thought is evident and the views of scholars considered.
- The connections are developed and explored rather than being simply comparative.

 TASK

In groups, comment on the extracts above.
- What do you see as the strengths and weaknesses of each example?
- To which aspects of human experience are connections made? (Use the introduction given in chapter 2 and the specification to help you to identify them.)
- Think of some other connections that might have been made.

Exam tip!

Make as much use as you can of the evidence and examples you come across when exploring the various issues within other aspects of human experience. You will see that many issues will arise more than once. For example, the issue of gender could emerge more than once as an aspect of human experience in a study of the Celtic Church. Make as much use of your research as you can.

TASKS

Find out about issues surrounding the care of marginalised people in a **variety of** political and social contexts.

Identify the issues concerning the role of religious organisations in caring for these people.

Comment on the view that all issues of social welfare are the responsibility of governments rather than religious groups.

Endnotes

[1] Ryan, J, *Irish Monasticism, origins and early development*, Four Courts Press, Dublin, 1992, p4

[2] Mk 10:17–31

[3] See for example Rom 7:18–23

[4] Ryan, *Irish Monasticism origins and early development, op cit*, p9

[5] See Chapter 2 of this book as well as C41; 42; 47

[6] De Paor, *Patrick Pilgrim Apostle of Ireland, op cit*, p125

[7] Hanson, *The Life and Writings of Saint Patrick, op cit*

[8] Ryan, *Irish Monasticism, op cit*, p91

[9] Oulton, JEL, *The Credal Statements of Patrick, op cit*, Preface

[10] Bieler, L, *The Life and Legend of Patrick, problems of modern scholarship*, Dublin, 1948, p65

[11] Ryan, *Irish Monasticism, op cit*, p63

[12] Chadwick, *The Age of the Saints in the Early Celtic Church*, Llanerch publishers, Wales, p37

[13] *ibid*, p39

[14] *ibid*, p50

[15] *ibid*, p92

[16] See the discussion later in this chapter on monastic sites.

[17] Stokes, GT, *Ireland and the Celtic Church*, 2nd edition, London, 1888, pp178–179

[18] Henry, F, *Irish Art in the Early Christian period*, London, 1947, p60ff

[19] Ryan, *Irish Monasticism, op cit*, p106

[20] Translation by Burkitt, FC, *Journal of Theological Studies*, Vol 27, 1925, p42

[21] Ryan, *Irish Monasticism, op cit*, p112

[22] *ibid*, p113

[23] Chadwick, *The Age of the Saints*, p116

[24] ibid, *p5*

[25] Ryan, *Irish monasticism, op cit*, p106

[26] Ryan, J, 'The monastic Institute' in *A History of Irish Catholicism*, Vol 1, Gill & Macmillan Ltd Dublin, 1971, p10

[27] As quoted in Scherman, K, *The Flowering of Ireland, op cit*, p108

[28] Ryan, 'The Monastic Institute' in *A History of Irish Catholicism, op cit*, p13

[29] See Chapter 1 to remind yourself of the *nemed* social class.

[30] The record of his death at 33 years may have been a literary device to increase his saintly reputation having lived the same number of years as our Lord.

[31] Taken from the 10th century tales of the voyage of Brendan.

[32] Ryan, *Irish Monasticism, op cit*, pp124–125

[33] ibid, p249

[34] Vitae Sanctorum Hiberniae

[35] Walker, GSM, (ed), *Sancti Columbani Opera* 1957 pp140–142

[36] Gwynn, EJ, & Purton, WJ, (ed) *The Monastery of Tallaght*, 1911, p115ff

37 Gougaud, L, *Christianity in Celtic Lands,* Four Courts Press Dublin, 1992, p93

38 Hamlin, A, & Hughes, K, *The Modern Traveler to the Early Irish Church,* Spck London, 1977, p26

39 *ibid*, p31

40 The Cathach is preserved in the Library of the Royal Irish Academy, Dublin.

41 Reference to the use of Bede as source material are from Hughes, K, *Early Christian Ireland: an Introduction to the Sources,* Hodder & Stoughton Ltd, 1972, pp201–202

42 Hughes and Hamlin, *The Modern Traveller to the Early Irish Church, op cit,* p12

43 Hardinge, L, *The Celtic Church in Britain,* Spck London, 1972, p167

44 Charles-Edwards, TM, *Early Christian Ireland* Cambridge University Press, United Kingdom, 2000, p121

45 Hughes and Hamlin, *The Modern Traveller to the Early Irish Church, op cit,* pp6–7

46 Charles-Edwards, TM, *Early Christian Ireland,* p122

47 Gougaud, L, *Christianity in Celtic Lands,* p95

48 *ibid,* p96

49 Ryan, *Irish Monasticism, op cit,* p408

50 *ibid,* pp407–408

51 Nowhere is this combination more apparent than in the *Life of Columbanus* as recorded by Jonas.

52 De Paor, L and M, *Early Christian Ireland,* Thames & Hudson, London, 1958, p52

53 See Chapter 5 for more detail with which to reference your responses.

54 See Chapter 2 of this book.

55 This topic is covered in more detail at A2 level and is dealt with in Chapter 7 of this book.

56 Skene, WF, *Celtic Scotland: A History of Ancient Alban,* Vol 11, Edinburgh, 1886–90, pp12–13

57 Gougaud, *Christianity in Celtic Lands, op cit,* p87

The Penitentials

Chapter 4

LEARNING OUTCOMES

Knowledge, understanding and evaluation of:

— the features of penitential practice

— the texts of Finnian, Columbanus, and Cummean

— the impact of the penitentials

— the penitentials as historical sources

INTRODUCTION

This chapter focuses on the system whereby sin was acknowledged and dealt with within the Church. Sin, as the failure of the Christian to live up to and live out the teachings of Christ, has always been an issue with which the Church has grappled.

This study involves both an examination of the texts themselves and the system of penitential practice which they facilitated.[1] Kenney provides us with a useful working definition of the penitentials as: "A little book containing a schedule of the expiatory works (penance) to be imposed for the various sins for which penitents might wish to make atonement."[2]

1. THE PRACTICE OF PENANCE IN THE EARLY CHRISTIAN CHURCH

In order to fully understand and appreciate the contribution and impact of Celtic penitential texts and practice, we must first examine the system of penance which they gradually replaced.

Jesus had always extended forgiveness to those who had done wrong and the forgiveness of weakness was very much a Christian virtue; however, in the early Christian Church there was a particular understanding of the nature of sin among those who had accepted Christian baptism and professed to be 'dead' to the old life of sin. From the earliest times in the Christian Church, Christians were encouraged to regularly confess their failings, *"Confess your faults to one another"*, James exhorts.[3] Most historians accept however that, in the main, it was the penance which was public while the confession of sins remained a private affair between the penitent and the bishop.

It was believed that just as baptism had eradicated the stain of sin, then forgiveness could only really be given once more in the lifetime of a Christian; indeed Ambrose ruled, *"As one baptism, so one penance."*[4] As McNeill observes, there was "a desire to maintain the Church as a body of people of unpolluted holiness".[5] This is supported by the tone of Paul, who says that the wicked man is to be dealt with by the church *"gathered together"*, and that punishment is to be inflicted *"by the many"* so that the *"spirit might be saved"*.[6] In order to emphasise the seriousness of sinful actions after baptism, penances were often very debilitating and involved the almost complete public exclusion of penitents from religious services.

By the fourth century it seems that 'stations' or 'order of Penitents' were in use, whereby penitents were given particular positions at church meetings or liturgy. The lowest grade of penitent seems to have been positioned outside the door of the church. Some were in the vestibule and were required to leave after the sermon and were referred to as 'the hearers'; others 'the kneelers', were positioned at the rear of the congregation and were required to kneel when others stood during the service. There is some evidence to suggest that they wore sackcloth and had ash on their heads[7.] Meanwhile, the 'co-standers' mingled with the congregation but were not permitted to receive communion.[8] Sozomen also speaks of the public nature of fifth century penance when he says: *"the place of those who are in penance is conspicuous: they stand with downcast eyes and with the bearing of mourners. When the Divine Liturgy is concluded ... with wailing and lamentation they cast themselves prostrate on the ground. So also the whole congregation of the Church with loud crying is suffused with tears ... meanwhile in private each spends as much time as the bishop has appointed in voluntary self-affliction. On the appointed day, having discharged his penalty like some debt, he is absolved from his offence and takes part in the assembly with the people."*[9]

The result of this system was that the young virtually never confessed their failings and confession was generally left until nearer death. This meant that many lived a sinful life until old age, when fear of eternal damnation drove them to confess. This concerned Tertullian to some extent, when he laments against those who postponed or shunned the practice completely: *"Is it better to be damned in secret than to be absolved in public?"*

In addition to the public identification of the penitent, the actual penances prescribed were often debilitating. The very act of receiving the sacrament had further implications, such as prohibition from marriage, Holy Orders or joining the military. It should be pointed out however, that more minor sins do not seem to have been subject to such a regime. Harsh penances seem to have been applied to quite serious sin including the sin of fornication, which posed a particular problem for the Church as it was not punishable by civil law yet was considered highly immoral in Christian law.[10]

 TASK

Think about and discuss as a class or in small groups:

"Christian commitment should be taken very seriously and the wrongdoing of those who profess themselves to be Christian should be treated with the utmost seriousness by the Church."
Do you agree or disagree?

2. THE ORIGINS OF THE PRACTICE OF PENANCE IN THE CELTIC CHURCH

Most scholars agree that there is little evidence to suggest that the system of public penance described above was ever practised in the Celtic Church.

- The first reference we have to the treatment of those considered guilty of serious sin comes from Patrick's address to Coroticus. Patrick both publicly condemns and excludes Coroticus. We may surmise from this that Patrick had the system of public penance in mind when he wrote the *Letter*.

- Patrick himself has a much heightened sense of his own sinfulness and emphasises the necessity of conversion from sin. Both of these are recurring themes throughout his *Confessio*.

- Gougaud suggests that when Theodore arrived in England to take over the archbishopric of Canterbury, "he ascertained that public penance and the solemn reconciliation of Penitents with the Church were practices unknown in that country". Gougaud further argues that "it is very likely that they were equally unknown in the Celtic Churches."[11] Warren disagrees, and suggests a number of examples of public confession of sins, although these may well have been a purely voluntary expression of sorrow on the part of the penitent.[12]

- It seems obvious that the custom of confession in the monasteries played a part in the introduction of a new system of penance in the Celtic Church. Columbanus' Rule suggests that confession of faults was made twice a day, before dinner and again before bedtime. The penalties imposed for breaches of monastic rule in the Celtic monasteries indicate that such penance could also be extended to the laity for sins committed. The idea that the overcoming of sin was central in attaining Christian discipleship and perfection was passed to the laity by the monastic institutions. In Ireland, the monasteries had a unique administrative and pastoral role among the laity. Both Adomnán and Jonas speak of numbers of penitents who retire to the monastery for penitential advice and to complete penances. The penitentials were then, in part, an extension to the laity of monastic discipline.

• The concepts which formed the basis of Irish secular law also had a role in the development of a new form of penitential practice in the Celtic Church, namely those of compensation and surety. Indeed, it will become apparent later in this chapter just how influential Brehon law appears to have been in the formation of the Celtic penitentials. It incorporates the idea that an offence can be made good by the agreement to pay a fine to compensate the injured or aggrieved party. It took into account the status of the one offended as well as the offender. As we shall see, this idea is very much reflected in the penitentials. Thomas O'Loughlin argues that "the Penitentials were an extension of their basic legal attitude into the realm of the sacred".[13]

Conclusion

• There is little evidence to suggest public penance was ever practised in Ireland.

• Patrick had an awareness of the need for repentance of sin and no doubt his spirituality influenced that of the Celtic Church.

• Patrick also, in his address to Coroticus, set the precedent that those who were Christian and continued to sin would be dealt with by the Christian Church.

• Monastic discipline and the spirituality of striving for Christian perfection was easily extended to the laity.

• Secular law formed the basis of the idea that wrong against another had to be paid for and was probably influential in the formation of penitential literature.

The change from public to private penance at a glance:

Public penance as practised in the Early Church	The new private system
Available as a once-off event, that was perceived as an extraordinary one	Available repeatedly, perceived as a normal element of the Christian life and indeed encouraged frequently so that the Eucharist might be worthily received
Usual minister of penance was the bishop	Penance was usually ministered by the priest
Necessitated by major sin	Necessitated because of human tendency to sin repeatedly, and in minor as well as serious ways
Penance was imposed in a punitive way to pay for the sin committed	Penances were remedies for the sin, which was perceived as a sickness
Penance was given as a means to recovering the status given at baptism	Penance was part of the discipline of ongoing Christian discipleship, enabling one to resume the journey towards spiritual wholeness
Emphasis was on maintaining the baptismal state	Emphasis was on the continuous and lifelong journey of the Christian disciple

3. THE PENITENTIAL TEXTS – AN OUTLINE

Remember that the penitentials themselves were handbooks for the use of confessors who engaged, as part of their ministry, in facilitating the forgiveness of penitents' sins. They were essentially a guidebook for such a minister.

The Penitential of Finnian

This was most likely, though not conclusively, penned by Finnian of Clonard, written perhaps, in the view of McNeill, before the middle of the sixth century.[14] It is the earliest existing Irish penitential and is an original work, important in the view of

Connolly because "it is the first comprehensive, discriminating and precise penitential produced in the Irish Church".[15]

He seems to have intended the work to be of use to his own monks and explains within the text that he writes out of love for his fellow monks. He claims to have used both Scripture and other *"learned sources"*. It is not clear what these learned sources are but Bieler believes he certainly made use of Cassian.[16] Kenney argues that "he made use of the Bible and some early Irish Canons".[17] It is also important to acknowledge his association with Gildas. He apologises for his own limited ability and encourages others to follow him in this endeavour, so that his ideas may be developed. He states his motive as the salvation of sinners.

The text is fifty three canons in length and seems to be easily divided into two main sections. Canons 1–30 deal with the sins of clerics while canons 31–48 deal with the sins of laity. McNeill believes he does "little more than codify current usage", rather than see his work as a departure from the current practices known to him in the Church.[18]

The significance of his work is that, for the first time, we have an availability of penance to the laity. The canons are progressive in that they deal first with less serious sins, moving on to those which are more serious. He also includes an opening paragraph which deals generally with guilt and penance and sin of the heart where, for Finnian, sin always originates. The intention, rather than the external action itself is of the utmost importance, as well as the intensity and speed of the expression of sorrow on the part of the penitent.

McNeill also observes that "considerable emphasis is laid upon sexual sin" and the belief that was current at the time, as suggested by Payer, that women were usually the cause and source of such sin.[19] Finnian strives to protect the permanence of marriage and the sanctity of the married state.[20]

He asserts his belief that the doing of penance absolves the penitent from guilt and in this sense the main message of his penitential is one of hope; that there is no sin which can be committed for which there is not a corresponding remedy.

The Penitential of Columbanus

This text shows significant dependence on that of Finnian. It seems that the text itself was compiled on the Continent and therefore exercised considerable influence on the practice of penance there. Ó Fiaich believes that this penitential was written either at Luxeuil or Annegray.[21] Laporte found that it was one single document but was divided into three parts, one for monks, one for clerics and one for laity.[22] In this sense, Charles-Edwards argues that it is comprehensive in character, but disagrees that it is one document. Instead he instead presents it as, "three separate attempts to produce concise Penitentials for monks, clerics and laity".[23] It consists of forty two canons, with up to five sub divisions.

Kenney believes, despite its dependence on earlier Irish ecclesiastical legislation, that it is "stamped with the personality of Columbanus" and is "logical and severe ... displays considerable intelligence, good judgement and sense of justice and of proportion".[24] Columbanus' Penitential occupies a singularly important place in the century that lapsed between Finnian and Cummean. There appears to be less of a chasm between the laity and the clergy since the writing of Finnian's Penitential. The latter at times seemed to suggest that the laity could be guilty of every imaginable sin, while Columbanus' Penitential illustrates close parallels between the clergy and the laity.

The Penitential of Cummean

Cummean's Penitential has been dated to the mid-seventh century. It was probably written by Cummean the Tall (c 662) and it is argued to be the most comprehensive of all the penitentials, perhaps written around 650. It can be divided into two parts – one of which is a prologue on the remission of sins, where Cummean sees penance in medicinal terms. This is followed by eight chapters which prescribe penances for the eight deadly sins: gluttony, fornication, avarice, anger, dejection, languor, vainglory and pride. For these eight vices, eight remedies are proposed.

The second part of the penitential is made up of three chapters, dealing with lesser offences, the misdemeanours of boys, and questions concerning the sacred host.

He gives a detailed explanation of the principle of curing contraries by their contraries and emphasises the role of the Confessor as someone who has diagnostic skills, which he must use to uncover the root cause of the sin. The fact that Cummean is at pains to point out that all that he says is based on the teachings of the fathers who have gone before him, O'Loughlin takes to be an indication of his awareness of the "novelty of the Irish system".[25]

This text shows a greater depth compared to earlier penitentials and was most probably transmitted to Britain and Europe.

4. THE FEATURES OF CELTIC PENITENTIAL PRACTICE

This section examines the main features of the practice of penance in the Celtic Church.

Private penance

The system was private and confession was to a person of the penitent's choice, rather than a bishop. The importance of this privacy is emphasised in the *Martyrology of Oengus* (c 800), wherein one of the four sins for which no penance is said to atone was the revelation of sin confessed to an *anamchara*. The penances too were more private, in that there was no requirement to sit in the 'order of penitents' or 'stations' and penitential exercises, such as fasting, could be carried out privately by the penitent. In addition, there does not seem to have been any public reconciliation ceremony restoring the penitent to the Eucharist. Instead, absolution appears to have been granted after the completion of the period of penance. However, it may be worth noting that by the nature of some of the penances given, they did have a public dimension; for example, in cases where penitents had to leave kin and *tuath* to go into exile or to complete penance in a monastery, or in the instance of a penitential requirement to approach the one offended to express sorrow or make reparation.

Repeatable penance

Penance and reconciliation was available repeatedly, as often as one sinned and felt the need for forgiveness. In fact, sinners were encouraged to confess frequently and in full, so that they could frequently avail of the Eucharist.

Types of penance

Some specific penances were employed frequently, for example, prayer, (in particular the recitation of psalms), fasting and almsgiving. However, McNeill notes that the compilers of the texts could at times be quite inventive in determining the penitential acts required of a sinner, such as the requirement of the monk penitent to stand *crosfigil* for many hours while reciting specific psalms.

Graded penance

The penitential books graded the penances which could be assigned by a confessor. The status of the sinner and the seriousness of the sin were taken into account when apportioning penances. A person with a higher status, particularly a cleric, was judged to have sinned more seriously than another of lesser status, even though the sin may have been the same. This recognised the influence that such a person might have on others, given their role and status in society. In addition, those whose knowledge was deemed greater, also had a greater degree of guilt. This is most clearly seen in the separate classification by Cummean of the sins of boys.

Compensation

Compensation of the victim was also prescribed in the penitentials. This satisfaction was to be paid to the victim or to the victim's family and was perceived to be of value in encouraging the penitent to turn the sin into a virtue. It was useful in ensuring that some good came from the original wrongdoing.

Sins of thought

These were also to be confessed. Great importance was attached to the intention of the wrongdoer at the time of the sin.

Anamchara

The confessor was known as an *anamchara*, meaning soul friend. Scholars such as McNeill, Connolly and Hardinge see this institution as having its origins, at least partially, in druidism.[26] The druids themselves acted as counsellors and advisors to kings. McNeill and Gamer point out that the *anamchara* was "with reasonable probability, a racial institution of great antiquity".[27] The Desert Fathers also encouraged the practice of opening one's heart to another as a means of attaining *heyschia* or peace of the heart. Connolly calls this "the tradition of heart speaking to heart".[28] The role of the *anamchara* was less to pass judgement than to act as a guide to the penitent in order to help them overcome the difficulties they were experiencing in the Christian journey and to develop a closer relationship with Christ. The role of the *anamchara* is perhaps best reflected in the words of Haltigar of Cambrai:

"Nobody can help the man who has fallen beneath a burden, unless bowing down he gives him a hand: no doctor can heal wounds if he is afraid of infection. Likewise, no priest can heal the wounds from which a sinner suffers, and take away the sin if he does not suffer and pray and weep with him."[29]

It seems that within monastic discipline every monk was expected to have a soul friend with whom to explore the depths of his conscience. The importance of the *anamchara* is well attested to in Celtic literature of the period; in some places attributed to Brigit, in other places to Comgall: *"anyone without a soul friend is like a body without a head"*. In other texts, the advice is clear as to the value of the *anamchara* to the penitent: *"as the floor is swept every day, so the soul is cleansed every day by confession"*.[30]

Sin as a sickness

Sin was perceived as a sickness and penance as a medicine for souls. Indeed, Bieler argues that "isolated medical metaphors occur in almost all the texts".[31] Penance in the Irish penitentials was never a negative pursuit but was always purifying and curative. The penitent was always perceived to be a sick soul in need of a cure; penance was not only to cure his own sickness, but also that caused to others who were hurt by his sin. The confessor was urged to correctly diagnose the underlying cause of the sin confessed, and only then could the correct cure be prescribed. He should therefore take account of all the symptoms of the penitent before him, for example, the circumstances of the sin, the intention behind it, and the frequency with which it occurred. The metaphors of sickness and medicine are intrinsically linked with the feature below.

Contraries by their contraries

Contraries were cured by their contraries, that is, to cure a vice by employing its opposite virtue. This principle can be traced to the Methodist school of medicine originating in 50BC. Alexander of Tralles, a Methodist medic, states:

"the duty of a physician is to cool what is hot, to warm what is cold, to dry what is moist and to moisten what is dry".

In the adoption of this principle into penitential practice however, the Celtic monks are indebted to John Cassian's Colloquies (c 360–435). In employing Cassian's doctrine the vice was eradicated and was also replaced by virtue.

Commutation

The system of commutation was also employed, that is, 'the paying over of something in the place of something else'. This practice could be used to shorten the period of penance (especially where the duration of that penance was impractical), sometimes by making the penance more severe, or by exchanging, for example a penance of fasting for one of almsgiving, perhaps in the case of an aged or infirm penitent. Some commentators see this as one of the more dangerous legacies of Celtic penance, paving the way perhaps for the later abuse of indulgences. In later centuries an entire table of possible commutations were devised.

Reconciliation comprised four main components:

- Contrition – a heartfelt, purposeful sorrow for the wrongdoing and its consequences, and a sincere willingness to turn one's back on the sin of the past and return to God.
- Confession – an admission to another of the wrong done, which is a sign of one's true contrition. Confession was also cathartic and cleansing. It was to be full and free and was aided by the purposeful interrogation of the *anamchara*.
- Satisfaction – an attempt to right the wrong, to make reparation for it with the purpose of healing the sinner and undoing the damage his sin has done.
- Absolution – granted after the completion of the period of penance. It incorporates the notion of the wiping away of the sins, a cleansing of the person and a re-admittance to Eucharist.

 TASK

Think about and discuss whether these four components are always necessary for full reconciliation to occur. Consider them in both the context of interpersonal relationships and political situations.

Some Textual Examples

Feature	Penitential of Finnian	Penitential of Columbanus	Penitential of Cummean
Private	Sins are to be absolved in secret by penance and by every diligent devotion of heart and body.		
Repeatable		Confession of sins should be frequent and always before going to Mass, lest we approach the altar unworthily.	
Types of Penances	If a cleric commits murder and strikes down his neighbour, he must become an exile from his country for ten years, three years of this on bread and water with salt.	He who slanders or who willingly hears a slanderer, let him do penance with three special fasts.	He who hoards what is left over until the morrow, shall give these things to the poor ... he shall be cured by alms and fasting.
Status	If anyone has plotted in his heart to strike or kill his neighbour, if he is a cleric he shall do penance for half a year ... but if he is a layman he shall do penance for seven days.	If any cleric has struck his neighbour in a quarrel and spilt blood, let him do penance for a whole year; if a layman, for forty days.	A boy of ten years who steals anything shall do penance for seven days, but if at the age of twenty years, he happens to commit a small theft, for twenty or forty days.
Compensation	If a cleric commits murder ... he shall make satisfaction to the friends of him whom he slew, and he shall render to his father or mother compensation .... and say "Lo, I will do for you whatever you ask, in the place of your son."	If any ... has shed blood in a brawl, let him be compelled to restore all the damage ... let him first attend to his neighbour's work ... let him do penance for forty days on bread and water.	He who by a blow in a quarrel renders a man incapacitated ... he shall meet the injured man's medical expenses, make good the damages for the deformity and shall do his work until he has healed and do penance for half a year.
Sins of thought	But if he frequently entertains evil thoughts ... he shall seek help from God by prayer and fasting day and night until the evil thought departs and he is whole.	If anyone has sinned in thought ... and has been ready in his heart to carry out these sins; let him do penance for the greater ones, half a year, for the lesser ones forty days on bread and water.	He who long harbours bitterness in his heart ... shall correct himself by fasting according to the decision of a priest.

Feature	Penitential of Finnian	Penitential of Columbanus	Penitential of Cummean
Anamchara		Thus let his guilt be wiped off by the priest.	But this is to be carefully observed in all penance: the length of time anyone remains in his faults; what learning he has received; by what passion he is assailed; how great is his strength; with what intensity of weeping he is afflicted ... by warning exhortation, teaching, instruction, leadest him to penance, correct him of his error ... be their salvation thy glory.
Medicine for souls	If one has sworn a false oath ... it is better to do penance and not despair ... by the medicine of penance, prevent perpetual pains in the future ... do penance for seven years.	For doctors of the body compound their medicine in diverse kinds ... so should spiritual doctors treat with diverse kinds of cures the wounds of the soul.	The eight principal vices shall be healed by the eight remedies.
Curing of contraries by contraries	But by contraries, as we said, let us make haste to cure contraries and to cleanse away faults from our hearts and introduce virtues in their places.	The talkative person is to be sentenced to silence; the disturber to gentleness; the gluttonous to fasting, the sleepy fellow to watchfulness.	
Contrition, Confession, Satisfaction, Absolution.	In weeping and in tears ... shall implore the mercy of the Lord.	After making satisfaction let him be restored to the altar after the judgement of the priest ... let him do penance and let his guilt be wiped away by the priest.	

Exam tip!

Remember that good responses are well referenced. Try to use a range of references to support the points you make in your answers.

 PRACTICE ESSAY TITLE

a) Explain the main features of penitential practice with reference to the texts of the period. (35)

Your answer may make reference to some of the following:
- The differences between the old and the 'new' system
- A definition of 'penitentials' and an outline of the texts
- Private and repeatable features
- The role of the *anamchara*, sins of thought and deed
- Types of penances given and the system of commutation
- Medicine for souls and the cure of contraries by their contraries
- Contrition, Confession, Satisfaction and Absolution
- Textual examples of the features
- The views of scholars

b) Explore the view that the penances assigned by the Celtic penitential texts were too harsh. Justify your answer. (15)

You could make reference to some of the following in your answer:
- A comparison with the penances assigned in the 'old' system
- Penances tailored to individual need
- Penitents were 'cured' of the fault
- Penances which compensated the victim
- Reference to very harsh penances such as long fasts and exile
- The views of scholars

5. THE ROLE AND IMPORTANCE OF THE PENITENTIALS IN THE CELTIC CHURCH AND SOCIETY

There can be little doubt about the far-reaching importance of the Celtic system of penitential practice both on the development of the Celtic Church and on the society of which the Church was part. Not all scholars agree that the influence of the penitentials was always a positive one. Charles Plummer, for example, sees them as, "in truth, a deplorable feature of the medieval Church".[33] Kathleen Hughes agrees that "they are certainly not very congenial reading".[34] Nonetheless, they were to have a huge impact both on the Church in Ireland and on the Continent, as well as on the evolution of the science of moral theology in the centuries which followed.

Facilitators of the new system

The primary function of the penitential books was to facilitate the spread of the new system of private penance.

Extension of monastic spirituality

The penitentials were one of the fruits of Celtic monasticism and in this sense the Irish monastic Church was key to the evolvement of Celtic penance, whereby, as Corish remarks, "the Irish monks extended to the laity the frequent spiritual counselling of the cloister".[35] The monks were very clear on what behaviour was in keeping with the Christian life and that which fundamentally damages one's relationship with God, so they designed "lists of penitential exercises to restore this relationship to full spiritual health".[36] This was the fundamental spiritual function of the penitentials. The penitentials were the means by which monastic spirituality could be extended to the laity, whereby they, like the monks, were encouraged to strive to overcome selfish tendencies and to strive for Christian perfection.

The Lough Derg Penitential Beds *(Photo courtesy of Cathal O'Connor, with the kind permission of Monsignor Richard Mohan, Prior of Lough Derg)*

137

Pastoral care

Because of the relationship between monastic spirituality and penitential discipline, the penitentials also had an important role in fostering close pastoral relationships between the monasteries and the local community. Many penitents retired to the monasteries to complete their penances. Adomnán's *Life*, for example, tells us of monastic penitents arriving at Iona while others were consigned to Hinba to carry out penances assigned to them.

Supported secular law

The penitentials and secular law had a mutually beneficial relationship. Most scholars identify close relationships between the penitentials and secular law. Some, such as McNeill, see the origin of some penitential features within Brehon law itself, such as the payment of compensation, the imposition of fasting, the consideration given to the extent of injury and the status both of the sinner and the person injured. Connolly agrees that "many penitential texts contain canons from civil law, and indeed the Irish monastic authors may well have used the Brehon codes as models for their own texts".[37] In this sense, the penitentials succeeded in marrying together various elements from differing traditions. In turn, the penitentials would have been a support to secular law. It is clear, for example, that vengeful feuding and vendettas would have been limited by penitential practice. Finnian, in his treatment of the sin of murder, legislates that, in keeping with the premise of Brehon law, the murderer is asked to offer himself and his services in a practical way to the family of the one he has murdered, ie to carry out the tasks and duties of the murdered one. This also meant that the victims' loved ones must also overcome any hatred or vengefulness they may feel towards the murderer. In this sense then, the penitentials sought to "break the cycle of sin and foment real reconciliation", bringing about the greatest possible good from the situation.[38] Kathleen Hughes reminds us that unlike secular laws which only really consider how the injured party might be compensated, the penitentials aimed to cure the sinner.[39]

Hence the social dimension of reconciliation is emphasised in the penitential practices of Irish Christians. In a society where warfare was commonplace, it is likely that the penitentials would also have contributed to the creation of political stability. Furthermore, they may have provided a means of ridding society of 'undesirables' and those who had committed heinous crimes against the community by the imposition of the penance of exile.

Educative

The penitentials had an important educative function. Student priests were expected to commit them to memory. Clergy were also educated in the importance of developing the ability to probe and interrogate penitents constructively in order to uncover the underlying vice which caused the sin in the first place and thus diagnose the appropriate cure. In this sense, the penitentials enhanced the relationship between priest and people. Hughes is a little critical of the penitential's attempt to 'list everything' and Le Bras feels that they reflect an "arbitrary fixing of tariffs and the transference to relationships with God, of a system of legal compilations".[40] Nonetheless, they were an important tool in preparing the confessor to face whatever situation he may be called upon to deal with in the confessional. They were equally educative of the laity, not only in terms of sinful attitudes and behaviour to be avoided, but also in pointing out the virtues that the good Christian should strive to develop. In this sense, as Gabriel le Bras argues, "we have every reason to believe that the vigorous policy of the Church raised the moral level of the Christians".[41]

Individually tailored

The penitentials were individually tailored to meet the need of individual penitents, taking into account age, status, intent and knowledge of the demands of Church teaching. Cummean, in particular, makes a distinction between the sins of a small boy and the sins of the youth of twenty years. In this sense they met the needs of a whole variety of people in an equal variety of contexts. While so doing, they also ensured parity of treatment of all sinners; for instance the penance of fasting could be applied equally to all penitents regardless of social class.

Eradicating paganism

The penitentials also had a role to play in the gradual eradication of pagan practices which, it seems, continued to be present at least a century after the mission of Patrick.[42] For example, the penitentials condemn the practice of magic and of 'keening' or wailing for the dead. Cummean prescribes hefty penances for those who consume human blood or urine. Clearly, as Connolly argues, they seek to "suppress some of the more bizarre and macabre druidic practices, rites and customs".[43] Corish agrees that "it is very hard to over-estimate the importance of this practice of regular penance in the slow task of making society Christian".[44]

Creating good from evil

According to Connolly, the aim of some penances was to bring about the greatest possible good, even out of a situation which was originally evil. The prescription of almsgiving as a penance reminds all Christians, not just penitents, of their obligation to the poor, and "encourages the spirit of generosity and kindness to others".[45]

Addressing sexual morality

The penitentials also addressed the area of sexual morality. Payer found that thirty-seven percent of Finnian's Penitential is made up of "sexually related canons" and that "one of the most striking features of the penitentials is their treatment of human sexual behaviour".[46] The sin of abortion was addressed by Finnian who prescribes half a year's penance for a woman who has *"by her magic destroyed the child she has conceived"*. Overt homosexual activity is also penalised. The penitentials seek to uphold the institution of marriage, portraying it as the only morally acceptable context for sexual intercourse. Within this however, the penitentials also perceive the purpose of married sexual relations as the procreation of life, and encourage continence between married couples at times when conception would be unlikely. This has led many scholars to be critical of the contents of the penitentials; Plummer arguing that "it is hard to see how any one could busy himself with such literature and not be the worse for it".[47] However, Finnian's Penitential in particular seems to encourage self-control and requires the confessor to take into account the efforts made by the penitent to exercise self-control. In this sense, the penitentials would have curbed the use of aphrodisiacs, which would have implied intent and warranted a more severe penance. It is important that we see the penitentials as products of their own time in this regard, when Augustine and Jerome felt that sexual desire was most dangerous because it overwhelmed the will to such an extent that it was a major reason for man's disobedience of God. It is perhaps for this reason, as Brundage argues, that "the penitentials, by and large, took a gloomy view of the sexual proclivities of both men and women".[48]

Building community

Although some scholars are critical of the individualistic emphasis of the penitentials, they did also seek to build up the sense of Christian community and fraternity within the Church, as reflected by Cummean in his emphasis on the importance of prayers of intercession for the penitent. Through such prayers, it was possible that forgiveness could be attained.

Care of the vulnerable

As we have already seen, the penitentials reminded Christians of their obligation to care for the poor. They also sought to protect other vulnerable groups. Finnian's Penitential prohibits the sexual misuse of female slaves. He legislates that the man who has intercourse with his slave women is to sell her, and do a year's penance; if she is pregnant by him, he is to set her free.

Hope and comfort

The penitentials are great documents of hope because the assumption that lies beneath the text is that whatever the sin committed, there is a remedy; as Finnian intones, *"there is no crime which cannot be expiated through penance"*. In this sense, O'Loughlin argues that they "must have been of psychological benefit to the penitent, conveying trust in God's mercy and removing the sense of hopeless dejection".[49] Furthermore, Christians would have derived comfort from the 'sturdy realism' of the penitentials: that discipleship does not so much demand perfection as repentance, and that imperfect discipleship can be repaired.[50]

It seems appropriate to conclude with the words of H S Lea, writing in the nineteenth century:

"Crude and contradictory as were the penitentials in many things, taken as a whole, their influence cannot have been but salutary. They inculcated ... lessons of charity and loving kindness, of forgiveness of injury and of helpfulness to the poor and stranger as part of the discipline by which the sinner could redeem his sins. ... They were not confined to the repression of violence and sexual immorality and the grosser offences, but treated as subjects for penance, excess in eating and drinking ... and in many ways the physical nature of man was sought to be subordinated to the moral and spiritual ... [At] the present day it is impossible to trace directly what civilising influence they may have exercised on the peoples subject to them ... [but] they exercised [such] influence."[51]

 TASK

In groups discuss the strengths and weaknesses of the penitential practice of the Celtic Church.
Consider in your discussions what benefits they might have for Christians today.
Give feedback to the class.

6. THE INFLUENCE OF THE PENITENTIALS ON THE CHURCH ELSEWHERE

Introduction

We have seen that the penitentials had an important role to play in the Church and society in which they originated, but what influence did they have on the Church beyond?

While on the one hand the penitentials have been hailed as one of the most innovative features of the Celtic Church, there has been some argument as to whether the system of auricular confession and penance as it evolved in the Celtic Church actually originated there.

As we have explored, the origins of Celtic penance lie within the monastic system, to some degree. While Patrick may have been invoking the system of public penance in the case of Coroticus, it seems unlikely that the Celtic Church thereafter would depart so radically from a system introduced by him. However, as Gougaud pointed out, there is little in the way of further evidence to suggest that the system of public penance was ever practised in the Celtic Church. Neither is there, on the other hand, any evidence to suggest that Patrick did indeed introduce the system of private penance into the Irish Church. We have also seen that some features of Celtic penitential practice were borrowed from the Church on the Continent, for example, the curing of contraries by their contraries and the Cassian classification of the *ogdoad* of deadly sins. In addition, in their treatment of sexual sins, the penitentials clearly reflect the ideas current in the wider Church at the time on the sanctity of marriage and the purpose of sex as exclusively for the procreation of children, as illustrated by James Brundage.[52] Is it then true to say that the penitentials had a limited influence on the Church beyond Celtic shores and in fact borrowed ideas and practices already present in the Church at the time?

This certainly seems to be the view of Galtier who argues that even if public penance was the normal and usual practice in the Church, there were instances when the Church did indeed grant pardon for sins without subjecting penitents to the full requirements of canonical penance.[53] In this sense then, the practice of private penance was not introduced to the Church on the Continent by the Celtic monks.

Private penance on the Continent – views of theorists

Galtier defines public penance as being the practice whereby penitents were required to sit in the 'order of penitents', and argues that where this practice was not observed then the practice of penance was private. That is not to say that two separate systems existed but rather that the decision not to require the penitent to sit in the order of penitents really was at the discretion of the bishop.

Galtier further presents in support of his argument, that there was a very positive reception given to the practice of private penance on the Continent, which would, in his view indicate that Christians there were already familiar with it to some extent. Galtier cites this practice in certain churches in the region of Gaul and if Patrick was familiar with it, or indeed studied in the Continental Church in Gaul, then he may have become acquainted with the practice and brought it with him to Ireland.

Mitchell agrees that "it is impossible to suppose the eminent and holy men who were originally responsible for the method ... should have acted independently of and contrary to what they knew to be the theory and practice of penance throughout Christendom".

Mitchell is sceptical, however, that Patrick, even if he was aware of instances of private penance, would have radically departed from what was the normal practice of the universal church at the time.[54] Mitchell also argues that if we accept Galtier's definition of 'private' penance, then "the existence of private penance on the continent prior to the coming of the Irish monks can hardly be called into question".[55] McNeill is clear in his conviction that "the Celtic penitentials came, not to conflict with an established penitential discipline but to fill what was almost a total vacuum, and to inculcate penance among those who had not been accustomed to it in any form".[56]

Nonetheless, the meagre evidence presented by Galtier and his rather limited definition of public penance as the expectation to sit in the order of penitents, does not justify the view that public penance had really ceased to be the norm by the time of Patrick.

The role of the Celtic penitentials

Poschmann agrees that it is unlikely that any form of private penance was commonly available in the Church of Western Europe before the Celtic monks. He does accept that it was permissible in exceptional circumstances, for example, granting pardon to the dying without the full canonical requirement but that it was largely due to the efforts of Celtic monks that the private practice was introduced into the Continental Church for all.[57] McNeill agrees that "the Celtic missionaries ... introduced into Europe, the penitential literature and practiced the administration of penance according to Celtic usage".

Galtier does accept that it was because of the work and efforts of Celtic peregrini that the system of private penance became universal practice in the Church.

In particular, the contribution of Columbanus must have been noteworthy in terms of the influence of Celtic penitentials on the Church beyond the Celtic isles. Columbanus produced the bulk of his Penitential in Luxeuil, and Gabriel Le Bras argues that many of the penitentials of the seventh and first half of the eighth century "are taken in whole or in part from Columbanian sources and lack, almost all of them, the slightest originality".[58] Loening agrees that private penance was made available to the laity in the seventh and eighth centuries through the influence of Columbanus and other missionaries and "gradually transformed into a universal ecclesiastical institution".[59] Jonas' *Life of Columbanus* evidences this, that Columbanus, *"strove to make confession more frequent, chiefly in the cloisters, but also among pious laymen"*.

Jonas also tells us that prior to the Columban Penitential, penance was neglected in Gaul. He clearly regarded Columbanus as "the restorer of penitential discipline in the Vosges region".[60]

In the view of McNeill and Gamer, the Celtic penitentials also influenced the Anglo-Saxon Church and are clearly echoed in the Theodorian penitentials.[61]

Le Bras also argues that the presence of the Celtic penitentials can be seen in the English penitentials but under the name of Bede or Egbert, and also in the Spanish penitentials at the end of the eighth century.[62] Le Bras concludes that "the Irish have contributed more than any other people in the dark ages to the progress of the moral conscience in the West".[63]

Gougaud is also "quite certain that they exercised an important influence in the legislation of the Frankish Church" and that they "were copied and recopied in the course of many centuries". Hughes agrees that "many of the texts survive in Frankish manuscripts" and that "Brittany was clearly a centre of dissemination".[64]

Oakley argues, with the agreement of Lea, that the influence of Celtic penitentials in terms of order and discipline was considerable in civilising the rude pagans among whom the Celtic missionaries worked.[65]

Criticism of Celtic penance

It is important to remember that the influence of the penitentials was not always positive, although any substantial opposition to them was 'late' to appear. The system of commutation, *arreum*, which arises from an Irish word, was later to give rise to abuse. The abuses were connected to the practice of almsgiving, which was apparently becoming popular as a means of purchasing immunity from punishment.[66] There is some evidence to suggest that vicarious penance was another abuse which crept in, probably arising from Cummean's provision that "a righteous man" could perform penance for those who do not know the psalms and are not able to fast. The Council of Chalons (813) ordered the total elimination of the books known as the penitentials *"of which the errors are as certain as authors are uncertain"*. In 829, the Council of Paris directed that they should be burned as anti-canonical. However, from 850 onwards there was a revival in the influence of the Celtic penitentials, which were to have from then until the present day, a lasting influence on the practice of penance within the wider Church.

Conclusion

- Most scholars agree that the practice of private penance arose in the Celtic Church primarily out of the practice of monasticism.
- They were influenced by writings and thought current in the wider Church at the time.
- Galtier argues that private penance was sometimes available on the Continent and, to some extent, Poschmann agrees.
- All accept that because of the influence of the Celtic monks, private penance became the norm in the Church as a whole.
- Later Continental penitential literature borrowed heavily from the Celtic books.
- Celtic penitential practice had a huge civilising influence on the now almost pagan Europe.
- The influence of the Celtic penitentials was not always positive. Some provisions were open to abuse, but on the whole their influence was profoundly positive and long-lasting.

PRACTICE ESSAY TITLE

Give an account of the contribution of the Celtic penitentials to the Celtic Church and society. (35)

In your answer you may make reference to some of the following:
- The features of Celtic penance
- The relationship of the penitentials to secular law
- The impact of the penitentials on clerical education and that of the laity
- Their contribution to the development of monasticism
- Their role in the eradication of paganism
- The importance in encouraging positive behaviour
- Examples from the texts
- The views of scholars

Using the notes in section 6 to help you, try this question:
Explore the view that the Celtic penitentials also contributed to the development of the Church elsewhere. Justify your answer. (15)

7. THE IMPORTANCE OF THE PENITENTIALS AS HISTORICAL SOURCES

Modern historians have attempted to use the Celtic penitentials in a variety of ways to gain insight into the period in which they were written. Although they are valuable written sources from an otherwise obscure period in history, they are of limited usefulness in some regards. In evaluating their worth we need to bear in mind the context out of which they evolved and the purpose for which they were written.

Social histories

The penitentials are not so useful to social anthropologists as source material in telling us about human behaviour at the time. Although they do cover an amazing range of behaviours, as Kathleen Hughes observes, "they do not even tell you what sins were popular at the time ... since they attempt to list everything".[67] Neither do they give us information on the frequency with which certain, or indeed any, of the penances were applied. We do not know either the degree of compliance of penitents to the penances prescribed or to the advice given by the *anamchara*. Nora Chadwick is of the view that "many of these cases are the webs spun in the casuistry of the monkish brain ... unnatural sins, thought up in the cloister by the tortuous intellect of the clerical scribe ... searching for every contingency that his casuistry can produce, so that nothing, however remote, may pass unprovided for".[68]

Some historians of canon law perceive the penitentials to be inferior to more formal church canons. Stickler, for example, sees them as mere collections of "rude customs".[69] Le Bras agrees, albeit in a more positive vein, that "they are witnesses ... of the structure and customs of Ireland".[70] Others, for example, Poschmann and Osborne,[71] who are more specifically interested in the history of the sacrament of penance, see them as precursors to later penitential developments and discussions, rather than being of any great historical significance themselves. In short, this school of thought views them as mere "stepping stones" which can be "subsumed ... into the history of the sacrament".[72]

Insight into growing theology

However, Connolly argues that an appreciation of the historical context out of which the penitentials emerged is vital. They clearly reveal the insight of the Celtic monks into the mystery of God's forgiveness, their perception of sin as a sickness; in short, the penitentials show us how the early Celtic monks perceived the Christian moral life.[73] O'Loughlin believes the penitentials to be all the more valuable because they show us that the "dark period after Patrick" is "one of vigorous intellectual growth".[74]

Existence of paganism

The penitentials show us that the Celtic Church was slow to eradicate pagan traditions and practices in the century or two after Patrick. They tell us of the practice of magic and of 'keening' or wailing for the dead, although, on a more cautionary note, to what extent these practices remained current, is unknown.

Britain and the Continent

Kathleen Hughes observes that the "penitentials are one of the sources, which illustrate Irish connections with Britain and the continent" at this time.[75] We have seen the borrowing of the thinking of both Cassian and Caesarius of Arles in previous sections, showing a dissemination of ideas from the Continent to Ireland. The British Penitential of Theodore shows a heavy reliance on Irish penitential writing, possibly on that of Cummean, while the later Old Irish Penitential borrows in turn from Theodore, showing a close and mutually enriching relationship between the Irish and the British Church.

Monks and the laity

The penitentials give a valuable insight into the life and structure of the Irish Church of the time. The fact that they make provision for lay penance indicates the intricate relationship between the laity and the monastic community. In addition, many monasteries have lay penitents attached to them, with the *anamchara* resident within the monastery; the penitentials highlight the constant interaction between the monastic Church and the lay community surrounding it.

Secular clergy

The penitentials indicate that the priest rather than the bishop was the minister of reconciliation and that with the penitential in hand he had some autonomy as such. While much has been written about the monastic structure of the Celtic Church, Corish's study of the penitentials shows that "they envisage the pastoral clergy as non-monastic".[76] He cites that Columbanus' Penitential lists the bishop as the highest ecclesiastical dignitary, while the abbot is not mentioned at all. In addition, Corish points out that:

- both Finnian and Columbanus' texts highlight that the penitent can only be reconciled and *"restored to the altar ... by the decision of a bishop or a priest"*.

- Finnian is clear that monks are forbidden to baptise and that clerics on the other hand have an obligation to baptise *"from the flock committed to his care"*.

The penitentials then, are vital sources for the period, illustrating the close relationship between monastery and laity, and the pastoral roles undertaken by secular clergy in the period with which we are concerned.

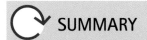

SUMMARY

In the early Church, it was normal and usual practice that reconciliation was allowed once in a lifetime, and penances were of a public nature.

⬇

Through the efforts of the Celtic monks, private, repeatable penance was made available to clerics, monks and laity. Penitential texts were written to facilitate the 'new' system.

⬇

Although not all scholars agree on their benefits, the penitentials had a profound effect on the Church and society at the time. They, for example, facilitated the spread of auricular confession, encouraged positive behaviour, helped educate the clergy, developed the role of the monasteries, supported secular law, repressed sexual immorality and paganism.

⬇

Although scholars differ on the extent to which they were influential, the Celtic monks ensured that auricular confession became common practice in the Church at large.

⬇

The penitentials were useful historical sources, telling us about the practice of penance at the time, the relationships with other churches, and the role of secular and monastic clergy.

◎ OTHER ASPECTS OF HUMAN EXPERIENCE

Concept of penance and forgiveness of sin in Christian churches other than your own

An evaluation of the contribution of the Truth and Reconciliation Commission

The ecumenical movement

Forgiveness and reconciliation

An exploration of the concept of sin from a range of perspectives

Challenges in the process of political reconciliation and peace making

Examples of individuals such as Nelson Mandela and Archbishop Desmond Tutu

The work of organisations which work for reconciliation

You will be asked to consider how the ideas of penance, reconciliation and forgiveness can be applied to other aspects of human experience.

The article and suggestions overleaf could be used as stimuli to help you develop your own ideas.

From The Times, 7 March, 2006, by Simon de Bruxelles

Vicar grappling with grief stands down over bombers who took her daughter's life

"It's hard to preach forgiveness when I feel far from it myself"

Even the Rev Julie Nicholson's Christian faith has not helped her to forgive the suicide bombers who took her daughter's life. Perhaps that would be too much to expect of any mother.

Exactly eight months since the London bombings on 7 July last year, Mrs Nicholson has given up her job as an inner-city vicar because she feels unable to preach a message of peace and reconciliation when she does not feel it in her heart.

Jennifer Nicholson, her talented, vivacious, 24-year-old daughter, was one of 56 people who died in the bombings.

Her mother, vicar of the parish of St Aidan with St George, in Bristol, has suffered the double bereavement of losing not just her daughter but also the vocation that she loved. Mrs Nicholson said: "It's very difficult for me to stand behind an altar and celebrate the Eucharist, the Communion, and lead people in words of peace and reconciliation and forgiveness when I feel very far from that myself. So, for the time being, that wound in me is having to heal."

She said: "I am looking for a way in which I can still have priestly ministry when there are some things I can no longer practise, or I can't currently practise, and for me that's about integrity.

"In terms of my ministry, a colleague and a friend recently said priesthood begins in the world not in the Church, and I was very relieved to hear that because what I am trying to do now is redefine my priesthood."

The Bishop of Bristol, the Right Rev Mike Hill, a personal friend of Mrs Nicholson, said he understood that her faith had been shaken by the events of 7/7. "I think these situations in life shake the faith of everybody because they immediately bring into focus the 'why' question. Unfortunately, there's no simple Elastoplast answer to that question," he added.

Jennifer, a gifted musician, was one of seven people killed by Mohammad Sidique Khan. Mrs Nicholson and her husband, Greg, were on holiday in Wales at the time. She has never discussed her daughter's death publicly and did not speak at her funeral at Bristol Cathedral in August.

Bishop Hill expressed anger on her behalf in his address when he told the 1,000 mourners: "There are few human words that can adequately express what we feel about people who indiscriminately carry out apparent acts of senseless violence against innocent civilian populations and, unbelievably, do so in the name of God. Such delusion, such evil, is impossible for us to begin to comprehend."

Mrs Nicholson says that not only could she not forgive the killers, she does not want to forgive. She said: "I will leave potential forgiveness for whatever is after this life. I will leave that in God's hands."

Every day she says the name of Mohammad Sidique Khan. "I have a certain amount of pity for the fact that four young people felt that this was something they had to do but I certainly don't have any sense of compassion. Can I forgive them for what they did? No, I cannot.

"I believe that there are some things in life which are unforgivable by the human spirit. We are all faced with choice and those four human beings on that day chose to do what they did."

She said, "I rage that a human being could choose to take another human being's life. I rage that someone should do this in the name of a God. I find that utterly offensive. We have heard a lot in the media about things causing certain groups of people offence and I would say that I am hugely offended that someone should take my daughter in the name of a religion or a God."

Despite her daughter's death, Mrs Nicholson has remained positive, assuring friends, "I just want you to know that there is still goodness in this world." [77]

 TASK

In groups or as a class, discuss the view that reconciliation is always a difficult process.

Suggestions for your file

- Research the issues involved in reconciliation between Christian denominations and world religions. Keep up to date with the latest developments.

- Compile some notes on the **processes, difficulties and successes** of two different situations in which reconciliation between groups and communities was achieved. For example, you could look at the Northern Ireland Peace Process and perhaps the process of reconciliation in South Africa. Use the archive material of on-line newspapers to gather facts, figures and useful quotation.

- Find out about the work of particular individuals who have worked to achieve reconciliation. These will be useful to use as evidence and examples in your exam responses. However, avoid telling the story of that person's actual life.

- Find out about the understanding of sin and reconciliation in a range of Christian denominations and in other world religions. Use the internet to help you.

Keep your file up to date. Always look out for interesting articles which highlight issues that might be useful in exam questions on other aspects of human experience. Use them to inform and influence any arguments you might wish to make and try to avoid just describing the work of people, organisations, or events that you have researched.

Endnotes

1 The translations of the texts referred to here are from Bieler, L, (ed and trans), *The Irish Penitentials*, Dublin Institute for Advanced Studies, Dublin, 1963

2 Kenney, JF, *The Sources for the early History of Ireland: Ecclesiastical an Introduction and Guide*, Columbia University Press, 1929, p236; the use of the word penance is mine.

3 James 5:16

4 Ambrose De Penitentia, 11, 10 PL, Col 250

5 McNeill, JT, *The Celtic Penitentials*, ACLS History e-book reprints, 1923, p27

6 See 1 Cor 5 , 2 Cor 2:6, 2 Cor 2 :7

7 Jerome Ep 30

8 The Councils of Nice and Ancyra both refer to such practices.

9 Sozomen, *Historia Ecclesiasticus vii 16* in Watkin, A, *The Great Chartulary of Glastonbury*, Butler and Tanner, Frome, 1947, p424

10 Murder did not pose such a problem as to some extent it was also addressed and punished severely by secular law which was undoubtedly of more concern to penitents than any sanction the Church could impose.

11 Gougaud, *Christianity in Celtic Lands, op cit*, p283

12 Warren, FE, *Liturgy and Ritual of the Celtic Church*, Oxford, 1881, p148ff

13 O'Loughlin, T, *Celtic Theology*, Continuum, London, 2000, p56

14 McNeill, *The Celtic Penitentials, op cit*, p38

15 Connolly, H, *The Irish Penitentials and their significance for the Sacrament of Penance Today*, Four Courts Press, Dublin, 1995, p32

16 Bieler, L, (ed), *The Irish Penitentials*, DIAS, Dublin, 1975, p4

17 Kenney, *The Sources for the Early History of Ireland, op cit*, p241

18 McNeill, *The Celtic Penitentials, op cit*, p39

19 Payer, PJ, *Sex and the Penitentials: the development of a sexual code 550–1150*, Toronto, 1984

20 *ibid*

21 Ó Fiaich, T, *Columbanus in His Own Words*, Veritas Publications, Dublin, 1974, p69

22 Laporte, J, *Le Penitential de Columban*, Tournai, 1958

23 Charles-Edwards, TM, *The Penitential of Columbanus* in *Columbanus, studies on the Latin Writings*, ed M Lapidge, Boydell Press Suffolk, 1997, p218

24 Kenney, *The Sources for the Early History of Ireland, op cit*, p200

25 O'Loughlin, *Celtic Theology, op cit*, p62

26 See McNeill, *The Celtic Penitentials*; Connolly, *The Irish Penitentials* and Hardinge, *The Celtic Church in Britain*

27 McNeill, JT, and Gamer, H, *Medieval Handbooks of Penance: A Translation of the Liber Poenitentiales* and selections from related documents, Columbia University Press, New York, 1938, p25

28 Connolly, *The Irish Penitentials, op cit*, p14

29 *ibid*

30 As translated in Plummer, *Vitae Sanctorum Hiberniae, PARTIM Haectenus Inediate*, Oxford 1910, xxx

31 Bieler, *The Irish Penitentials, op cit*, p46

32 *ibid*

33 Plummer, C, (ed), *Venerablis Baedae Opera Historica*, Vol 1, Clarendon Press Oxford, 1896, ppclvii-clviii

34 Hughes, *Early Christian Ireland: Introduction to the Sources, op cit*, p84

35 Corish, P, 'The Christian Mission' in *A History of Irish Catholicism*, Vol 1, ed P Corish, Gill & Macmillan, Dublin, 1971, p12

36 Connolly, H, *The Irish Penitentials and their significance for the Sacrament of Penance Today, op cit*, p1

37 *ibid*, p3

38 *ibid*, p71

39 Hughes, *Early Christian Ireland: an Introduction to the Sources, op cit*, p87

40 Le Bras, G, *The Irish Penitentials* in *The Miracle of Ireland*, ed Daniel-Rops, Clonmore & Reynolds, Dublin, 1959, p116

41 *ibid*, p124

42 The Penitential texts of Finnian, Columbanus and Cummean, as well as *The First Synod of Patrick*, all refer to pagans and pagan practices evident in Ireland at the time.

43 Connolly, *The Irish Penitentials, op cit*, p42

44 Corish, P, 'The Christian Mission' in *A History of Irish Catholicism, op cit*, p12

45 *ibid*, p52

46 Payer, *Sex and the Penitentials, op cit*, p61

47 Plummer, C, (ed), *Venerablis Baedae opera Historia*, Vol 1, 1896, pclviii

48 Brundage, JA, *Law, Sex and Christian Society in Medieval Europe*, University of Chicago Press, 1987, p152

49 O'Loughlin, *Celtic Theology, op cit*, p57

50 *ibid*, p59

51 Lea, HS, *History of Auricular Confession and Indulgences in the Latin Church*, London, 1896

52 Brundage, J, *Law, Sex and Christian Society in Medieval Europe, op cit*, pp152–162

53 Galtier, P, *Revue d'histoire ecclesiastique*, 1937

54 Mitchell, G, *The Origins of Irish Penance in Irish Theological Quarterly*, p5

55 *ibid*

56 McNeill, *Celtic Penitentials, op cit*, p152

57 Poschmann, B, *Penance and the Anointing of the Sick*, (ed & trans Courtney), London, 1963

58 Le Bras, *The Irish Penitentials, op cit*, p116

59 Loening, E, *Geschichte des deutschen Kirchenrechts* Strassburg, 1878, p468ff

60 McNeill, *Celtic Penitentials, op cit*, p44

61 McNeill, JT, and Gamer, H, *Medieval Handbooks of Penance: a Translation of the Liber Poenitentiales and selections from relayed documents*, Columbia University Press New York, 1938

62 McNeill, *Celtic Penitentials, op cit, p44*

63 *ibid*, p126

64 Hughes, *Early Christian Ireland: Introduction to the Sources, op cit*, p89

65 Oakley, TP, *English Penitential Discipline and Anglo-Saxon Law*, New York, 1923, pp193–196; Lea, HS, *History of Auricular Confession*, 11 London, 1896 pp106–107

66 McNeill, *Celtic Penitentials, op cit*, p154

67 Hughes, *Early Christian Ireland: An Introduction to the Sources, op cit*, p84

68 Chadwick, *The Age of the Saints, op cit*, p148

69 Stickler, AM, *The Case for Clerical Celibacy*, San Francisco, 1995, p42

70 Le Bras, *The Irish Penitentials, op cit*, p123

71 Poschmann, *Penance and the Anointing of the Sick, op cit*, pp122–138; Osborne, KB, *Reconciliation and Justification: The Sacrament and its Theology*, New York, 1990, pp84–89

72 O'Loughlin, *Celtic Theology, op cit*, p49

73 Connolly, *The Irish Penitentials, op cit*, p1 & p37

74 O'Loughlin, *Celtic Theology*, p66

75 Hughes, *Early Christian Ireland: An Introduction to the Sources, op cit*, p88

76 Corish, *The Christian Mission in A History of Irish Catholicism, op cit*, p7

77 www.timesonline.co.uk See this web page for related and relevant links which will help you make connections to other aspects of human experience.

Chapter 5

Missionary Outreach In Britain

LEARNING OUTCOMES

Knowledge, understanding and evaluation of:

— the career of Colmcille/Columba*

— Colmcille's contribution to the development of the Church

— the peregrini in Britain

* Colmcille is also commonly referred to as Columba.[1] Throughout this chapter the names will be used interchangeably.

1. THE SIGNIFICANCE OF COLMCILLE IN THE DEVELOPMENT OF THE CELTIC CHURCH

Introduction

Chadwick hails Colmcille as "the greatest saint of the Celtic Church".[2] Not all historians of the age would agree. Colmcille is certainly one of the most controversial of the era, and continues to generate debate today.

To understand Colmcille the man, and to fairly interpret his actions, we must understand the background from which he came.

- He belonged to the Cenél Conaill, which was a branch of the great Uí Néill ruling dynasty. As such, he may have been eligible for the High Kingship of Ireland. No doubt, many of his formative years would have been spent in the company of the political elite of the day. In these surroundings it is likely that Colmcille would have acquired the skills of those with whom he associated. At the very least, it is likely that he had a political awareness that other youths of his age would not have possessed and, given his possible destiny, these political abilities may have been actively fostered by those involved in the early years of his care.

- It is also important to remember that Colmcille is active about a century or so after the mission of Patrick and so is one of the earliest saints of the infant Celtic Church. As such, he would have been aware of and perhaps influenced by the surviving pre-Christian elements of that society: the importance of the tribe, ongoing warfare and recurring pagan and superstitious observances.

- During the early part of his career, Colmcille emerges as an illustrious student. Anecdotal evidence suggests that because of this he drew the personal attention of Finnian, who singles him out for ordination to the priesthood. It seems that Finnian wished him to be advanced to the office of bishop and so sent him to Etchen, a bishop in Meath, who, by mistake, ordained him only as a priest. Colmcille saw this as the intervention of Divine Providence and apparently vowed to always remain a priest. Adomnán, who wrote the *Life of Colmcille*, tells us that the young Colmcille was:

"Devoted from childhood to the Christian novitiate and the study of philosophy ... he was angelic in aspect, refined in speech, holy in work, excellent in ability, great in council."

In spite of these abilities, Colmcille was not to carve out for himself a particularly distinguished monastic career in his native Ireland, but by the age of forty-two left Ireland and sailed to the Island of Iona.

The Career of Colmcille at a glance

Birth Date	7 December 521
Where	Gartan, (meaning 'little field'), County Donegal
Name	Christened Criomhthann 'fox';
	Later called Colmcille meaning 'dove of the Church'
Parents	Father: Feidlimidh, great-grandson of Niall of the Nine Hostages, after whom the great Uí Néill tribe was named
	Mother: Eithne, possibly a descendant of Cathair Mór, a king of Leinster
Education	Firstly, under his foster Father Cruithnechan, an Irish Pict
	Also studied under the Christian bard Gemman at Leinster
	Introduced to monastic experience when with Finnian of Clonard. Here he was ordained priest
	Completed his education under Mobhi at Glasnevin
	Had some association with Finnian of Moville and Enda of Aran

Monastic foundations	Derry in 546 at the age of 25
	Smyth suggests he founded Durrow in Offaly in the 580s[3]
	Iona, approximately 563
	Other associated foundations: Kells, Swords, Drumcliffe, Moone and Tory[4]
	Some scholars associate Colmcille with up to fifty monastic foundations
Key events	561: Battle of Cúl Dreimne
	562: Synod at Teltown to discuss and perhaps revoke the excommunication of Colmcille
	13 May 563: landed on Iona, visited King Bruide, gained tenure of Iona, engaged in evangelising work from there for next 34 years
	574: Consecrated Aedán king of Dál Riata
	575: Attended the Convention of Druim Cett, involved in negotiating status of the bards, the release of the hostage Scandlán, and the independence of the Scottish Dál Riata
Death	June 597

Colmcille's departure to Iona

No other event in the life of a saint of Celtic Ireland at this time has invited such speculation as the circumstances surrounding Colmcille's departure from Ireland.

Colmcille left Ireland and sailed to the island of Iona in May 563. Adomnán in his *Life of Colmcille*, dated this departure in the context of the Battle of Cúl Dreimne, saying it was two years after the battle that Colmcille left Ireland, *"planning to become an exile for Christ"*.

Adomnán thereby implies that the decision to leave was a voluntary one on the part of Colmcille, and that his motive was to be an exile for the love of Christ.

Nonetheless, Adomnán does place the departure firmly within the context of Cúl Dreimne and it is this that has given rise to the assumption that Colmcille was somehow involved in the battle. Moreover, it is this involvement that may have had something to do with his departure from Ireland. Three theories abound as to what that involvement might have been:

a) Columba, in his eagerness to develop his scriptural knowledge, is said to have copied, without gaining permission from its owner Finnian, a manuscript of the Psalter and Gospels which Finnian is said to have brought from Rome. Finnian, claiming copyright on the document, is said to have angrily demanded the copy made by Colmcille. Colmcille refused his request and appeal was made to King

Diarmuit at Tara. Diarmuit, in keeping with Brehon law, gave a verdict following the maxim: *"to every cow belongs her calf, to every book its copy."*

Colmcille, allegedly incensed by the king's decision, roused his clansmen, the northern Uí Néill, against Diarmuit and the southern Uí Néill. The Battle took place at Cúl Dreimne near Sligo and the northern Uí Néill was victorious. It is said thereafter that Molaise, the *anamchara* of Colmcille, assigned him the penance of expulsion from Ireland to convert as many souls to Christ as were lost in battle. Skene disputes the truth of the story claiming it to be inconsistent with the tradition, supported by Adomnán, that there was huge affection between Colmcille and Finnian.[5] However, Adomnán does say that Colmcille had been blameworthy *"for some venial and quite excusable causes,"* albeit that he doesn't specifically mention this incident. Finlay is sure that Adomnán omits something here which was not to his liking.[6]

Tradition suggests that this copy may well have been the *Cathach* attributed to the pen of Colmcille. Close studies of the text, surviving with half of its pages lost, leave open the possibility that the *Cathach* was written by Colmcille.[7]

b) A second account, mentioned in the *Annals of Tigernach*, shows Colmcille's involvement to be more politically motivated. Curnan had caused the death of his competitor at the games at Tara and had fled to Colmcille for protection and sanctuary. He was subsequently snatched and slain by Diarmuit. Colmcille then found himself as Curnan's protector – duty bound to avenge his death – and so rose up the force of his clan against Diarmuit.

c) The third possible reason for Colmcille's involvement in the battle suggests that Colmcille was angered by the still-present pagan traditions observed at the Festival of Tara. It was festival which marked the inauguration of Diarmuit, and Colmcille felt duty bound to ensure the eradication of pagan practices by defeating Diarmuit in battle.

Colmcille's role in battle

The *Annals of Ulster* tell us that victory for the Northern Uí Néill was achieved through the prayerful intercession of Colmcille but leave his involvement in the battle at that.

Evidence presented by Smyth of scarring on Colmcille's body may be suggestive of a more personal involvement. Perhaps, given the family background of Colmcille, it is reasonable to presume that at some stage in his life he was involved in warfare. Warring and faction were an integral part of society at that time and so it is important to judge Colmcille not within the conventional framework in which we consider sainthood, but as very much a man of his own time.

Simpson accepts that Colmcille was involved in this battle and refers to him as "an exiled strife-monger" who, riddled with guilt about the huge loss of life during the battle, left Ireland and landed on Iona.[8] Finlay, too, argues that it is quite unbelievable "that a Celtic prince with Columba's background would have hesitated to use the weapon he knew well how to wield."[9]

Was Colmcille exiled?

Whether Colmcille was, as Simpson holds, actually exiled for his alleged part in this battle is also open to debate. There is some record of a Synod being held at Teltown, County Meath, at which the matter seems to have been discussed. A decision might have been made at some time that Colmcille should be excommunicated but was then reversed. Indeed, Adomnán tells us that Columba was:

> "*Excommunicated by a certain synod … not rightly, as afterwards in the end became clear.*"

We are told nothing of who called or attended the Synod. Was Colmcille excommunicated? Was he exiled by Molaise and told to never again return to Ireland? Were these the real reasons for his mission to Iona?

It is important to point out that two years had lapsed from the Synod to Columba's departure. We would assume that had he been exiled it would have taken effect immediately.

It is also important to acknowledge that Adomnán presents his motive as being for "*the love of Christ*" and in addition cites his return to Ireland on ten different occasions.

Conclusion

- Adomnán places Columba's departure from Ireland within the framework of the battle of Cúl Dreimne, giving rise to questions surrounding the departure of Colmcille.

- Some evidence suggests the possible expulsion of Colmcille for his part in the battle which was, perhaps, later revoked.

- Certain theories have been suggested regarding the possible nature of Colmcille's involvement in the battle.

- There is no definitive evidence proving conclusively the nature of Colmcille's part in the battle, or indeed if he was involved at all. In addition, there is no conclusive evidence to suggest that warfaring was related in any way to his departure.

- At the very least, we can accept that this battle represented some kind of turning point in the life of Colmcille. Certainly, as Finlay remarks, Colmcille "was a man in whom secular ambition often conflicted with the urge to preach the word of God."[10] Finlay accepts that there was a real confrontation with the king and the conflict Colmcille felt between religious vocation and politics came to a head, with this event becoming a kind of personal crisis point for him.[11] McNeill agrees that it may have "represented for him, a crisis between monastic missionary dedication and a return to the mores of his warrior ancestors."[12] In fact, Colmcille may simply have wanted to remove himself from any pressure exerted by his royal kin to become involved in their battles.

- Colmcille's motive may have been to be *"an exile for the love of Christ"*; to engage in the evangelisation of pagan Scotland; and perhaps to attempt to revive the strength of the ailing tribe of his kinspeople, the Scottish Dál Riata, who had suffered serious defeat at the hands of the Picts. Skene believes it was this reason, as much as any other, which called forth his mission to Iona.[13]

 TASK

Summarise the arguments and evidence surrounding the reasons for Colmcille's departure from Ireland. Use these as revision notes.

2. THE MISSION OF COLUMBA

Colmcille departed from Ireland in 563 and landed on the Western coast of what is now Scotland. He was to labour there for the next thirty four years of his life.

The foundation at Iona

The foundation on Iona was itself significant. It lay right on the border of Irish and Pictish territory, on the line which divided the Christian Scots of Argyll from the pagan Picts. Therefore in a religious and political sense, the foundation was strategically important for the mission of Columba.

As we have seen, Colmcille may have had mixed motives for leaving Ireland and travelling to this area. It is noteworthy that he did not go further afield, to Europe and beyond, as his fellow travelling monks did. In one sense, Columba left Ireland but remained with the Irish. John Ryan accepts that "it was an obvious duty of Irish churchmen to minister spiritually to their own countrymen who had settled beyond the sea."[14] A colony of the Dál Riata, who were kinspeople of Colmcille, had settled in the area and had been militarily and politically challenged by the neighbouring pagan Picts. The king of the Dál Riatan colony had been slain by the Picts, and so it was forced into a defensive position.

It could be that Columba saw in this area a double challenge: to come to the aid, politically speaking, of his own people; and an opportunity to evangelise the pagan Picts of the area. In this sense the phrase of Adomnán is most apt that Columba was in a real sense a *"soldier of the Church"*.

There is some evidence to suggest that both the Picts and the Dál Riata claimed ownership of Iona. According to the *Annals of Tigernach*, it was Conall of the Dál Riata who granted Iona to Colmcille, while according to Bede, it was granted by Bruide, king of the Northern Picts. The island of Iona stretched approximately three miles from north to south and about one and a half miles wide at its widest point, totalling about three thousand acres. It may have happened that Colmcille came across Iona, noted its sheltered position from the prevailing winds, and that despite its rockiness, its pasture was fertile. He was perhaps promised by Conall undisturbed occupation. This would have been important given Iona's vulnerable border position. There is certainly no historical record of any attack on Iona once Colmcille was established on it. Perhaps when the Picts were later converted to Christianity, Bruide formally granted it to him.[15]

It may have been the case, as Finlay suggested, that Colmcille actually spent up to two years on the mainland before taking up occupancy of Iona, and that negotiations to secure tenure were quite protracted.[16] During this time, Finlay further argues that Colmcille could have been working towards the conversion of the tribes who lived closest to Iona.

The foundation of Iona, lying as it did in a politically sensitive area, illustrates clearly the negotiating skills, political sensitivity and foresight of Columba.

The mission at Iona

As with other aspects of Columba's career, the nature and extent of his missionary endeavours are a source of disagreement among historians of this period. However, as we have just seen, the mission of Colmcille would have been a most difficult and challenging one, given the political situation he found himself in. Although the Picts would have been a Celtic tribe, customs would have been different from those in Ireland. There would have been a language barrier, and while Colmcille took with him his identity as an Uí Néill, he no longer had a buffer of support – the political power of that tribe – as he would have had in Ireland.

We know that Colmcille laboured at Iona for thirty four years, yet the details of his work in that area are disappointingly scant. Although many poems and a rule have been attributed to the pen of Columba, there are no surviving documents which can, with total confidence, be attributed to him and which might have shed light on that mission. What we do know is that Iona became the mother Church of the entire area.

Visit to Bruide

In order to smooth out some of the difficulties that his mission would face, Columba first set out to visit King Bruide of the pagan Picts. To do so he would have had to journey across the great Glen of Alba. Part of the journey would have been

The abbey on Iona. *(Photo Wesley Johnston)*

he view from Iona island. *(Photo Wesley Johnston)*

on water and then through forest and wilderness. Finlay describes the journey as potentially "suicidal", had Columba not had the prior permission of Bruide himself.[17] To truly appreciate the significance of the visit, it is important to remember that Bruide was a pagan king of a pagan people and the enemy of the Dál Riata, which was a clan of Colmcille. It is possible that it was Columba's family background as an Uí Néill that gave him the status of a visiting statesman and intrigued Bruide. Certainly his royal descent would have made him a 'power player' politically. Most scholars agree that the meeting must have had a political agenda as well as a religious one. Bruide may well have been aware of this in advance and so permitted the visit of Columba and his monks. Certainly, it seems likely that Bruide somehow saw the visit as advantageous to himself. Although in dispute with the Dál Riata, he may have been more concerned with the rising power of the Angles from Northumbria to whom some parts of his kingdom would have been vulnerable, and perceived that a united front with the Dál Riata may have afforded him some protection.

It seems, according to Adomnán, that Colmcille's visit to Bruide was a success, although he makes no claim that Bruide was converted by Colmcille. Bede however does make claim of Bruide's conversion by Colmcille. Skene accepts that Columba had some authority at the king's court and that Bruide, a convert himself, greatly facilitated the spread of the faith throughout his kingdom.[18] Most historians accept that Colmcille's reasons for visiting Bruide were politically and religiously motivated. Skene and Stokes both see the visit as some kind of response to the challenge facing the Christian Dál Riata,[19] while Henderson goes further, suggesting that Conall of the Dál Riata may have asked Colmcille to make this "conciliatory approach" to the Pictish king to ease the situation of his people.[20] Certainly, he did secure tenure of Iona, and gained Bruide's permission to preach in his kingdom. At the very least Bruide seems not to have persecuted Colmcille. It is important to note however that Columba's visit was also at the very least, the first step in improving relations between the Picts and his kinspeople, the Dál Riata. It not only created the right conditions for a lasting peace but also improved conditions for his own people in the region. It is this dimension of Colmcille's work that caused McNeill to comment, "by his royal lineage and his superior personal gifts, he was well qualified for the political aspects of his role."[21]

Extent of Colmcille's mission

We are somewhat in the dark as to the extent of Colmcille's mission. Adomnán neglects to give us much detail on the matter. He does make it clear that Columba needed an interpreter, so clearly some of Colmcille's work is among the pagan Picts. He only refers in a haphazard way to journeys into Pictish territory: *"Beyond the dorsal ridge of Britain… [when Colmcille was] sojourning in the province of the Picts".* He certainly recounts one visit to Skye where Colmcille baptises a chief.

Simpson, for example, disputes the extent of Columba's work in pagan Pictland and

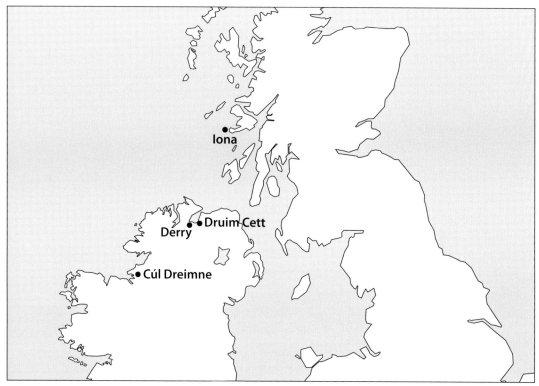

Map showing the location of Iona.

believes a lot of his labour to be among his own people, the Dál Riata. Finlay agrees that "Iona was the main ground of the saint's activities" as mention of any activity in Pictland is so infrequent in Adomnán.[22]

Simpson further argues that Pictland was not entirely pagan at the time of Columba. He claims that St Moluag founded churches at Rosemarkie, Mortlach and Clova.[23] Simpson believes that most of the evangelisation of Pictland was carried out by Ninnian. He traces Ninnian's footsteps across the northern counties of Aberdeenshire and Caithnesshire and associates him with the beginnings of Christianity in the Orkneys and Shetland. In this way, he presents the extent of the work of Colmcille as being much overrated. There is some evidence however, to suggest that the area of Ninnian's mission had once again lapsed into paganism before the mission of Columba. Finlay, while accepting Simpson's argument on the extent of Colmcille's mission, also believes that "material evidence ... indicates that the Pictish people were not Christian".[24] McNeill is of the view that in light of the lack of evidence for the boundary of the mission of Columba, we need to "recognise that he was less of a pioneer, in the absolute sense, than has been popularly believed".[25] Perhaps it is not in these terms that we should evaluate Colmcille.

Statesman and saint?

Columba was also a king-maker. In 574, eleven years after the arrival of Columba, King Conall of the Dál Riata died. Due to the efforts of Colmcille, the position of the Dál Riata was much stronger. The Picts no longer appeared an immediate threat and Colmcille had opened the lines of communication between himself and Bruide, the former enemy of his people. The immediate heir to the throne would have been Eógan – the cousin of Conall – who was said to be close to Columba. Although reportedly a personal friend, Colmcille seems to have sensed an inadequacy in Eógan, in terms of statesmanlike qualities. Columba certainly had high ambitions for the kingdom of the Dál Riata and had noted the military skills of Eógan's brother Aedán. The story is told in Adomnán:

> One night whist staying on the island of Hinba, Colmcille had an angelic vision in which he was directed to ordain Aedán as king. Refusing the order out of love for Eógan, the angel lashed the saint with a whip, leaving a bruise that remained with Columba the rest of his days. He said to Colmcille:

> "Know for certain that I am sent by God, in order that thou mayest ordain Aedán king, which if thou wilt not do, I will smite thee again." The Angel revisited Columba on three consecutive nights with the same message. Colmcille returned to Iona and subsequently consecrated Aedán king.

The story may have been fabricated by Adomnán to justify the behaviour of Columba, or it may have been the case that Columba surely felt himself to be acting on the will of God, communicated to him in one way or another.

The decision was not a popular one and strife resulted. Eógan would have been the more obvious choice for succession and many at the time must have been shocked by the decision. The *Annals of Tigernach* speak of a great slaughter "of the allies of the sons of Gabhrán", which may have been a reference to an ensuing battle. It certainly has served to fuel the fire of criticism from Columba's detractors. Finlay ponders whether, "in a crisis involving political decision, the prince did not take precedence over the prelate, the warrior over the saint".[26]

Nonetheless, it must be pointed out that Aedán proved to be an excellent leader, both consolidating and expanding the power of the Dál Riata, and returning to them a status which had long been lost. It could be argued that this environment provided a much better seed-bed for missionary outreach than the one on which Colmcille started. The Dál Riata, wherein was situated the spiritual heart of Columba's mission, could now become "the religious centre of the Celtic world".[27]

Druim Cett

In 575 Columba and Aedán attended the Convention of Druim Cett, near Derry. There were three issues on the agenda:

- The freeing of Scandlán Mor, who had been taken hostage by Aedh, king of the Irish Dál Riata.

- The position of the poets, who were under threat of banishment because they had abused their privileges.

- The relationship between the Scottish and the Irish Dál Riata, the balance of which may have been affected by the growth of Aedán's power.

The conference provides us with another example of Columba's statesmanship.

The outcome was certainly a triumph for Aedán and the Scottish Dál Riata. Up until now, the Scottish Dál Riata had probably been little more than a province of the Irish kingdom, and one which had been much diminished under the attacks of the Picts. Under Aedán, it had perhaps become stronger than the kingdom from which it originated. This meant that Aedán became generally independent from the Irish kingdom. It seems that Aedán perceived this to be a licence to expand his power and this may have marked the foundation of the kingdom of Scotland.[28]

It also appears that the release of Scandlán was secured, while a compromise was reached with regard to the poets – whereby they would be subject to greater discipline and reduced in number.

McNeill believes that Columba's influence at the synod was "dominant",[29] while Bannerman believes that Colmcille was merely in attendance as Aedán's advisor and that his prominence there is exaggerated because of "magnification" of the saint in the centuries after his death.[30] While Finlay accepts that Columba's role may have been purely advisory, he argues that "there are times when Columba's actions, or their outcome, makes him look more hawk than dove ... and Druim Cett was one of them".[31] Whatever one's view, as a result of Druim Cett, Aedán's kingdom emerged with greater independence and Columba "became a legend for more than his saintliness".[32]

Further disputes

Colmcille may possibly have been involved in two more battles.[33] It seems that in 579 there was a dispute between Comgall and Colmcille about the church at Ross-Torathair, near Coleraine, taken up by the Uí Néill on Columba's behalf. Then in 587 there was a battle between the Northern and Southern Uí Néill because, once again, Columba's sanctuary – this time at Leim-an-eich – was violated by Cuimin's slaughter of Baodan.

It is important to note that references to these battles appear in sources later than Adomnán and the reliability of the information must be questioned.[34]

TASK

Think about and discuss the view that religious leaders should never involve themselves in politics.

- You could consider this in both contemporary and historical contexts.
- Use the headlines below to help you start.
- Use your ideas to help prepare connections to other aspects of human experience.

Blair acted like a 'white vigilante' by invading Iraq, says bishop

Tony Blair came under attack from two of the Church of England's most senior figures yesterday for acting "like a white vigilante" and for lacking humility in forging ahead with the war on Iraq.

From The Times, September 20, 2006

Bishop speaks out against 'draconian' refugee policies

Bishop Patrick O'Donoghue, who chairs the Bishops' Conference, Office for Refugee policy, has spoken out against the "restrictive and draconian deterrence measures" governments of the developed world apply against refugees.

A man of his time

We need to be mindful of judging Colmcille as a man of his own time rather than from ours. Reeves reminds us that the ancient priesthood had no aversion to taking part in war, and cautions that we must "bear in mind the complexion of the times and the peculiar condition of society, of which civil faction seemed almost part and parcel".[35] Finlay sees the saint as reminiscent of Old Testament prophets who frequently intervened in the affairs of state. Colmcille cannot really be judged as bearing any similarity to later religious leaders who meddled in secular affairs, such as Wolsey, who was perhaps more enraptured by the esteem that power could bring rather than with serving his Church.[36] McNeill too agrees, that seventh century abbots "were often called upon to participate in the troubled affairs of their era ...".[37]

It is prudent to conclude that in the long term, Columba's political involvements brought peace and prosperity, and thereby ensured secure and solid foundations on which a strong Church could be built. Indeed, Máire Herbert believes, "the most important aspect of the achievement of Colmcille was the fact that he bridged the divide between secular and ecclesiastical realms of interest [showing] the potential for mutual benefit arising out of co-operation between church and dynasty".[38]

TASK

Make a list of the political involvements of Colmcille. Discuss the reasons you think he may have had for his actions.

Do you think Colmcille was right? In your view do they lessen or enhance his reputation as "the greatest saint of the Celtic Church"?

Make notes on your discussion.

3. COLMCILLE THE SAINT

It is crucial to remember that Colmcille chose to turn his back on what could have been an illustrious political career in the Uí Néill dynasty. By doing so, he brought a new status to the religious life. He was first and foremost a priest and a monk, faithful always to his ordination.

Columba's Church was very much a missionary Church and it was his aim to establish a living and vibrant faith throughout the land. In fact, it was to become the centre of a vast area of missionary activity as well as a renowned seat of learning.

Colmcille was a man of incredible practical gifts. He knew that his mission would be impossible where there was faction and political instability, and so by establishing a Christian Church he also secured peace between warring tribes.

The foundation at Iona gave rise to many daughter houses, not least Lindesfarne, but for long after the death of Columba, Iona was the outpost of the Celtic Church in the area and the "citadel and retreat" of Celtic missionaries.[39]

Adomnán tells us that: *"He could not pass the space of even a single hour, without applying himself either to prayer, or reading, or writing, or else to some manual labour."*

His stark asceticism is well attested to in Adomnán's *Life* even to the extent of lying upon a stone for a pillow. We are also told: *"He endured hardships of fasting and vigils without intermission by day and night; the burden of a single one of his labours would seem beyond the powers of man."*

Colmcille's desire for peace is best illustrated in his final words to his monks: *"This, dear children, is my last message to you – that you preserve with each other sincere charity and peace."*

The final hours of his life paint a vivid picture of Colmcille's sanctity; he ends his life as he began it, copying the Word of God, ending at verse 10 of Psalm 34: *"They that seek the Lord shall not want any good thing".*

To the very end of his days Colmcille remained a simple monk who served his faith and his people with humility and sincerity. Whatever ambition he possessed, he used in the interest of the Church and his people.

Conclusion

Any evaluation of Columba depends very much upon one's perception and interpretation of all that he achieved. He has been dismissed as a "vindictive, passionate, bold man of strife, born a soldier rather than a monk, and known, praised and blamed as a soldier" by writers such as Montalembert,[40] while others, such as Skene, perceive him to be more angel than soldier. The choice perhaps does not have to be an either/or one because Colmcille was, as we have seen, both statesman and saint. In any assessment we make, we need to remember the caution of Reeves to bear in mind the complexity of the times in which Columba lived when perhaps "to be amiable would not have won him much success".[41] Under Colmcille, the Church and the state almost became one entity and through his labour, "Christianity became the bond which would unite these turbulent nations, and establish among them, an abiding peace".[42]

 PRACTICE ESSAY TITLE

a) Give an account of the contribution made by Colmcille (Columba) to the development of the Celtic Church. (35)

   In your answer you could make reference to some of the following:
   • His early life and monastic foundations in Ireland
   • The foundation at Iona
   • The nature and extent of his mission
   • The impact of the political decisions he made
   • Adomnán's *Life of Colmcille*
   • The views of scholars

b) Explore the view that Colmcille (Columba) was more 'strife-monger' than peace-maker. Justify your answer. (15)

   In your answer you could make reference to some of the following:
   • The Battle of Cúl Dreimne
   • Other battles associated with the saint
   • Adomnán's *Life of Colmcille*
   • Political involvements of Colmcille
   • The views of scholars

4. PEREGRINI IN BRITAIN

The Church established by Colmcille was to endure for centuries after his death. Bede tells us that Columba "left successors distinguished for their great charity, divine love and strict attention to discipline".[43] The little island monastery of Iona became the mother house of numerous monasteries created by her sons. The seventh century was to see the height of her fame – the centre of a huge area of missionary activity. Colmcille had spearheaded the great missionary outreach of the Celtic Church. In the view of Kenney, the achievement of Colmcille's followers in Christianising their Anglo-Saxon neighbours "is from the viewpoint of world history the most momentous achievement of the Irish section of the Celtic Church".[44]

Peregrination is 'the pilgrimage for Christ'. It follows then that the peregrini were 'pilgrims for Christ.' However, Gougaud rightly warns against this literal translation of the word in this context. Pilgrimage implies journey to a shrine, which is the 'object of the devotion of the pilgrim'. It implies that once the visit had been made the pilgrim returns home and 'resumes his usual life'. The early Celtic peregrini were not then, strictly speaking, pilgrims in this sense of the word, because in most cases they were to leave their home, never to return. More often than not they also left without a particular destination in mind; their final halting place was often not a religious shrine but a place in much need of religion.[45]

The background to the missionary outreach

Just as the Christian faith was beginning to flourish in Ireland and paganism was evaporating, Britain was being invaded by the Angles, the Saxons, the Jutes and other pagan tribes, from the region of north Germany.[46] Paganism had now taken root in a large part of Britain, while the Christian Church was greatly reduced to small pockets in Wales, Cornwall and some parts of Scotland. The Christians were desolate in the face of the barbaric pagan advance and morale was too low to engage in the evangelisation of the invaders.

The invaders were, however, to receive the faith from two different sources: the mission of Saint Augustine sent from Rome in the year that Colmcille had died, and his subsequent successors; and the missionary outreach of the Celtic monks of Iona. Whereas Columba had mainly evangelised in Pictish territory, the Ionian monks now moved southwards towards the territory of the Saxon.

The personalities

Aidan

The name of Aidan "marks the period of the great expansion of the Columban Church".[47]

Oswald, son of the king of Bernicia, had been in banishment with his brothers since the slaying of his father. During this time he became Christian, and is said to have spent time on Iona. Oswald regained the throne of his father, after praying for victory beside a cross he had erected at the side of the road. He immediately sent to Iona to request of the abbot Segéne a monk who would be willing to preach the Word of God in his Kingdom. Corman was chosen initially for this work. He soon returned, dejected by his lack of success and regaled the community with stories of the difficult time he had had with the Angles. One monk spoke up and said that clearly too much had been expected of the pagan Angles and that the maxim of St Paul regarding *"milk for the babes"* needed to be applied.[48] This monk was Aidan, and he was immediately chosen to replace Corman.

Aidan was consecrated bishop and chose as his see the island of Lindesfarne – close to Bamburgh, the capital of Oswald's kingdom – and is now known as Holy Island. Bede was full of admiration for Aidan whom he calls *"a man of singular meekness, piety and moderation"*. At Lindesfarne, though bishop, Aidan remained in his heart a monk and ruled his island foundation as abbot. Bede pours forth his admiration for Lindesfarne, which was to become in the words of Lightfoot: "the true cradle of English Christianity".[49] It became "a second Iona" with its missionaries penetrating deep into England.[50] Gougaud agrees that it was the most powerful centre of religious influence in England.[51]

Meanwhile, Oswald was an excellent king who soon gained ascendancy. In spite of his growing power, Aidan and he remained close friends, with the king accompanying Aidan on his mission and acting as interpreter for him. Under the influence of Aidan, Oswald became a most humble and pious leader, who was known to frequently request that food be brought from his table to the poor of his kingdom.

Oswald was defeated when at battle with Penda in 642. This defeat was a personal loss for Aidan and would have been a threat to the entire Christian mission. It is said that Aidan went and retrieved the head of his beloved Oswald from the battlefield and laid him to rest at Lindesfarne. Penda and his army came to Bamburgh and lay siege to the royal household there, as Aidan and his monks watched anxiously. Penda's army set fire to the demolished houses of Bamburgh. The devastated Aidan cried out in prayer: *"See, Lord what ill Penda is doing!"* Thereupon the wind changed direction and turned the fire back upon the pagans who beat a hasty retreat. Oswy, the brother of Oswald, gathered resources and re-conquered the kingdom in 655. He offered little support for Aidan's mission. Oswald's cousin and enemy, Oswin, king of Deira, did however offer him support. Aidan became as close to him as he had been to Oswald. Aidan thus "transcended the political basis of his mission ... and managed to cross the divide between the two feuding dynasties".[52]

Ecclesiastically, if not militarily, therefore, Northumbria became a unified single kingdom.[53] Aidan remarkably, kept on excellent terms with successive Northumbrian kings, without compromising himself or the Gospel. Ryan believes that it was his "transparent sanctity which made this possible".[54]

Although very much a part of the royal court, Aidan remained aloof from the feasting and excess which would have been a part of it. Bede gives some wonderful anecdotal evidence as to the humility of Aidan. Apparently Aidan travelled everywhere on foot so that he could easily talk with those he would meet on his evangelising journey. King Oswin, concerned for Aidan's comfort on bad roads, presented him with a fine mare for his journey. One day Aidan met a beggar on his travels and gave him the fine (and expensive!) animal with all its dressing. A displeased Oswin asked Aidan to explain his actions, to which Aidan replied: *"O King, is that son of a mare dearer to you than that son of God?"* Oswin repented and promised, *"never again to ask how much of our money you give to the sons of God"*.

Oswin was assassinated by an envoy sent by Oswy, and twelve days later, on 31 August 651, Aidan himself dies of grief and old age.

McNeill notes that by the time of Aidan's death, the tide had definitely turned against paganism. Lightfoot argues that "it was not Augustine but Aidan who was the true apostle of England".[55] Aidan's love of the poor endeared him to commentators of the day; his austerity and asceticism inspired many who were to come after him. Even Oswy, who succeeded Oswin, was to change his ways and become the champion of the faith in his kingdom. Aidan and his followers restored Christianity to the areas that had lapsed and won over new areas that their predecessors had not been able to conquer.

Finian

Finian succeeded Aidan to the bishopric and abbacy of Lindesfarne. His abbacy was to last for ten years. One of Finian's achievement was the rebuilding of the church at Lindesfarne, which he perceived to be more worthy of an episcopal see. Bede tells us he built a church of wood, which was thatched with reeds. Finian was to increase the frontiers of Christianity, bringing it beyond Northumbria. He succeeded in baptising the son of Penda, the slayer of Oswald, as well as Sigebert, king of the Saxons. Ryan tells us that "in virtue, in zeal, in ability as an organiser, he was worthy of St Aidan, so that the Church in Northumbria grew and prospered".[56]

Finian also sent his monks out from Lindesfarne, most notably Cedd whom he consecrated as bishop to the Saxons. Cedd laboured hard, founding a number of churches and monasteries in Essex and ordaining bishops.

Cedd's brother Chad carried on his work in the kingdom of Mercia. Bede tells us that he was devoted to *"keeping the Church in truth and purity"*. He, like Aidan, travelled not on horseback but on foot.

Colman

Colman succeeded Finian at Lindesfarne. He held the episcopacy for three years and his leadership is strongly associated with the Synod of Whitby, after which he left Lindesfarne and retired to Mayo.

Comgall

Comgall of Bangor, himself a Pict, assisted Colmcille in his mission to the Picts.

Canice

Canice also cooperated with Colmcille in his missionary work before founding his own church, after which the city of Kilkenny is named.

Blaan

Blaan was born about 565 near Kingarth, five miles from Rothsay, where it appears that his uncle St Catan had founded an important monastery. Blaan's best known monastery was at Bute, in the parish of Kingarth. Although there is some uncertainty regarding whether he was a Pict or Briton, he is known to have trained as a monk at Bangor under the Abbot Comgall. The regard in which Blaan was held is evident in the numerous church dedications to him in Strathclyde, Dunblane and in the Pictish Highlands. James Hutchinson Cockburn sees these dedications as evidence of a "correspondingly wide and effective ministry".[56a]

Fursa

Fursa came from Ireland and ministered to the East Anglians and converted many by example and teaching. He established a monastery at Burgh Castle. Bede tells us that in desiring to be a hermit, he left his brother Foillán in charge of his foundation.

John Richard Green says that Irish Christianity "flung itself with a fiery zeal into battle with the mass heathenism which was rolling in upon the Christian world".[57] John Ryan acknowledges that while the conversion of Scotland was due to the efforts of the Britons and the Irish, the contribution of the Irish monks "far outdistanced" that of the Britons.[58]

 PRACTICE ESSAY TITLE

a) Give an account of the missionary outreach of the Celtic Church in Britain. (35)

In your answer you could make reference to some of the following:

- The achievements of Colmcille
- The influence of Iona
- The foundation of Lindesfarne
- The mission of Aidan
- The activities of other peregrini such as Blaan, Cedd, Chad, Canice, Finian, Fursa

Try on your own:

b) Explore the view that the achievements of Aidan match those of Colmcille. Justify your answer. (15)

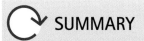 **SUMMARY**

Colmcille was the first of the Celtic peregrini.

He left Ireland under questionable circumstances.

He combined political ability with the qualities of sainthood.

He established a close relationship between Church and State.

His monks had a huge impact on the re-evangelisation of Britain.

Lindesfarne in particular was an important daughter house. It in turn became a centre of missionary outreach.

A number of Celtic monks were prominent in the evangelisation of Britain.

OTHER ASPECTS OF HUMAN EXPERIENCE

The following are suggestions of connection you could make to other aspects of human experience. You should use them as stimuli to produce and develop your own connections. Use also the notes you made from the discussion task earlier in the chapter.

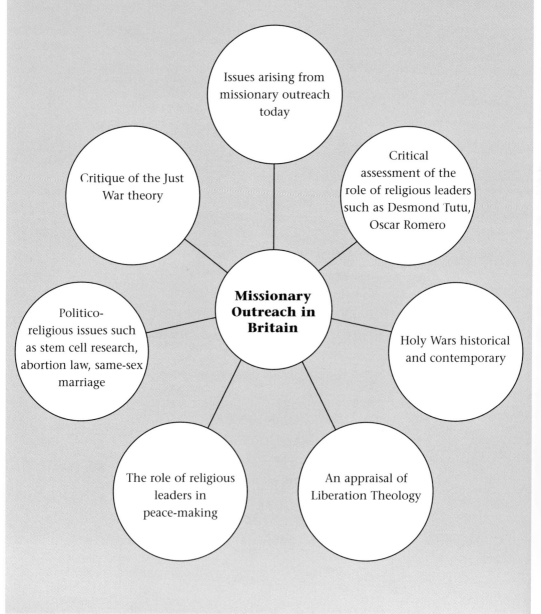

Tony Blair: I want to spend my life uniting faiths

From www.guardian.co.uk, 29 May 2008

Tony Blair today said he wanted to devote the rest of his life to promoting understanding between the world's religions.

Does religion fit here?

The former prime minister recalled how his Christian faith gave him the strength to take tough decisions during his spell in Downing Street. Blair said religion inspired him even when he thought he had little political support.

Blair was wary of talking about religion during his time in Downing Street for fear of being seen "as a nutter", he told a BBC documentary last year.

Alastair Campbell, his former communications director, famously told an interviewer from Vanity Fair: "We don't do God."

The former prime minister, a committed Anglican since his days as a student at Oxford in the 1970s, converted to Catholicism after his departure from No 10 last year.

He told how religion helped him during difficult periods as prime minister, saying: "The worst thing in politics is when you're so scared of losing support that you don't do what you think is the right thing.

"What faith can do is not tell you what is right but give you the strength to do it."

But he made the central importance of his faith clear when he said: "I think faith gives you a certain strength and gives you a support in doing a job as difficult as leading a country and gives you that strength and support."

In a rare comment about his faith during his time in Downing Street, Blair said in 2006 that he accepted that he would be judged by God.

"If you believe in God, [judgment] is made by God as well," he said. This was wrongly interpreted to mean he had sought divine approval for the Iraq war.

 TASK

Read the article above.

Many argue that Colmcille was both a man of politics and man of God. In groups or as a class consider the view that in order to serve the common good, **political** leaders must not be influenced by religious faith.

Consider a range of views. Gather evidence and examples to support your answer.

Think about the statement in both historical and contemporary contexts. (For example, you could find out about and discuss the role of the Emperor Constantine in the history of the Roman Empire and the Christian Church.)

 TASK

Colmcille's role in war and conflict is somewhat unclear. Read the article below.

In groups or as a class, think about and discuss, the view that:

1. The role of religion in conflict is a complex one.

2. War on religious grounds can never be justified.

Remember to make notes on your discussion. Find evidence and examples to support arguments you make. Try to show that you are aware of a range of different views and arguments.

File your work to use in preparation for Section B of the exam.

Religious Wars: A Bloody zeal

Monday, 12 July, 1976 by Lance Morrow

The scenes are macabre. Religious images adorn vehicles and guns as Christian soldiers, some of them wearing crosses around their necks, storm Moslem strongholds. Moslem soldiers, in their turn, strip or mutilate the bodies of dead Christian soldiers, tie them to cars and drag them through the streets. In the vicious war in Lebanon, religion is a palpable presence—though allegiances are complex and contradictory; some Christians are backing the leftist Palestinians, while the Syrians, mainly Moslem, support the rightist Christian forces. Still, the air crackles with a certain primitive energy of zealots in a holy war.

Fighting and dying under religious flags go on with a violent persistence elsewhere around the world. Protestants and Roman Catholics in Ulster trade killings in a kind of perpetual motion of futility. Arabs and Israelis stand tensely at borders of territorial, cultural and religious dispute. In the Philippines, Moslem separatists are in rebellion against a Christian majority. Greek-Cypriot Orthodox Christians confront Turkish-Cypriot Moslems across a sullen truce line. Pakistan separated from India because Moslems feared the rule of a Hindu majority.

Why, at this point in the 20th century, the strange vitality of what seem to be religious wars? Agnostic societies find it difficult to understand why anyone would think religion worth fighting about.

These conflicts are, of course, more complicated than religious fanaticism; they have a great deal to do with economic discrimination, battles for political power, questions of deeply laminated social difference. Nor do the wars involve religious doctrine – except in oblique, complex ways. A Belfast pub is not blown up to assert the Real Presence or the Virgin Birth. Many of the terrorists are atheists anyway. In such places as Ireland and Lebanon, religious leaders on all sides have prayed and pleaded for an end to the fighting. But the violence persists with a life of its own, like a hereditary disease. It is an anomaly of such conflicts that organized religion is powerless to stop them.

The wars arise in part from fears about identity and survival. Two factors, sometimes contradictory, are at work: 1) deep, real, material interests lie just beneath the surface of most of today's ostensibly religious conflicts; 2) religion, not as a doctrinal crusade but as an identifying birthright, a heritage, is persistently present to complicate every issue, to enforce an "us-them" hostility. Religion, always a receptacle for ultimate aspirations, can enlist the best and worst in its congregations. In conflict, religion can be used – or perverted – to call up supernatural justifications for killing. In 1915 the Bishop of London asked his congregation to "kill Germans, to kill them, not for the sake of killing, but to save the world, to kill the good as well as the bad, to kill." Though the issue in Northern Ireland has much to do with colonial policy, religion serves as an identifying element. Protestants like the demagogue Ian Paisley have kept the "religious threat" alive by constantly referring to the dangers of "popery" and "Romanism".

Endnotes

[1] Usage varies. He is generally referred to as Colmcille in the Catholic tradition and Columba in the Protestant tradition.

[2] Chadwick, *The Age of the Saints of the Early Celtic Church*, Llanerch Publishers, Wales, 1960, p1

[3] Smyth, AP, *Warlords and Holy Men: Scotland, AD80–1000*, London, 1984

[4] See, for example, Hanson, WG, *The Early Monastic Schools of Ireland*, Cambridge, 1927, p15

[5] Skene, WF, *Celtic Scotland*, Vol 1, Edinburgh, 1886

[6] Finlay, I, *Columba*, p96

[7] The text had been preserved in its damaged condition. In the 11th century it was encased in a wooden box and again, at a later date encased in silver. In 1813, it was opened, made legible and left in the Royal Irish Academy, Dublin.

[8] Simpson, WD, *The Historical Saint Columba*, Aberdeen, 1927, p35

[9] Finlay, I, *Columba*, Victor Gollancz Ltd, London, 1979, p93

[10] *ibid*, cited in the Foreward

[11] *ibid*, pp83–84

12 McNeill, *The Celtic Churches, op cit*, 4, p90

13 Skene, *Celtic Scotland, op cit*

14 Ryan, J, 'Irish Missionary work in Scotland and England', in *The Miracle of Ireland*, ed Daniel-Rops, Clonmore & Reynolds Ltd, Dublin, 1959, p97

15 The visit to Bruide will be dealt with in detail in the second paragraph to follow.

16 Finlay, *Columba, op cit*, p105

17 *ibid*, p122

18 Skene, WF, *Celtic Scotland,* Vol 2, Edinburgh, 1886–87, p86

19 *ibid*, p84; Stokes, GT, *Ireland and the Celtic Church*, London, 1888, p122ff

20 Henderson, I, *The Picts*, New York, 1967, pp44–45

21 McNeill, *The Celtic Churches, op cit*, p90

22 Finlay, *Columba, op cit*, p140

23 Simpson, *The historical Saint Columba, op cit*, pp18–21

24 Finlay, *Columba, op cit*, p122

25 McNeill, *The Celtic Churches, op cit*, p95

26 Finlay, *Columba, op cit*, p146

27 *ibid*, p151

28 This is the view expressed by Finlay, *ibid,* p160

29 McNeill, *The Celtic Churches, op cit*, p97

30 Bannerman, JWM, *Studies in the History of Dalriada*, Edinburgh 1974, cited in Finlay, I, *Columba*

31 *ibid*, p160

32 *ibid*, p162

33 As Cited in Finlay, *ibid,* p163

34 A poem, *The Altus Prosator*, in the *Leabhar Breac* which has been attributed to the pen of the saint has a preface which comments that the poem was composed because Colmcille was "beseeching forgiveness for the battle of Cúl Dreimne and the other battles that were gained on his account".

35 Reeves, W, *The Life of Saint Columba (Adomnán)*, Edinburgh, 1874, pxviii

36 Finlay, *Columba, op cit*, p165

37 McNeill, *The Celtic Churches, op cit*, p101

38 Herbert, M, *Iona, Kells and Derry, the History and Hagiography of the monastic Familia of Columba*, Clarendon Press, Oxford, 1988, p35

39 McNeill, M, *Iona, A History of the Island with Descriptive Notes*, Blackie & Son Ltd, Glasgow, 1920

40 Cited in Finlay, *Columba, op cit*, p186

41 Reeves, *The Life of Saint Columba, op cit,* pxvii

42 McNeill, *Iona: A History of the Island with Descriptive Notes, op cit*

43 All excerpts from Bede's *Ecclesiastical History* in this chapter are taken from Colgrave & Mynors edition, Clarendon Press, Oxford, 1969

44 Kenney, *The Sources for the Early History of Ireland: Ecclesiastical, An Introduction and Guide, op cit*, p225

45 Gougaud, *Christianity in Celtic Lands, op cit*

46 Refer to Chapter 1 to refresh your memory on the collapse of the Empire.

47 Finlay, *Columba, op cit*, p193

48 1 Cor 3:2. Paul was referring to the need to introduce the faith gently and in a manner appropriate to the cultural background and understanding of the converts in question.

49 Lightfoot, JB, *Leaders of the Northern Church*, London, 1890, p16

50 Finlay, *Columba, op cit*, p196

51 Gougaud, *Christianity in Celtic Lands, op cit*, p137

52 Charles-Edwards, *Early Christian Ireland, op cit*, p315

53 *ibid*

54 Ryan, J, *Irish Monks in the Golden Age*, Clonmore & Reynolds Ltd, Dublin, 1963, p41

55 Lightfoot, *Leaders of the Northern Church, op cit*, p9

56 Ryan, J, 'Irish Missionary work on Scotland and England', in *The Miracle of Ireland*, ed Danel-Rops, Clonmore & Reynolds Ltd, Dublin, 1958, p100

56a Cockburn, J, *The Celtic Church in Dunblane*, Dunblane, Scotland, 1954, pp49–85

57 Cited in Finlay, *Columba, op cit*, p42

58 Ryan, 'Irish Missionary work in Scotland and England', *op cit*, p98

Chapter 6

The Historical Patrick

1. THE HISTORICAL PATRICK

Introduction

This unit involves a study of the person of Patrick within a particular time and place in history. The main sources we have on the person of Patrick are his own writings. From these we can gain much insight into the person of Patrick – his spiritual journey, the difficulties he faced and his response to them. But what they tell us about Patrick in time and place is more limited. Indeed, Kenney explains that when we search Patrick's writings for historical facts we are confronted with "an exasperating incoherence which leaves the meaning constantly in doubt."[1] Patrick may be a much more obscure figure than many would like to admit.

What we know:

- He was born in Roman Britain.
- He came from an affluent clerical background.
- His father was a minor official.

- He was captured by Irish raiders at the age of sixteen.
- He lived as a slave in Ireland for six years.
- He escaped by making a journey of 200 miles to the coast and securing passage on a boat with pagans.
- He was called to return to the Irish in a series of dreams and visions.
- He returned to preach the Gospel, in pagan areas, enduring much difficulty and hardship.
- He was criticised by other clerics.
- He perceived his mission to be successful and was committed to it until death.

What we do not know:

- Patrick's birth and death date.
- The date of Patrick's mission to the Irish.
- The location of his captivity.
- The extent of his missionary activity.
- The place of his clerical training.

Séan MacAirt refers to the fifth century as the "lost century", because of the absence of any historical information. With the exception of the writings of Patrick – the *Letter* and the *Confessio* – and Prosper's reference to the arrival of Palladius, we are still in the era of pre-history. Even within the two documents, which are the most important we have, there are no dates given and only two place names mentioned. Creating an historical record or autobiography was not the primary concern of Patrick. O'Rahilly points out that:

> "the last thing the saint could have imagined, would be that many hundreds of years later, the document would be scrutinised again and again with a view to gleaning biographical details of the writer's life."[2]

The problem is compounded by the fact that 200 years passed between the time in which Patrick actually lived and the time he was first written about.

Daniel Binchy remarks that the quest to uncover the *acta* of the historical Patrick is "much labour and little profit." He argues that "the most essential pieces of the Patrick puzzle have been lost and are unlikely to be rediscovered."[3] Nonetheless, historians have tried, with varying degrees of success, to uncover the historical Patrick. The 'pieces of the Patrick puzzle' that concern most Patrician scholars are his dates and his geography.

2. THE GEOGRAPHY OF PATRICK

Three locations concern us when considering Patrick's geography. These are Silva Focluti (the Wood of Foclut), Bannavem Taburniae and Gaul.

A satisfactory investigation could shed light on the location of Patrick's hometown, the place of Patrick's captivity, and the location of Patrick's ecclesiastical training.

Bannavem Taburniae

Many attempts have been made to locate Bannavem Taburniae. The Roman place name no longer exists and many scholars feel the quest for it to be futile. The fact that it is the only British place name that Patrick gives us has ensured that it is of interest to historians.

It is generally accepted that three criteria must be met in determining the location of Patrick's home:

- It would have to be within easy reach of the west coast of Britain in order to facilitate easy access for Irish raiders. Charles Thomas would add to this the criterion that it would be opposite the place of Patrick's captivity in Ireland.[4]

- Patrick had a strong sense of his Roman identity, which means the location of his home would need to be in a strongly Romanised part of Britain. Bannavem Taburniae would then have to be south of Hadrian's Wall.

- Patrick's father, Calpurnius, was a decurion (collector of taxes). To hold this job, he must have been living near a town with a civil administration centre.

Bearing these in mind, different suggestions have been put forward for the location of Bannavem Taburniae. Muirchú, writing in the seventh century, tells us that Bannavem Taburniae was identified as Ventre, although this does not help with our identification.

Bieler does however, take this into account when he reconstructs the name as Bannaventa Taburniae. If he is right, then there was a place called Bannaventa, a small Roman settlement in Northamptonshire. The name of this settlement was then taken and given to a place just outside Daventry. This area is in the midlands and would not be very accessible to Irish raiders.

Other suggestions have been made including Dumbarton, which would be too far removed from Roman influence, and even Boulogne in northern France.

Charles Thomas believes the only area to fulfil all three criteria would be the North West corner of Britain.[5] He points out that the home of Patrick was a *vicus*, which can be taken to mean a small settlement or village. This would need to be close to a larger town, which would have had a civil administrative centre in which Calpurnius might have worked.

Thomas concludes that the only place in the North West at this time would have been Carlisle. He argues that this solution "entirely outweighs that of Daventry, Dumbarton or elsewhere." It is also far enough north to explain the poor quality of Patrick's Latin. Historically this vicus was identified as Bewcatle, six miles north of the wall, or Birdoswald, which is still only fifteen miles from Carlisle.

Some scholars take a linguistic approach, breaking the name up into compounds:

Banna	The name of a fort on Hadrian's Wall.
Venta-	Probably means meeting place.
Taburniae	May come from the word 'bern' which means mountain pass.

This would mean that the area is a small settlement of some kind, south of Hadrian's Wall, on or near a mountain pass. This may be the area around the Greenhead Pass, which is still in close proximity to Carlisle.

Dark warns us that any attempt to locate Bannavem Taburniae is based on assumptions and so can never be conclusive. However, he believes the only place in Britain that we can say with certainty suffered from frequent raids by the Irish in the fourth and fifth century were the areas of South Dorset and the Cotswolds.[6] Most scholars would concur that Bannavem Taburniae is indeed somewhere in the Severn Valley.

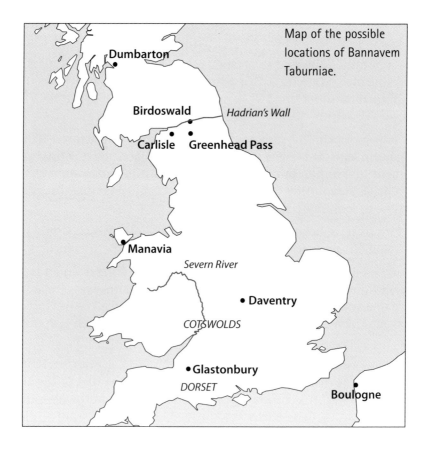

Map of the possible locations of Bannavem Taburniae.

TASK

Summarise the main arguments presented for the location of Bannavem Taburniae.

Silva Focluti (the Wood of Foclut)

The location of Silva Focluti has also been the subject of historical debate. It arises in the 'call' narrative in Patrick's *Confessio*.

> *"As I read the beginning of the Letter, I seem to hear the voice of those who were by the wood of Foclut which is near the western sea and they cried as with one voice, Holy Boy we are asking you to come and walk among us again." (C23)*

> Hanson believes that the title given to Patrick 'Holy Boy' is a nickname Patrick may have been given during his time as a slave.

The question: is this the place of Patrick's captivity? Bury, O'Rahilly and Hanson assume that it is. The use of the word *"again"* implies a return to the area.[7] Mohrmann agrees that the correct interpretation of Patrick's words suggests that "they are heard from the mouth of people from a part of the country that Patrick seems to have known from his captivity".[8]

This raises the further difficulty of reconciling the two suggested locations of Slemish and Mayo, both of which are traditionally held as the place of Patrick's captivity.

Some have suggested that Patrick is speaking metaphorically and his real meaning is that the people even at the furthermost point of Ireland (as the west coast is from Britain) were calling him to return.

On the other hand, it could be a place Patrick had heard of, but never been to as is the view of Bieler, who believes Patrick experienced the call of the Irish people generally, rather than the call of people from one specific area.[9]

Where is it?

Tírechán, writing in the late seventh century, identifies Silva Focluti it with the area around modern Killala in County Mayo. Some are sceptical of this identification because Tírechán himself was from this area. Others believe that it is the earliest identification we have and so we should accept it as genuine.

Patrick gives one clue in the *Confessio* as to the location of Silva Focluti. He tells us it was near the western sea. Hanson believes that Patrick does give us further clues in his own writings, as to the location of his captivity.

In the escape story Patrick tells us that he had to travel to a ship that was perhaps 200 miles away (C17). If we accept that he was returning to Britain then if he were in the West of Ireland he may have had to make such a journey from the northern coast of Mayo to the coast of Wicklow or Wexford, travelling diagonally across Ireland.[10]

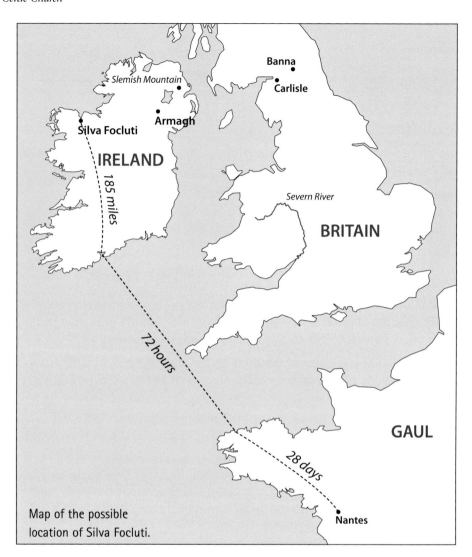

Map of the possible
location of Silva Focluti.

Slemish

There is also a strong tradition of long standing that Patrick tended the flocks as a slave boy on Mount Slemish. We do know that the place of Patrick's captivity was on a mountain.

Hanson argues that this would not 'fit' the evidence of the escape story. An escape from Slemish would have involved a walk of twenty or thirty miles to a ship, rather than two hundred. He insists that "we must accept the plain evidence of his own words and place his captivity in Co. Mayo near the border with Co. Sligo."[11] Muirchú, also a seventh century source, does however believe that the place of Patrick's captivity is Slemish.

Meanwhile, Bury, O'Rahilly and Hanson all reject the location of Slemish as being part of the Armagh legend. Nonetheless, Slemish is a mountainous area while the area suggested around the town of Killala is a plain. Many insist that the Slemish tradition cannot be dismissed and point to Patrick's captivity somewhere in the north-east of Ireland. Morris identifies it with Faughal near Cushendall; MacErlean believes it to be Magherafelt.[12]

Concannon and Philbin suggest a compromise. Both localities can be accepted because Patrick changed master. Healy and Newport White offer a similar compromise by suggesting an escape from captivity in the north-east to the west of Ireland.[13] The likelihood of such an escape in fifth century Ireland however is open to serious question.[14]

We cannot know for certain of the place of Patrick's captivity and while we should not accept something as historical fact on the basis of tradition, neither can tradition of long standing be easily dismissed.

 TASK

Summarise the main evidence and arguments for the location of Silva Focluti.

Gaul

Despite Patrick's protestations about his inadequate education, he would have had to undertake clerical training in order to prepare for his ordination and subsequent consecration as bishop. Scholars are in disagreement as to the location of this training. Some argue that Patrick was a British bishop, trained in Britain and responsible to the British Church. Others believe he had strong associations with the Continent and may have been trained there.

Gaul	Britain
Patrick says he wishes to visit Gaul to see the brethren. This may have been a desire to visit friends he had made there during training.	Binchy believes this was merely a desire to visit the holy men of Gaul, of whom he had heard much.[15]
The escape from Ireland involved three days' sailing, more likely to be to Gaul than Britain.	Carney disagrees that Patrick could have been in Gaul at this time.[16]
Muirchú, writing in the seventh century, tells us of Patrick's stay in Gaul for some 30 years.	O'Rahilly argues that this is actually a confused account of the training and ordination of Palladius.[17]

Gaul	Britain
Language expert Christine Mohrmann believes the colloquial expressions in Patrick's Latin are from the Continent before 450.[18] He did not however have a monastic experience there.	Binchy argues that given Patrick's unsophisticated Latin, it is unlikely that he would have spent a long time on the Continent. Had he trained on the Continent for a long time, it is unlikely that the British bishops would have been so critical of his lack of learning.
	Hanson believes his Latin is that of the British Church and he is "wholly the product of the British church."[19]
	Jackson agrees that Patrick's Latin was "the living language spoken in Britain ... which may have been similar to that spoken in Gaul."[20]
Michael Herron believes that the high regard Patrick has for monasticism comes from a long stay in a monastery in Gaul.[21]	Duffy agrees that Patrick was more likely to have received his clerical training in Britain rather than Gaul.[22]
Thomas accepts he picked up these sayings in Gaul, but during a visit of two or three years there after his escape from Ireland. He did not, in the view of Thomas, study in Gaul.	

Conclusion

- It is very difficult to determine the location of Patrick's hometown in Britain. Even Muirchú, writing in the seventh century, is not certain of its location. Most accept that it is somewhere in the Severn Valley.
- Silva Focluti is the only place name in Ireland mentioned by Patrick. For this reason it has been the subject of much debate, particularly by those who believe it to be the place of Patrick's captivity. Two strong traditions are held as to its location: Slemish and County Mayo.
- Patrick also mentions Gaul and a desire to visit there. This had led some historians to assume that he had already spent a significant portion of his life there, probably while undergoing clerical training. Others argue he came direct from the British Church and was directly responsible to British bishops.
- The unresolved debate has led many to assume that some of the details of the life of the historical Patrick are forever lost to the historian. Others may well argue that the most important aspects of the person of Patrick are preserved for us for eternity in his own writings.

3. THE DATING OF PATRICK'S MISSION

Introduction

Patrician scholars, almost without exception, place Patrick's mission to the Irish in the fifth century. This is most clear from the *Letter to Coroticus*, which gives one vital clue:

> "This is the custom of the Christians of Roman Gaul: they send suitable Christian men to the Franks and the other heathen nations ... to ransom baptised people who have been captured." (L14)

Clovis, who was the first Frankish Christian king, died c 511–512 and is conventionally dated as having been baptised around 496. The Franks were therefore pagan for most of the fifth century, clearly suggesting a fifth century dating for Patrick's mission.

The differences emerge when attempting to be more exact. There are a number of problems in dating the mission of Patrick more precisely.

- There are no dates given in Patrick's own writings.

- There are different death dates given for Patrick in the annals.

- Known disciples of Patrick died well into the sixth century, eg Mochta died 535.

- Palladius came to Ireland in 431 as the first bishop to the Irish. Prosper implies he is still active in 434. Muirchú places his death within a year of his arrival. Patrick makes no mention of him in his writings.

- None of the early writings of the Celtic Church, ie either the penitentials, Bede or Columbanus actually mention Patrick at all.

The term 'annals' suggest that they were kept yearly, recording the events of the previous 12 months. But the annals recording fifth century events were not drawn up then. The annals only begin to record contemporaneously from the seventh century onwards at the earliest. Some argue that entries concerning fifth century events were entered on the basis of strong tradition going back to that century. Others are more sceptical. Most scholars accept that interpolation did occur in the annals.

What the annals tell us [23]

432	The year of the Lord 432 ... Patrick reached Ireland in the ninth year of Theodosius Minor ... so reckon Bede and Marcellinus in their chronicles (*Annals of Ulster*).
432	The fourth year of Loeghaire – Patrick came to Ireland in this year (*Annals of the Four Masters*).

457	Old Patrick yielded his spirit (*Annals of the Four Masters*).[24]
461	Some place the death of Patrick in this year. (*Annals of Ulster*)
492	The Irish say that Patrick the Archbishop died. (*Annals of Ulster*)
493	Patrick ... in the 122nd year of his age resigned his spirit to heaven (*Annals of the Four Masters*).

While all the annals are unanimous in suggesting 432 for the arrival of Patrick, the different death dates suggested, add to our difficulty in dating the mission of Patrick with certainty.

Historians suggest different dates for the mission of Patrick

 TASK

Before reading on, return to the commentaries on Patrick's writings in Chapter 2. Read through them carefully to refresh your memory on what they may tell us about Patrick.

432–493

The first dating, argued by **Healy**[25] is based on a view that Patrick came to Ireland in 432, commissioned by Pope Celestine, worked in Ireland for just over sixty years and died on Wednesday 17 March 493, aged 120 years.

432–461

Bury presented what is now called the traditional dating for Patrick.[26] His case was strengthened by the later work of **Hanson**.[27]

Hanson constructed his arguments from looking at the internal evidence in Patrick's own writings:

- Patrick's pride in his Roman identity indicates that he grew up in Roman Britain, before the collapse of the Empire – therefore in Hanson's view before 410. This suggests a mission in the first half of the fifth century

- *Confessio* 9, 10 and 13 all emphasise Patrick's deficient learning, which was interrupted by his capture at sixteen. He had benefited from Roman education up to that point, probably before Rome withdrew its troops and money from Britain just after 408.[28]

- Patrick's writings tell us that his father held the position of both deacon and decurion. **Hanson** argues that there is no evidence of decurions or municipal councils existing after 410. Patrick's father most likely held this position between 388–395. At other times generals had attempted to close down the tax loophole.

- Patrick was possibly captured in the great raid of 405, as he tells us that he was taken away with *"so many thousands"*

- The theme of judgement day, which runs throughout his *Confessio,* was influenced by the experience of living through the collapse of Rome after an attack on the city in 410. This was taken by many Christians to be a sign that the end of the world was near. **Hanson** writes that "had Patrick been writing in the 480s or 490s the impact of such a relatively distant event would have been less."[29]

- In *Letter* 14, Patrick refers to the gold coin solidus, which **Hanson** believes was not minted in Britain after 410, and was completely out of circulation by the second half of the fifth century.

- The further we progress into the fifth century the more war-torn Britain became. Therefore it seems more unlikely that the Church would finance a mission to another barbarian country. The mission was more likely to have been organised between 430 and 460.

- **Hanson** believes Coroticus to have been a king of Strathclyde who reigned between 410–440. Patrick wrote to him between 430–440.

For **Hanson,** the 461–493 dating "is not supported by the evidence in Patrick's writings, but rest upon not very convincing external evidence … I conclude therefore with some confidence that it is sounder to place Patrick's career in the first half of the fifth century … returning to Ireland as bishop about 430 and dying about 460."[30]

Christine Mohrmann, an expert on early Christian Latin, believes that the Latin of the *Confessio* is more likely to belong to the first half of the fifth century rather than after 450, so linguistically speaking, the traditional dating is more likely for the mission of Patrick.[31]

461–493

Some scholars suggest different dates for the internal evidence identified by Hanson and argue that an alternative chronology of these events could indicate a dating in the second half of the fifth century.

Charles Thomas believes that we cannot know for certain that formal education and local government had completely broken down in Britain by 410 as Hanson assumes. He believes that town life continued well into the fifth century.[32]

Dolley argues that there was a spate of raids around the 430s, with a major raid taking place in 440, which may have captured Patrick.[33]

Thomas points out that there was a further attack and destruction of Rome in

457, which might have been the one experienced by Patrick.

Thomas holds that Coroticus may have been a Welsh prince of Cardiganshire, who reigned from 460 onwards.

Thomas believes that the *Letter to Coriticus* was written between 465–475 and that Patrick wrote the *Confessio* some time after 480. He concludes that "the annalistic dates from his death that cluster around the early 490s, may reflect with some reality, the tradition that he dies before the end of the century."[34]

In 1942, **Thomas O'Rahilly** delivered his **Two Patricks** lecture and suggested a later dating for Patrick's mission, albeit still within the fifth century. He took into account the evidence of both fifth and sixth century annals and concluded that Patrick, the author of the *Confessio* and *Letter to Coroticus*, arrived in Ireland in 461 and died in 492/3.

For more detail on O'Rahilly's argument, see the Two Patricks Theory on p192.

A common representation of Patrick, bishop of Ireland. *(Photo courtesy Cathal O'Connor)*

456/7–493

This is the view of **James Carney**.[35] He believes Patrick was born in 418, taken captive in 434, escaped in 440, and returned in 456 (5 April). He claims the *Confessio* was written in 489 and that Patrick died in 493, on 17 March.

350–430

Mario Esposito[36] presents a more diverse dating of 350–430 for Patrick of the *Confessio* and *Letter*. Patrick precedes Palladius, coming to Ireland sometime between 390–395, although not as a bishop. He was only so 'by popular acclaim'. This allows Prosper to rightly refer to Palladius as "the first bishop to the Scotti who believe in Christ". Patrick the Briton then converted the first Irish Christians. He believes the *Confessio* was written about 420 and the *Letter to Coroticus* a few years later.

Esposito's theory does solve the problem of why the humble Patrick didn't mention at all the work of Palladius, but it is rejected by most Patrician scholars. Certainly if Patrick were only bishop by popular acclaim, he would hardly have had the authority, which he was anxious to 'put on record' in his *Letter*, to excommunicate Coroticus.

 TASK

Divide into two groups. One group should compile the arguments and evidence for the 432–461 dates for Patrick. The other group should compile the arguments and evidence for the later dating for Patrick.
Present your arguments to the class.
Which is the more convincing? Give reasons for your opinion.

 PRACTICE ESSAY TITLE

a) Outline and explain the issues involved in uncovering the historical Patrick. (30)
   In your answer you may make reference to some of the following:
   • Lack of historical information in Patrick's writings
   • Silva Focluti
   • Bannavem Taberniae
   • Gaul
   • Two death dates
   • Historical inferences in Patrick's writings
   • The views of scholars

b) Critically assess the view that Patrick's writings teach us little about the person of Patrick. (20)

In your answer you may refer to some of the following:
- Autobiographical details in Patrick's *Letter* and *Confessio*
- Personality of Patrick
- Spiritual life of Patrick
- Views of scholars

Use what you learned at AS Level to help with this question.

4. THE TWO PATRICKS THEORY

 TASK

Before reading on, return to Chapter 1 and read again the section on Palladius.

Introduction

The Two Patricks lecture was delivered by Thomas O'Rahilly on 20 March, 1942. It is a summary of studies undertaken by O'Rahilly in the years 1934–35.[37]

O'Rahilly's interest initially was in the fifth and sixth century annals. It was while studying these that O'Rahilly first noted the discrepancies surrounding the dating of Patrick. He admits that "the history of Christianity in the fifth century bristles with difficulties, many of them of chronological order." He is hopeful, nonetheless, that "the most serious of our difficulties [regarding Saint Patrick] will resolve themselves quite readily once we get our chronology right."[38]

Bury suggested, as we have seen, a 432–461 date for Patrick, which was held as the 'official' dating of Patrick's mission from 1905. O'Rahilly believed that Bury's limitations lay both in the fact that he was not an Irish language scholar, and that he had not looked at sixth century annals when compiling his chronology. Had he done so, O'Rahilly is sure he would have revised his opinion.

The starting point for a Christian mission to Ireland is the reference of Prosper to the sending of Palladius in 431. This date is beyond question and marks the beginning of Irish history as well as the official introduction of the Christian faith into Ireland. No other date regarding the Christianisation of Ireland is certain.

Discrepancies with dates

While studying the annals, O'Rahilly noted the recorded death dates of the accepted contemporaries of Patrick in the sixth century annals, for example that of Mochta.

We know for example, that Mochta was a disciple of Patrick from two sources: firstly Adomnán, in the Second Preface, refers to Mochta as:

> *"a certain stranger, a Briton and a holy man, disciple of the holy bishop Patrick. Mochta by name."*[39]

Then the *Annals of Ulster* record Mochta's death under the year 535[40] and quote the beginning of a letter written by Mochta in which he refers to himself as *"sancti Patrcii discipulus"*:

> *"The sleep of Mochta, Patrick's disciple on 20 August. So he wrote in his own letter: 'Mochta the priest, a sinner, disciple of holy Patrick, would offer salutation in the Lord'."*

In addition to the recorded death of Mochta, O'Rahilly noted that from 488 until 544 the annals recorded the death of over twelve bishops who were confirmed in other sources to be known contemporaries of Patrick. This led O'Rahilly to ask the question: "if Patrick died in 461, how do we explain the fact that so many of his fellow workers die fifty, sixty or even seventy years later?"[41]

O'Rahilly, unlike other scholars,[42] believes that the annals "are the safest and most trustworthy guide that we possess".[43] If we assume that the sixth century annals are correct, then "what justification is there for the general opinion that Patrick died in 461?"

An explanation

Some attempts have been made to explain this discrepancy by suggesting that some of the dates are wrongly recorded, or recorded late to exaggerate the lifespan of the saint in question. Sometimes there was also a tendency to 'move' the significant dates of saints to correspond with the lives of other important figures such as, for example, Pope Leo or Germanus or King Loeghaire. However, it is highly unlikely that the obits of so many such saints would be 'moved', in some cases by up to seventy years. Whatever explanations are put forward, Binchy is of the view that "taken *en bloc*, their combined testimony is most formidable."[44]

It is clear that the 492/3 death date for Patrick would 'fit' with the obits of his contemporaries. However, accepting the 492/3 death date for Patrick calls into question the 432 date cited for the arrival of Patrick. Bury argues that this date was "certain" and "rested upon clear and unvarying tradition."[45] He had rejected the 492/3 death date as an attempt to equate the lifetime of Patrick with that of Moses, but O'Rahilly argued that the 492/3 date is as likely to be valid as the 461 death date. He believed that instead the 432 arrival date should perhaps be questioned.

Two missionaries?

There has always been a tradition, going back to the seventh century and continuing into the ninth century, of two missionaries called Patricius, working in Ireland in the fifth century. The following sources record such a figure, for example, the *Stowe Missal* which lists saints commemorated in the Mass begins with the saints:

"*Patricii, Patricii, Secundii, Auxili, Iserinini …*".

The *Law of Adomnán* and the *Martyrology of Oengus* also refer to an 'older Patrick'; and *Fiaccs Hymn* states that:

"*When Patrick went aloft, he fared first to the other Patrick; together they ascended to Jesus the Son of Mary.*"

This is contemporary evidence that "there was a belief that there was an older Patrick who declined to go to heaven until he could be accompanied by his junior namesake."[46]

As we have already seen, the annals record:

"*the repose of Sen Phátric as some books tell.*" (*Annals of Ulster*)

"*Sen Phátric yielded his spirit.*" (*Annals of Inisfallen*)

There is some argument as to whether the word 'Sen' in Irish, translated to 'Senex' in Latin means 'older' in years or 'senior' in terms of being a title of dignity, that is, more venerable, or 'having primacy over'.[47] Most scholars accept that in this context the term is used to refer to a figure who is chronologically older.

The idea of the Two Patricks then was not a new one. Binchy believes that the theory of the Two Patricks "is at least as old as the middle of the eighth century."[48] Bieler, although accepting an 'earlier' Patrick of the *Confessio*, believed that the 493 death date referred to a 'junior Patrick.'

Several attempts have been made to identify the Sen Phátric, although they do not concern us here. By the ninth century the differentiation between the two figures had lessened considerably before disappearing altogether. For O'Rahilly, the two death dates exist quite simply because there were two Patricks.

Palladius

O'Rahilly then turned his attention back to Palladius. As we saw earlier, there are no fifth century Irish records of Palladius beyond the annalistic entry, copied from Prosper, which records his arrival in 431. O'Rahilly explains that this is because the Latin name ' Palladius' never really took root in the Irish language, so "there was no genuine Irish tradition of any missionary named Palladius."[49]

O'Rahilly points out that there are notes in the appendix of Tírechán's *Brief Account*, in the *Book of Armagh* which speak of: "*Palladius, also called Patricius*".

This leads O'Rahilly to assume that Palladius' full name was Patricius Palladius – Patricius being quite a common name at this time. In Ireland he was referred to by his first name, while in the Chronicles of Prosper his surname is used. Palladius is then, Sen Phátric. Bury, on the other hand, dismisses Sen Phátric as "a mere phantom".

The dating of the mission of Patrick the Briton and the mission of Palladius.
Courtesy of Cathal O'Connor

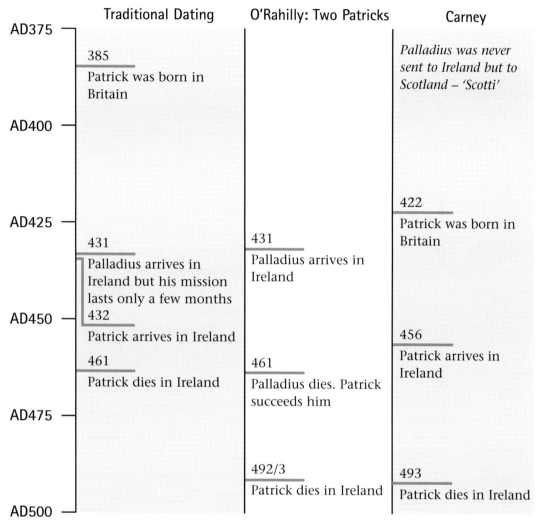

	Traditional Dating	O'Rahilly: Two Patricks	Carney
AD375			
	385 Patrick was born in Britain		*Palladius was never sent to Ireland but to Scotland – 'Scotti'*
AD400			
AD425			**422** Patrick was born in Britain
	431 Palladius arrives in Ireland but his mission lasts only a few months	**431** Palladius arrives in Ireland	
AD450	**432** Patrick arrives in Ireland		**456** Patrick arrives in Ireland
	461 Patrick dies in Ireland	**461** Palladius dies. Patrick succeeds him	
AD475			
		492/3 Patrick dies in Ireland	**493** Patrick dies in Ireland
AD500			

A composite Patrick

O'Rahilly believes that because both missionaries were of the same name, one composite Patrick emerged; the works of the two Patricks merged into that of one figure and the work of Palladius was attributed to Patrick the Briton. Hence the memory of Palladius *per se* has become subsumed into that of Patrick of the *Confessio*.

O'Rahilly then explains the 432 arrival date. It is this, he argues, not the 492/3 death date, which is interpolated. The church of Armagh claimed both Patrick the Briton as their founder and primacy over all the churches of Ireland. They wished to glorify the missionary contribution made by Patrick the Briton, and wanted to associate him as closely as possible with the origins of Christianity in Ireland. Hence his arrival date was pushed back to 432 and Muirchú persuaded readers of his narrative that Palladius had died within a year of arriving in Ireland to accommodate it. O'Rahilly believes that the confused story of the consecration of Patrick in Gaul by Amator was actually an account of Palladius' consecration, either concocted by Muirchú, or showing that by that time in the seventh century some merging of the two figures had already begun to take place.

O'Rahilly's chronology then suggests that Palladius came to Ireland in 431, laboured for approximately thirty years, and died in 461. Patrick the Briton, who wrote the *Letter to Coroticus* and the *Confessio*, came to Ireland shortly thereafter, laboured for around the same amount of time, as is implied in *Fiacc's Hymn* and dies somewhere around 492/3. The 432 arrival date for Patrick the Briton is fictitious. All of Palladius' work is attributed to Patrick the Briton.

Summary

- There are two recorded death dates for Patrick in the annals – 461 and 493. The annals record the arrival of Patrick in 432.
- The deaths of Patrick's contemporaries are recorded in the sixth century annals, some as much as seventy years after the 461 death of Patrick. This means the death of Patrick the Briton is more likely to have occurred in 492/3.
- This raises the question of the 461 death date. There is no further mention of Palladius after 431, except in the notes of Tírechán's *Brief Account*, which tells us that Palladius was also called Patricius.
- There are records going back to the seventh century of a Sen Phátric (older Patrick). There is clearly a very old tradition of two missionaries called Patrick, living and working in Ireland in the fifth century.
- The 432 date for the arrival of Patrick was established by the Armagh Church in order to minimise the contribution of Palladius and associate Patrick the Briton with the beginnings of Christianity in Ireland.
- O'Rahilly believes that Palladius is the Sen Phátric figure and that the 461 death date belongs to him.
- O'Rahilly's chronology would thus be:

  431–461 for the mission of Palladius

  461–492/3 for the mission of Patrick

  O'Rahilly takes these annalistic dates to be approximate.
- Not all scholars agree that Palladius was the Sen Phátric or that O'Rahilly's chronology is accurate.
- The 432–461 dating for the mission of Patrick is still strongly held.

The strengths

- If we accept O'Rahilly's theory, then it allows us to accept both death dates given in the annals.
- It also sheds light on the figure of Sen Phátric, referred to in so many early Irish sources.
- It offers an explanation for the comment in the notes to Tírechán's *Brief Account* that Palladius was also known as Patricius, which is the earliest evidence we have of the existence of two Patricks.
- It would furthermore explain the implication in Prosper's reference in AD434 that Palladius' mission was ongoing and successful.

The criticisms

- Carney, of course, would dispute O'Rahilly's identification of Palladius with 'the elder Patrick', because as we have seen he believes Palladius to have laboured in Scotland rather than Ireland.
- Nonetheless, it is a weakness of O'Rahilly's theory, that if Palladius did minister to the Irish for thirty years, that the unassuming Patrick the Briton did not mention him. Murphy replies that Patrick did not even mention those who assisted him in his own mission, much less a predecessor and anyhow "a man writing under deep emotional strain to defend himself against unjust accusations, is unlikely to find time for tributes to others."[50] It could be of course, that *Confessio* 51 is such a reference to Palladius.
- Ryan's objections are more credible. He points out that Palladius is very much associated with Auxilius and Iserninus. Why then did they not become his successors, or if not, another Gaulish bishop? If Palladius had a long mission of thirty years, it does seem odd that an unknown Briton would have become successor to him.
- We could also assume that had Palladius' mission lasted thirty years, his work would have involved, as Patrick's did, the ordination of native clergy. If so, it raises the question of why a native Irish bishop could not have become his successor.
- Christine Mohrmann, commenting on the Latin of Patrick, makes the following observation on an earlier mission to the Irish:

  "If Patrick had found in Ireland a Christian Latin tradition, then he could and would have drawn on it; he would not have been so helpless in the way that he expresses himself in Latin ... after thirty years of Continental missionaries... there would certainly have been an established Latin tradition... everything in Patrick's Latin points to a beginning and to isolation."[51]

• Hanson is critical of O'Rahilly's chronology. He believes its major weakness to be that "it discounts internal evidence about him in favour of later tradition … it is not supported by any evidence in Patrick's writings … and rests on a hypothesis, [that much attributed to Patrick happened in fact to Palladius] which can only be called farfetched…".[52]

Even when taking into account the weaknesses within the Two Patricks Theory, Binchy believes that O'Rahilly's suggestion "is the least improbable of the theories which at present hold the field."[53] He believes that within it, "most of the chronological and biographical difficulties … will resolve themselves."[54] It is possible though, as Binchy believes, that the Two Patricks Theory illustrates the truth that the evangelisation of Ireland was the work, not of one glorious national apostle but of two or even three missionary figures.

 TASK

Think about and discuss:

Do you think the Two Patricks controversy lessens the respect due to Saint Patrick, the national Apostle of Ireland? Give reasons.

 PRACTICE ESSAY TITLE

a) **Explain and consider the relationship between Patrick and Palladius. (30)**

In your answer you may make reference to some of the following:
• Prosper
• The annalistic evidence
• *Fiacc's Hymn, Stowe Missal, Martyrology of Oengus*
• Tírechán's memoirs
• Sen Phátric
• Patrick's contemporaries
• The views of scholars

b) **Critically assess the view that the Two Patricks Theory solves the 'puzzle' of Patrick. (20)**

In your answer you may refer to some of the following:
• The dating of Patrick
• The geography of Patrick
• The views of Carney, Esposito, Bieler, Bury and Mohrmann
• The strengths and weaknesses of the theory

5. OTHER TEXTS ATTRIBUTED TO PATRICK

Introduction

We know for certain that Patrick the Briton penned two texts sometime in the fifth century. No serious challenge has been mounted as to the authenticity of these texts.

The question has been raised as to whether Patrick wrote anything else. He may well have done. We do know, for example, that he wrote two letters to Coroticus; we only possess the second of these. Some scholars argue that his style is so awkward and his confidence in his own writing ability so low, that it is unlikely that he would have written more than these.

Nonetheless, other documents exist which have been attributed to Patrick. The questions are:

> Are they actually from the pen of Patrick?
>
> If not, why would his name be added?
>
> What do they tell us?
>
> Are they historically valuable to us?

The First Synod of Patrick

What is it?

The First Synod of Patrick is a circular letter written to the clergy of Ireland concerning ecclesiastical organisation and the discipline of clergy. It contains thirty four canons in all, seventeen of which deal with clerical discipline, although mainly in terms of regulation and instruction rather than as penance. For example, clergy are told to reside in their own diocese, and not to accept alms from pagans. Sometimes it is referred to as a 'circular.' It is introduced in the words: *"Here begins the synod of the bishops, namely, Patricius, Auxilius and Iserninus."*

Did Patrick write them?

The views of scholars differ on the authorship of these canons. Hadden and Stubbs argue that they cannot be Patrician and believe that they were written as late as the eighth century.[55] They reached this conclusion having analysed canon 33, which states that clergy travelling from Britain without full letters of recommendation will not be allowed to minister in the Irish Church. They believe that this was most likely to be written at a time when the Irish Church had become estranged from the British Church and that this was in the eighth century.

J T McNeill disagrees with this interpretation, instead taking the canon to mean that all travelling British clergy with the proper accreditation would be welcomed in Ireland.[56] He also argues that, where there are penitential canons,[57] these are of a period earlier than the main body of the Celtic penitential texts, because they do not emphasise the privacy of reconciliation nor do they contain any references to compensation or commutation, both of which are features of the later penitential texts.

Bury argues that the canons were accepted very early on as the work of Patrick and he tends to agree that they are authentically Patrician.[58] He believes that the canons were promulgated at a Synod in Leinster by Patrick and his co-authors – who were either already or afterwards to become bishops. Kenney agrees that "as a whole it has every appearance of being what it purports to be."[59]

Bieler also accepts the canons to be the authentic work of Patrick, with some later additions to the main text.[60] Kenney believes that the likelihood of later interpolation was great but that "the character of the major part of the text would not thereby be impugned."[61] Bieler puts forward the following reasons for his view:

- Church life has not yet settled into a pattern of routine and the basic duties of clergy have to be clarified to them, in the manner of 'stating the obvious'; for example, *"a deacon must not absent himself without the permission of his priest; each lector ought to make sure in which Church he is to sing ... bishops must consecrate newly built churches before offering Mass in them for the first time."*

- The references to paganism suggest an infant church very much in the making; for example, Christians are told that *"no offering is to be accepted from pagans."*

- The Church for which it legislates is diocesan, which Bieler argues was no longer the case in the sixth century.

- Some of the formulae used are comparative to the acts of councils and synods held in fifth century Gaul, and are not found in any of the later Celtic penitentials. In fact, where a penance is laid down for a serious breach of discipline in these canons, it is the penance of excommunication, which was the practice of the ancient Church. This supports a fifth century rather than a later dating.

Bieler believes that the canons were drawn up in 439 and 459 at a meeting with Patrick and missionaries in the south of Ireland to discuss what attempts could be made to pool their efforts. They also intended to set out clearly the status of bishop and the appropriate relationship between clergy and their bishop.

Disputing Patrician authorship

Christine Mohrmann disputes that the Circular Letter (*First Synod*) could possibly contain the words of Patrick, based on the style of Latin used.[62] Nonetheless, Bieler explains the difference in style between these and the *Confessio* and *Letter to Coroticus* by arguing that they were written by Auxilius and Iserninus and then approved by Patrick, for wider use.[63]

Hanson believes that because Patrick makes no mention of other bishops in Ireland at the time, it is highly unlikely that there would have been a Synod of bishops at this time. Furthermore, he argues that the material in *The First Synod* reflects that the clergy had been slotted into complex Irish society – a situation at odds with the one Patrick suggests where he clearly perceived himself, and was presumably then treated, as an outcast.[64]

Daniel Binchy initially believed the canons of *The First Synod of Patrick* to have been compiled in the seventh century.[65] He argues that it is clear that Patrick worked completely alone and had he known of the work of Iserninus and Auxilius, it would not have been his style to pass it over without comment. Convinced by the arguments of Kathleen Hughes,[66] he later accepted a dating of the second half of the sixth century.[67] Both of these historians then, clearly dispute Patrician authorship of these canons.

Hughes, followed by Binchy, suggests the following as reasons for a dating of the second half of the sixth century:

- The Church depicted in the canons is much too well organised to be a first generation missionary Church. For example, the Church is already formed into dioceses, whose boundaries are clearly defined; within each diocese there are smaller subordinate churches with priests in charge of them, while churches are being built and consecrated under the authority of bishops.

- Formal monasticism exists, and has moved beyond the individual practice of asceticism as described by Patrick in the *Confessio*. Monks live under the rule of an abbot and are not to travel without his permission.

- Paganism is still prevalent, which negates a later date of the seventh century and beyond, as formerly suggested by Binchy, Hadden and Stubbs. We are told that Christians are not to accept alms from pagans, and that pagans swear before their own diviners. Belief in vampires, witches and various forms of magic is also denounced.

- The canons also imply that by secular law, clergy are recognised as being among the noble grades of society because they are, according to Canon 8, to act like the "paying surety" who is usually a lay person. Binchy believes this type of surety was only introduced after Christianity had arrived and been established.[68] The integration of the clergy into the noble grades of society happened later, not in the missionary Patrician Church.

- Christians are told to avoid the secular law courts in the settlement of disputes, whereas in the seventh century provision is made for Christians in secular law and there is also much more adjustment of secular law to accommodate the Church.

- The Church is a diocesan one rather than a monastic one as was the case in the seventh century, but had not yet fully occurred in the sixth.

- The canons tell us that the ministry of British clergy was being rejected, which would be unusual if it were an infant missionary church with a likely shortage of clergy.

Liam de Paor argues that the "attribution to Patrick, Auxilius and Iserninus cannot be taken at face value [because the document] appears to incorporate, rather repetitiously statutes from several synods or councils."[69] On this basis, he believes it to be no earlier than the seventh century.

Patrick Corish[70] has no problem with a fifth century dating for the canons, but does not accept Patrician authorship. Like Mohrmann, Corish disputes that the quality of the Latin can be identified with the writer of the *Confessio* and the *Letter to Coroticus*. The content is also markedly different from that of Patrick's two previous writings. Like Binchy, he asserts that, "Patrick is his own man. He does not share authority. There is no mention of other bishops."[71] The world of the Church in this document is different from the one portrayed in Patrick's writings. While Patrick is clearly evangelising, this document is organising. Patrick mentions numerous converts but does not tell us of any structure in place for them.

Corish does accept that they could well be the work of Auxilius and Iserninus. These clerics are associated with Kilashee in North Leinster and Aghade, near Tullow in the South, around the middle of the fifth century. Corish believes that they were sent from Gaul, and that they may have been contemporaries of Patrick but working independently of him. Patrick in the *Confessio* is very much the bishop, and in the *Letter* he does not share his authority with any others.

Corish agrees with Kathleen Hughes that the contents of the canons reflect a second generation Church, probably that originally formed as part of the mission of Palladius. He believes that Auxilius and Iserninus succeeded Secundinus as clerics of the church in Leinster, thus making that church a second generation Christian Church in the fifth century.

 TASK

Can you think of any reasons for the addition of Patrick's name to documents that he may not have written?

The historical value

At its very least, *The First Synod of Patrick* is a record of the very earliest days of the Church in Ireland, and as such is a remarkably useful document.

Bieler believes that if we accept this document as authentic, as he does, then it adds to the information that we already have in the *Confessio*.[72] In *Confessio* 51, Patrick makes a possible allusion to other sacramental ministries.[73] Could this be a reference to the ministries of Auxilius and Iserninus? If we accept it as being from the fifth century then it points to the existence of a number of bishops, each with jurisdiction in his diocese but not in the dioceses of other bishops.

The First Synod of Patrick also give us some insight into the particular circumstances of the Irish Church at the time, for example:

- the continued fight against paganism and the code of conduct expected of a Christian in all dealings with pagans;
- the fight against liberating captives by force rather than with ransom[74];
- the difficulty in organising the Church along Continental lines, that is, the idea of attaching a bishop to a particular diocese;
- that married clergy were recognised.

It tells us that there was interaction between British clergy and the Irish Church in the fifth and sixth centuries. It is also possible from the evidence of *The First Synod* that British clerical refugees were fleeing from the barbarian invasions on Britain and sought refuge in Ireland, and that guidelines had to be laid down for their conduct.

Summary

- There can be no conclusive proof that *The First Synod of Patrick* was co-written by him in the fifth century.
- Established Patrician scholars, such as Bury and Bieler, accept Patrick's authorship, but only when they exclude so many later 'interpolations' as to discredit them as a fifth century source, in the view of Dumville.[75]
- Corish accepts it as a fifth century document drawn up by Auxilius and Iserninus for the second generation Leinster church. He believes Patrick's name was later added.
- Hughes and Binchy believe it was neither written by Patrick, nor written in the fifth century, proposing instead a sixth century dating. Hadden and Stubbs believe it to be eighth century while de Paor accepts a seventh century dating.
- Mohrmann, an expert on ecclesiastical Latin, does not believe it could have been written by the same person who wrote the *Letter* and *Confessio*.
- Even if we do not accept Patrician authorship, it is still a document of great historical importance.

The Dicta Patricii (The Three Sayings of Patrick)

The Three Sayings of Patrick are found as a Prefix to the *Collection of Tírechán* in the *Book of Armagh*.

- The First Dictum or Saying reads:

"The fear of God I had as my guide through Gaul and Italy and the islands of the Tyrrhene Sea."

- The Second Dictum states:

"From the world you have gone to Paradise, thanks be to God."

• The Third Dictum states:

"Church of the Irish, nay of the Romans, in order that you be Christians as are the Romans, you must sing in your Churches at every hour of prayer that praiseworthy utterance: Kyrie eleison, Christe eleison. Let every Church that follows me sing: Kyrie eleison, Christe Eleison, Deo gratias."

Tírechán used as a source the *Book of Ultán,*[75a] in which he found the first saying. The *Book of Ultán* contained some truth no doubt, but also some legendary material. By the seventh century the Three Sayings were accepted as being Patrician.

The Authorship of the First Saying

Historically speaking, the First Saying is probably the most important and if written by Patrick would suggest evidence of his Continental training, which is by no means agreed by all scholars.

Bieler accepts the First Saying as genuine, given that there is no real case against it.[76] He cites that the language is quite similar to that used by Patrick in the *Confessio*. He does, however, accept the possibility that the words could be a later imitation of Patrick's style.

Binchy is of the view that the Saying could not be considered genuine because, "scholars now reject the whole story of Patrick's sojourn in Lérins".[77]

Bieler holds that the saying does not specifically refer to Lérins or any other area in the Tyrrhene Sea, nor does it suggest any prolonged stay on any of the Tyrrhene islands. Bieler appears to be arguing that whether or not one believes that Patrick did spend any significant length of time in this area, the argument surrounding this issue is a separate one, and should not affect our judgement of this Saying as genuine. He does accept that Patrick did train on the Continent under Germanus and when there, may well have visited Lérins and other holy places. Bieler, Mohrmann and Joseph Duffy all accept that Patrick's Latin was Continental in style.

Hanson does not accept that this First Saying is authentic, arguing that it "does not recall either Patrick's style or vocabulary".[78] He dates the Saying to some time in the seventh century.

There is no consensus of opinion on the authenticity of this Saying.

The authorship of the Second Saying

The Second Saying is to be found in the *Letter to Coroticus* and the term "thanks be to God" was one frequently used by Patrick. The authenticity of this Saying then is not in question, but it is of little historical use as it tells us nothing new either about Patrick or the period we study.

The authorship of the Third Saying

Many scholars, including Hanson, reject the idea that Patrick could have written these words. Certainly they are not reminiscent of the language and tone of either the *Confessio* or the *Letter*. In the *Letter* and the *Confessio*, Patrick very much sees himself as working and living among a barbarian people and seems to frequently differentiate his own, more civilised Roman identity from the barbarous identity of those among whom he works. Some argue, therefore, that he would not have addressed the Irish Christians as "Romans". He is clear in the *Letter* that *"they despise us because we are Irish."*

Bieler, however, is not so sure that the Third Saying can be dismissed so easily. He believes that it is clear from the *Letter* and the *Confessio* that Patrick sees Roman and Christian as being one and the same thing. In this sense then, once the Irish had become Christian, they also had assumed the status of being Roman and civilised.[79]

Binchy, however, raises questions about the use of the Kyrie prayer, arguing that it was introduced into the Church for the first time by Pope Galasius (492–496), about thirty years after the 'official' death of Patrick.[80] Bieler believes it may have been current in the Jerusalem Church and had been brought back by pilgrims in the early fifth century.

The reference to *Christe Eleison* is generally taken to have been introduced much later by Pope Gregory the Great. There is no use of the Kyrie prayer in Patrick's writings.

Considering the late date of *Christe Eleison* and the exhortation to the Irish to be like the Romans, this 'Saying' may have been attributed to Patrick in the seventh century, perhaps after, or around the time of the Paschal Controversy, to encourage the Celtic Christians to assume more Roman practices. It would be useful in this regard to attach the name of Patrick to the plea.

The Lorica or 'Breastplate of Saint Patrick' is familiar to millions of Christians of all denominations world wide. It is a morning prayer calling on the protection of the Holy Trinity against all kinds of evil.

It is written in a variant of the ancient Irish language which, linguistic experts are certain, was not in use until some centuries after Patrick's death.

The first time its recitation is mentioned is the eleventh century. Muirchú, writing in the seventh century, does not mention it, nor does the ninth century tripartite *Life of Patrick*.

Summary

- The Three Sayings were being attributed to Patrick by the mid-seventh century.
- The Second Saying is taken from the *Letter to Coroticus* (with minor changes) and is of very limited historical value.
- The First and Second Sayings generate the most scholarly debate.
- The First is historically very important as it may suggest evidence for Patrick's Continental training. (See also p179 on the historical Patrick.)
- Bieler believes the First might well be genuine, although accepts there may be some doubt about its authenticity.
- Hanson rejects the First Saying on the basis of its un-Patrician language.
- Binchy also discounts it as Patrick's.
- Binchy and Hanson reject the Third Saying. The exhortation seems to be more like the Romans, hinting at a seventh century dating as is suggested by Hanson.

 PRACTICE ESSAY TITLE

a) Identify and consider the issues involved in the authorship of *The First Synod of Patrick* and the Dicta Patricii. (30)

In your answer you may refer to some of the following:
- A definition of *The First Synod of Patrick*/Three Sayings
- Style of writing and language
- References to monasticism
- References to church organisation
- Views of scholars
- Possible reasons for the addition of Patrick's signature
- Gaul/Lérins
- The Kyrie Prayer

b) Critically evaluate the claim that these writings add no value to a study of Patrick. (20)

In your answer you may refer to some of the following:
- Debate surrounding Patrick's education
- Other bishops in Ireland at the time of Patrick
- Patrick as an administrator and organiser
- The value of the *Letter* and *Confessio* as a source on Patrick

↻ SUMMARY

The 'historical' Patrick is usually taken to refer to Patrick in time and place.

⬇

The Patrick puzzle has two dimensions: his dates and his geography.

⬇

Patrick's writings give us no dates and only three place names: Bannavem Taburniae, Silva Focluti, and Gaul.

⬇

Numerous attempts have been made to locate Bannavem Taburniae, with suggestions ranging from Daventry, the West Country, and Carlisle.

⬇

Silva Focluti may be the place of Patrick's captivity in Ireland. Some believe it to be Slemish, others accept County Mayo and dismiss Slemish as part of the Armagh legend.

⬇

Scholars are divided on whether Patrick had his ecclesiastical training on the Continent. Some accept that this is where his 'missing years' were spent.

⬇

Difficulties arise when dating the historical Patrick. Some use inferences in his writings to establish the date of the mission. External evidence suggests two death dates to add to the confusion.

⬇

O'Rahilly's Two Patricks Theory may provide a possible explanation for these and solve problems caused by references to, for example, an older and younger Patrick.

⬇

Some other texts produced around the period have been attributed to Patrick. Scholars differ as to their authenticity.

⬇

The First Synod of Patrick is an historically important document but adds little to our knowledge of Patrick except to suggest that he may not have been alone in his mission to the Irish. The First Saying may be historically important because if authentic, it suggests a Continental training for Patrick.

⬇

Any discussion on the historical Patrick means dealing in uncertainties. Although historians strongly believe in the chronology they present, it is probably not possible to be certain about much that happened in the fifth century.

Endnotes

1 Kenney, J, *The Sources for the Early History of Ireland* op cit, p160

2 O'Rahilly, T, *The Two Patricks: A Lecture on the History of Christianity in Fifth century Ireland*, Dublin Institute for Advanced Studies, Dublin 1942, p30

3 Binchy, D, *Patrick and His Biographers: Ancient and Modern, op cit*, pp8–9

4 Thomas, *Christianity in Roman Britain to AD500, op cit*, p310

5 *ibid*, pp310–314. Most of the arguments concerning the location of Bannavem Taburniae are taken from the summary given by Thomas in these pages.

6 *ibid*, p23

7 Hanson, *Life and Writings, op cit*, p26

8 Mohrmann, *The Latin of Saint Patrick, op cit*, pp20 &23

9 Bieler, *Life and Legend, op cit*, p59

10 *ibid*

11 *Ibid*, p27

12 Art. Cit. (ed) *The Problem of 'Silva Focluti'* in Irish Historical Studies 1943

13 *ibid*

14 See Chapter 1: The Social and Political conditions in Ireland before the mission of Patrick

15 Binchy, *Patrick and His Biographers, op cit*, p82

16 Carney, *The Problem of Patrick, op cit*, p66

17 O'Rahilly, *The Two Patricks: A Lecture on the History of Christianity in Fifth century Ireland, op cit*, p42

18 Mohrmann, *The Latin of Patrick, op cit*, p54

19 Hanson, *Life and Writings, op cit*, p42

20 Jackson, *Language and History, op cit*, pp80–94

21 Herron, *Sages, Saints and Story tellers*, ed D Corráin, *op cit*, pp76–85

22 Duffy, *Patrick in his own words, op cit*, p42

23 These excerpts are taken from De Paor, L, *Saint Patrick's World*, 1993

24 The slight divergence in dates between the various annals is common. It is accepted by most scholars that it arose when different methods of computing dates were used. For our purposes 457 might well be equated with 461.

25 Healy, J, *The Life and Writings of Saint Patrick*, Dublin, 1905

26 Bury, *The Life of Patrick and His Place in History, op cit*

27 Hanson, *Saint Patrick His Origins and Career, op cit*; and *The Life and Writings of the Historical Saint Patrick*, 1983

28 Hanson, *Life and Writings, op cit*, p21

29 *ibid*, p23

30 *ibid*, p25

31 Mohrmann, *The Latin of St Patrick, op cit*, p54

32 Thomas, *Christianity in Roman Britain, op cit*, p319

33 Dolley, M, *Roman Coins from Ireland and the date of Patrick*, Proc Royal Irish Academy, 1976, pp181–190

34 Thomas, *Christianity in Roman Britain, op cit*, p345

35 Carney, *The Problem of Saint Patrick, op cit*

36 Esposito, M, *The Patrician Problem and a Possible Solution*, HIS X, 1956, p131–155

37 O'Rahilly, *The Two Patricks: A Lecture on the History of Christianity in the Fifth Century, op cit*

38 *ibid*, pp5–6

39 Sharpe, R, (trans and ed), *Adomnán's Life of Colmcille*, Penguin Classics

40 Annalistic references are taken from De Paor, L, *Saint Patrick's World, op cit*

41 O'Rahilly, *The Two Patricks Lecture, op cit*, p7

42 Binchy in *Patrick and His Biographers Ancient and Modern* (*op cit*) for example, questions the reliability of annalistic evidence.

43 O'Rahilly, *The Two Patricks Lecture, op cit*, p7

44 Binchy, *Patrick and His Biographers, op cit*, p112

45 Bury, *The Life of Patrick and his Place in History, op cit*

46 Binchy, *Patrick and His Biographers, op cit*, p125

47 Fr Shaw's interpretation is cited in Binchy, *Patrick and His Biographers*, pp116–122

48 *ibid*, p126

49 O'Rahilly, *The Two Patricks Lecture, op cit*, p9

50 *Ibid*, cited on p145

51 Mohrmann, *Latin of St Patrick, op cit*, p54

52 Hanson, *Life and Writings, op cit*, p25

53 *ibid*, p143

54 *ibid*, p156

55 Hadden & Stubbs, *Councils and Ecclesiastical documents relating to Great Britain and Ireland* 11, London 1878, pp328–331

56 McNeill, *Celtic Penitentials*, ACLS History E-Book Reprints, 1923, p26

57 Canons 1, 6, 14, 15, 19, 21, 22, 26, 27, 32

58 Bury, *The Life of Saint Patrick*, p168 & p236ff

59 Kenney, J, *The Sources for the Early History of Ireland, op cit*, p169

60 Bieler rejects canons 8, 11, 14, 15 on grounds of language and historical content.

61 *ibid*

62 Mohrmann, *Latin of St Patrick, op cit*, p2

63 Bieler, L, 'St. Patrick and the Coming of Christianity' in *A History of Irish Catholicism*, ed P Corish, Gill & Son, Dublin, 1967, pp16–17, p82

64 Hanson, *Life and Writings, op cit*, p14

65 Studia Hibernica 11, 1962, pp45–49

66 Hughes, *Early Christian Ireland: Introduction to the Sources, op cit*, pp68–70

67 Studia Hibernica, VIII, 1968, p53

68 Binchy, D, 'Celtic Suretyship, a fossilized Indo-European Institution?' in *Indo-European and Indo-Europeans: Papers presented to the Third Indo-European Conference*, 1963, published Philadelphia 1970, pp355–367

69 De Paor, *Saint Patrick's World, op cit*, p135

70 Corish, P, *The Irish Catholic Experience: A Historical Survey*, Gill & Macmillan, Dublin 1984, pp2–3; 'The Christian Mission' in *A History of Irish Catholicism*, Gill & Macmillan Ltd, 1971, pp2–3

71 *ibid*

72 *ibid*, p83

73 See Chapter 2 of this book.

74 Identified by Bieler, *St Patrick and the Coming of Christianity, op cit*, p89

75 Dumville, D, (ed), *St. Patrick AD493–1993*, The Boydell Press, Suffolk, 1993, p175

75a Ultán was Tírechán's master.

76 Bieler, 'St Patrick and the Coming of Christianity', in *A History of Irish Catholicism, op cit*, pp10–15

77 Binchy, *op cit*, p43

78 Hanson, *Saint Patrick: His Origins and Career*, Clarendon Press, Oxford, 1968, p36

79 *ibid*, p13

80 Binchy, *op cit*, p43

The Development Of Celtic Monasticism

Chapter 7

LEARNING OUTCOMES

Knowledge, understanding and evaluation of:

— the nature of episcopacy

— monastic spirituality

— the characteristics of the Celtic Church

---

1. THE NATURE OF EPISCOPACY

Introduction

The term episcopacy comes from the Greek word *episkopos* which literally translated means 'overseer'. However, in a religious context it refers to a form of church government that is hierarchical and where bishops have authority over dioceses and the priests who work in the parishes within those dioceses. It is generally believed that such authority comes directly from the authority that Christ gave to his apostles. The term given to this is Apostolic Succession, and until the Reformation, episcopacy was the main form of government in the Christian Church.

There are central questions regarding the nature of episcopacy, which we need to address:

- What was the nature of episcopacy from the beginnings of the Celtic Church?

- What evidence is there to suggest that the organisation of the Celtic Church changed?

- What reasons can be suggested for that change?

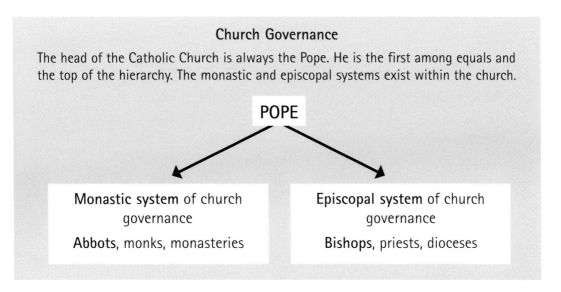

Church Governance

The head of the Catholic Church is always the Pope. He is the first among equals and the top of the hierarchy. The monastic and episcopal systems exist within the church.

POPE

Monastic system of church governance

Abbots, monks, monasteries

Episcopal system of church governance

Bishops, priests, dioceses

Although the term 'episcopacy' might be a new one to you, we already know quite a lot about the nature of episcopacy in the Celtic Church.

Patrick, in the view of Hanson, had a very high sense of the authority of his office as bishop.[1] In the *Letter to Coroticus,* Patrick declares most solemnly his status as bishop to the Irish.[2] He uses the full weight of the authority of the office of bishop to denounce the actions of Coroticus and his men and to excommunicate them. He himself speaks of ordaining a native clergy[3] and in the *Letter,* he refers to *"a presbyter I have known from childhood."*[4]

He speaks most highly of the ascetic life in his *Confessio* and indeed encourages his converts to embrace it. There is no evidence, however, that these ascetic practices were in any way organised into a formal structure, and as we have seen, the *"monks and virgins for Christ"* of whom he speaks with so much pride were probably individuals practising asceticism privately in their own homes.[5] Patrick did not establish monasteries.

The First Synod of Patrick, whether we accept a fifth, sixth or seventh century dating, legislates for a church governed by bishops who resided in dioceses, the boundaries of which were clearly defined.

The earliest sources written about Patrick also suggest an episcopal Church. Tírechán claims that Patrick consecrated 450 bishops but only names forty two.[6] Patrick himself does not mention the consecration of any bishops, but if he did, as Tírechán suggests, ordain native bishops, then these bishops must have been in charge of very small territories and so could not have been very powerful figures. Neither Muirchú or Tírechán give us much information about monks or monasteries. Tírechán indeed frequently refers to bishops when speaking of religious figures. When a kind man saves Patrick from a plot to kill him, Patrick prophesies in reward, *"there shall be bishops and priests of thy race"*. In other places the prediction was made: *"there shall be good bishops here"*.[7]

The *Annals of Ulster* tell us that the three bishops, Auxilius, Iserninus and Secundinus, came from the Continent to assist Patrick in AD439.[8] However, it was native bishops, rather than these, who succeeded Patrick.

Patrick certainly would only have been familiar with an episcopal structure of government and would undoubtedly have imposed this on the Irish Church.

Ryan argues that the conclusion we must draw from the earliest sources is that "the tradition they enshrine is strongly clerical and Episcopal as distinct from monastic".[9]

The eighth century *Catalogus* refer to all of the First Order of Irish saints as being bishops up until approximately AD544:

> *"The First Order of Catholic Saints was in the time of Patrick; and then they were all bishops, distinguished and holy and full of the Holy Ghost, 350 in number, founders of churches. They had one head, Christ and one chief, Patrick."*[10]

The change from episcopal to monastic organisation

Introduction

The form of government in the Celtic Church changed from episcopal to abbatial. This is mainly because the structure of the church changed from episcopal to monastic.

Patrick did found an episcopal Church and the sources suggest that it remained that way for about a century after his death. From around the mid-sixth century the Celtic Church began to depart from the structure imposed upon it by Patrick; it began to take on a monastic structure. Chadwick believes that "the differences in organisation of the Church conceived by the Patrician writings and that of the monastic church of the sixth century is a fundamental one, even though we must insist that this difference is one of emphasis and organisation, never of belief or spiritual prerogative".[11]

Although Kenney refers to the changes that took place in the Irish Church as "a revolution", the process was probably more gradual than is sometimes suggested and was not complete until later in the eighth century.[12]

What were the reasons for this change?

There is no doubt that monasticism became very popular from the sixth century onwards. Nonetheless, in the view of Kathleen Hughes, "this does not account for the change in constitution". Even if bishops had fully embraced the monastic lifestyle, as many of them had, this still does not explain why the diocesan structure was not retained.[13] The popularity of the monastic lifestyle then does not adequately explain the change in the organisation and structure of the church.

• Absence of cities

The Church that Patrick founded was episcopal in structure because that was the form of organisation found in the Church on the Continent. In the Continental Church, the see of the bishop was in the cities, which then became the administrative centre of that province. In Ireland, because of the absence of cities, the boundaries of the diocese corresponded with that of the *tuath*. In this sense then, though Patrick had established an episcopal Church, the Church in Ireland had never had Roman organisation. So, from the outset, the Irish church would have to evolve in its own way. Chadwick agrees, "that the rapidity with which [monasticism] spread and gained complete predominance must have been largely due to the fact that there had never been a Roman occupation".[14]

• A dual legacy

Chadwick also suggests that because of the growing popularity of monasticism, Patrick may have had some difficulty in establishing a strong episcopal structure in the Irish Church as "that form of church government was in the fifth century felt to be old-fashioned, and somewhat out-moded and was losing prestige before the spread of monasticism and asceticism."[15] Ó Cróinín argues that the Irish Church inherited "a dual legacy" from the Church on the Continent as a church governed by bishops who had considerable sympathy with the monastic lifestyle as a means of attaining holiness. Many of these bishops may even have had monastic training.[16] The process of 'transformation' from episcopal to monastic structure need not "have been as traumatic as some have supposed".[17]

Sheehy agrees that early missionaries who came from Gaul to Ireland brought with them a system of church organisation whereby monks and clerics lived a similar lifestyle.[18]

• Clerical families

John Ryan agrees that from the very beginning the larger episcopal settlements were organised in a way that closely resembled monasteries. Indeed, "in prominent foundations like Armagh, Trim and Sletty, the clergy lived under their bishop ... [They] thus became by force of circumstances, a religious family in which the bishop was princeps or head".[19] Although these were not monasteries in 'externals', they would have differed little from monasteries.[20] Ryan believes that this would have meant that "the transition to formal monasticism would be very easy".[21] Because prominent churches like Armagh clearly held monastic practices and virtues in such high esteem, the monastic structure could "sweep the country unchecked".[22] Even Patrick's 'own church', Armagh, did not insist on episcopal government.

Rapid and uniform changes?

Kathleen Hughes warns against oversimplifying the changes in the government of the early Irish Church, "which were neither rapid or so uniform".[23] She argues that the diocesan Church was never, in the seventh century, completely replaced by a monastic one, and that bishops remained important. The transition was however, more or less complete by the eighth century. She offers the following reasons for the change in structure[24]:

- The native Irish idea of kin. The Irish word for 'abbot' was *comarba* which means 'heir.' Abbots of monasteries were quite literally 'heirs' of the founder and generally belonged to the same family dynasty. In the case of Iona, all abbots up to AD724, with the exception of the sixth and the tenth century abbots, belonged to the Uí Néill. Secular law seems to suggest that if an heir could not be found from among the founder's family group, then he must come from the family of those who donated the monastic land; if that search failed he must then come from the family of the *manaig* (the monastic tenants).

  'Kin' or family was the basic group in Celtic society. Land stayed within the family, passing down the male line.

  Hughes accepts, however, that the same law of inheritance could equally apply to diocese and bishop.

  Abbots were celibate, so it was not their sons who would have become their heirs. It was probably their nephews or more distant relations who inherited the abbacy.

- The native institution of kingship also influenced the development of monasticism. The head of a great monastic paruchiae was like an over-king. In the seventh century the Uí Néill had established a confederation of *tuatha*. Monasteries too established such confederations of subject monasteries, all connected to the same founder.

  An over-king could represent a number of *tuatha* which had joined together to form an alliance. Tribute was paid to the over-king.

  In these ways monasteries adapted themselves to Irish secular practices and so were well suited to the nature of Irish society at the time.

- If families were very enthusiastic about the ascetical lifestyle, they could and did endow the monasteries, donating the family land to an existing monastery or turning land over for the building of a new monastery. The ownership of land was well protected by Irish law. Inheritance of land within the family could not be compromised. The land must stay within the family. It could not be given outside the family unless consent was obtained from the whole kin group. In some cases whole families did join the monasteries, donating their land.

  These families could then become *manaig*. Sometimes smaller churches also sought to merge with more powerful ones and so they too turned over their estate. On the other hand, Hughes notes that prominent ecclesiastical churches were always located very close to pagan sanctuaries. She believes that these were financially supported by funds which had been used for the upkeep of the pagan sanctuaries. In this way then, the episcopal churches were funded by a limited estate, while the monasteries had "unlimited powers of expansion".[25]

According to the *Life of Saint Samson*, his family gave their land for the building of his monastery. Samson's father said: *"Let not only me and you, as is fitting and proper serve God, but let us link together all our children in the service of God, and let all that is ours become wholly God's."*

Plague

Liam de Paor suggests that the episcopal Church in Ireland had very close connections with the Church on the Continent, and that during the 540s, Europe had been badly contaminated by plague. The small Irish episcopal churches also succumbed to the plague and were wiped out.[26] Monasteries were semi-closed institutions and so were to a large degree protected from infection. This theory may explain the demise of the episcopal Church but does not fully account for the rise of monastic dynasties.

A haphazard development

A more radical view suggests that there was really no organisation to speak of in the early Celtic Church. Sharpe is of the view that "there is no evidence pointing to a clearly defined hierarchical structure ... in short no evidence that the growth of the church or its organisation were the subject of any form of control".[27] This view is not supported, however, by the evidence we have of the various church synods. These were convened discuss various matters of ecclesiastical discipline, for example, *The First Synod of Patrick*, or indeed the Synod of Teltown (c 563) at which the excommunication of Colmcille was discussed.

Summary

- There was a change in the structure, organisation and government of the Celtic Church from the mid-sixth to the eighth century.
- There was no structure in which to build an episcopal Church in Celtic Ireland.
- Patrick himself clearly encouraged the monastic ideal, which in turn may have influenced the larger episcopal churches to gather communities of clerics around them and devote themselves to ascetic practices.
- Monasteries modelled themselves on the secular customs and practices of kin and kingship.
- Monastic paruchiae had access to greater resources than the episcopal Church. Monasticism grew in stature and popularity due to the generosity of its

benefactors; kings often donated huge expanses of land and lent their support to a particular monastery.

- Episcopal churches on the other hand, were only able to rely on the resources of the 'geographically defined diocese' in which their see was situated.
- The Christian Church, if it were to survive in Ireland would have to adapt itself to a very new type of environment and in this sense the monastic structure adopted by the Church in Ireland at that time became "an Irish solution to an Irish problem."[28]
- It was this unique form and structure that came to be referred to as 'the Celtic Church'.

 PRACTICE ESSAY TITLE

a) Analyse and discuss the nature of episcopacy in the Celtic Church. (30)

Your answer could include reference to some of the following:
- The Church founded by Patrick
- Evidence from annals and *Catalogus*
- Abbot/bishops
- Monastic paruchiae
- Reasons for the change from episcopal to monastic structure, such as endowment, kinship, kingship
- The views of scholars

Try this one later.

b) Comment critically on the view that the Celtic Church was more innovative than conservative. (20)

Your answer may include reference to some of the following:
- The adoption of a monastic structure
- Penitentials
- Paschal Controversy
- Similarities between Roman and Celtic Christianity
- The views of scholars

The roles of abbot and bishop in the Celtic Church

As we have seen, bishops were the figures in which authority was vested in the Church throughout the Christian world. This was based on the authority Christ invested in the Apostles. The same seems to be true of all the early leaders of the Celtic Church.

Most historians agree with Ryan that "the Episcopal constitution of the Church was observed as a matter of course."[29]

The *Book of Armagh* tells us of the leaders of the Church at Trim, one of the earliest foundations, that "these were all bishops and rulers venerating holy Patrick and his successors."[30] The *Book of Armagh* is generally believed to have been compiled in the eighth century, so for Ryan this means "that not merely during the period ascribed to the First Order of Irish Saints, but thereafter until the eighth century the rulers of the Church at Trim … were all bishops." It would seem that the same was true of other very early, fifth century churches, such as Armagh and Sletty.

The *Annals of Ulster* tells us that all of Patrick's successors at the church of Armagh were bishops up until 547. The prominent churchmen up to around sixty years after the death of Patrick were all bishops:

467	The repose of *bishop* Benignus, Patrick's successor
468	Iserninus the *bishop* dies
481	The repose of Iarlath, third *bishop* of Armagh
490	Cormac, *bishop* of Armagh and successor of Patrick died
512	Dubthach, *bishop* of Armagh died
525	Aillil, *bishop* of Armagh died
547	Dubthach, *abbot* of Armagh dies

These records illustrate a very important change in the leadership of early episcopal churches such as Armagh. From around the middle of the sixth century, the title given to primates in the church was 'abbot' rather than 'bishop'.

The *Book of Leinster* sheds more light on the change. In this source, Cormac, who succeeded Iarlath as leader of the church at Armagh, is recorded as an abbot, not a bishop. Indeed, the term used is *primus abbot* or 'first abbot.' Thereafter in this source, all the leaders of the church of Armagh were recorded under the title of Abbot, even though, in the *Annals of Ulster* the same individuals bear the title bishop.

What does this mean in terms of the government of the Celtic Church at this time?

We can only assume that the leaders of the church at Armagh were abbots as well as bishops and that the titles seem to have been used interchangeably. In one of the oldest churches in Ireland then, the ruler was both an abbot and a bishop. It is important to note though, that there was never an instance in the case of Armagh, where the leader of that church was an abbot but not a bishop. It would seem that the bishops in that church added monastic duties to their episcopal ones and came to rule over their church as an abbot would his community, while at the same time retaining his episcopal title.

John Ryan believes that around the time of the reign of Cormac, the church of Armagh re-organised itself along monastic lines.[31] Thus at Armagh, the form of government was both episcopal and abbatial from around the mid-sixth century. He emphasises that the ruler of the church at Armagh was always a bishop, even if he also used the title abbot. Kathleen Hughes agrees that at least up to the early eighth century, Armagh was governed by a bishop. However, she argues that "by 800, men thought of the rulers of Armagh as abbots even though they might still be occasionally in bishops orders, for by this time, the character of the office had changed."[32] At the church at Fern, Cilléne is recorded as being both bishop and abbot.

Abbatial leaders

In the Celtic Church the government of the Church came to be in the hands of abbots for a certain period of its history. This means that the form of government within the Celtic Church for some of the period which we study was abbatial rather than episcopal.

> Abbatial government generally refers to the authority given to abbots. Abbots General are usually the head of a religious order or congregation. The term Abbot means 'father'.

In other prominent churches, leadership was exercised by people who were not bishops at all. Ryan claims that "the abbatial mode of government was predominant outside of Armagh."[33] Finnian of Clonard was consecrated a bishop, but he ruled as an abbot and it was as an abbot that he became renowned. Other leaders of the period were priests and abbots (presbyter abbots), but not bishops. Ciaran of Clonmacnois, Colmcille, Brendan of Clonfert and Comgall of Bangor are all examples of such abbatial leaders. Bede's *Ecclesiastical History of the English People* tells us of the island of Iona:

> "*This island always has an abbot for its ruler, who is a priest, to whose authority the whole province, including its bishops are subject – an unusual order of things in which they follow the example of their first teacher, [Columba] who was not a bishop, but a priest and monk.*"[34]

The *Catalogus* claims that in the Second Order of Saints after Patrick, there were many presbyter abbots and fewer bishops. In addition, the annals from the mid-sixth century onwards, recording the death of church leaders, record fewer bishops and more abbots. This source shows that abbots and not bishops were perceived to be the rulers of the Church at this time.

More powerful abbots

Abbots could rule over more than one foundation and often had a huge paruchiae under their administration. Paruchiae Colmcille, for example, covered Colmcille's monastic foundations in Ireland as well as Iona, making him and his successors some of the wealthiest abbots of the period. They acted as kind of 'overlords' of all the monastic foundations, which owed allegiance to one founder. This contrasted sharply with the authority of bishop, which as we saw in *The First Synod of Patrick*, could not proceed beyond the boundaries of his own diocese, lest he encroach on the diocese of another bishop. It is easy to see how the abbot became materially more powerful than the bishop.

Chadwick points out that the power base of Irish bishops differed significantly to that of bishops on the Continent; in the Continental churches bishops resided in densely populated urban areas, while in Ireland the office of bishop could never flourish because there was no natural basis for the development of territorial sees.[35]

Independent rulers

Most of the monastic foundations with which we are familiar, are ruled by abbots without interference from bishops. We will see a good example of the independent rule of abbots in the Celtic Church, in the career of Columbanus,[36] who goes ahead with the establishment of his monasteries without first asking the permission of the bishops in whose diocese he was situated. This was because, in the Celtic Church, the bishop did not have any administrative authority over abbots and it was abbots rather than bishops who were in control of the lands and districts covered by that monastery. Often in the texts of the period, the abbot is referred to as *princeps,* indicating his executive functions. The legislation shows that he receives bequests of land, collects burial fees on behalf of the church and had to give his permission before a body could be moved from the monastic burial ground. In this sense, "the abbot was the administrative head of the church".[37]

The authority held by abbots appears to have been recognised by the Pope and other Roman clerics at the time of the Paschal Controversy. The Roman bishops, writing between 605 and 617, address *"the bishops and abbots of Ireland"*. In 640 Pope John IV wrote to the ecclesiastics of Ireland who are in the main, abbots. The wider Church was clearly aware that in the Irish Church, abbots as well as bishops were figures with some authority and had to be consulted. Abbots clearly occupy a prominent position in the public life of the Church.

Role of the bishop

This is not to say that there were actually fewer bishops in the Celtic Church at this time. Presbyter abbots could not confirm or ordain clergy; they could not consecrate churches or bless holy oils for use in the sacraments. Some monasteries then, chose one of the monks to be raised to the rank of bishop and he would then meet the sacramental needs of that monastic community. Ryan points out however, that "the powers [of that monk] would be restricted to the sacred functions".[38] Chadwick believes that sometimes two or three bishops lived in one monastery.[39] The abbot of that community, not the bishop, retained sole authority. Indeed, one story told in Adomnán's *Life of Colmcille* shows that on some occasions, an abbot may intervene in the affairs of the bishop. Adomnán recounts how an abbot persuaded a bishop to ordain a candidate for the priesthood whom the bishop clearly did not think suitable. The bishop, keen to exonerate himself from total responsibility, insisted that the abbot also 'lay hands' on the head of the candidate on whom he reluctantly bestows priestly orders![40]

Bishops then probably had not declined in number, but because they no longer had administrative authority they were not the recognised and recorded leaders of the Church from about the middle of the sixth century. We also have to bear in mind that the annals – the main source for the period – were drawn up in the monasteries and are therefore more likely to record monastic rather than episcopal history. As Ryan observes, the evidence is meagre and had we access to fuller source material we might well find that bishops were more numerous and prominent than at present they appear to be.[41]

The penitentials also shed some light on the nature of episcopacy in the Celtic Church. Corish argues that they show that the pastoral care of the laity was in the hands of non-monastic clergy. For example, Finnian and Columbanus both make it clear that the penitent can only be admitted back to the Eucharist on the decision of a bishop or priest rather than a monk or abbot. In Finnian's Penitential, monks are forbidden to baptise.[42] The bishop and secular clergy then, clearly still retain a role of great importance. Adomnán's *Life of Colmcille* also gives insight into the esteem in which the office of bishop is held. When a bishop from Ireland visited the community at Iona, Colmcille insisted that it would be he, rather than Colmcille himself, who should officiate at the Eucharist.

Special dignity

In civil law the bishop remained more important than the abbot. He had dignity equal to that of king and had a higher honour price than the abbot. The eighth century Rule of Patrick also shows that the bishop remains a figure of authority:

"Every tuath should have a chief bishop to ordain its clergy, to consecrate its churches, to give direction to its chiefs and nobles, and to sanctify and bless their children after baptism. For the tuatha and territory which have no bishops to perform these functions see the law of their faith and belief perish."[43]

Corish argues that the bishop, from earliest times, was perceived as having the fullness of sacramental order and that it is difficult to see how the pre-eminence of the role of bishop could become obscure, no matter what administrative authority had been passed to the abbot.[44]

Summary

- The Church founded by Patrick was an episcopal one divided into dioceses, loosely based on the *tuath*. This is confirmed by Tírechán's *Brief Account*.
- Patrick encouraged the monastic ideal but did not found monasteries or organise the church in a monastic pattern.
- Patrick had a highly defined sense of the authority of the office of bishop.
- Early sources, such as *The First Synod of Patrick*, reflect an episcopal Church.
- From the mid-sixth century onwards, the government of the Celtic Church was in the hands of abbots, according to the annals. Fewer bishops are recorded as positions of authority.
- Some leaders held both the title 'abbot' and 'bishop' but were known as abbots rather then bishops. Bishops do not have authority over abbots.
- Sometimes monks became bishops to meet the sacramental needs of the community.
- Bishops remained important, and had a vital sacramental function.
- In secular law bishops had a higher dignity than abbots.
- Source material is scarce and was drawn up in a monastic setting. The true number of bishops is probably not known to us.
- Abbatial government was unique to the Celtic Church but seems to have been recognised by the Roman Church at the time.

 TASK

Think about and discuss the questions arising from the issue of religious authority today. Your discussion could reflect some of the ideas below. Make notes on your ideas to help you with evaluation questions and synoptic tasks.

> There is no right or wrong or ultimate Truth. There is no 'right' way of doing things. One choice is valid as another.

> All decisions should be based on worldly rather than religious values. Religious values should not influence decisions.

> I don't think religion should or can limit my choices. I am free to choose any lifestyle I desire.

- Find out about *secularism, individualism* and *relativism.* Match each of the statements above to the correct term.
- You might also want to consider the issue of authority within religious

organisations from the perspective of Christian traditions other than your own or within that of other world religions.
- Use what you have found out and the notes from your class discussion to complete the following evaluation task:

Critically evaluate the view that religious authority is still controversial. (20)

2. MONASTIC SPIRITUALITY

 TASK

Return to Chapter 3.
Read again about the nature of monasticism and the daily routine of the Celtic monks.
A lot of what you have already learned will be relevant to this topic.

Spirituality (in the sense which is relevant here) is concerned with matters of the spirit – that part of human beings that is beyond the physical being. It is also associated with deep religious experiences and can be concerned with 'finding the true self', and by becoming free of the ego, which can be perceived as the 'lesser' self.

In turn, monastic spirituality was a complex mix of pragmatism, asceticism and learning. The main features of monastic spirituality are as follows:

Community-centred

Monastic spirituality was community-centred. As we saw in Chapter 3, monasticism focused on withdrawal from the world, but combined this with close involvement in the life of the local community. Esther de Waal argues that "they were rural people, for whom the clan, the tribe and kinship was important; a close knit people who thought of themselves in a corporate way as belonging to one another."[45] Sometimes this was reflected in the site of the monastery itself. Most of the monasteries that were later to become important were situated on major routes. For example, Bangor was situated near the southern coast of Belfast Lough and Clonard was founded on one of the major tributaries of the Boyne. The *Life of Saint Cronán* tells us that he moved his monastery because people could not find him:

"I will not be in a desert place where guests and poor people cannot easily find me, but I will stay here in a public place."[46]

Hines-Berger also points out that: "The Celts seemed to have a natural disposition for community ... life shared together in and around the monastery became the ordinary way in which the Christian life was lived."[47]

TASK

Go back to Chapter 3. Find the different ways in which the monasteries involved themselves in the lives of the local communities in which they were situated. You should include, for example, their spiritual role, their educative role, their role as providers of sanctuary and hospitality.

Ascetic

Monastic spirituality was severely ascetic, much more so in the Celtic Church than elsewhere. As we have seen, fasting, silence, deprivation of sleep were all common features of monastic routine. Breaches of monastic rule were sometimes punishable by lashes and blows. Prayer was intensified by standing *crosfigil* or immersing oneself in cold water for long periods. It was believed that it was the body which led the person to sin and by subjugating it in such a way, spiritual perfection could be achieved.

Learning-centred

Monastic spirituality was learning-centred. Learning for the Celtic monks was a way of centring one's mind on God, and lifting one's mind towards God. For that reason, study of the scriptures was central to monastic learning. The copying of scriptures in vivid colour and ornate decoration was a way of giving glory to God. The Celtic monks also saw the provision of learning as a way of bringing others to know God. For this reason, they welcomed into the heart of their communities those who sought learning, and this learning they gave without charge. In a legend told about Cumméne,[47a] when asked what he would most like for his church he replied:

> *"I should like it full of books, for them to go to students, and to sow God's word in the ears of everyone, so as to bring him to heaven out of the track of the devil."*[48]

Care of the marginalised

Monastic spirituality was particularly concerned with the marginalised. Richard Woods argues that "an outstanding feature of Celtic spirituality concerns its active political character, which is to say, its commitment to social justice ... . Justice and charity were the main hinges of Celtic social action."[49] Through the provision of hospitality, no stranger in need was ever turned away. Provision for the poor was especially important. Brigit's foundation at Kildare became renowned as the City of the Poor, and she reportedly told the king of Leinster:

> *"If I had riches as great as yours, I should happily give them all away to Christ's poor."*

Cogitosus' *Life of Brigit* is filled with tales of just such generosity. Similarly, Aidan of Lindesfarne was also famed for his attitude to the poor.

TASK

Read Chapter 5 to find Bede's recollection of one incident which shows Aidan's care for the poor.

Care for those marginalised was also extended to sinners. As we have seen, the penitentials were an extension of monastic discipline to the laity and it was to the monasteries that the laity often retired to complete their penance. The monasteries also provided the *anamchara* who was a soul friend to the sinner. His role, far from judging, was to 'walk with' the sinner. Connolly agrees that "the minister is viewed above all as the fellow traveller, fellow pilgrim, fellow sufferer ... a companion",[50] "... always conscious of their own sinfulness ... what we might call today 'wounded healers'".[51]

Gender inclusive

Celtic monastic spirituality was also gender inclusive. It would be wrong to assume that they were egalitarian institutions but they were inclusive of women and many women were prominent in the monastic movement itself. Sellner argues that "a ... distinct characteristic of the Celts was their appreciation of women's leadership and gifts."[52]

 TASK

Read Chapter 3 to find examples of the role afforded to women in Celtic monasteries.

Women had a role in liturgy, and the spirituality of the Celtic monks had a sense of the feminine, often referring to Jesus as "the son of Mary". *Fiacc's Hymn* speaks of Patrick's ascension into heaven to be united with "Jesus, son of Mary." The *Life of Saint Senán*, describing a request made to the saint from a woman wishing to join his community, gives insight into the perception of the feminine common in the monastic setting:

> "Christ is no worse than you. Christ came to save women no less than men. He suffered for the sake of women no less than for men. Women have given service and ministry to Christ and his apostles. Women enter the heavenly kingdom no less than men."

There were probably even more monastic foundations established by women than are recorded because women could only have a life interest in land, which upon her death passed back to her family. This would have been the case with many of the women's foundations. Kildare, Killeedy, Clonbroney and Killeavy are the most prominent female foundations of the era; many others no doubt existed but broke up on the death of the saint because of Irish inheritance laws.

Oneness with nature

Oneness with nature was also a central aspect of monastic spirituality. Woods argues that "the monks great scholarly achievements were matched by an equally great love of beauty, especially in nature." Celtic monasteries, as we have seen, were often sited in central locations. Paradoxically, they can also be found in remote places. An examination of some of these sites would suggest that the aim of the founding monks was not only to withdraw from the world but also to withdraw to the solitude of the lonely place with nothing to distract from the beauty of the surroundings. One of the most dramatic of such sites is the one on Skellig Michael, built on a triangle of rock, which rises very sharply out of the sea eight miles off the Waterville Peninsula in County Kerry. Although the peak rises to 715 feet above sea level, in rough or misty weather the monastery would have been completely lost to view from the mainland. Even today, visits to the perfectly preserved site are only possible when the weather permits. The community here must have been a contemplative one, where prayer was inspired by exposure to the raw beauty of all that surrounded them. The Celtic monks appreciated this beauty and serenity, as Thomas O'Loughlin tells us: "this universe has all over it ... the tell-tale signs of something infinitely greater, beyond it, before it and giving it purpose. In each thing there are the footprints of the Creator."[53]

Hines-Berger agrees: "for Celtic Christians God was a key part of all things natural and beautiful."[54]

Other monasteries were also founded in remote places, for example Inishmurray,

Little Skellig (left) and Skellig Michael (right) illustrate the desire of the Celtic monks to seek out the lonely place. *(Photo Norman Johnston)*

The steps to the monastery on Skellig Michael are cut into the rock of the island. *(Photo Norman Johnston)*

four miles off the Sligo coast. As well as the island sanctuary, which seems particularly appealing to the Celtic monk, there were also mountain-top hermitages such as Slieve Donard, and the top of Mount Brandon, the hermitage founded by St Brendan. These monks lived out their response to the call to holiness "near cliff and cloud, within sight of rocks, waves and islands, open to wind and sea".[55] It is important to note that they communed with nature and through that communion communicated with God. Their relationship was oneness with nature rather than exploitation of it.

Poetry written in the monasteries also reflects this spirituality. A poem written about Saint Brigit tells us that she "sat the perch of a bird upon a cliff."[56]

The oneness with nature felt by the monk scribes in the scriptorium is illustrated in this poem scribbled in the margins of a scriptural text:

Over my head the woodland wall
Rises; the ousel sings to me.
Above my booklet lined for words
The woodland birds shake out their glee,
There's the blithe cuckoo chanting clear
In mantle grey from bough to bough!
God keep me still! For here I write
A scripture bright in great woods now.[57]

TASK

Consider and discuss in class the relevance of monastic spirituality to the theme of 'holiness'.

Think in a synoptic way about how aspects of Celtic monastic spirituality may connect to your other areas of study.

Make notes on your discussion.

Journeying

Esther de Waal identifies 'journeying' as an important aspect of monastic spirituality. She argues that "the monastic life had always been that of continual conversion, moving through the never ending transformation of the old into the new."[58] The journey was a journey into one's self to bring about personal conversion and transformation, but also a journey out of one's self to bring about the conversion and transformation of others. She argues that the peregrination was not a word or a concept found anywhere else in Christendom. Indeed, "the monasteries looked inward to the saints and outwards to the world around them."[59]

Pilgrims on Lough Derg *(Photo courtesy Cathal O'Connor, with the kind permission of Monsignor Richard Mohan, Prior of Lough Derg)*

PRACTICE ESSAY TITLE

a) Identify and consider the nature of Celtic monastic spirituality. (30)

Your answer may refer to some of the following:
- Centrality of community
- Asceticism
- Oneness with nature
- Love of learning
- Gender inclusivity
- Care of the marginalised

b) Critically assess the view that the Christian Church today has much to learn from the spirituality of the Celtic monks. (20)

Your answer could include reference to some of the following:
- Asceticism in the Church today
- Ecology and the environment
- The role of the Church in education and learning today, eg faith schools etc.
- Role of women in the Christian Church today
- Care of the poor and marginalised today

3. THE CHARACTERISTICS OF THE CELTIC CHURCH

This topic necessitates an overview of the Celtic church during the period covered by the specification. In this sense it provides a good opportunity for revision at the end of the course. You should return to it again when you have completed the course. The diagram opposite suggests an approach you could take to this topic.

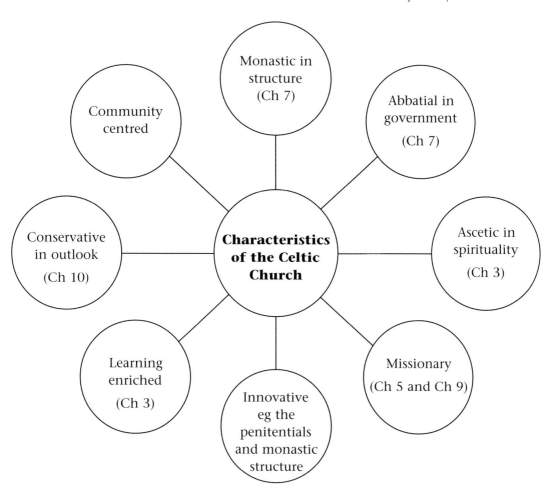

 TASKS

Read back through the chapters indicated in the diagram above.

a) Write up a paragraph on each of the characteristics shown. Remember to include the views of scholars.

b) Can you think of any other characteristics which could be added to the list? File your work away and return to it again when you complete the course.

c) Write a conclusion to your piece which you think best sums up the Celtic Church of this period.

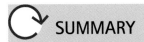

SUMMARY

The Celtic Church as founded by Patrick had an episcopal structure, ruled by bishops and divided into dioceses.

Evidence suggests it remained this way for around a century after Patrick's death.

Around the middle of the sixth century the sources reflect a change in structure.

Abbots seem to become more important and more numerous than bishops.

A number of reasons have been suggested for the change in structure, from those explaining the demise of the episcopal Church to suggestions that monasticism was better suited to Irish society.

Celtic monasticism had a unique spirituality – ascetic, community-centred, gender-inclusive, learning-enriched, nature orientated, caring for the weak.

It is possible to identify key characteristics of the Celtic Church of the period – innovative yet conservative, ascetic, missionary, monastic and abbatial.

Endnotes

1 Both the Roman Catholic and Anglican churches still have Apostolic Succession.

2 Epistle 1

3 See *Confessio* 38, 50 and 51

4 See *Letter* 3

5 Read the commentary to the *Confessio* in Chpt 2.

6 Most scholars would accept that this number is at least a little extravagant. Even if we accept the forty two names cited, this too would be an achievement of some magnitude, given the geographical conditions Patrick would have faced in Ireland.

7 Tírechán's *Brief Account* as quoted in Ryan, *Irish Monasticism*

8 Remember that some scholars see these as the assistants of Palladius rather than Patrick.

9 Ryan, *Irish Monasticism, Origins and early development, op cit*, p92

10 Todd, *The Life of Patrick*, p88,

11 Chadwick, N, *The Age of the Saints in the Early Celtic Church*, The Riddell Memorial Lecture Series, Llanerch publishers, Wales, 1960, p22

12 Kenney, *The Sources for the Early History of Ireland: Ecclesiastical, An Introduction and Guide, op cit*, p324

13 Hughes, *Early Christian Ireland: An Introduction to the Sources, op cit*, p72

14 Chadwick, *The Age of the Saints, op cit*, p33

15 *ibid*, p34

16 Ó Cróinín, D, *Early Medieval Ireland 400–1200*, Longman, London, 1995, p149

17 *ibid*

18 Sheehy, M, Irish Theological Quarterly, xxix 1962, pp136–144

19 Ryan, *Irish Monasticism, op cit*, p95

20 *ibid*, p96

21 *ibid*

22 *ibid*, pp102–103

23 Hughes, K, *The Church in Early Irish Society*, London, px

24 Hughes, *Early Christian Ireland: An Introduction to the Sources, op cit*, pp72–75

25 *ibid*, p75

26 De Paor, L, *Early Christian Ireland*, Thames and Hudson, London, 1958, p56

27 Sharpe, R, 'Some Problems concerning the organisation of the church in early medieval Ireland' in *Peritia* iii 1984, p241

28 Ó Cróinín, D, *Early Medieval Ireland 400–1200, op cit*, p167

29 Ryan, *Irish Monasticism, op cit*, p98

30 Todd, *The Life of Patrick*, p153

31 Ryan, *Irish Monasticism, op cit*, pp101–102

32 Hughes, *The Church in Early Irish Society, op cit*, p69

33 *ibid*, p172

34 Bede's *Ecclesiastical History of the English People*, Colgrave & Mynors (ed & trans), 1969, p222–224

35 Chadwick, *The Age of the Saints in the Early Celtic Church*, Riddell Memorial Lectures, Llanerch publishers, Wales, 1960, p77

36 See Chapter 9 of this book.

37 Hughes, K, *Introduction to a History of Medieval Ireland* in *Church and Society in Ireland*, ed D Dumville, Valiorum Reprints, London 1987, p19

38 Ryan, Irish Monasticism, *op cit*, p179

39 Chadwick, *The Age of the Saints, op cit*, p77

40 Adomnán's *Life of Colmcille* 1.36 Richard Sharpe (ed &trans), Penguin Classics

41 Ryan, *Irish Monasticism, op cit*, p170

42 Corish, P, 'The Christian Mission' in *A History of Irish Catholicism*, Gill &Macmillan Ltd, Dublin 1971, pp6–7

43 Quoted in 'Saints, Kings and Vikings' in *The Irish Catholic Experience, A Historical Survey*, ed P Corish, Gill & Macmillan Ltd, Dublin, 1984, p7

44 *ibid*, p8

45 De Waal, E, *The Celtic Way of Prayer*, Doubleday Press, New York, 1997, pxxii

46 Quoted in Hughes and Hamlin, *The Modern Traveller to the Early Irish Church*, Spck, London, 1977, p28

47 Cited in Hines-Berger, S, 'An Irish Journey into Celtic Spirituality', www.americancatholic.org/messenger/mar2001

47a Cummène was abbot of Iona in 657 and was a kinsman of Columba.

48 Quoted in Hardinge, L, *The Celtic Church in Britain*, Spck, London, 1972, p191

49 Woods, R, 'The Spirituality of the Celtic Church', in www.spiritualitytoday.org, p7

50 Connolly, *The Irish Penitentials, op cit*, p178

51 *ibid*, pp159–160

52 Sellner, E, 'Heavenly Fire: Celtic Spirituality and Imitation of the Future', www.aishlingmagazine.com

53 O'Loughlin, T, *Journeys on the edges: The Celtic Tradition*, Orbis Books, New York, 2000, p35

54 Hines-Berger, *op cit*, p3

55 Hughes and Hamlin, *The Modern Traveller to the Early Irish Church, op cit*, p21–22

56 *ibid*, p20

57 Flower, R, *Poems and Translations in The Irish Tradition*, Oxford, 1947, p116

58 De Waal, E, *The Celtic Way of Prayer, op cit*, p1

59 *ibid*, p163

Hagiography

Chapter 8

LEARNING OUTCOMES

Knowledge, understanding and evaluation of:

— the features of hagiographical writing

— the content and purpose of Adomnán's *Life of Colmcille*, Muirchú's *Life of Patrick*, and Cogitosus' *Life of Brigit*

— the historical value and reliability of hagiography

INTRODUCTION

As part of the huge literary output of the Celtic monasteries, there emerged a genre of literature which was by no means unique to the Celtic Church. These productions were 'Lives' of the saints, whose contribution to the Church at that time was deemed to be remarkable. The term given to this type of religious literature is 'hagiography.

1. WHAT IS HAGIOGRAPHY?

The word 'hagiography' literally translated means 'writing about saints'. Hagiographies were not biographies in the conventional sense. Instead they were a panegyric[1] of the saint, that is, a writing in praise of them. For this reason only certain aspects of the saint's life would be recorded.

Indeed, Kathleen Hughes states: "Hagiography is not a history. The author is not concerned to establish a correct chronology. He is not interested in assembling and examining evidence and coming to a conclusion which takes the evidence into account."[2]

The focus of the writing is on emphasising the saint's holiness, not in the sense of stressing his morality but by stressing the supernatural abilities of the saint in terms of miracle, prophecy, and visions. "The essential proof of an individuals sanctity was his power to work miracles."[3]

The three hagiographies which concern us here are: Muirchú's *Life of Patrick*, Adomnán's *Life of Colmcille* and Cogitosus' *Life of Brigit*.

It is important to understand that all writing of this genre will have particular features in common, certain 'compositional characteristics'. Nonetheless, we must guard against the tendency "to lump all the Lives together as if they belong to a common pattern. Almost every Life is quite a complex production."[4] So while all hagiographers share a common purpose – to glorify the saint about whom they write – each author also had his own particular purpose in mind. It will be important to appreciate this purpose in order to truly understand each production.

The general purpose of hagiographical writing

- All hagiographies aim to edify the saint about whom they are written. Fustel de Coulanges argues that they were written "to demonstrate the sanctity of their subject, and to make known his worth as a saint, in the interest of the church or monastery which claimed him as their patron."[5]
- Some hagiographies are written to promote the interests of a particular monastery or church.
- Some hagiographies are written for economic reasons, to make claim to property or to draw greater attention to the important relics of that church and, from which it then "made its fortune."[6]
- Some hagiographies aim to teach the community for which they are written or indeed the wider Church. In these cases the moral and spiritual qualities of the saint may be more pronounced. As Gougaud says, these hagiographies abound in "narratives of marvellous incidents, or striking traits of virtue, calculated to impress the mind of the reader and stir up his feelings to reverence and emulation."[7]
- Some hagiographies are written simply at the request of that monastic community.

All hagiographies will, to a greater or lesser degree, reflect some or all of these purposes.

The conventions of hagiography

Although the individual Lives have their own unique purposes and some "are more spiritually aware than others",[8] they do reflect the same compositional characteristics.[9]

1 The saint is usually very ascetic.

2 The saint shows an affinity with nature and the animal kingdom. Jacques Chevalier has said, *"Celtic Christianity, sombre and forbidding in aspect, often violent and of mixed nature, reveals itself, on closer acquaintance, as animated throughout by the love of nature ... by a winning familiarity with our 'unknown brothers', animals or angels."*[10] Nowhere is this affinity with nature and the animal kingdom more evident than in the Lives of the saints.

3 The Life will tell us more about the time in which it was written than about the time of the actual saint. Reference will be made to political issues of the author's day and religious practices more likely to be current at the time of writing than at the time of the saint.

4 The saint has a tendency towards malediction (the pronouncing of curses) on those who disregard or offend him or her. These incidents are intended to show the power of the saint.

5 There will be very little genuine, detailed historical or biographical information on the saint. There will be gaps in chronology and little genuine information on, for example, the family background of the saint.

6 Anything which is likely to portray the saint in a negative light will either be omitted altogether or fleetingly alluded to in a non-committal way.

7 Miracles are frequently performed by the saint which are commemorative of those performed by Christ. For example, the multiplication of food and drink (miracles of plenty), the raising of the dead to life, and the calming of storms. Sometimes these miracles are borrowed from one Life into another. For the hagiographers, these miracles provide a strong body of evidence for the sanctity of his saint.

8 The author employs the methods of secular story telling. The Celts loved a good story and the hagiographer was conscious of his responsibility to entertain and amuse his audience. Indeed, "there was no people whose taste for the extraordinary and the fantastic was so keen as that of the Celts."[11] In this way, Bieler sees hagiographies as "continuing the tradition of heroic literature."[12] Gwynn comments: "the Christian miracle takes the place of the traditions, mythological or tribal, of the secular legends and numerous are the points of resemblance between the methods of the miracle working saint and those of the magician of pre-Christian times."[13] Many of the details are also deliberately exaggerated in order to "incite laughter".[14]

TASK

Go through the texts of Muirchú, Adomnán and Cogitosus.
Try to identify stories which you think may have been told in such a way as to amuse or entertain.

9 The saint is often portrayed as having a greater likeness to a Celtic hero of pagan times than to a saint. They are often portrayed as warriors, engaging their opponents in physical contests to prove their prowess because this is the standard by which a pagan hero was judged in secular story. Deeply entrenched in Irish culture was the idea that a man of honour must be prepared to fight to prove his superiority.[15] In some cases the saint appears to assume the characteristics of a pagan god or goddess. Some stories show the saint 'shape-shifting' for example, that is, taking on another form – an ability attributed to the *sid* and some gods and goddesses. It is important to note that some of these stories of the 'heroic age' go back to Iron Age times and were being committed to paper for the first time in the Celtic monasteries. It is not surprising therefore that their own religious literature would take on some of the character and flavour of the great stories of pagan heroes past.

10 Despite the lack of historical information about the saint in question, the hagiographies often contain large quantities of other historically valuable information that is given in a way which is incidental to the main story. The author may, as an aside, digress from the main story to describe the church building, or the ceremony surrounding the arrival of a guest, or the methods used to plant, plough and harvest crops at a monastery. The hagiography may tell us details of the ruling dynasties of the day and disputes which arose that are not referred to in other historical sources. Therefore hagiographies are often, almost in spite of themselves, very important historical sources. Kenney agrees that each work usually forms "a true picture of the hagiographer's own age. It is of the social conditions of that age. It is in its ideas, its customs and manner of living, that the historian will find authentic record in the Lives of the saints."[16]

Exam tip!

Make sure that your responses include concrete examples of these features within the particular text you are asked about.

To help you to do this you should copy and complete the table opposite and overleaf.

Features	Muirchú's Life of Patrick	Adomnán's Life of Colmcille	Cogitosus' Life of Brigit
Ascetic	Patrick withstands long periods in the ice cold water, while the boy Benignus could not	Colmcille used a stone as a pillow	
Affinity with nature and animals			Brigit tames the wild fox to entertain the king and hangs her cloak upon a sunbeam
Malediction			A millstone on which Brigit performed a miracle refuses to grind the corn of a druid
Historical gaps		No details on the missionary activity of Colmcille	
Omission of 'damaging' material		Vagueness on events surrounding Colmcille's departure from Ireland	
Miracles of biblical proportion			Brigit was asked by some lepers for beer, but had none. She blessed the water that had been prepared for the baths and transformed it into the best beer.

Features	Muirchú's Life of Patrick	Adomnán's Life of Colmcille	Cogitosus' Life of Brigit
Secular story telling mechanisms	The story of the contest between Patrick and the wizards and the conversion of Loeghaire is the high point of Muirchú and represents the triumph of Christianity over paganism		
Likeness to warrior hero or pagan god			Brigit seems to have been confused with the pagan goddess Brigit
Important incidental information	The presence of a 'north' church at Armagh and perhaps reference to surviving pagan cult of the deer		

2 MUIRCHÚ'S *LIFE OF PATRICK* [17]

The Author

Muirchú means 'sea-dog' and his tribal territory was Tuath Mochtaine close to Armagh. He was a member of the ecclesiastical family of Armagh. He attended the Synod of Adomnán in 697 with Aed of Sletty who between 662 and 668, during the reign of the abbot Ségene, had incorporated his church into the paruchiae of Patrick at Armagh. His *Life of Patrick* must have been written some time after that, in the second half of the seventh century. Some sources locate Muirchú's church at Wicklow, others suggest he has associations with County Down. Certainly Sletty, Armagh, Wicklow and Down all feature in his work.

The structure of the work

The first part of the book replicates Patrick's *Confessio*, with the exception of adding that Patrick's mother was called Concessa and that his surname was Sochet. Morris believes his use of the *Confessio* and the *Letter to Coroticus* to be both "sober" and "scholarly".[18] The *Life* also contains the story of Patrick's supposed stay in Gaul for a period of approximately thirty years and his subsequent consecration as bishop to the Irish on hearing news of the death of Palladius. Many scholars believe that Muirchú had a written source at his disposal for this section. Some argue that this was actually a description of the consecration of Palladius and illustrates the confusion between the lives of the two men which was evident in the seventh century. Other scholars such as Bury, rebuild Patrick's career, taking this material into account.

The second section begins the story of Patrick's arrival in Ireland. The style of this section is very different from what has gone before, "becoming more rhetorical and the story more amusing. Perhaps this change marks the end of the written sources and the beginning of oral legend".[19] Patrick arrives in Ireland at Inverdee, which in the view of Kenney, is because Muirchú's own church was there and the journey made from there to Armagh actually reflects a journey made by the author himself.[20] Interestingly, the first convert made by Patrick, according to Muirchú's account is that of Dichu at Saul. In the view of Doherty, the story was intended to link Patrick with the ancestios of the family which controlled Saul.[21] There is a very long section describing the contest between Patrick and Loeghaire's wizards. The high point of this narrative is the conversion of Loeghaire, which Muirchú recounts in very dramatic fashion, "as if it were a summary of some saga."[22] It also contains the story of the grant of Armagh to Patrick by Dáire. Indeed, Muirchú's account is at its most detailed around the area of Armagh, Antrim and north Down.

The third section appears as a 'second book'. Some scholars believe it was added to Muirchú's original work by a redactor. It tells the story of the death of Patrick and explains his burial at Downpatrick. Bieler believes these stories to be the work of Muirchú,[23] while others believe they were added later by the Armagh lawyers. Their purpose seems to be to put an end to any dispute about possession of the relics of Patrick, and to perhaps explain why Armagh, founded by Patrick as his primary church, did not possess the body of Patrick.

The sources used by Muirchú

1 Muirchú certainly used Patrick's *Confessio*. Some argue that he may also have had at his disposal Patrick's first, and now lost, *Letter to Coroticus*.

2 He may have used a copy of the *Hymn of Secundinus* which praised the work and virtues of Patrick and which may have been written in the lifetime of Patrick.

3 The Circular Letter/*The First Synod of Patrick*.

4 Muirchú may have used information given to him by Aed of Sletty at whose request he writes the *Life*. McNeill[24] and some others believe that Aed himself had written a document about Patrick based on his own research and that Muirchú had this at his disposal.

5 He may have relied on the records of Cogitosus, whom he describes as his "father". Both Cogitosus and Aed may have known people in their youth who would or could have conversed with others who knew Patrick. These would have been part of an extensive body of oral tradition available to Muirchú.

6 Ryan believes that there was "an Old Irish Chronicle reaching from A.D. 437–661",[25] which could have been used by Muirchú.

7 Muirchú, in the Preface to his *Life*, refers to a number of *Vitae Patricii*, so he may well have been able to work from these early biographies which are no longer extant.

8 He may have used a written narrative outlining Patrick's time in Gaul. O'Rahilly believes that the details of the story told by Muirchú and indeed Tírechán, "must ultimately go back to a written document embodying information obtained in Gaul, not later than the seventh century, by some monk who had visited Auxerre and had had access to the church records preserved there."[26] Hanson disputes this on the basis that no such details are included in the *Life of Germanus* by Constatius, who would doubtless have been able to access the record of the church of Auxerre.[27]

9 Hanson also argues that Muirchú had no other written source but the *Confessio* and disputes the idea that Muirchú would have had at his disposal any earlier 'lost' writings of Patrick. He argues that "the difficulty and embarrassment which Patrick plainly experienced in expressing himself in Latin in his two surviving works do not encourage us to think that he is likely to have written more than these."[28] He believes that aside from the *Confessio*, Muirchú's only other sources would have been oral tradition preserving stories about Patrick's association with different churches and great people, "who had left an impression on the popular mind, such as Amator, Germanus or Loeghaire."[29] Olden believes his method of proceeding was very simple. It was to follow the *Confessio* a certain way and then tack on the legendary matter.[30]

The purpose of Muirchú's *Life of Patrick*

Introduction

An understanding of the reasons for which Muirchú wrote is crucial to a comprehension of his *Life*. Muirchú's intention in writing the *Life of Patrick* would have been similar to that of all hagiographers, that is to glorify and praise the saint, to emphasise his sanctity by the citation of prophecy, miracle and vision.

However, the particular purpose of Muirchú's *Life of Patrick* was a little more complex than that. Political and ecclesiastical politics of the day dominate the work, and an awareness of them is vital to an overall understanding of this work.

Muirchú places the bulk of the work carried out by Patrick in the Northern half of the country. Most modern scholars agree that this is most likely the location of

Patrick's mission. In the fifth century, at the time of Patrick, the northern part of Ireland would have been part of the territory of the Ulaid, the tribe after whom the province of Ulster takes its name. By the time of Muirchú however, the Ulaid had experienced a decline in fortune at the hands of the Uí Néill and had shrunk considerably in size. This posed a problem for Muirchú, in that he had little desire to associate his saint with a humiliated and declining power.

Patrick and the Uí Néill

One of the purposes in writing was therefore to associate Patrick, not with the Ulaid but with the Uí Néill. To this end, Muirchú builds up to a huge climax with the story of the conversion of Loeghaire, the Uí Néill king, at Tara. Doherty points out that:

"Tara was not a 'capital' in the strict sense of a city, but it was an important inauguration site and kings who had been inaugurated there, rose to considerable power … [and] had managed to dominate the entire country."[31]

The timing of this event at the Paschal Vigil is important. The centrality of the Easter Vigil was lost a little until the mid-twentieth century. In Muirchú's time it was the central moment in the whole liturgical year and was a very elaborate ritual based on fire and light. It towered above other ritual gatherings at Easter and dwarfed other festivals such as Christmas. Muirchú's audience would have appreciated this grand climax of the Patrick story.

"Holy Patrick said to the king: 'If you do not believe now you will die on the spot; for the wrath of God descends on your head.' And the king, shaken in his heart feared greatly, as did the whole city with him.

King Loeghaire summoned his elders and his whole council, and said to them: 'It is better for me to believe than to die.' And he took the advice of his company and followed it: he believed on that day and turned to the eternal Lord God. Many others also believed on that day."

This is all the more interesting because the Uí Néill were the kinspeople of Colmcille, and as such, one would imagine should lend their favour to that paruchiae.

The story is tactically very important to the author because it shows that the Uí Néill owe their Christian faith to Patrick and therefore should favour the church of Patrick (Armagh) and lend it their support.

Patrick and the church at Armagh

Muirchú's purpose was also to associate his saint with the church of Armagh. His work forms part of the propaganda of that church. As we have seen, he himself was a church man of Armagh and was requested by Aed of Sletty to write the *Life of Patrick*. Aed had also given over his own church to Armagh. If Armagh was to justify its claim to be the most important church in Ireland, the authority of which should be

Hill of Tara *(Photo courtesy of Cathal O'Connor)*

recognised by all other churches, then it would have to be shown to be the church chosen by Patrick as his own. Muirchú therefore tells, in detail, the story of the grant of the land at Armagh to Patrick by Dáire. He makes it clear that Patrick had proper legal title to the site.

> *"There was a certain wealthy and honourable man in Airthir whose name was Dáire. Holy Patrick asked him to give him a place for the exercise of religion. The rich man said to the holy one: 'What place do you want?' 'I ask' said the holy man 'that you give me the hilltop known as Druim Sailech [Armagh] and I will build a church there.' But he did not wish to give the hilltop to the holy man; but he gave him another place on lower ground … . Patrick settled there with his people. After some time there came an ostler of Dáire's leading his horse to graze on the Christian's meadow. The pasturing of the horse on his land annoyed Patrick, who said 'it was stupid of Dáire to place brute animals on the small place he has given to God, to disturb it.' … The following morning the ostler came back to tend to the horse and found that it was dead. He went home sadly and reported to his master: 'Look: that Christian has killed your horse. The intrusion on his church annoyed him.' And Dáire said: 'Then he must be killed. Go now and kill him.' Just after they had gone out, sudden death struck Dáire – more quickly than it could be told. His wife said: 'This death is caused by the Christian. Someone go out quickly and curry favour with him for us; and you will be saved. Those who have been sent to kill the Christian must be stopped and called back.' … [Patrick]*

blessed water and gave it to them saying: 'Go: sprinkle some of this water on your horse, and take it with you.' And they did; the horse came back to life and they took it with them. When Dáire was sprinkled with the holy water, he was brought back to life and health ... And Dáire came along and bore the cauldron to Patrick, saying to him '... I now give you that piece of land you previously asked for, insofar as it is mine. Live there.' And that is the city now called Armagh."

 TASK

Read the full story of the grant of Armagh to Patrick by Dáire and the story of the contest between Patrick and Loeghaire's wizards. Identify all of the hagiographical conventions present in the stories.

Triumph of Christianity over paganism

Muirchú also wished to illustrate the triumph of Christianity over paganism at the hands of Patrick and his work is filled "with echoes of conversion/deliverance events from the Scriptures."[32] The wizards are shown, early in the narrative, predicting the arrival of the new faith and prophesying its triumph at the expense of their own religion. Muirchú presents a detailed story of the contest between the saint and Loeghaire's wizards, who are the enemy of Patrick. Patrick's powers are shown to be greater than theirs and the story culminates in the death or defeat of the wizards and the conversion of Loeghaire, which symbolises "Ireland's night of deliverance."[33]

Burial at Downpatrick

Muirchú had a problem in explaining why Patrick had died among the Ulaid and also needs to explain why the church of Armagh does not have the relics of Patrick. Although emphasising again in the story the favouritism shown by Patrick to Armagh, he balances the primacy of Armagh with the right of Downpatrick to retain the bones of the saint.

"... the day of his death drew near. An angel came to tell him of his death. So because of this, he sent word to Armagh, the place he loved best in the world, that many men should come to conduct him there, the place to which he wished to go. Then with his company, he began the journey he desired to make to that place – Armagh that he longed for. But by the wayside, there was a burning bush, which was not consumed (as had happened in the past to Moses). In the bush was the angel Victor who had been a frequent visitor to Patrick. Victor sent another angel to Patrick to forbid him to go where he wished to go, who asked him: 'Why do you set out on the road without Victor's counsel? Victor is summoning you about this. Turn aside and go to him.' And he digressed as he had been instructed, and he asked what he should do. The angel

answered him, saying:

'Go back to where you came from (that is Saul), and the four requests you have made are granted to you. (1) That your primacy will be at Armagh. (2) That whoever on the day that he is departing from the flesh, sings the hymn composed about you, will have you as judge of the penance due for his sins. (3) That the descendants of Dichu who kindly received you will earn mercy and will not be lost. (4) That on the day of judgement the Irish will be judged by you, so that you may sit in judgement on those whose apostle you were. Go back therefore as I tell you; and you will die and go the way of your fathers."

This occurred on the 17th March, the years of his whole life numbering one hundred and twenty; and it is commemorated throughout the whole of Ireland every year.

Muirchú, in the telling of the death story, not only gives justification for the absence of the Patrician relics at Armagh but also gains an advantage for Armagh in showing it to be the will of God through the grant of the angel that the church at Armagh have primacy.

In addition, he wishes to put a stop to the feuding which seems to have been ongoing over the body of Patrick. There appears to have been several attempts made by the Uí Néill to take possession of the body of Patrick, which had even led to war. Muirchú adds a story to deter anyone from interfering with the body of Patrick.

Patrick's final resting place is in Downpatrick, County Down. *(Photo courtesy of Cathal O'Connor)*

"When the angel came to advise him about his burial: 'Let two untamed oxen be picked and allowed to go wherever they will with the wagon carrying your body; and wherever they pause to rest, there a church will be built to honour your body.'... And under God's direction they went out to Dún Lethglaisse [Downpatrick, County Down], where Patrick is buried.

And the angel said to him: 'Let a cubit's depth of earth be placed in your body, so that relics will not be taken from it.' In recent times it was shown that this was done at God's command: because when a church was being built above the body, the men who were digging in the earth saw fire bursting forth from the grave, and they drew back in fear of the flaming fire."

 PRACTICE ESSAY TITLE

Appraise the contents and purpose of Muirchú's *Life of Patrick.* **(30)**

Your answer may include some of the following:
- A definition of hagiography
- An outline of the contents of Muirchú
- Hagiographical conventions with textual examples
- General aim of hagiography
- The specific intentions of Muirchú, with reference to text
- The views of scholars

The historical value and reliability of Muirchú's *Life of Patrick*

Introduction

Scholars differ greatly in their interpretations of hagiographical works, and especially in regard to Muirchú's *Life of Patrick*. Several questions must be considered when assessing the historicity of hagiographical texts:

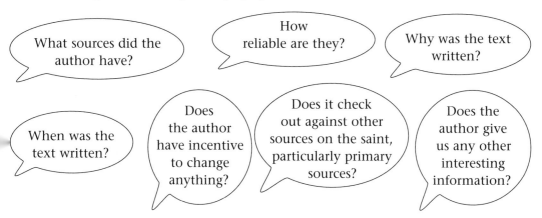

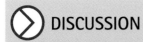 **DISCUSSION**

In groups, discuss Muirchú's *Life of Patrick* considering the questions above. Make notes on your discussion. Include textual examples where appropriate.

Time of writing

Muirchú's *Life of Patrick* was written toward the end of the seventh century, two hundred years after the mission of Patrick. This has obvious implications for the reliability of the information he gives about Patrick.

Sources and choice of material

Muirchú himself does not inspire confidence regarding the collection of material about Patrick in preparation of the *Life*.[34]

> "*My lord Aed, many people have attempted to reconstruct this history, following the tradition they received from the fathers* ... but they have found discrepancies in the story so often – and so many have expressed doubts – *that they have never arrived at a coherent narrative of events. Therefore it would not be wrong for me to say that* ... *I have taken a child's skiff out on this most* dangerous and deep sea of sacred history *and I have ventured boldly on the swell of mountainous waters* among the most acute perils, *into* an unknown ocean, *previously entered and experienced by no boat except one only – that of my father Cogitosus* ... *although with little skill*, from uncertain sources, *from* an unreliable memory *and weak judgement, and inelegantly.*"

This account of his difficulties, cited in the Preface to the *Life*, does not seem to indicate that Muirchú had many written sources at his disposal, but to be fair in our judgement, he clearly desires to write an accurate account and has earnestly tried to write what he thinks to be true. (See also pages 239–240.)

We must also bear in mind Muirchú's purpose in writing, which no doubt coloured the stories he chose to include and his manner of retelling them. Hanson suggests that it would not be inappropriate to use the methods of form criticism applied to biblical studies in assessing hagiography.[35] In the glorification of Patrick, Muirchú would have been anxious to discredit the work of Palladius and to this end tells the story of the failure of the mission of Palladius and the consecration of Patrick.

> "... *they were certain that Palladius, archdeacon of Pope Celestine, bishop of Rome* ... *had been consecrated and sent to be established in this island of wintry cold in order to convert it. But no one can receive from earth what has not been given by heaven: Palladius was denied success. For these wild and obdurate people did not readily accept his doctrine and he himself did not wish to spend a long time in a foreign country, but to return to him who had sent him. He left here having crossed the first sea and*

began his land journey, he ended his Life in the confines of the Britons. ... Patrick had the grade conferred on him by the holy bishop Amathorex. On the same day on which Patrick was consecrated, Auxilius, Iserninus and others received lower orders."

Inconsistencies

Morris believes Muirchú presents a "sober account of Patrick's stay in Gaul",[36] while Hanson disputes that there is any background material at all for Patrick's time in Gaul, and points out the "glaring inconsistencies" in the story.[37]

- If Palladius did not want to spend time in a foreign land, why did he set out at all?

- Why should he have left Ireland just because the inhabitants were initially not inclined to listen to him?

- Muirchú tells us that Patrick was accompanied by two others, Auxilius and Iserninus, yet Patrick gives the clear impression in the *Confessio* that he is a lone bishop to the Irish.

- Why would the Church at Gaul involve itself in the sending of a clergy from the Church in Britain to evangelise Ireland?

- Amator was actually the predecessor of Germanus so could not have consecrated Patrick after a period of thirty years studying with Germanus.

This is clearly a "jumbled narrative"[38] containing historical inaccuracy and statements which are inconsistent with the *Confessio*.

The story of the grant of Armagh cannot be considered to be historical either and has echoes of 'folklore' about it. It may well, however, be based on local tradition that the land for the church at Armagh had been given by Dáire.[39]

Gougaud comments that "pure invention on the narrator's part would have clashed with the local traditions, which it may be supposed were still alive and flourishing, even after a considerable lapse of time and would have called forth protest and denial."[40] Others may insist that the story was pure fabrication, forming part of Armagh's seventh century propaganda.

Little needs to be said on the truth of the 'Loeghaire' story. Certainly had it been true, it surely would have been the high point of Patrick's career and would no doubt have been mentioned by him in the *Confessio*. Binchy holds that the Tara monarchy did not become Christian for more than a century after this 'alleged' encounter.[41]

JB Bury[42] accepts a lot of the material in Muirchú as genuine and even produces an account of the career of Patrick based on its content. He accepts the intended journey to Rome, the stay in Gaul, and the contest with the wizards of Loeghaire.

Gwynn even suggests an amendment to the information given in the *Confessio* on the basis of a statement in Muirchú. In C23 Patrick says he heard the voices of the people of Foclut calling him to walk among them again. Gwynn argues it is wrong to accept the Wood of Foclut as the place of Patrick's captivity because Muirchú tells us it was Slemish.

Hanson argues that "if Muirchú had not described Patrick's place of captivity as Slemish, in Co. Antrim, it would never have occurred to anybody that the place was not 'the wood of Foclut, near the Western Sea'."[43]

Bieler believes that we should "accept as probable all traditions which existed at the end of the seventh century unless they are demonstrably false."[44] He also claims that "unless a later piece of evidence is in itself suspect, or runs counter to fifth century evidence that is unequivocal, it ought to be accepted",[45] but adds that, "except where they are based on the genuine works of Patrick, their evidence must be treated with the greatest caution."[46]

 TASK

Read through Muirchú's *Life of Patrick* again. Identify the content which seems to contradict the information given in the Confessio.

Esposito and Binchy are both sceptical about the seventh century traditions of Patrick and tend to reject most of them totally.[47] JB Morris is clear in his view as to how hagiographical material should be handled; we should always use "common sense, and its first precept is that over riding priority must go to the interpretation of contemporary statements".

Historical value

De Coulanges, writing in the nineteenth century, accepts a certain amount of elaboration in the Lives of the saints but argues that "we may be certain that the author did not invent, though he added certain virtues to his hero, he did not imagine the small details of his life ... what interests us is not the miracle, but the details that surround it ... what we need to look for are ... the facts that the hagiographer had no incentive to change."[48]

In kind with all hagiographies then, Muirchú does give important information on the social, religious and politico-religious history of the time in which he was writing.

- He tells us in an 'incidental' manner that there was a north church at Armagh in the seventh century, implying the existence of more than one church there.
- In the same narrative he describes the doe and its fawn which lie on the hill-top that Dáire eventually gave to Patrick. This gives an insight into the still extant tradition of the pagan cult of the deer associated with Armagh. In this sense, the *Life* "gives useful information on the remnants of paganism or superstition of

the period or of the writers own time."[49]

- His account also focuses on the ongoing dispute over the body of Patrick between the Airthir, supported by the Uí Néill, and the Ulaid. Muirchú tells us that at one point the Uí Néill were deluded into thinking that they had the body of Patrick. This is supported by the *Book of the Angel*, written in the eighth century, which claims that Armagh does indeed possess the body of Patrick.

Therefore hagiographies can "add substantially to our historical information and understanding",[50] and "even within Lives strongly tinged with legend it is not impossible to disengage some historical facts."[51]

Portrait of Patrick

Many scholars would dispute the usefulness of the *Life* as a source on Patrick. Hanson points out that Patrick emerges from the *Life* as "over-bearing, self-confident, truculent and irritable, whereas his writing reveals him as very anxious not to give offence or cause persecution for the Church."[52] Binchy agrees that "the humble servant of God who speaks to us so movingly in his own writings had become a hero of folklore ... this glorified Patrick is not merely the successor of the hero: he has inherited some of the more disagreeable characteristics of the very druids that were overthrown by him."[53] There is much emphasis on power and authority and clearly a 'half-pagan mentality' underlies this emphasis.[54] Indeed, "weighty evidence of a certain coarsening of the religious life is provided by the Vitae of the saints ... the contrast between the Patrick of the *Confessio* and the Patrick of Muirchú is startling."[55] In many hagiographies the saint appears to be "selfish, arrogant, unprincipled, blood-thirsty and self-seeking, devastating cursers; the very opposite of the notion of sanctity provided in monastic legislation."[56] Many therefore would agree with Daniel Binchy that "far from glorifying Patrick, they diminish him, and had his own writings perished, his biographers would effectively have obscured the true greatness of the man."[57]

It is important to retain a balanced view of such works, as Binchy reminds us: "This genre of literature, though it has great literary charm and is often useful as a reflection of the social and religious ideas of the age in which it circulated, is notoriously a stranger to historical accuracy or perspective. We must not of course dismiss such material out of hand."[58]

 TASK

Compare and contrast the portrait of Patrick which emerges from Muirchú's *Life of Patrick* and that which comes from his own writings. Find plenty of textual examples to support the points you make. File your notes for exam preparation.

PRACTICE ESSAY TITLE

a) Analyse and discuss the historical value and reliability of Muirchú's *Life of Patrick*. (30)

> In your answer you may refer to some of the following:
> - A definition of hagiography
> - Features of the writing with textual examples
> - The purpose of Muirchú
> - The dating and sources for the *Life of Patrick*
> - Comparison with Patrick's writing
> - Incidental information
> - The views of scholars

b) Critically assess the view that Muirchú's portrayal of Patrick is inspiring for the Christian reader. (20)

> In your answer you could refer to some of the following:
> - Use of miracle and prophecy
> - Asceticism
> - Prayer
> - Comparison with person of *Confessio* and *Letter*
> - The view of scholars

3. ADOMNÁN'S *LIFE OF COLMCILLE*

The author

Adomnán was the ninth abbot of Iona (AD679–704). He was a kinsman of Colmcille. He was a prominent figure in the Celtic Church, and very actively involved in trying to resolve the Paschal Controversy. He was a reputable biblical scholar and had also written a guide to the Holy Land, which was "both practical and well informed", in spite of the fact that he had never been there himself.[59] He promulgated his own ecclesiastical legislation in the form of Adomnán's Law in 697 at the Synod of Birr. It was the first example of a new type of Church law which was enforced on clergy and laity alike and protected women, children and the clergy.

The structure of the work

Adomnán divides his work into three separate books which deal with the saint's miracles. His work opens with a miracle similar in proportion to Christ's miracle at the wedding feast of Cana, and includes another in which Columba raises a dead child to life. His prophetic revelations show that Colmcille could foresee many events in the future. These gifts of miracle and prophecy were designed to show him as "a man joined to the Lord in spirit".[60] The Third Book of angelic visions is designed not only to show that as in biblical times God sends angels to his chosen ones, but in Adomnán's *Life*, Colmcille is frequently shown to be at one with the angels, conversing with them, thereby indicating that he was a man of heaven rather than a man of this earth.

 TASK

Read Adomnán's *Life of Colmcille*. Write a summary of the contents including something from the Preface and highlighting what you consider to be the main stories. Your summary should not be more than 500 words. Pay attention to the hagiographical conventions as you read.

Sources

Adomnán claims to have used written sources on Colmcille. Herbert is convinced that there was a written account of the miracles of Colmcille in existence at Iona in Adomnán's time, and that his account preserves "much of the simplicity of these testimonies". Herbert also believes that these were committed to writing within a very short space of time from their initial telling.[61] Although Adomnán does not acknowledge it as such, this is probably Cumméne's book on the miraculous powers of Saint Columba. Sharpe believes Adomnán is vague about this source because in Irish law, eye witness testimony is valued more highly than written source material.[62] It is to the eye witness accounts that Adomnán gives more emphasis. There is a marked contrast between the evidence produced from within the monastic community and that gained from other sources. It is from sources other than the Iona community that the more conventional hagiographical saint emerges.[63]

Family connections

Adomnán was a Cenél Conaill, a kinsman of Colmcille, and is likely from his earliest days to have had access to people who would have known the saint. No doubt his family had accumulated a considerable amount of lore about their distinguished kinsman Columba.

Adomnán also used his own experience to inform his audience about the greatness of Colmcille. His starting point is his own belief regarding the sanctity of Columba. He cites that he himself was granted immunity from the plagues during his time in

Northumbria because of the intercession of Colmcille. He similarly credits the saint with the ending of a period of drought at Iona. In addition, there were three separate occasions when travellers received the benefit of favourable winds when going on a journey because they prayed for the saint's intercession.

> *"[The miracle which by God's favour we are now about to recount took place in our own time and we witnessed it with our own eyes.] It happened about seventeen years ago. Right through the spring a severe drought lasted unrelieved so that our fields were baked dry. It was so bad that we thought that our people were threatened by the curse which the Lord imposed on those who transgressed ... we debated what should be done and debated on this. Some of our elders should walk around the fields that had lately been ploughed and sown, carrying with them saint Columba's white tunic and books which the saint had himself copied. They should hold aloft the tunic, which was the one he wore at the hour of his departure from the flesh and shake it three times. They should open his books and read aloud from them ... . When all these things had been done, on the same day – wonderful to tell – the sky which had been cloudless through the whole of March and April, was at once covered, extraordinarily quickly, with clouds rising from the sea, and heavy rain fell day and night."* (Bk 2; 44)

Oral tradition

Kathleen Hughes argues however, that his main source must have been oral tradition.[64] Adomnán tells us himself that he got much of his information *"after diligent enquiry ... from certain informed and trustworthy old men."*[65] He is also able in many places to name the source who had recounted the story to him, for example, the abbot Failbe. Much of the oral tradition used by Adomnán therefore came from within the monastery itself. Kenney points out that "genuine monastic tradition was a source of considerable authority ... the tradition of a permanent corporate community, whose members, in intelligence and literary education, must have been higher – in some cases far higher – than the mass of the population."[66] A smaller portion of the *Life* recounts stories which took place away from Iona and show that Adomnán was also aware of a body of oral tradition about the saint which existed independently of Iona.

Lives of other saints

Adomnán also used the Lives of other saints such as Athanasius' *Life of Anthony* and the *Lives of Martin of Tours* and *St Jerome*. Throughout his *Life of Colmcille*, he borrows examples of holiness or descriptions and phrases from these Lives and attributes them to his own saint. It should be noted however, that where he does so, he usually acknowledges the source of the borrowing, by stating, for example, this incident in the *Life of Colmcille* reminded him of something that had happened in the *Life of Germanus*. Just as the *Life of Martin* is divided into three books, so too is

Adomnán's *Life of Colmcille*. These Lives had a huge influence on Adomnán's writing and served the purpose of equating the stature of Columba with the other great saints of Christendom.

The purpose of Adomnán's *Life of Colmcille*

Adomnán is writing for his own community. This explains the scant historical detail in the *Life of Colmcille*. His community did not desire information on the founding of their monastery or other monasteries for that matter. All of this type of information about Colmcille would have been taken for granted. The focus is very much on the abbot Colmcille and how he lived the religious life among his monks. This motive also explains why we do not have details of Colmcille's evangelising work among the Picts. Adomnán was not concerned to write for a Pictish audience. Nor do we have the details of Columba's many political achievements, for Adomnán did not write for a political audience. Adomnán's purpose was very much a teaching one, to teach his community what their founder was like and to inspire them to emulate his holiness.

Reminder to Uí Néill

Adomnán wrote his *Life* at the time of the rise of the paruchiae Patrick and the paruchiae Brigit. Both the church of Armagh and the church of Kildare were making claims of supremacy. Although Adomnán is not making any such claims for the paruchiae Colmcille, he is anxious that his saint will not be forgotten. In particular, his *Life* is a reminder to the Uí Néill – who had just given their patronage to Armagh – that their own kinsman, Colmcille, was a good and holy man of equal stature to Patrick. Picard is of the view that "the decline of Iona had already begun, mainly because of its position on the Easter controversy".[67] However, it is important to note that this is disputed by Herbert who pointed out that Iona "did not feel obliged to join in the scramble" because they had both political backing and solid leadership which "placed them at the forefront of the Irish ecclesiastical scene at the time."[68]

Colmcille as king-maker

Adomnán portrays Colmcille as a king-maker and throughout the *Life*, there is a particular interest in kings. He had an Old Testament perception of kingship by Divine command. By presenting Colmcille as a king-maker, he is claiming the right of the successors of Columba to have a role as assistants to kings. This is made clear at the beginning of Book One.

> "*Some kings were conquered in the terrifying crash of battle and others emerged victorious, according to what Columba asked of God by the power of prayer. God who honours all saints gave this special privilege to him as to a mighty and triumphant champion, and it remained as true after he quit the flesh as it had been in this present life.*"

Adomnán wanted to make it clear that kings were dependent upon God and the Church.

Paschal Controversy and loss of prestige

We also have to remember that Adomnán wrote at the time of the Paschal Controversy. At the Synod of Whitby the authority of Colmcille had been called into question and Iona had since lost prestige. The *Life* is designed in that sense to bolster morale in the community and to remind everyone of the greatness of Colmcille. Adomnán also wanted to remind readers in Britain and Ireland of the important role played by Iona in the Christianisation of the North of Britain. It is important to note however, that Adomnán does not refer to the Paschal Controversy directly, such was the sensitivity of the matter within his own community. He himself had been convinced of the rightness of Roman practices and became an ambassador for them, convincing churches other than his own to yield. He wishes to show his own community that though he had converted to Roman methods, he remained devoted to the memory of Colmcille and wished to be seen as his biggest advocate. His only reference to the Paschal Controversy directly lies in Book 1 [3] where he recounts a prophecy of Colmcille:

> *"During the time that Columba stayed as a guest at Clonmacnois, he prophesied many things by the revelation of the Holy Spirit. Among them was the great dispute that arose years later among the churches of Ireland, concerning the differences in the date of Easter."*

"The Life was designed to restore perspective. It was the fact that Colmcille had lived a life of sanctity which was of central importance for his followers, not the fact that he had observed particular ordinances regarding the celebration of Easter or the wearing of the monastic tonsure."[69] Adomnán tells his community that there should be no more dissent, supporting his teaching with a prophecy of Colmcille concerning such dissent. He encouraged unity by the use of phrases such as "our" island of Iona and when referring to Colmcille, speaking of him as *"Noster patronus"*, *"Noster Colmcille"*. The *Life* was therefore to act as a unifying force for the Iona community, following the arguments of the Synod of Whitby.[70]

Conversion of Northumbria

Adomnán at one stage seems to address a Northumbrian audience, reminding them that they owe a considerable debt to Columba. He recounts the story of Oswald's important military success which was due to the intercession of Colmcille, and which resulted in the conversion of Northumbria to the Christian faith:

> *"... up until that time all that land of the English was shadowed by the darkness of heathenism and ignorance, excepting the king Oswald himself, and twelve men who had been baptised with him, while he was in exile among the Irish."* (Bk 1; 1)

Adomnán thus reminds his Northumbrian audience that they too should show their acknowledgement of Colmcille because it was to the saint that their Christianity was directly due.

The historical value and reliability of Adomnán's *Life of Colmcille*

Adomnán's *Life* was written within one hundred years of the death of Colmcille. When Adomnán claims to be able to trace the exact source of a story, we can believe him. It seems that, remarkably in the case of Colmcille, quite a reasonable amount of historical and biographical material survived.[71]

Adomnán was writing at a time of much scholarship at Iona. We know that some written records of traditions concerning Colmcille already existed at Iona. In addition to this, the annals were being drawn up at this time.

The author himself claims to only have used sound traditions concerning Colmcille:

"No one should think that I should write anything false about this remarkable man, nor even anything doubtful or uncertain. Let it be understood that I shall tell only what I learnt from the account, handed down by our elders, man both reliable and informed, and that I shall write without equivocation what I have learnt by diligent enquiry either from what I could find already in writing or from what I heard recounted without a trace of doubt by informed and reliable old men."

Adomnán the scholar

Adomnán himself was a scholar of some repute and was a prominent ecclesiastic in his own right. Corish argues that Adomnán's *Life of Colmcille* is "a very sophisticated construct", despite its division into three books, devoted respectively to his hero's prophecies, miracle and visions.[72]

Identifying sources

Adomnán goes out of his way to identify the source of his material:

"My predecessor, our abbot Failbe related all this to me, Adomnán without question. He swore that he had heard the story of the vision from the lips of king Oswald himself, who was relating it to Abbot Ségéne ...

This story was told me by a religious old man, a priest and soldier of Christ, called Oisséne mac Ernáin, from the line of moccu Néth Corb. I am in no doubt as to its truth. He had heard the story from Fintan mac Tulcháin himself, whose monk he was."

It is likely that the stories were retold because of the solid belief in the sanctity of Colmcille, which was held dear by those who first told them. Therefore, as Herbert argues, "mundane events take on the hue of the supernatural and chance remarks may be interpreted as prophetic pronouncements ... it is evident that the element of the marvellous ... lies in the interpretation of events rather than the nature of the events themselves."[73]

Other works acknowledged

Borrowing from other works are always acknowledged, which lends a certain integrity to his work.

> "For in this way saint Germanus was once attacked by legions of evil spirits as he sailed away from the bay of Gaul to Britain, in the cause of man's salvation. They rushed at him on the open sea, putting perils in his path, stirring storms and blotting out the daylight sky with a mist of darkness. But in an instant at St Germanus' prayer, the mist was wiped away, the storms were stilled and all perils ceased.
>
> Our own Columba, seeing the elements were roused to fury against him, called upon Christ the Lord."

Colmcille: a 'believable' saint

The portrait of Colmcille which emerges from the *Life* is a humane and gentle individual, a 'believable' saint, concerned for the well-being of others. As a result of Adomnán's *Life,* "Colmcille stands out as a clear cut historical personality against a background wherein his associates in sanctity, including the legend-encrusted Patrick and the half mythical Brigit, move as shadows in a land of twilight."[74] Although Colmcille does call down curses on those who disregard him, in the story below we see the rehabilitation of Erc the robber who had stolen from the community:

> "Once, when the saint was in Iona, he called for two of the brethren ... and gave them instructions.
>
> 'Take a boat now, across the Sound to Mull and seek out a thief called Erc from among the grounds near the sea. ... He has made himself a hiding place under his upturned boat, which he has camouflaged with grass. Here he tries to conceal himself all day so that by night he may sail across to the little island that is the breeding place of the seals we reckon as our own. His plan is to kill them, to fill his boat with what does not belong to him, is not his own.
>
> Erc was brought to the saint as they were instructed. On his arrival the saint addressed him:
>
> 'To what end do you persistently offend against the Lord's commandment and steal what belongs to others? If you are in need and come to us you will receive the necessities you request.'
>
> Fulfilling his words, so the man should not go home empty handed, he had some sheep slaughtered and given to the wretched thief instead of the seals." (Bk 1; 41)

Celtic Cross at Iona Abbey. *(Photo Wesley Johnston)*

In addition to this compassion, Colmcille does not engage in rivalry with other church leaders; many, for example Comgall, come to visit the saint at Iona and are warmly received.

Furthermore, Adomnán does not make any exaggerated claims concerning the success of Colmcille, unlike Bede who claims that the saint was responsible for the conversion of the pagan Picts:

> *"A priest and abbot named Columba, distinguished by his monastic habit and life, came from Ireland to Britain to preach the word of God in the provinces of the Northern Picts, which are separated from those of the Southern Picts by a range of steep and desolate mountains … . Columba arrived in Britain in the ninth year of the reign of the powerful Pictish king Bruide; he converted that people to the faith by preaching and example, and received from them the island of Iona on which to found a monastery."*[75]

Adomnán gives little detail on the missionary endeavours of Colmcille, although he does speak of visits into Pictland. In the story of Columba's journey to the court of King Bruide, we have a typical hagiographical narrative of a contest between the saint and the wizards of Bruide. Columba certainly wins the contest but Adomnán does not make any claim that he was successful in the conversion of Bruide.

Adomnán instead tells us that *"Colmcille stayed for some days in the territory of the*

257

Picts" and in other places refers only to a journey made by Colmcille, *"to the other side of Drium Alban"*. We do not know how numerous these visits were, but we do know that on two occasions Colmcille converted two individual families. He also tells us of Columba preaching to the Picts through an interpreter, but the claims of success for his saint are less grandiose than those Muirchú makes for Patrick. Kathleen Hughes is of the view that although Bede's account is generally accepted, "Adomnán's testimony is preferable and it fits in much better with archaeological evidence."[76]

> *"A little boat came in to land on the shore, bringing in its prow a man worn out with age. He was the chief commander of the warband in the region of Cé. Two young men carried him from the boat and set him down in front of the blessed man. As soon as he had received the word of God from Saint Columba, through an interpreter, he believed and was baptised by him."* (Bk 1; 33)

> *"During the time when saint Columba spent a number of days in the province of the Picts, he was preaching the word of life through an interpreter."* (Bk 2; 32)

It is the realistic account of the achievements of Colmcille which leads Ó Cróinín to declare that "pride of place among Irish hagiographers must go to Adomnán ... . Although the work suffers from many of the faults that disfigure medieval hagiography in the eyes of modern readers, Adomnán's *Life of Columba* far surpasses all the other seventh century Irish Lives, both as authentic portrait of its subject and in its value as evidence for the life of the church in Adomnán's own time."[77]

 TASK

Compare and contrast the portraits of Patrick and Colmcille as presented by their hagiographers. Give textual evidence and examples to support the points you make.

Everyday monastic life

It is this vast quantity of 'incidental' information that Adomnán gives which also impresses Kathleen Hughes in terms of its historical value.

He gives wonderful anecdotal evidence of the daily routine of life in the monastery, illustrating that the centre of that life was the daily worship in the church and that the monks were summoned to it by the ringing of a hand bell. We know that on Sundays and feast days the Eucharist was celebrated at the mid-day service. Work seems to have included agricultural work as well as the copying of books. Copies had to be checked most diligently:

> *"I beseech all those that may want to copy these books, nay I adjure them through Christ, the judge of the ages, that after carefully copying they compare them with the exemplar from which they have written, and emend them with the utmost care; and also that they append this adjuration in this place."*

The description of the reception of guests at the monastery is heart-warming:

"Go quickly and bring at once to us the pilgrims that have arrived from a far away place. They obeyed at once and took a boat over the Sound and brought the guests across. The saint greeted them with a kiss ... and they were shown to the guesthouse."

These are all background details which are "minutely sketched, and ordinary, even trivial events of community life [which] provide the setting in which the sanctity of Colmcille is revealed."[78] In addition, Adomnán names twenty of the monks of Colmcille's community. Overall, his work gives us "the chief record of the old Celtic monastic Church."[79]

News gathering

Adomnán names a number of important princes who came into contact with the saint and gives us details about them which we would not otherwise have known. This information is given to us in the form of prophecies by the saint about such people. He tells us that King Oswald had spent some time *"in exile among the Irish"*. Herbert believes that there was a practice of making a note of news of the world beyond the monastery, which arrived in Iona from visitors and monks returning from their travels.[80] This would explain the detailed accuracy of much information contained in the *Life*.

Many of the details given by Adomnán are supported by information given in the annals, and at times he elaborates on that information.[81] This has led Kathleen Hughes to lament: "One cannot help wishing that Adomnán had been writing an 'Ecclesiastical History of the Scots' instead of a saint's Life, so that we might have explicit accounts where we now only have tantalising allusions."[82] Kenney agrees that it is "a source of extraordinary value for contemporary conditions ... its statements of fact regarding the past seem, as far as they can be tested, to be remarkably accurate."[8]

The *Life* also lends considerable insight into Pictland at the time. We are told of the over-lordship of Bruide who has a *"sub-king of the Orkneys at his court."*[84] In this way, Adomnán's *Life of Colmcille* tells us many things which we would not otherwise know about Iona, Scotland, and to a lesser extent Ireland in the century between the saint's death and Adomnán's own lifetime.[85] The *Life* supplements the annals and in one case modifies Bede. For this reason it is "perhaps the most valuable monument of the Irish Church which has escaped the ravages of time."[86]

Gaps in knowledge

Nonetheless, having read Adomnán's account, we are still left with a number of gaps in our knowledge of the saint's monastic career. In particular, there is little information about Columba's time in Ireland before his departure to Iona and there is uncertainty surrounding the circumstances of that departure.

Other scholars are more dismissive of the work of Adomnán. Schoel, writing in the nineteenth century, argues that "it is so obscured by fables that one could scarcely believe that such nonsense could have been written in the seventh century when learning flourished at Iona."[87]

 PRACTICE ESSAY TITLES

a) **Outline and examine the contents of Adomnán's *Life of Colmcille*. (30)**

   Your answer may include reference to some of the following:
   - A definition of hagiography
   - An outline of the work
   - Adomnán's purpose in writing
   - The sources he used
   - Hagiographical features with textual examples
   - Views of scholars

b) **Critically assess the view that Adomnán's *Life of Colmcille* is a reliable historical source. (20)**

   Your answer may include reference to some of the following:
   - The purpose of hagiography in general
   - The date of writing
   - Some sources used and the referencing of Adomnán
   - Examples of historical content
   - The presence of miracle, prophecy, cursing, angelic visions
   - The views of scholars

4. COGITOSUS' *LIFE OF BRIGIT*

Introduction

Cogitosus' *Life of Brigit* stands in marked contrast to Adomnán's *Life of Colmcille*. Brigit was a figure who emerges from the very earliest years of the Christian Church in Ireland. An entry in the *Annals of Ulster*, probably interpolated, tells us that she was born in 457, but there are no less than three death dates suggested for the saint. We know that Muirchú had Patrick's own writings and maybe a written account of Patrick's stay on the Continent[88]; Herbert has shown that Adomnán had at his disposal monastic tradition concerning Colmcille, which had been committed to writing in a very early stage after its transmission. Cogitosus would have had no source-rich store of information regarding his subject.

We know that Muirchú's *Life of Patrick* was written between 680 and 700. He cites Cogitosus as his "father" and tells us he was the only other known writer of this genre in the Celtic Church. The *Life of Brigit* was therefore written before that, perhaps around 650. It was written in the Latin language, probably at Brigit's own monastery in Kildare.

The structure and characteristics of the *Life of Brigit*

Some historians question whether the *Life of Brigit* by Cogitosus had any real structure to speak of and suggest that it is instead, "little more than a series of miracles."[8] He begins his narrative with a prologue which is similar to the one Muirchú later produces.

The *Life* begins and ends with talk of issues of the time of the author himself – the seventh century – and has accounts of the many miracles of Brigit in between. In particular, miracles of plenty are common in this section:

> "*In the course of time, when she came of suitable age, her mother sent her to the dairy, to churn and make butter from cows' milk, so that she too would serve in the same way as the women who were accustomed to engage in this work. For a period, she and the other women were left to themselves. At the end of the period they were required to have produced a plentiful return of milk and curds, and measures of churned butter. But this beautiful maiden, with her generous nature, chose to obey God rather than man. She gave the milk to the poor and to wayfarers, and also handed out the butter. At the end of this period the time came for them all to make a return from their dairy production; and it duly came to her turn ... she had nothing to show, having given all away to the poor ... and she trembled with fear of her mother. Burning with the fire of indistinguishable faith, she turned to God in prayer. Through the bounty of his Divine Will, He ... answered her faith in Him by providing a plentiful supply of butter ... not only was her quota seen to be filled, but her production was found to be much greater than that of her fellow workers.*"

 TASK

Think about and discuss the importance of miracle as a mark of sanctity.
Discuss what other characteristics you would associate with holiness.
Can you find evidence of any of them in Cogitosus' *Life of Brigit*?

The nature theme in the Life of Brigit [90]

> "*Not long after wards, her parents in the ordinary way of the world, wished to betrothe her to a man. But heaven inspired her to decide otherwise: to present herself as a*

chaste virgin to God. ... She went down on her knees in the presence of God and the bishop, and she touched the wooden base that supported the altar. The wood retains to the present day the wonderful effect of that gesture long ago: it is as green as if the sap still flowed from the roots of a flourishing tree, and as if the tree had not long ago been felled and stripped of its bark. Even today it cures infirmities and diseases of the faithful.

I retell here another episode which demonstrates her sanctity; one in which what her hand did, corresponded to the quality of her pure virginal mind. It happened that she was pasturing her sheep on a grassy spot on the plain when she was drenched by heavy rain, and she returned home in wet clothes. The sun shining through an aperture in the building cast a beam inside which, at a casual glance, seemed to her to be a solid wooden joist set across the house. She placed her wet cloak on it as if it were indeed solid, and the cloak hung safely from the immaterial sunbeam."

It is also important to note that asceticism and mortification are absent from Cogitosus' *Life of Brigit.*

Animals in the Life of Brigit

Berschin argues that none of the other Latin Lives of the Middle Ages contain as many stories about animals as Cogitosus' *Life of Brigit.* In this way, he argues that Brigit "lives in an archaic world surrounded by animals, praising the invisible Creator through His visible creation to whom the animals are subject and for whom they live."[91] These stories usually involve miracles designed to show in Cogitosus' words:

"that the entire nature of the beasts and cattle were subject to her command. On another day, a certain person, not knowing the circumstances, saw the king's fox walking into the royal palace, and ignorantly thought it to be a wild animal. He did not know that it was a pet, familiar with the king's hall, which entertained the king and his companions with various tricks that it had learned – requiring both intelligence and nimbleness of body. He killed the fox in view of a large crowd. Immediately he was seized by the people who had seen the deed. He was accused and brought before the king. When the king heard the story he was angry and ordered that, unless a man could produce a fox with all the tricks that his fox had had, he and his wife and sons should be executed and all his household be committed to servitude. When the venerable Brigit heard the story she was moved to pity and tenderness ... and offering prayers to the Lord ... travelled across the plain... And the Lord instantly heard her prayers. He directed one of the wild foxes to come to her. And in the presence of the king and of the crowd [the fox] went through all the tricks that the other fox had performed, and amused the crowd in exactly the same way. The king was satisfied ... ordered that the man ... should be set free. Not long after Saint Brigit had procured the man's release ... the same fox, bothered by the crowds, skilfully contrived a safe escape ... fled through the plains and into the waste and wooded places and so to its den."

Pagan goddess Brigit

Most scholars claim that Cogitosus' *Life* may reflect some confusion with the pagan goddess Brigit. *Cormac's Glossary*, written around 900, records one such pagan goddess and it is thought that there were a further three sister goddesses of this name. Liam de Paor agrees that many of the stories included by Cogitosus are "not particularly Christian in form or content – probably retellings of old stories of pagan times ... told originally about the god or goddesses, of whom the most widespread name is Brig[id]."[92]

The purpose of the *Life of Brigit*

In his Prologue, Cogitosus tells us that he writes at the request of his community, who "press" him to write his account.

Cogitosus also writes to make claims on behalf of the paruchiae Brigit and to elevate Brigit to episcopal status. He tells us that:

> *"Kildare is head of virtually all the Irish Churches and occupies the first place, excelling all the monasteries of the Irish. Its jurisdiction extends over the whole island of Ireland from sea to sea.*
>
> *[Brigit] was concerned about the churches which adhered to her in many territories. She called on a famous hermit ... to leave his hermitage and his solitary life and to come and join her in that place, so that he might rule the church with her in Episcopal dignity. She continues to rule (through happy line of succession), venerated by all the Irish abbesses."*

Ó Cróinín[93] believes that Cogitosus' *Life of Brigit* is a very good example of a Life written "with a view to attracting popular interest and a corresponding inflow of pilgrims and wealth":

> *"What eloquence could sufficiently extol the beauty of this church and the innumerable wonders of what we may call its city, For 'city' is the proper word to use, since [Kildare] earns the title because of the multitudes who live there; it is a great metropolitan city ... it is the safest refuge among all the enclosed towns of the Irish. The wealth and treasures of kings are in safe keeping there, and the city is known to have reached the highest peak of good order. And who could number the varieties of people who gather there in countless throngs from all provinces? Some come for the abundance of feasts; others, in ill health, come for a cure; others come simply to watch the crowds go by; others come with great offerings to take part in the celebrations of the feast of Saint Brigit."*

The historical reliability and value of Cogitosus' *Life of Brigit*

- Cogitosus claims to have been using "written documents as well as people's memories". Most scholars believe that there were few written sources on Brigit, belonging as she did to the earliest period of the Christian Church in Ireland. Nonetheless, Kathleen Hughes has pointed out that Cogitosus' account and the later *Old Irish Life of Brigit* may both have used a common early source on Brigit. Cogitosus' written sources may have included some secular literature. He seems to have a fascination with the carriage of Brigit, which is very much a trait of Celtic stories. Traditionally, Continental Celtic princes took their carriages to the grave with them. It seems clear that there was some borrowing of ideas from other Celtic literature.

- It is also important to note that during the time of Cogitosus, Kildare was beginning to put together the annals and during the seventh century a scriptorium seems to have been quite active at Kildare. There would have been stories circulating about Brigit at this time, which Cogitosus may have availed of.

- Cogitosus' *Life* is important in its own right because it is "the first of such texts to have emerged out of the darkness of the seventh century."[94]

- Bieler refers to the scant detail on the saint herself. He briefly describes the saint's birth, childhood and vocation. "He does not even describe the saint's death, instead he tells as an eye witness some miracles performed after her death."[95] It may have been the case that after recounting such a huge amount of supernatural material in the *Life*, he could not possibly discuss the harsh and merely earthly reality of her death. His desire instead, was to show the presence of his saint just as strongly after her death.

"Many miracles were performed in her lifetime, before she laid down the burden of her flesh; many later. The bounty of the gift of God never ceased working wonders in her monastery, where her venerable body lies. We have not only heard tell of these marvels; we have seen them with our own eyes."

- Cogitosus' *Life* is an excellent source for seventh century affairs, particularly at Kildare. As we have already seen, the church there was growing in wealth and prominence. It had some involvement in secular affairs, both as an esteemed place of sanctuary and a place of safe keeping for the wealth of kings.

The church was also growing in size which necessitated the building of a new church which Cogitosus describes in great detail in his *Life*:

"In fact, to accommodate the increasing number of the faithful, of both sexes, the church is spacious in its floor area, and it rises to an extreme height. It is adorned with painted boards and has on the inside three wide chapels, all under the roof of the large building and separated by wooden partitions. One partition which is decorated with painted images and is covered with linen, stretches transversely in the eastern part of the church from one wall to the other and has two entrances, at its ends. By one entrance, placed in the external part, the supreme pontiff enters the sanctuary and approaches the altar with his retinue of monks. To these consecrated ministers, are

entrusted the sacred vessels for Sunday use and the offering of the sacrifice. And by the other entrance, placed on the left side of the above – mentioned transverse partition, the abbess, with her faithful virgins and widows, equally enters to enjoy the banquet of the body and blood of Jesus Christ ...

... The church has many windows, and an ornamented door on the right side through which the priests and the faithful of the male sex enter the building. There is another door on the left through which the virgins and the congregation of the female faithful are accustomed to enter. And so, in one great basilica, a large number of people, arranged by rank and sex, in orderly division, separated by partitions, offer prayers with a single spirit to the almighty Lord."

Cogitosus thus gives us the only extant detailed description of a seventh century church, much grander and more ornate than we otherwise might have expected. He also gives us a valuable description of the procedures applied to worship in a double monastery in the seventh century. This material stands in marked contrast to the abundant miraculous content in the *Life*.

 **SUMMARY**

Hagiography is a type of writing not unique to the Celtic Church. Celtic hagiography was to some extent modelled on early hagiographical material from the Church on the Continent.

Hagiographies were a type of writing, written in praise of the saint, evidencing their holiness by citing the miracles performed by them.

Each author had their own purpose and specific circumstances which gave rise to the production of the Life. Some writers wanted to make claims about the eminence of their own church or to gain financial benefit for that church by attracting pilgrims.

Although unique, all hagiographies (to a greater or lesser extent) follow the same compositional characteristics.

Some are more historically reliable than others, yet most probably contain very little in the way of genuine historical detail on the saint.

Most historians agree that all hagiography is a valuable historical source for the time in which it was written and for the 'incidental' information which they give.

They are also important for the cultural insight they give into the types of stories people liked to hear then, and their perception of what made a person holy.

Endnotes

1 This is the term used by both James Kenney and Kathleen Hughes to describe hagiographies and is generally taken to be a very appropriate description of this genre of literature

2 Hughes, *Early Christian Ireland: Introduction to the Sources, op cit,* p219

3 Kenney, *The Sources for the Early History of Ireland: Ecclesiastical An Introduction and Guide, op cit,* p299

4 *ibid*

5 De Coulanges, F, *Histoire de institions politiques de l'ancienne France, La monarchie franque,* Paris 1888, p9

6 *ibid*

7 Gougaud, *Christianity in Celtic Lands, op cit,* p53

8 *ibid*

9 These characteristics generally reflect the ideas of Kathleen Hughes and James Kenney.

10 Quoted in Gougaud, *Christianity in Celtic Lands,* p56

11 *ibid,* p53

12 Bieler, L, *The Life and Legend of St Patrick,* Clonmore and Reynolds Ltd, Dublin, 1948, p113

13 Gwynn, EJ *Some Saints of Ireland,* in *Church Quarterly Review, LXXIV,* 1912, pp64 & 202

14 Hughes, *Early Christian Ireland: Introduction to the Sources, op cit,* p220

15 Hughes, K, *Sanctity and Secularity,* in *Church and Society in Ireland AD400-1200,* ed D Dumville, Variorum Reprints, London, 1987, p29

16 Kenney, *Sources for the Early History of Ireland, op cit,* p297

17 All textual references are taken from the translation by de Paor, L, *Saint Patrick's World,* Four Courts Press, Dublin, 1993

18 Morris, *The Dates of the Celtic Saints,* op cit, p366

19 Hughes, *Early Christian Ireland: Introduction to the Sources, op cit,* p230

20 Kenney, *Sources for the Early History of Ireland, op cit,* p332

21 Doherty, C, *The Cult of Saint Patrick in Ireland and Northern France AD600-850,* ed JM Picard, Four Courts Press, Dublin, 1991, p84

22 Hughes, *Introduction to the History of Medieval Ireland* in *Church and Society in Ireland AD400-1200, op cit,* p16

23 Bieler, *The Life and Legend of Patrick, op cit*

24 McNeill, 'St. Patrick', Essay on 'The Earliest Lives of Patrick', pp118–119 quoted in Hanson, *Patrick, His Origins and Career, op cit,* pp88–85

25 Ryan, *Irish Monasticism, op cit,* p75

26 O'Rahilly, *The Two Patricks, op cit,* pp18–19

27 Hanson, *St Patrick, His Origins and Career, op cit,* p86

28 *ibid,* p89

29 *ibid,* p94

30 Olden, *The Church of Ireland,* p412, cited *ibid,* p91

31 Doherty, *The Cult of St Patrick, op cit,* p86

32 O'Loughlin, T, *Celtic Theology,* Continuum Press, London, 2000, p92

33 *ibid,* p96

34 The bold print is mine and does not appear in the translation by Liam de Paor.

35 Hanson, *The Origins and Career of Patrick, op cit,* p93

36 Morris, *The Dates of the Celtic Saints,* p342 and p 366 cited in Hanson, *ibid* pp87 and 88

37 Hanson, *op cit,* p90

38 *ibid*

39 *ibid,* p92

40 Gougaud, *Christianity in Celtic Lands, op cit,* p56

41 Binchy, D, *A pre-Christian survival in medieval Irish Hagiography* in *Ireland in Early Medieval Europe,* ed D Whitelock *et al,* Cambridge University Press, 1982, p166

42 See Bury, *The Life Of Patrick, op cit*

43 Hanson, *Origins and Career, op cit,* p91

44 Bieler, *The Life and Legend of Patrick,* p102

45 'The Lives of Saint Patrick and the Book of Armagh' in *St. Patrick,* ed J Ryan, pp61–62

46 Bieler, L, 'St Patrick and the Coming of Christianity' in *A History of Irish Catholicism,* ed P Corish, Gill & Macmillan, Dublin, 1967, p27

47 See Hanson, *St Patrick, his Origins and Career, op cit,* p83

48 *ibid*, p347

49 Gougaud, *Christianity in Celtic Lands, op cit*, p56

50 Hughes, K, *Early Christian Ireland: An Introduction to the Sources, op cit*, p232

51 Gougaud, *op cit*, p55

52 Hanson, *Origins and Career*, p92

53 Binchy, D, *Patrick and His Biographers: Ancient and Modern, op cit*, p58

54 Corish, P, 'The Christian Mission' in *A History of Irish Catholicism*, Vol 1, ed P Corish, Gill & Macmillan, Dublin, 1972, p46

55 *ibid*, p45

56 Hughes, *Sanctity and Secularity in the Early Irish Church* in *Church and Society in Ireland, op cit*, p28

57 Binchy, *A pre-Christian Survival in medieval Irish Hagiography in Ireland in Early Medieval Europe, op cit*, p168

58 *ibid*, pp95–96

59 Hughes, *Early Christian Ireland: An Introduction to the Sources, op cit*, p222

60 Sharpe, R, *Adomnán of Iona: Life of Columba*, Penguin Classics, 1995, p57

61 Herbert, M, *Iona, Kells and Derry, The History and Hagiography of the monastic Familia of Columba*, Clarendon Press, Oxford, 1988, pp20–21

62 Sharpe, *op cit*, p56–57

63 Herbert, *op cit*, p17

64 Hughes, *Introduction to the Sources*, p223

65 All textual references are taken from the translation of Richard Sharpe, Penguin Classics, 1995

66 Kenney, *The Sources for the Early History of Ireland: Ecclesiastical An Introduction and Guide, op cit*, p301

67 Picard, J, *The Purpose of Adomnán's Vitae Columbae*, p171, cited in Herbert, *Iona, Kells, and Derry*, p146

68 *ibid*

69 Herbert, *Iona, Kells and Derry, op cit*, p144

70 See chapter 10

71 Kenney, *op cit*, p304

72 Corish, P, 'The Christian Mission', *op cit*, p47

73 Herbert, *op cit*, p16

74 Kenney, *op cit*, p426

75 Bede's *Ecclesiastical History of the English People*, ed Colgrave & Mynors, Clarendon Press, Oxford 1969

76 Hughes, *op cit*, p225

77 Ó Cróinín, D, *Early Medieval Ireland AD400–1200*, Longman, London, 1995, pp208–209

78 Herbert, *op cit*, p14

79 Kenney, *op cit*, p425

80 Herbert, *op cit*, p22

81 Hughes, *op cit*, p224

82 *ibid*

83 Kenney, *op cit*, p301

84 *ibid*

85 *ibid*, p226

86 Reeves, W, (ed), *The Life of Saint Columba, founder of Hy; written by Adomnán*, Dublin: the Irish Archaeological and Celtic Society 1857; see Kenney, *op cit*, p429

87 Schoel, CG, *De ecclesiasticae Britonum Scttorumque historiae fontibus*, Berlin, 1851

88 Remember that not all historians accept that this was a valid source on Patrick the Briton.

89 Berschin, W, *Radegundin and Brigit* in *Studies in Early Irish Hagiography*, ed Herbert, O'Riain and Carey, Four Courts Press, 2001, p73

90 All quotations from Cogitosus' *Life of Brigit* are taken from the translation by de Paor, L, *Saint Patrick's World*, Four Courts Press, Dublin, 1993

91 Berschin, W, *op cit*, p72

92 De Paor, L, *Saint Patrick's World*, Four Courts Press, Dublin, 1993, p47

93 Ó Cróinín, D, *Early Medieval Ireland AD400–1200*, Longman, London, 1995, p210

94 Berschin, *op cit*, p72

95 Bieler, L, *The Celtic Hagiographer*, p247 cited in Herbert *et al* (eds)

Chapter 9

Aspects of Missionary Outreach

LEARNING OUTCOMES

Knowledge, understanding and evaluation of:

— the career and contribution of Columbanus

— the monastic Rules of Columbanus

— the contribution of the peregrini

INTRODUCTION

The Celtic peregrini were active in Europe in the Dark Ages, long after the collapse of the Empire when the barbarous tribes of Vandals, Goths and Huns had rampaged across the Continent, leaving devastation in their wake. Under the influence of the invaders, paganism had begun to raise its head again; almost all traces of learning and culture had disappeared and a weakened Church was under threat from heresy. Politically, there was unrest and constant warfare between opposing factions; violence was a constant feature of society on the Continent. Into this environment came "new invaders … unarmed white robed monks with books in their satchels and psalms on their lips, seeking no wealth or comfort but only the opportunity to teach and to pray."[1] The foremost of these was Columbanus.

1. COLUMBANUS

The Career of Columbanus at a glance

Birth	Born in Leinster in 543.[2] Parents of low social class.
Early Education	Study of grammar, rhetoric, geometry and Scripture.
Vocation	Attracted attention of local maidens, called "lascivious wenches" by Jonas. He sought advice from a local nun; she advised him to embrace the monastic life. His mother objected, prostrating herself across the doorway to beg him to stay. Columbanus stepped over her body.
Early Monastic Career	He studied at Cleenish, Upper Lough Erne, school of Sinnell, who was himself a student of Finnian of Clonard and Comgall. He studied the Bible, wrote a commentary on the psalms and some hymns. Went to Bangor and remained under Comgall for 25 years, progressed in his studies and acted as senior lecturer in the monastic school.
Missionary Outreach	He asked Comgall's permission to go on peregrinatio. Comgall agreed reluctantly and Columbanus, with twelve companions, set out and travelled through Brittany into Gaul in 591. He and his companions acted as itinerant preachers for a while before looking for a place to settle.
Early Monastic Foundations	The local king, probably Guntram, gave permission to choose a location for a monastery. He chose a remote spot, the abandoned fort of Annegray in the foothills of the Vosges close to Burgundy's border with Austraisa. Many came for the forgiveness of their sins and to receive penance. Another settlement was needed and was made at Luxeuil, eight miles away. Columbanus wrote his Monks' Rule, Community Rule and Penitential. Again, huge popularity necessitated a third foundation three miles north at Fontaines. He is reported to have had around 220 monks.[3]

Other Key Events	Columbanus incurred the anger of the French bishops because he had neglected to seek their approval to found monasteries in their dioceses and for his erroneous dating of Easter.
	He wrote to Pope Gregory the Great around 600 to defend himself. He also wrote to Gregory's successor Sabinian on the same matter.
	In 603 the French bishops called him to a council to explain his peculiar practices. He declined to attend, sending only a letter outlining his own preference for traditions of his own country.
	He denounced the immoral lifestyle of King Theuderic and refused baptism of the king's illegitimate children, causing his expulsion from Luxeuil and intended deportation back to Ireland. The year was around 612.
	At Nantes, Columbanus escaped. He wrote a letter of encouragement to his monks at Luxeuil. He made his way to Neustria and though well received, he moved on to Metz in Austraisa and gained King Theudebert's permission to evangelise in the lake country of Switzerland.
	He moved on to Bregenz at the eastern end of the Lake of Constance and made a monastic foundation here in 612.
	In 612–613, after an altercation with Gall, Columbanus leaves Bregenz and travels across the Alps to Milan.
	In Milan he delivered his thirteen sermons.
	He moved on into the heart of Lombardy and was offered a site for a monastery at Bobbio. He was actively involved in the Arian Controversy and wrote a long letter to Pope Boniface IV on the subject of heresy.
	Columbanus died at Bobbio on 21 November 615.
Other writings	Columbanus wrote six poems, the most famous of which was the *Carmen* or *Boating Song*, written while rowing up the Rhine to Switzerland.
	His sixth Letter was written in encouragement to a young disciple.

The background to the mission of Columbanus

The political condition of Frankish Gaul at the time of Columbanus was very unstable. Gregory of Tours finds just one good king, Guntram of Burgundy, who was king at the time of Columbanus' arrival among the Franks. Political strife, of which assassinations were a common part, was continuous, as territories were fought over. In the countryside the constant threat from rampaging armed barbarians meant that farmers were often forced to flee their land, with disastrous consequences for the poorly farmed land. In the cities people often lived under siege, which in turn brought the threat of plague.

King Guntram died in 593. The kingdom of Burgundy was given to his nephew Childebert who in turn, died two years later. The kingdom was then divided: Childebert's son Theudebert received Austrasia while his other son Theuderic inherited Burgundy. Clothair[3a] ruled Neustria. Alsace was added to the kingdom of Burgundy, causing bad relations. Both Theudebert and Theuderic were minors when they succeeded to the throne, and Theuderic in particular was heavily influenced by his grandmother Brunhilde, who relished her political influence in the kingdom of Burgundy.

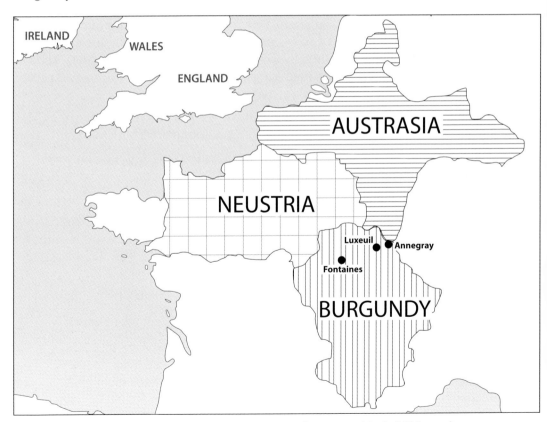

The geography of Columbanus' sojourn on the Continent (courtesy of Cathal O'Connor).

In terms of the faith, many suggest that the attitude was rather apathetic. Jonas implies that it was because of the negligence of the Frankish bishops that the faith had almost entirely disappeared in the region. Other commentators paint a picture of a "decadent and amoral Christian faith."[4] Some texts depict a worldly clergy, supporting the power struggles of the local princes in exchange for a fee. Other clergy were demoralised by the resurgence of paganism and the threat of heresy. It was against this background that Columbanus set to work.

Significance and impact of Columbanus

The Sources

Columbanus is a Celtic saint who is very accessible to us in the modern age. There are two reasons for this. Unlike Colmcille, a huge amount (though probably not all) of Columbanus' writings have survived. Through these writings we can paint quite a clear portrait of the man. It is the sheer volume of his writings that in the view of Ó Fiaich "places him head and shoulders above all his contemporaries as the first great Irish man of letters."[5] In addition, we have the *Life of Columbanus*, written by Jonas. Many commentators take Jonas' *Life of Columbanus* to be fairly reliable. Jonas entered Columbanus' monastery at Bobbio, not later than 618, only three years after the death of Columbanus. He knew and interviewed many of the saint's contemporaries and disciples. He also travelled to Luxeuil and interviewed Eustasius, the Abbot there. Jonas was in an excellent position to gain a wealth of reliable factual information about the life of Columbanus.

Monasticism

Columbanus made a very significant contribution to the development of monasticism on the Continent. Although monasticism had already been established on the Continent, there is no evidence of the practice of a formal written rule.

The Rules of Columbanus

Columbanus' Monks' Rule and Community Rule are the earliest existent Celtic monastic rules we have. For this reason, they are historically very important for the information they give on the essence and routine of Celtic monasticism in the sixth and seventh century. It is important to note that they were not in themselves innovative. The general principles and practices of monastic life were the same everywhere but each abbot would have given different emphasis and interpreted them with greater or lesser severity. Columbanus' Rules are probably a replica of the Rule of Comgall at Bangor.[6] They did give a formal structure to monasticism on the Continent and for the first time gave monasticism on the Continent a formal constitution.[7] Metlake is of the view that although the chapters on Obedience and

Discretion in the Monks' Rule are almost copied verbatim from Cassian and Saint Basil, Columbanus "stamps his Rule with the mark of his personality and distinguishes it from all others."[8]

- The Monks' Rule outlined the virtues and inner attitudes and disposition expected of the monks. Ó Fiaich believes that "its tone is balanced and tolerant throughout."[9] The Rule advises that:

  "... nothing must be refused in their obedience by Christ's true disciples, however hard and difficult it be, but it must be seized with zeal, with gladness ...

  ... greed is a leprosy for monks ... thus then nakedness and the disdain of riches are the first perfection of the monks ... few things are true necessities without which life cannot be led.

  ... the nurture of righteousness is in silence and peace ... in many words sin will not be lacking.

  How dangerous vanity also may be ... vanity and proud self-esteem are the destroyer of all good things."[10]

- The Community Rule lays down the structure and routine of the daily life of the monks as well as suggesting penalties for the breach of the Rule. To the modern reader, it is perhaps not difficult to see why the Rule of Columbanus was replaced in the mid-eighth century, with the milder Rule of Benedict. Some commentators claim that the Rule of Benedict was even used in Columbanus' own foundations; others suggest the mixed Rule of Columbanus and Benedict became the norm. Benedict, for example, recommended the recitation of twelve psalms each night, while Columbanus' Rule requires three hundred and thirty. Columbanus allows around half the amount of food as permitted by Benedict. Benedict made much greater allowance for those weakened by illness than did Columbanus, allowing them, for example, to eat meat. Columbanus does not suggest any such relaxation. Strangely though, rather than alienating people, Columbanus' Rule attracted more and more disciples to his monasteries, necessitating three foundations in France to accommodate their number. In 817 at the request of Louis the Pious, the Council of Aix-la-Chapelle made the Rule of Benedict compulsory for all monasteries in the area.

  Some are critical of the Rules of Columbanus because they lack detail. There is no direction, for example on the election of an abbot; the time for going to bed and for rising are not given; nor is there a prescribed amount of time allotted for study, manual work or prayer. Columbanus is prescriptive only about the recitation of the Divine Office, which was to be shorter in winter than in summer.

  "He who utters a loud speech without restraint, unless where there is need, with an imposition of silence or fifty blows.

Thus him who has not kept grace at table and has not responded Amen, it is ordained to correct with six blows.

And him who has not blessed the spoon with which he sups, with six blows."

Independence for the monasteries

Columbanus also gained exemption from episcopal control. He set up his monasteries within the dioceses of local bishops without asking their permission and ruled them in an entirely independent manner. By ruling as abbot over all three of his French foundations, he also contravened the restriction that an abbot could only rule over one house and so carried to the Continent the Celtic system of monastic paruchiae. In this way, he ensured the growth of his monasteries. Indeed in 628, after the death of Columbanus, Honorius put Bobbio under Papal jurisdiction, the first example of the privilege of monastic freedom.

Celtic flavour

Columbanus brought to the Continent, monasticism that had a distinctly Celtic flavour. His monasteries did not in any way submit to the values of the secular world even while they provided service to it; their renowned asceticism remained as strong as ever. Columbanus and his monks were often hungry to the point of starvation and sometimes reliant on the goodwill of visitors to bring them provisions. It was from the monastery of Luxeuil and its many sister monasteries that the Celtic monks in the Continent gained their great reputation for holiness.

 PRACTICE ESSAY TITLE

Using the notes above to help you, try the following evaluation:
Critically evaluate the contribution made by Columbanus to the development of monasticism. (20)

Private repeatable penance

One of the most important contributions Columbanus made to the development of the Church on the Continent was the provision of private repeatable penance. By doing so, "he provided a discipline, at once private and accessible that was entirely new to France".[11] However, because Columbanus' Penitential draws heavily on the Penitential of Finnian, Columbanus is more of a reformer than an innovator in this regard. It seems that the Penitential of Columbanus was the first Irish penitential to be used on the Continent. In the view of Ó Fiaich, for this reason, *"it had a significant influence on the development there of the new theology of the Sacrament of Penance."*[12] (Read Chapter 4 for more detail on the Penitential of Columbanus.)

Defender of the faith

Columbanus was a tremendous defender of the faith. He was quick to involve himself in the controversies of his day. These were many, in a Church torn by heresy.

Jonas tells us that *"wherever he went he preached the Gospel."* McNeill agrees that in his sermons Columbanus appears to us as *"an earnest proclaimer of the Christian message."*[13] It was particularly during his time in Italy that he participated most fully in the theological controversies of his day. In Milan he delivered his thirteen sermons in defence of the Trinity. These were clearly intended to address the heresy of the Arians current in the Church at that time.

Columbanus was very distressed by the divisions he found among Christians in Italy. The first of his thirteen sermons gives evidence of his orthodoxy:

> *"Let each man who wishes to be saved, believe first in God the first and last, one and three, one in substance, three in character … for whom you must not seek a beginning or an end … who shall boast of knowing the infinite God? … Therefore let no man venture to seek out the un-searchable things of God, the nature, mode and cause of his existence."*

The Arian Controversy centred on the relationship between the Father and the Son. They claimed that the Father had always been but the Son had not. He was created by the Father and was not equal to, or the same as the Father. He was neither truly God nor truly man. Furthermore, God was so different from humanity that it was not possible for humans to know him in any way.

A tower of peace and unity

Columbanus was also a strongly ecumenical figure. Just as attacks on the truth of the faith appalled him, divisions among Christians deeply saddened him. After leaving Luxeuil, Columbanus settled in Lombardy, living among those who had separated themselves from the Church and others who were embroiled in the Arian controversy. Here he worked tirelessly to bring these people back to the Catholic faith: just one example of Columbanus' ecumenical nature. Separation and hostility between Christians was a source of grief for Columbanus.

Many of his Letters reflect his concern for Christian unity. The Letter to the French Bishops ends:

> *"We are all members of the same body, whether Gauls or Britons, whether Spaniards or descendants of other nations. Let us therefore rejoice in the Unity of the faith … in Jesus let us love one another, encourage one another, correct one another, visit one another and pray for one another…".*

In his Letter to Boniface he pleads:

> *"Consign the old quarrels to silence and oblivion … forgive one another that there may be joy in heaven upon your peace and unity … I cannot understand how Christian can*

quarrel with Christian about the faith … that all may be one, that there may be one fold of Christ, that peace may be restored … to the whole Church."

He was immensely tolerant of difference and did not see it as an obstacle to unity among Christians. His only desire as far as the Easter Controversy was concerned was to be left alone to follow the tradition of his fathers.

Man of principle – objections to Theuderic's lifestyle

Columbanus was a defender of moral values. Although he was on friendly terms with Theuderic, he did not allow this to stop him from being an open critic of Theuderic's lifestyle, particularly his personal relationships. The story goes as follows:

The king, although unmarried had many concubines at his Court, with whom he had four illegitimate children. Columbanus convinced him of the immorality of his ways and persuaded him to take a wife. In 607, he asked Witteric, king of the Visogoths for the hand of his daughter. However Brunhilde was angry at the interference of Columbanus, and according to Jonas, *"fearing that if he married, she would lose much of her dignity and power"*. She hatched a plot to diminish the influence the monk could have over her grandson. She visited Columbanus at Luxeuil, bringing with her the four sons of the king and asked for his blessing upon them. This would have conferred a legitimacy of sorts on the children of the king, in the eyes of the people. Columbanus was furious and angrily denied the blessing saying, *"Know this, that these boys should never hold the kingly sceptre for they are the offspring of harlotry."* The humiliated Brunhilde swore her revenge. She ordered the monks not to leave the monastery and forbade any of the people to assist them in any way.

Columbanus decided to visit the king in person but waited in the courtyard instead of entering the monastery. The king, declaring *"it is better to honour the man of God by furnishing him with all he requires, than to provoke the wrath of God by offending His friends"*, ordered a feast to be sent to Columbanus. Columbanus refused, saying, *"the Almighty rejects the gifts of the wicked"* and smashed the plates and goblets into pieces on the pavement. The king and his grandmother were greatly humiliated. Brunhilde convinced Theuderic to return his fiancée to her father and reinstall his mistresses. Columbanus apparently wrote a letter to the king threatening excommunication. Brunhilde resolved to get rid of Columbanus and incited Theuderic to demand entrance into the cloister. He did so saying *"why do you not grant free access to your monastery to every Christian?"* Columbanus replied, *"it is not our custom, but we have a guesthouse for the fitting entertainment of all who come to us."* The king continued to insist and Columbanus continued to reproach him. Theuderic exiled Columbanus.

Columbanus clearly believed that he could "dispense with the powerful; he accepted the gifts of kings but he attacked their morals."[14] We could argue that Columbanus should have told himself that the lifestyle of the king was none of his concern, and that it was not his place to call the king to task. Surely the bishops of the land could have tried to influence the king? This was not the nature of the man however, and he saw that there was an issue of morality at stake. He acted, in the words of Metlake, "with characteristic impetuosity and disregard of consequences."[15] He certainly appears to lack the diplomatic skills of Colmcille and it caused him his time in Luxeuil. However, Dubois believes that Columbanus is the most fearless of all the Irish saints.[16] It certainly did take some courage to "rebuke rulers with the power to put him to death."[17] He was aware of the social and political responsibility of the leaders of his day and so was outspoken against them when he felt they needed correction.

In typical hagiographical style, Brunhilde suffered the consequences of her plotting against Columbanus. The old queen, who must have been around seventy at the time, was tied by her hair, an arm and leg, to the tail of a wild horse and so met her death.

TASKS

Think about and discuss whether you think the action of Columbanus was correct.
Should he have tried to placate the king so he could remain in Luxeuil?
Do you think religious leaders today have an obligation to comment on the behaviour and lifestyle of secular leaders?

Controversy with French bishops

Columbanus was also involved in controversy with the French bishops.

- He ignored their jurisdiction by establishing his monasteries without their consent.
- His monks wore a tonsure, which was different from that worn on the Continent.
- He used the Celtic method for calculating the date of Easter. This meant that his monastery celebrated Easter at a time that was different from the rest of France.

Ó Fiaich believes that in this regard "he left himself open to a charge of unorthodoxy".[18] The evidence from the Letters of Columbanus suggests that the dispute was prolonged. Charles-Edwards believes that not all bishops were opposed to Columbanus and some seem to have used him as their spiritual advisor.[19] When challenged by them, Columbanus wrote to Gregory in appeal. He initially defended the Irish methods of dating Easter, but then changed tact, requesting that the Irish should be allowed to follow their own customs. Columbanus' background meant that he was tolerant of difference, while the French bishops felt him to be divisive to the unity of the Church. Charles-Edwards agrees that in the eyes of the French "the Irishman was a source of division; the majority of the bishops were probably opposed to his continued influence."[20] Columbanus' reply by letter to the summoning to the Council at Châlon-sur-Saône is written with some irony and some would say arrogance, thanking God that for his sake, *"so many holy men have been assembled"* and then he adds with deep sarcasm, *"would that you met more often."*[21]

Admonishing the Pope

Columbanus also saw that it was his right to admonish the Pope. He feared that the Pope had not taken a harsh enough line in dealing with the schism and heresy of the day. His concern is that the Papacy should be beyond suspicion and hint of scandal. He was worried that any perceived indecision on the part of the Pope would weaken the Papacy. In this regard we can interpret his 'rebuke' of the Pope as an illustration of the tremendous esteem he had for Papal authority. He believes he has the right to address the Pope in such a manner because he comes from a country whose orthodoxy had always been beyond question and where the faith has always been preserved in its purity. His concern for the danger in which he sees the Church is clear:

> *"Watch, for water has now entered the vessel of the Church, and the vessel is in perilous straits.*
>
> *In our island there are no heretics … no schismatics. Here the Catholic faith is preserved as intact as it was delivered to us by you, the successors of the apostles.*
>
> *Watch over the peace of your Church, come to the aid of your sheep … speak to them with the voice of a true Pastor … Be vigilant at your post day and night. If you do not wish to lose the honour due to your apostolic office, preserve the apostolic faith; confirm it by your testimony; fortify it by a written instrument … Take care, when He comes, He finds you not neglectful of your duty … for you have taken upon yourself the care of many … For the love of God I beg of you to defend your good name, which is being torn to shreds among the nations … Such being the dignity of your See, you ought to take care not to prejudice it by any act of yours."*

No aspect of Columbanus' career had caused so much debate among scholars as this epistle to the Pope. Some believe his outspokenness to have gone too far, others that he wrote "out of zeal for the Truth and zeal for the honour of the Holy See".[22] Dubois argues that "even in the heat of his keenest controversies with the Papacy; he never lost his sound sense of orthodoxy."[23] Hauck agrees that "by his appeals to the Pope, Columban explicitly recognised the right of the Pope … his mandates a legal binding force."[24]

Multi-faceted character

As Metlake says, "we must remember that there were two sides to Columban's character ... he was eager, wilful, dauntless and passionate [but] like most of the Celtic saints he possessed a full share of tenderness of character."[25] This gentleness is most clearly seen in both his Letter to his disciples, written from Nantes after his expulsion from Luxeuil, and in the Letter written to a young disciple.

Letter to disciples at Luxeuil from Nantes:

"... keep Waldelenus always; if he is there with the community, may God dwell with him, may he be humble and give him my kiss, which then in his hurry he did not receive. For what advantage is it to have a body and not to have a heart ... For you know already the smallness of my knowledge, like a drop, you have learnt that all advice is not suitable for all, since natures are diverse and men's types differ widely from each other ... I wanted to write you a tearful Letter ... but have used another style, preferring to check rather than to encourage tears ... so my speech has outwardly been made smooth and my grief is shut up within."

Letter to a young disciple:

"My son that needs instruction, you ask to be taught ... my dearest sons must often be taught and instructed ... be simple in faith, trained in character, exacting in your own affairs, unconcerned in those of others, pure in friendship ... agreeing about truth ... kindly in griefs, slow to anger ... gentle to the weak. ... Let this be your model, beloved boy and dear secretary. [26] Happy and blessed you will be, admirable boy, if you fulfil all of this."

Conclusion

As Walker says: "it is the misfortune of commanding characters to arouse consuming hatreds; and Columbanus, by the outspoken freedom of his language and the tenacious independence of his mind, was plunged into animated quarrels for the greater portion of his active life."[27] Such was the force of his personality and the volume of his literary output that he stands out as the most influential of the peregrini. Columbanus is indeed a character "complex and contrary."[28] He stands out as the most influential of the peregrini. He is a figure of many contradictions; while always seeking the lonely place for himself, he also sought to influence those in public life and to "enter into dispute wherever he believed that wrong had been committed."[29]

The presence of Columbanus in Burgundy did much to transform the spiritual condition of its inhabitants. People flocked to Luxeuil in order to do penance and to be reconciled to the Church. The example of Columbanus and his monks inspired the local people to want to change their ways. His work brought about something of a reformation of the Church in France.

Over fifty three monasteries and hermitages adopted the Columban Rule in the seventh century. The personal influence of Columbanus was huge. After his death, his ideas concerning the status of the monasteries and the practice of penance were spread by the work of his disciples. Many of those who had positions of influence also championed the ideals of Columbanus. For example, Gougaud draws attention to Wandrille who resigned his rank as count and gave himself up in solitude to prayer and ascetic practices, which "remind us strongly of the ascetic practices of the monks". "It is likely", it had been said, "that Wandrille's thoughts were haunted by the memory of Columban".[30]

Columbanus has certainly "left a mark on human history, imponderable but real … his writings remain as an abiding memorial to the genius of his soul."[31]

 PRACTICE ESSAY TITLE

a) Explain and consider the contribution made by Columbanus to the development of the Celtic Church. (30)

> Your answer may include reference to some of the following:
> • The career of Columbanus
> • His monastic Rule and Penitentials
> • Exemption of the monasteries
> • His contribution to Church unity
> • The views of scholars

Using the notes given in the section above to help you and using your own opinion, try the following task:

b) Critically assess the view that Columbanus was too outspoken. (20)

2. OTHER CELTIC MISSIONARIES ON THE CONTINENT

Introduction

The main work of conversion throughout Europe was done by Celtic monks. We know this as historical fact, though the historical detail is scant and "abounds in obscurities and contradictions."[32] Many of these peregrini are obscured by the greatness of Columbanus and little was preserved in the way of written sources. Many of the Lives of these saints were compiled as late as the twelfth century and contain very little genuine and reliable information. Nonetheless, the persistence to the present day of strong cults of these saints and the abundance of towns, cities and villages named after them right across the Continent is strong testimony to their achievements.

We often hear of the peregrini travelling in groups of twelve. This is no doubt a reflection of the scriptural sending out of the twelve. However, it was also for practical reasons. These were "turbulent and violent ages."[33] It would not have been sensible to undertake such a journey alone or even in a small group, particularly on foot as so many would have done. Many sources from the period tell us of the poverty and exhaustion of the peregrini, almost to the point of total deprivation. Others, for example Fursa, lost their lives on such journeys.

Peregrini in Switzerland

Gall

We know that Gall was brought to the monastery at Bangor by his parents at a young age. He was one of the twelve who had accompanied Columbanus when he departed from Bangor. He also remained with Columbanus when he was exiled from Luxeuil and travelled with him as far as Switzerland.

Just after 610 he had an altercation with Columbanus. Columbanus expressed his desire to leave Switzerland and travel through the Alps into Italy. It would have been a long and hazardous journey. Gall had fallen ill and begged his abbot to remain in Switzerland. The *Life of Gall* tells us that Columbanus:

> "*thinking that Gall was held back by love of a spot endeared to him by many labours and was shirking the fatigue of a long journey, said to him: 'I know brother, that now it seems to thee a heavy burden to endure toil and weariness for my sake. Nevertheless, this I enjoin on thee ere I depart, that so long as I am alive in the body, thou shalt never take upon thee to celebrate Mass.'*"

The saint remained and Columbanus continued on his journey. When Gall heard of the death of Columbanus, he sent a deacon to Bobbio to enquire how the saint had died. The deacon returned with the staff of Columbanus. Columbanus had requested, before his death, that it be sent to Gall as a symbol of his forgiveness.

Gall – a model missionary

Gall, as part of Columbanus' band of companions, had been very zealous and almost violent in the fight against paganism. But his own mission was conducted using 'gentle persuasion', making friends among those he hoped to convert and gaining the support of local rulers.

McNeill credits Gall with being "a model missionary, not unlike his much admired contemporary, Aidan of Lindesfarne. Like Aidan, he went among the people, carrying his message to their homes."[34] It was by his example of holy living that pagans were converted to Christianity and that bad Christians were inspired to become better Christians. Gall's reputation for holiness spread throughout the whole region around the Lake of Constance.

His endeavours have earned him recognition as "the greatest figure in the founding of the Swiss church", even though in history he tends to be a little overshadowed by Columbanus with whom he spent many years.[35]

Where Columbanus was "a pioneer, a prophet, a legislator, a born leader of men…. [who] welcomed conflict, even with bishops and kings … Saint Gall on the other hand seems to have been meek and mild in spirit, unassuming, unambitious."[36] Gall had no ambition for himself, retaining only a small band of helpers and refusing the abbacy of Luxeuil when it was offered to him on the death of Eustace, the successor of Columbanus. He also declined the offer of the bishopric of Constance in 616, which was offered to him by the Duke of Alemanni whose daughter had been healed by the prayers of Gall. Instead Gall passed the position to his deacon John. The only existing writing from the pen of Gall was the Latin sermon he preached at the consecration of John.

By the time Gall died in 645, the territory had become largely Christian. There are over forty parishes dedicated to the saint.

Gall, seeking solitude and peace, constructed for himself a cell in a desert place in the valley of the Steinach stream, which flows into the Lake of Constance. It was here that he spent his last years and had his final resting place.

Peregrini in Gaul

Fursa

Fursa was born, according to his *Vitae* (Life), on the shores of Lough Corrib in Galway. Tradition also associates him with both Louth and Kerry.

He left Ireland for Britain after about ten years' labour in Ireland. He founded a monastery at Burgh Castle in East Anglia.

Bede pays tribute to him:

> "Renowned among his people, according to worldly standards, yet more eminent because of the heavenly gift of grace."

Sometime around 644–645, having been consecrated bishop, he landed first in Brittany[37] and rejecting pleas to remain there, went on to Neustria and built a monastery at Lagney on the Marne, east of Paris.

As the time of his death approached, it is said that Fursa desired to return to England, but he died, possibly in 649, while travelling at Mézerolle, in north Gaul.

The monastery had a succession of Irish abbots for a century after his death. The death of one such abbot, Móinán MacCormaic, is recorded in the *Annals of Ulster* as the *"Abbot of Fursa's monastery in France."*

The generation or so after his death, this monastery in north-eastern Gaul became known as the Paruchiae Fursa. His body was taken to Péronne and it was here that his memory remained strongest. His body retained its uncorrupted state, drawing many pilgrims to Péronne.

Although his achievements are not comparable to those of Columbanus, his contribution is important in terms of the monastery, which was later built at his burial place. It is because of this monastery that Péronne became known as Perrona Scottorum – 'Péronne of the Irish' or in the *Annals of Ulster* as *"the city of Fursa"*, and remained so until its destruction by the Norsemen in 880.

In the view of Ní Mheara, "Fursa is quite the most remarkable Irishman to leave his mark on France in the wake of Columban."[38]

Foillan and Ultán

Fursa had two brothers named Foillan and Ultán, who had followed him to the Continent. They went first to Péronne and then were given a settlement at Fosses by Itta. This benevolence of the nobility to the Irish peregrini was common at this time. Einhard was still calling this foundation the *"monastery of the Irish"* in the ninth century. The brothers preached in the Artois and Flanders regions and penetrated the area around the Ardennes forest.

Foillan was killed with three companions while travelling between Nivelles and Fosses, while returning from a visit to his brother Ultán. After a long search, Foillan's mutilated body was found buried in a piggery.

Gougaud believes that Ultán was still at Fosses in 659, possibly as an abbot and probably went on to become abbot of Péronne.[39] He died in 686.

Gobán

Gobán had accompanied Fursa. King Clovis gave him land for a hermitage in the forest area to the west of Laon. He remained in this area for many years until he was murdered in his oratory by the Vandals in 670. Around the site of his hermitage, grew the hamlet of Saint Gobain.

Peregrini in Austria and Germany

Killian

Irish missionaries, along with the Franks, were involved in the conversion of Bavaria. According to tradition, Killian came from Mullagh on the border of counties Cavan and Meath. He left Ireland in 643 with twelve companions. He was known as the apostle of Franconia having spent many years there. He chastised Duke Gosbert of Thuringia because he married the wife of his deceased brother. However, at the command of the new duchess, Killian was put to death with two of his companions at Würzburg around 689. Their relics were preserved there in the eighth century and they were celebrated as martyrs throughout Germany, where Christians were much fewer in number than in Gaul.

Tomás Ó Fiaich points out two other Celtic martyrs in Germany who seem to have been forgotten.[40] Bishop Marin was put to death on 15 November 697, in Wilparting and his deacon Anian is reported to have died of natural causes on the same day. They were placed in a tomb in front of the altar in the church in Wilparting.

With their strong liking for islands, some Celtic monks were said to have discovered a small island in the Rhine, approximately five miles below Strasbourg. On this island, Honau, they founded a monastery dedicated to St Michael.

Peregrini in Italy

More surprisingly perhaps, there were also Irish missionaries in Italy, many of whose names are not known to us. The most well known was, of course, Columbanus. Cataldus also worked in Tarentum in the south of Italy.

Even before Columbanus, Ursus had spent time in the area of Digne, Southern France before travelling across the Alps to Aosto, where he was bishop. He faced down challenges from Arian heretics, and preached and taught widely in the region. Although the dates of his mission are far from certain, his mission must have been some time in the sixth century, certainly no later than the second half.

Fridian,[41] reputedly the son of an Ulster king, founded a monastery at Lucca around 560 and became bishop there. Like Ursus, he too struggled with Arians in his diocese.

Peregrini in Brittany

Efflam, apparently an Irish prince, supposedly died in Brittany in 512 in the monastery he had founded there. There is a strong cult of Efflam in which stories are told of his self-sacrifice, giving up his title, wealth and beautiful bride for the peregrinatio. The church in which his body is buried became a great centre of pilgrimage. The remains of his hermitage have long since disappeared but his name lives on in the busy seaside resort of Saint-Efflam. A granite cross which marked the spot where he docked in Brittany and which was allegedly erected by him, was knocked down when the allied forces landed in 1944. Only a stump of the cross remained, but in 1993, in a grand ceremony, 'The Mid-Way Cross' was erected once more.

Brioc and Budoc landed at Plouba. Brioc is said to be the son of an Ulster ruler, but his heritage is uncertain. Budoc is thought to be the son of a fugitive of Brittany who had settled in Ireland.[42]

Legends and stories surround the name of Saint Rónán in Brittany. He lived as a hermit off the coast of Léon, before moving on to the forest of Nevit where he incurred the wrath of some of the locals. He then decided to return to his native Ireland to die, but died on the peninsula of Hillion. His body is said to have been interred near his hermitage in the forest of Nevit. The town of Locronan grew up around the saint's cell.

The cult of Saint Fiachra is also a colourful one in Brittany. Although the details of his life are obscure, he is thought to have died in France in the second half of the seventh century.[43] Devotion to him throughout Brittany is widespread, particularly in Morbihan where there are still annual processions to the Chapelle Saint Fiacre. Gurunhuel in the north of Brittany also has a parish dedicated to Saint Fiachra. He is credited with building the first hostel for Irish pilgrims on the Continent.

There is also a tradition of the 'Seven Holy Brothers' from Ireland, who came to Brittany in the fifth century. They worked around the Bay of Saint-Malo, which was later named after one of these seven. The brothers are also commemorated in many place names in the area.

Peregrini in the Slavic countries

Celtic monks who remain unnamed also played an important and pioneering role in the Christianisation of the Slavic lands. Excavations uncovered a late eighth century church, very similar to that at Glendalough and certainly Irish in structure and design. McNeill is of the view that "such a building would naturally have been preceded by a good few years missionary work."[44] In fact, "these Celts were the earliest missionaries to operate in Moravia with lasting success."[45]

Other peregrini who are assumed to be Irish

Some missionaries have been given Irish identity, which in the view of Gougaud, is doubtful.[46] Other scholars accept their Irish heritage.

One such monk is Gibrian, one of seven brothers and three sisters who settled on the banks of the Marne and Fridolin, who founded the monastery of Säckingen on the Rhine.

Caidoc and Fricor are also named as Irishmen, although Gougaud points out that the former of these has a name associated with Brittany.[47] It is not certain whether these were Irish in the view of Gougaud, who emphasises that when medieval hagiographers were compiling the Life of a saint, if he was uncertain of the individual's nationality, "he did not hesitate to make him one of those Scotti,"[48] "with whom", in the words of Strabo "the custom of travelling into foreign lands has now become almost second nature."

Trudpert, who worked in south-eastern Germany, was also thought to be Irish.

3. THE REASONS FOR PEREGRINATIO

Introduction

To a large extent we can agree with Ní Mheara that "the peregrinus remains an enigma, his inner motivation a source of wonder to all ages."[49] Indeed, many reasons have been suggested for the tremendous missionary outreach of the Celtic Church at this time.

As we have seen, Gougaud points out that the peregrini were not pilgrims in the strict sense of the word.[50] Their exile from their own country was voluntary and in addition to this they often engaged in missionary work. We cannot assume in all cases that evangelisation was the primary motive for their journey.

Exam tip!

Good responses will have evidence and examples to support their answers. Refer to the careers of individual peregrini in your discussion.

A search for the lonely place

Peregrinatio may well have been an ascetic act. John Ryan identifies Celtic monasticism as combining both the "anchoritical and apostolic" ideals.[51] It may well have been then, that some monks found themselves more drawn to solitude than community life and became peregrini out of such a desire for the lonely place. Adomnán's *Life* tells of the attempts made by Cormac úa Liathán, abbot of Durrow, to embark upon the ocean, in search of 'solitude', and who on one occasion got lost in the Arctic region. Chadwick sees this withdrawal for a lifetime, or for a period of one's life, as being "one of the most important features of early Irish asceticism, and its chief legacy to after ages."[52] Millet argues that "it seems certain that the Irish monks were more concerned with solitude, prayer and meditation than they were with making converts."[53] This was true in the case of Columbanus who desired "the salvation of many and a solitary place of my own."

An act of martyrdom

Some scholars have argued that this *"separation for the sake of God, from everything he loves"*,[54] was an act of 'white martyrdom'.[54a] There is some evidence for this in the *Cambrai Homily*, an Irish sermon on Jesus' teaching: *"If anyone wants to be a follower of mine, let him deny himself and take up his cross and follow me."*[55]

Stancliffe argues that the Irish were "interested in the idea that certain practices could count in lieu of martyrdom".[56] Robin Flower sees the separation from all that one loves for God's sake, as "perfect pilgrimage", the leaving of homeland in both body and soul to travel abroad as a peregrini.[57] Malone, too, sees peregrinatio as the "crowning act of Martyrdom".[58] Therefore peregrination could be viewed as an act of supreme self-sacrifice, especially given the 'familiar' basis of Irish society.

To share the faith

It is possible that the peregrini were motivated by missionary zeal – a desire to share their asceticism or even their faith with others. Lawlor believes that the circumstances in which they found themselves drove these peregrini into missionary work. However, "speaking generally, the primary idea of the word peregrination is not evangelistic labour, but exile from the mother country and its temptations, for the purpose of leading a life of austerity."[59] Nonetheless, they could have been following the Gospel command to *"Go teach all nations … as the Father has sent me, so am I sending you."* It is important to note that the peregrini appear to have cut off all contact with the monastery from which they came, so the evangelisation work undertaken was not organised or directed from there.

For the love of God

The peregrini may also have left Ireland to seek greater unity with God. The hagiographies of the age are littered with phrases such as *"for the love of God"*, *"in the name of God"*, *"for the love of Christ"*, *"for the love of heaven."*[60] An Anglo-Saxon chronicler in 891, while speaking of the arrival of Irishmen on the Cornwall coast, describes them as:

> *"men who had stolen away, because they wished for the love of God to be on pilgrimage, they cared not whither."*[61]

Some have argued that as monasticism was an escape from one's social responsibilities, then peregrinatio was also a selfish act – concerned with the salvation of one's own soul.[62] Chadwick disputes that the peregrini were self-centred, and that they were instead "God centred"; "a loving attention upon God" being the true objective of peregrination in the Celtic Church.[63] This is most aptly reflected in an ancient Irish poem:

> *"To go to Rome/ Is much trouble, little profit;/ The King [of Heaven] whom thou seekest there,/ Unless thou bring Him with thee, thou wilt not find."*[64]

Love of adventure

Allen points out that the Celts had a characteristic love of wandering and adventure which probably had something to do with the departure of so many from Ireland at this time.[65] Saint Brendan the Navigator may well be one example of such 'wanderlust' and love of adventure. We need to remember, however, that the peregrini were not strictly nomadic and most were quick to put down roots or establish their own monastic foundations, clearly evidenced in the *Life of Columbanus.*

Penance

Exile was often prescribed as a penance, which as we saw, was possibly the case with Colmcille. Certainly, in the Celtic Church, island sanctuaries in particular were places of pilgrimage and Chadwick sees them as closely related to peregrinatio.[66] Saint Brendan, who by his negligence caused the drowning of a youth, is ordered to become a wanderer by Ita, according to the *Life of Brendan*, in order to bring souls to Christ. The Brehon laws also recognise the authority of the *anamchara* to prescribe pilgrimage and exile. It may not necessarily have been prescribed by a confessor, but may have been a voluntary act of penance on the part of an individual to exile themselves from those that they loved.

Escaping paganism

Ian Finlay argues that the underlying motive for those of the peregrini who travelled to the Continent was "to tear themselves free of those pagan roots which are so constantly showing themselves".[67] While we can agree that paganism did not disappear from Celtic Ireland overnight, the lands they travelled to were equally, if not more pagan, than the one they left behind.

Reliance on God

Peregrinatio was also an act of faith. As we saw, in the words of the Anglo-Saxon Chronicler "they stole away ... they cared not whither."

Hughes describes them as "a guest of the world, without stability ... without oars or rudder."[68] Often these travellers had no particular destination in mind, seeing the end of the journey as being God's will for them. Millet finds that it is "striking, the absolute confidence they all had in God, when they gave themselves up to the waters ... they accepted beforehand that it was His will, and at the same time they accepted the destination He had in store for them."[69] If it is His will then He will provide all that they need for the journey, so it was an act of total reliance on Divine Providence.

An impulse

In the earlier days of the Celtic Church, it could well be that peregrinatio was an act of total spontaneity, the *"prompt and unhesitating response of the individual to a call from God to be up and away."*[70] But as the environment around the pilgrim changed, so did the reason for travel. It seems that greater and greater numbers of monks left the Church with the express reason of sharing the Christian faith.

To repay

We must also consider that these Celtic peregrini were following the example of Patrick who perceived himself to be *"an exile for the love of God"*. It may also be that the early Celtic Christians wanted to repay the debt of the gift of faith given to them from the British Church and more indirectly from Europe. So, in this sense, peregrinatio may have been an act of gratitude.

Greater challenge

Some argue that as the Church became more established in Celtic Ireland, the monks became more and more concerned not to fall into the sin of complacency and so seek more difficult challenges. Millet points out that "certain ascetics could not be content ... with communal life, severe as it was. This it was which led them to search for a desert on the ocean."[71] Given however the particular austerity of the Celtic monasteries, this seems to be an unlikely reason, except perhaps in the cases of certain individuals who felt particularly called to such a degree of asceticism.

Conclusion

There are many reasons for the vast numbers of peregrini who left Ireland in the sixth and seventh century for the Continent. Given the sheer number of them, it is difficult to believe that all of these monks were carrying out a penance imposed by a confessor. Most scholars are of the view that evangelisation was not the primary motive of the peregrini. This seems to be borne out by the frequent practice of seeking the lonely place in which to construct a small hermitage. They could not however, resist reaching out to meet the spiritual needs of the people, although choosing to live apart from them. Perhaps they were profoundly influenced by the example of the foremost of the *"exiles for the love of Christ"* – Patrick himself. It may have been his legacy to them, that self-denial of this kind should be deeply embedded in their spirituality. Given the real danger into which they travelled, the peregrinatio must have been both an act of asceticism and the ultimate act of trust in God. For some, such as Killian and Fursa, they paid the ultimate sacrifice of their very lives.

 TASK

With reference to the careers of individual peregrini, and to the information given above, make notes on what you consider to be the most likely reason for the peregrinatio undertaken by each one.

4. THE IMPACT OF THE CELTIC PEREGRINI ON THE CONTINENT

Introduction

The outreach of these peregrini was markedly different from that of the peregrini to north Britain. Unlike their counterparts who had travelled to Scotland and evangelised from Iona and Lindesfarne, these monks travelled into unknown territory, the natives of which were of a different race, language and custom to themselves. Unlike the North Britain missionaries, the Continental peregrini had little hope of ever going home again. The activity of the peregrini in Europe was "the most important religious and cultural phenomenon"[72] of the early Middle Ages.

John Ryan agrees that what was achieved by the Irish monks was "an object of wonder."[73] We need to bear in mind the challenges of travelling in that time, in order to truly understand their achievements. In the 'global village' of today, with "every capital city around the corner" the distances covered by the peregrini seem slight.[74] In their own time however, the expanse of territory covered would have been vast and would perhaps be comparable to a trek today, mostly on foot, into the heart of the African jungle.

The Celtic peregrini covered Gaul, Belgium, Switzerland, Austria, Southern Germany and Northern Italy, in a period stretching from the late sixth century to the mid-eighth century.

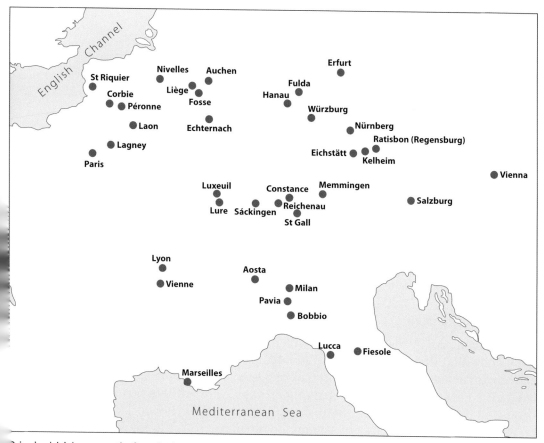

Principal Irish monastic foundations and ecclesiastical centres in Continental Europe

Facing the challenges

As we have seen, the condition in which the Celtic peregrini found the Continent in a desolate condition. The barbarian invasions had been culturally destructive and the influence of the pagans seemed dominant. The Church itself was fighting the threat of heresy from within and the clergy were too overwhelmed by the loss and destruction they had witnessed to know where to begin, in terms of mission, in this new and strange environment.

The Celtic monks knew that the challenges that faced them were complex and so their mission was to operate on several fronts[75]:

- Mission to evangelise a pagan people
- Mission to those who had fallen into heresy
- A sacramental mission to those who were Christian but had no clergy to minister to them
- Mission to a Christian people whose clergy were so demoralised and inactive that they could not minister to them

 TASK

Think about and discuss the challenges facing the Christian Church in terms of their mission to people today.
What are the similarities and differences between contemporary challenges and those faced by the peregrini?
Make notes on your discussion.

A lasting faith

The peregrini realised the need to build a strong Church which would withstand the challenges it faced long after their departure. When they settled in specific regions they immediately evangelised the youth and enlisted their services in further missionary work, thus ensuring that Christianity became "indigenous and self perpetuating."[76]

Care of the vulnerable

The peregrini carried the essence of Celtic monasticism with them to the Continent. They knew that their mission should involve praxis as well as orthodoxy, and were actively involved in meeting the myriad of needs of the people among whom they lived. As Ní Mheara comments, "Arriving on the Continent in a period of change, confusion and human misery, the Irish put charity first."[77] Beside each hermitage and oratory was a hospice, a place of asylum, designed to protect those who were most vulnerable.

TASK

Some people argue that the role of the Church in mission is to preach and evangelise. It is the role of the government or the United Nations to meet material, social and political needs.
Do you agree or disagree?
Research and discuss the different ideas about what mission should involve today. Make notes on your research and discussion.

Education

We cannot overlook the contribution made by the Celtic peregrini to the sphere of learning on the Continent. The monasteries founded by them on the Continent were centres of learning and Christian culture and focused on asceticism and faith. Standards had become lax and all civilisation eroded, so the interest in learning brought by the Celtic monks was gratefully received. The learning which engaged the Celtic monks and those who attended the monastic schools was not merely restricted to religious education, but also included science, philosophy and literature. The monastic schools were endowed by the kings and princes of Europe who sent their children there to be educated. In this way they supplied the continent of Europe with a "superabundance of religious life."[78]

Private penance

One of the most noteworthy contributions made by the Celtic monks to the Church on the Continent was the practice of frequent confession, penance and reconciliation.

Their revolutionary system of penance was to have a profound and lasting effect on the development of moral theology. The main features of the system became the established practice of the universal Church because of the efforts of the Celtic peregrini on the Continent.

 TASK

Go back to Chapter 4 and revise the practice of public penance as well as the main features of the Celtic system. Use what you have read to develop this point.
Not all scholars agree that the Celtic monks did bring private penance to the Continent. Find out more and use the information to inform exam responses on the influence of the peregrini on the practice of penance in the Church on the Continent.

Celtic monasticism

The Celtic peregrini were hugely influential in the development of monasticism on the Continent. They brought with them the spirit of Celtic monasticism. All of the monasteries founded by them were based on Celtic monastic rule, with its emphasis on asceticism and self-sacrifice, love of learning and the duty of hospitality. In this way, the distinctive elements of Celtic monasticism became established monastic practice on the Continent, until eventually the harsher Columban Rule was replaced by the more gentle Benedictine one.

For some of the clergy of the Continental Church, Celtic monastic practices were not all positive: "... *the Celtic ... Episcopal organisation, their abbot-bishops, their monastic clergy, ... their tonsure*" all gave cause for concern and needed reform.[79] The difficulty caused by this was most clearly seen in the career of Columbanus, who incurred the anger of the French bishops because of his neglect of their authority – acting instead on his own (greater) abbatial authority. In Brittany however, Celtic monastic practices, including the tonsure, remained until Louis the Pius forbade them in 818. By this time, the Rule of Benedict had been substituted for Celtic monastic practices in any case, and the Roman coronal tonsure became an established monastic custom everywhere.

 TASK

Re-read Chapter 7. Pay particular attention to the roles of abbots and bishops in the Celtic Church.
What difficulties would this cause for the Celtic monks on the Continent?

Wandering bishops

The work of the peregrini and its results were to span the next three centuries. In the words of McNeill: "That one small island should have contributed so rich a legacy to a populous continent remains one of the most arresting facts of European history."[80]

However, by the eighth century, not all agreed that the influence and legacy of the Celtic peregrini on the Church on the Continent was a positive one in every respect.

A considerable number of Celtic monks worked throughout Frankish territories from the sixth to the ninth century. These were abbots and abbot-bishops who governed their monastery and a diocese at the same time, or who had episcopal duties only within a monastery. Quite a few Celtic peregrini were held in high esteem by the Continental clergy; some were given a diocese of their own and came to oversee some of the most important sees in Continental Europe. Others were criticised by their Continental counterparts who noted how ill-at-ease the Celts felt within the confines of ecclesiastical discipline. Many peregrini preached widely throughout the regions and sometimes moved on to another place when they felt that their work was done. The practice of *episcope vagrants* or 'wandering bishops' was in contravention of canon law and was "a source of constant scandal among the foreign churchmen".[81] Although they had been consecrated bishops before leaving their own country, they had never been attached to any diocese and "roamed ceaselessly from place to place, without any authorisation."[82]

This judgement of Celtic episcopacy by the Continental Church may seem a little harsh if we consider that the majority of peregrini immediately settled down and got to work in one vicinity – only leaving the place of their labour after many years of work or because changing circumstances forced their departure. Despite this, they were certainly looked upon with suspicion by their Continental colleagues.

Ultimately, there may have been some 'undesirable' characters among Irish exiles of the period, especially in light of the practice of prescribing exile as a means of penance for serious sin.

Imposing a structure

While the Celtic monks evangelised widely, they did not organise or structure the Church. It was not until the mission of the English Saint Boniface, in the eighth century, that an ecclesiastical structure was imposed on the region that had been evangelised by the Celts. He was hostile to those Celts who remained outside the hierarchical 'Roman' system, that is, 'the wandering bishops' who ordained clergy and consecrated other bishops wherever they went. While a missionary Church required clergy to travel from place to place in order to evangelise, by the eighth century the Church on the Continent was no longer missionary and these wandering Celtic monks were now perceived to be "a serious menace to unity and order."[83] There was some suspicion on the part of the 'Roman establishment' towards those who came from Ireland. By the eighth century, there was a decree from the first Germanic General Council, held at the request of Saint Boniface in April of 742, that any 'unknown' clergy, either bishop or priest, should not be allowed to minister until they had been examined in Council and had been given permission by the local bishop.[84]

Saint Boniface's efforts to bring the Celtic peregrini into line were fruitful only after his death. Boniface became the consolidator of the Celtic pioneering efforts, bringing their flock under greater hierarchical control. Schaff believes that "he reaped the fruit of their labours and destroyed their further usefulness." In this sense, he argues that had Boniface employed a more "liberal church policy", he may have continued to make greater use of the many gifts of the Celtic peregrini.[85]

In a ninth century canon promulgated at the Council of Chalon-sur-Saône, the Celtic clergy are named specifically: *"There are certain places, Scots who pass themselves of as bishops and confer holy orders; such ordinations are null and void ..."*.

Celtic Easter

One of the most divisive aspects of the Celtic peregrination on the Continent was the Celtic method of dating Easter.[86] Indeed, as Gougaud points out, "their Easter customs were in the eyes of the French, reprehensive irregularities calling for urgent and radical reform."[87] It was this particular Irish custom which caused the most friction between the Irish peregrini and the clergy of the Church on the Continent and was perceived at the time to somewhat threaten the unity of the Church. In the case of Columbanus, the Celtic custom of dating Easter lost him the support of the French bishops who may otherwise have tried to support his mission from Luxeuil when he was exiled by the king. It was this kind of "obstinate adherence to religious custom which was characteristic of the Celts", and caused grave suspicion of them on the Continent, perhaps putting a dent in their otherwise huge sphere of influence.[88]

 PRACTICE ESSAY TITLE

Try this question when you have completed this section.

Critically assess the view that the influence of the Celtic peregrini on the Church on the Continent was divisive. (20)

Your answer may include reference to some of the following:

- The condition of Europe at the time
- Evangelisation
- Monasticism
- Penitential practice
- Learning and culture
- The dating of Easter
- Nature of episcopacy
- The views of scholars

Brittany – a lasting influence

The influence of the Celtic peregrini in Brittany was huge. There were still heathens in Brittany in the sixth century. British clergy had already visited the area although Gougaud feels that their travels were more a means of practising asceticism than to evangelise:

> "They are rarely found in contact with the natives ... and the missionary zeal which led so many Scots to cross the seas, does not seem to have animated these early Christian monks to the same degree."[89]

The Irish influence was felt particularly strongly in the monastery of Landévennec, described by Ní Mheara as "a cradle of Christian culture."[90] It existed first as a place of refuge and gradually became a great centre of civilisation and learning. It was here, more than anywhere else in Brittany, that the Irish monastic element was predominant.

Interestingly, the evidence suggests that Celtic practices remained in Brittany long after the issues had been resolved and Roman usages adopted in Britain and Ireland. It does not seem to have created any controversy though and it was not until the ninth century that Brittany "shed some of its peculiarly Celtic characteristics."[91]

Largillère tells us: "The priests who came … found in Brittany a virgin soil and a population wholly unsettled which had scarce taken up its abode and had as yet no social organisation."[92] The Celtic monks were free to act independently and set up churches wherever they saw the need. The main focus of the Celtic monks in Brittany was to give the infant Breton Church an ecclesiastical organisation and to provide a strong base for a pastoral ministry. "Worship, preaching and the administration of the sacraments formed their chief business, for in the regions … everything had to be started afresh."[93]

 PRACTICE ESSAY TITLE

a) Identify and consider the contribution made by the peregrini to the development of the Church on the Continent. (30)

> Your answer may include reference to some of the following:
> - The careers of individual peregrini
> - Monasticism
> - Penance
> - Evangelisation
> - Learning and culture
> - Dating of Easter
> - Episcopacy
> - The views of scholars

Try this question on your own, using the notes you made from your earlier discussion.

b) Critically discuss the view that the mission of the Church has not changed. (20)

Conclusion

The period between the sixth and the ninth century was a period of expansion for the Celtic Church. In many ways it was their great period of glory, when they were at the very peak of their most generous missionary activity. They displayed a remarkable enthusiasm for the salvation of souls and the winning of converts. They were in many regards, "true pioneers of the Gospel".[94] They saturated Europe with monasteries, hermitages, churches and schools, encouraging the virtues of asceticism, poverty, chastity and love of learning.

In the latter part of their missionary outreach, the benefits they brought were perhaps overshadowed by some of the difficulties they caused to the Church on the Continent in their wake.

Nonetheless, these peregrini "remain a lasting glory to their country and their faith."[95]

James Westfall Thompson concludes that "the weight of Irish influence on the Continent is incalculable. It penetrated the still unchristian regions of Europe. … For three hundred years the light of Ireland flamed, shedding its rays upon Scotland, England and the Continent, until diminished in the darkness of the Norse invasions."[96]

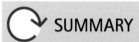 **SUMMARY**

> The period of the sixth and seventh century was one of huge missionary outreach by the Celtic monks.

> It arose for a variety of reasons, eg asceticism, penance, search for solitude. The peregrini may not have had the clear intention of evangelising.

> The influence of the peregrini on the Continent was massive in terms of evangelisation, practice of penance and education.

> A number of their practices did irritate some established clergy, eg dating of Easter.

> Columbanus, though controversial, was the most influential of the peregrini because of both the volume of his writing and his readiness to engage in conflict for what he saw as a just cause.

Endnotes

1 McNeill, *The Celtic Churches*, *op cit*, p155

2 There is some discrepancy over the date of Columbanus' birth. Others accept 563 as the correct date. The date given here is the one accepted by Walker.

3 This is the estimate given in the *Life of Saint Valericus*, a disciple of Columbanus.

3a Clothair was the son of Chilperic and Fredegune (the enemy of Brunhilde). He inherited Neustria from his father and his territory continued to be a rival power to Burgundy and Austrasia which were both under the influence of Brunhilde. On the death of Brunhilde in 613 and later her grandsons Theuderic and Theudebert, Clothair also inherited Burgundy and Austrasia.

4 Scherman, K, *The Flowering of Ireland*, Victor Gollanz Ltd, London, 1981, p174

5 Ó Fiaich, *Columbanus in His Own Words*, Veritas, Dublin, 1990, p61

6 Laporte points out that the entire Antiphonary was a direct replica of the one at Bangor.

7 Metlake, G, *The Life and Writings of Saint Columban*, Philadelphia 1914, Facsimile Reprint, J.F.M.Books, Felinfach, 1993, p68

8 *ibid*, p70

9 Ó Fiaich, *Columbanus in His Own Words*, *op cit*, p66

10 All excerpts from the writings of Columbanus in this chapter are from the translation by Walker, GSM, *Sancti Columbani Opera*, Dublin Institute for Advanced Studies, Dublin, 1957.

11 Walker, GSM, *Sancti Columbani Opera*, Dublin Institute for Advanced Studies, Dublin, 1957, xxiv

12 Ó Fiaich, *Columbanus in His Own Words*, *op cit*, p65

13 McNeill, *The Celtic Churches*, *op cit*, p7

14 Guillemain, B, 'The Irish Saints in France' in *The Miracle of Ireland*, Daniel-Rops (ed), Clonmore & Reynolds Ltd, Dublin, 1959, p71

15 Metlake, G, *The Life and Writings of Columban*, a Facsimile Reprint, Felinfach, 1957, p149

16 Dubois, Marguerite-Marie, *Saint Columbanus* in *Irish Monks in the Golden Age*, ed J Ryan, Clonmore & Reynolds Ltd, Dublin, 1963, p44

17 McNeill, *The Celtic Churches*, *op cit*, p168

18 Ó Fiaich, *Columbanus in His Own Words*, *op cit*, p29

19 Charles-Edwards, *Early Christian Ireland*, *op cit*, p369

20 *ibid*, p 371

21 Ó Fiaich, *op cit*, p30

22 Metlake, *op cit*, p212

23 Dubois, *op cit*, p44

24 Hauck, A, *Kirchengeschichte Deutschland's* Vol 1, Leipsic 1904, p281

25 Metlake, *op cit*, p84

26 The secretary of Columbanus to whom this letter is addressed could have been either Domoal or Chagnoald, who both held that position.

27 Walker, *op cit*, xxxi

28 *ibid*, xxxii

29 *ibid*

30 Gougaud, *Christianity in Celtic Lands*, *op cit*, pp144–5

31 Walker, *op cit*, xxxiv

32 Ní Mheara, R, *In Search of Irish Saints*, Four Courts Press, Dublin, 1994, p9

33 Gougaud, *Christianity in Celtic Lands*, *op cit*, p174

34 McNeill, *op cit*, p169

35 *ibid*

36 Hertling, L, 'Saint Gall in Switzerland' in *Irish Monks in the Golden Age*, ed J Ryan, Clonmore and Reynolds Ltd, Dublin, 1963, p72

37 See pp285–286 for more on the peregrini in Brittany.

38 Ní Mheara, *op cit*, p54

39 Gougaud, *op cit*, p148

40 Ó Fiaich, T, 'Irish Monks on the Continent' in *An Introduction to Celtic Christianity*, ed J Mackey, T & T Clark Ltd, Edinburgh, 1989, p126

41 Not all historians accept Fridian's Irish heritage.

42 The *Life of Guenolé* tells us that after the arrival of the pagan tribes, ships took people who wished to escape the ensuing persecution from Brittany to Ireland.

43 See pp283–284 for more on the peregrini in France.

44 McNeill, *The Celtic Churches*, *op cit*, p174

45 Dittrich, Z, *Christianity in Greater Moravia*, Gronigen 1962, p41

46 Gougaud, *Christianity in Celtic Lands*, *op cit*, pp158–163

[47] *ibid,* p159

[48] *ibid,* p163

[49] Ní Mheara, *op cit,* p11

[50] Gougaud, *Christianity in Celtic Lands, op cit,* p130 See also Chapter 5 of this book.

[51] Ryan, *Irish Monasticism, op cit*

[52] Chadwick, *The Age of the Saints in the Early Celtic Church,* Llanerch Publishers, Wales, 1960 p82

[53] Millet, RP, 'Peril on the Sea' in the *Miracle of Ireland,* ed Daniel-Rops, Clonmore & Reynolds Ltd, Dublin, 1959, p56

[54] Stancliffe, C, 'Red, White and Blue Martyrdom in Ireland' in *Early Medieval Europe,* ed D Whitelock *et al,* Cambridge University Press, 1982, p23

[54a] White martyrdom is a martyrdom without blood, without the violent taking of life.

[55] The sermon was found sandwiched between two chapters of canons in a copy of the *Collectio Canonum Hibernensis,* which was then copied into the main text of canons by a scribe. The sermon had been dated to late seventh or early eight century.

[56] *ibid,* p38

[57] Flower, R, *Irish Tradition,* Oxford 1947, pp19–21

[58] Malone, E, *Spiritual Martyrs and Irish Monks,* American Benedictine Review 2, 1951, p393–409

[59] As cited in Gougaud, *Christianity in Celtic Lands, op cit,* p131

[60] Adomnán, Jonas and Bede all use these phrases when speaking about missionary outreach.

[61] Hughes, *Sanctity and Secularity in the Early Irish Church* in *Church and Society in Ireland AD400–1200, op cit,* p25

[62] See, for example, Dill, S, *Roman Society in the Merovingian Age,* London 1926, p358; Meissner, JLG, *Celtic Christianity in the Church of Ireland AD432–1932,* Dublin 1932, p79

[63] Chadwick, *The Age of the Saints, op cit,* p84

[64] Translated by Kuno Meyer, *Ancient Irish Poetry,* London, 1913, p79

[65] Allen, PS, *The Romanesque Lyric: Studies in background and development,* Chapel Hill N.C., 1908, p159

[66] *ibid,* p102

[67] Finlay, I, *Columba,* Victor Gollancz Ltd, London, 1979, p47

[68] Hughes, 'Sanctity and Secularity in the Early Irish Church' in *Church and Society in Ireland AD 400-1200, op cit,* p25

[69] Millet, *op cit,* p54

[70] McNeill, *The Celtic Churches, A History, AD 200–1200, op cit,* p155

[71] Millet, *op cit,* p54

[72] Ó Fiaich, T, 'Irish monks on the Continent' in *An Introduction to Celtic Christianity,* ed JP Mackey, T & T Clark Ltd, Edinburgh 1989, p101

[73] Ryan, J, 'The Achievements of Our Irish Monks' in *Irish Monks in the Golden Age,* ed J Ryan, Clonmore & Reynolds Ltd, Dublin, 1963, p100

[74] *ibid,* p101

[75] *ibid*

[76] McNeill, *op cit,* p175

[77] Ní Mheara, *In Search of Irish Saints,* p9

[78] Ryan, *op cit,* p113

[79] Gougaud, *op cit,* p122

[80] McNeill, *op cit,* p175

[81] Gougaud, *op cit,* p164

[82] *ibid*

[83] McNeill, *op cit,* p172

[84] This was decreed at a separate Council of Soissons in 744.

[85] Schaff, P, *History of the Christian Church Vol 4,* New York, 1910, p98

[86] See Chapter 10.

[87] Gougaud, *op cit,* p122

[88] *ibid*

[89] *ibid,* p111

[90] Ní Mheara, *op cit,* p31

[91] McNeill, *op cit,* p151

[92] Largillère, R, *Les Saints,* Brest, 1896, p182 cited in Gougaud, *Christianity in Celtic Lands,* p120

[93] Gougaud, *ibid,* p118

[94] *ibid,* p421

[95] *ibid,* p170

[96] Westfall Thompson, J, & Johnson, EN, *An Introduction to Medieval Europe, 300–1500,* New York, 1937, p216

Chapter 10

Issues of Controversy

LEARNING OUTCOMES

Knowledge, understanding and evaluation of:

— Celtic and Roman Christianity

— the claims of Armagh to primacy

---

1. THE PASCHAL CONTROVERSY

Introduction

The Paschal Controversy centred on the dating of Easter. It is important to note that debate concerning the correct method of dating Easter had been ongoing in the Christian Church for some centuries. The controversy had become quite serious in the second century when the Quatrodeciman heretics were excommunicated. This group celebrated Easter on Jewish Passover.

Easter is of primary importance in the Christian Church because it celebrated the very lynchpin of the Christian faith – the Resurrection of Christ. For this reason it is easy to see why it was so important that all Christians, no matter where they are in the world, would celebrate Easter at the same time. The dating of Easter was also a matter of some practical importance. It was a movable feast and the date of it, in turn, affected the date of other movable feasts in the Christian calendar, such as Lent and Pentecost.

The problem

It was important that the date, which marked the celebration of the Passion, Death and Resurrection of Jesus, should somehow keep association with the date of the Jewish Passover,[1] which, for Christians, marked the occasion of Jesus' death. The Jews calculated this by lunar months rather than solar calendar months. Passover was always on the 14th day of the month of Nisan, which was the day of the full moon in the first Lunar month of Spring, after spring equinox. Since no one knew exactly when the full moon would fall, the Jews used a lunar calendar of 354 days to calculate it.

The Christian Church moved away from solely using Jewish calendars and began to use methods that would reconcile the lunar calendar with the solar calendar. The various Christian communities each developed their own Paschal Tables for calculating the date of Easter.

> Paschal Tables were used to work out cycles of years which would repeat indefinitely and so enable the Church to be aware of the date on which Easter would fall in advance.

Because of the resulting divergence, the Council of Arles met in 314 and declared that Easter must be celebrated on the same day throughout the world.

It seems that this did not happen and in 325 the Council of Nicea decreed that Easter be celebrated on the same Sunday throughout the Christian world. There were still divergences.

The Paschal cycles of the Alexandrian Churches were based on a cycle of 19 years. The Church in the West devised Tables based on a cycle of 84 years. These were used for some time until inaccuracies emerged in this method in 444 and again in 455. Victorius of Aquitaine was commissioned to draw up a new Paschal Table. His table was based on a cycle of 532 years. This system was adopted in the West and remained in use in Gaul until the eighth century. Unity between East and West however, was not achieved until the introduction of the Dionysiac cycle around 525.

The 84-year-cycle was the one that was probably brought to Ireland by both Palladius and Patrick. It remained in use there and became known as the 'Celtic 84'. Ireland's remoteness from the Continent and the collapse of the Roman Empire made contact between the Churches very difficult, and meant that Ireland probably did not hear of further changes made in the use of Tables. In fact, the Victorian calendar was not used uniformly across the Church in any case. In 577 the Victorian calendar calculated Easter as falling on 18 April; the Alexandrian calendar determined that Easter was on 25 April; and the Spanish Church computed an Easter date of 21 March. In 597, Gregory of Tours complained that he was celebrating a Latin Easter while people around him were celebrating the Greek. It is clear then that divergence of practice and confusion over the date of Easter was not unique to the Celtic Church.

There is no record of concern about Ireland's divergence in the method used for computing the date of Easter. The irregularity does not seem to have caused any controversy until the late sixth and seventh century. It was during this time that the greatest difference emerged between the Celtic date for Easter and that on which Easter fell elsewhere. Also at this time, the Celtic monks embarked on the peregrinatio. When they brought their peculiar practices with them to the Continent, there was conflict with the local clergy.

Meeting with Augustine

In Britain, again, conflict only arose with the convergence of the mission of the Celts and the Roman mission of Augustine. Augustine, a monk from Marseilles, was appointed by Pope Gregory the Great to undertake a mission to pagan Anglo-Saxon England. It seems that Gregory had given him authority over the British bishops, ordering him to *"correct the obstinate."*[2] The Irish believed that Easter could fall between the fourteenth and the twentieth of the lunar month, which meant that technically, if Easter Sunday happened to fall on 14th Nisan then it would be celebrated on Jewish Passover. Such diversity was also a constant reminder of division in the Church. Given that the decrees of Arles and Nicea had appealed for unity in the celebration of Easter, continued diversity was interpreted as an "outward sign of refusal to accept the rulings of Rome and her claim to authority over the Western Churches."[3]

In 602 Augustine held a conference with the *"bishops and teachers of the English people"*, at a place which became known to Bede as Augustine's Oak. Augustine, perhaps in an attempt to assert Roman authority over the Celts from the outset, did not rise to greet them when they arrived. The Celtic monks were offended at what they took to be both a lack of respect and arrogance on the part of Augustine. Bede tells us that Augustine said to them:

> *"You do many things which are contrary to our customs, or rather to the customs of the universal Church; nevertheless, if you are willing to submit to me in three points, we will gladly tolerate all else that you do, even though it is contrary to our customs. The three points are: to keep Easter at the proper time; to perform the sacrament of baptism ... according to the rites of the holy Roman and Apostolic Church, and to preach the word of the Lord to the English people in fellowship with us."*

The picture painted by Bede suggests that this meeting was handled very badly and that the Roman case was presented in a way that was somewhat "tactless if not arrogant."[4] He tells us that *"it is said that, Augustine, the man of God, warned them with threats, that if they refused ... they would have to accept war from their enemies and ... would one day suffer the vengeance of death at their hands."* As a result, the Celtic clergy were antagonised from the beginning.

On the Continent, Columbanus had also fallen into conflict over the Celtic method of dating Easter. In 600 he wrote to Pope Gregory on the matter and also to his successor Sabinian. He was summoned to a meeting with the French bishops in 603 to address the issue.

Appeal to the Celts

In 605, Laurentius of Canterbury "came to realise that in Ireland as well as in Britain, the life and profession of the people was not in accordance with church practice in many things."[5] Concerned at how bitter the dispute had already become, he wrote a circular letter to the Irish bishops and abbots, outlining the Roman argument on the dating of Easter:

> "… before we knew them we held the holiness of both the Britons and of the Irish in great esteem, thinking they walked according to the customs of the universal Church. But now we have learned from bishop Dagan when he came to this island and from Abbot Columban when he came to Gaul that the Irish did not differ from the Britons in their way of life. For when Bishop Dagan came to us he refused to take food, not only with us but even in the very house where we took our meals."

There does not seem to have been any immediate response to this appeal.

In 628 Pope Honorius wrote to *"the nation of the Scots"* whom he saw as few in number, and living *"at the ends of the earth"*. He appealed to them not to consider themselves wiser than all other Churches regarding the dating of Easter.

In the 620s and 630s in the south of Ireland there was a growing desire to resolve the issue and if necessary to adopt Roman practices. There were quite frequent visits between the Church in the south of Ireland and the Continent, which convinced a number of prominent clergy from the south of Ireland to conform to Roman practices.

Synod at Mag Léne

In 629–30 a Synod at Mag Léne, near Durrow, seriously considered accepting Roman practices. One abbot, Fintan, from the northern part of Ireland, whom Cummian[5a] refers to as a *"whited wall"*, challenged the decision. As a result, a deputation was sent to Rome to clarify some issues. It returned in 632 completely convinced of the rightness of Roman practices.

Letter of Cummian

In 632/3 Cummian sent a letter to Segéne, abbot of Iona, presenting the Roman point of view. His main fear was that of being *"cut off from the universal Church"*:

> "The Hebrews, Greeks, Latins, and Egyptians are all agreed: only the Britons and the Scots stand out, these peoples 'who are almost at the ends of the earth, and, as I might say, a pimple on the chin of the world.' What can be felt worse for Mother Church than to say: Rome is mistaken; Alexandria is mistaken; Antioch is mistaken; all the world is mistaken; the Scots and Britons alone have sound wisdom?"

Southern Ireland conforms to Roman practices

By 636 Roman practices had been adopted by the churches in the southern part of Ireland.

In 640, Pope John IV wrote to the *"doctors and abbots of the Scots"*, but seems to have wrongly associated them with the Quatrodeciman heresy. The Quatrodecimans were a second century sect who celebrated Easter on the 14th Nisan, on Jewish Passover.

> *"… some of your province, in opposition to the orthodox faith, are striving to revive a new heresy out of an old. In the darkness of ignorance they reject our Easter, on which Christ was sacrificed, and contend that it should be celebrated on the fourteenth moon with the Jews."*

Events in Northumbrian Royal household

In England there was relatively little strife over the Easter question and things had remained as they had been left at Augustine's Oak. However, events were to come to a head when the dispute entered the Northumbrian royal household. King Oswy of Northumbria had been brought up with Celtic practices and had married the princess Eanfled who herself was devoted to Roman practices and had in fact been baptised on Easter Day, by Roman calculation. Bede tells us that:

> *"When the king had ended his own fast and was keeping Easter, the queen and her followers were still fasting and celebrating Palm Sunday."*

It is easy to see that this would have caused great inconvenience in the royal household as well as confusion among the Christians of the kingdom. We have to remember that the Lenten fast was very strictly observed and would have involved, at the very least, abstention from meat and fish. Christian married couples would also abstain from sexual relations during the Lenten period.

Meanwhile, the king came under pressure to resolve the Easter question – for political reasons:

- Aldfrith, the king's son, held the sub-kingdom of Deira and was ambitious to rule over all of Northumbria. He saw the opportunity to weaken his father's influence in Bernicia and so conquer his father's kingdom. Aldfrith had formed a friendship with the cleric Wilfrid – who had been educated at a Celtic monastery, but as a result of a later visit to the Continent, changed allegiance to Roman practices. Aldfrith was impressed by the position held by Wilfrid and began to put pressure on his father to resolve the issue. He felt sure that his father would retain his Celtic usages and so his power would diminish as a result.

- Agilbert, bishop of Essex, was supportive of the position and efforts of both Aldfrith and Wilfrid and gave Wilfrid the abbey of Ripon, thus increasing Wilfrid's status and influence. Under pressure from Aldfrith, who saw an opportunity to divide and conquer his father's kingdom, Oswy called the Synod of Whitby in 664.[6]

Exam tip!

The account above explains in detail the topics that you will need to understand in order to do well in your exam. You should not attempt to reproduce all the details that are given here. Instead make sure that you understand what the Paschal Controversy was really all about and then summarise the main points. Choose a few brief quotations from the original sources to use as evidence. Be clear also on the sequence of events. Keep your notes and use them for exam revision.

 PRACTICE ESSAY TITLE

a) Analyse the events which led to the calling of the Synod of Whitby. (35)

Your answer could include reference to some of the following:
- A summary of the different Paschal cycles in use in the Church
- Synod of Mag Léne and Letter of Cummian
- Deputation to Rome
- Meeting with Augustine
- Events in the Northumbrian Royal household

Try this one later.

b) Critically evaluate the claim that the Synod of Whitby was a 'milestone in the history of the Celtic Church'. (20)

Your answer may include reference to some of the following:
- The Romanisation of the Celtic Church
- Conformity of practice and liturgy
- The impact on the churches in the north and the south of Ireland
- Monastic and abbatial character
- Conformity of Iona
- Assertion of Papal authority

Events at the Synod of Whitby

Introduction

Whitby is about twenty miles north of Scarborough, on the North Sea coast. It was the location of a double monastery, the abbess of which was Hilda, kinswoman of Oswy and devotee of Celtic practices. Hilda was a very influential figure and had a reputation as the nurturer of the leaders of the northern Church. At the Synod of Whitby however, she appears to have taken a back seat.

Bede is our main source for the events of Whitby. One of Bede's concerns was the unity of the Church and a deep desire to see the English Church at one with the Roman Church. His account of the events at the Synod of Whitby reflect this interest, and the controversy "occupies much space in the history and forms one of his central themes: could the English Church accept her position as the true and loyal offspring of the Roman Church, free from any taint of heresy or particularist error?"[7]

The People involved

The Celtic Party	The Roman Party
Colmán of Lindesfarne	Wilfrid
Bishop Cedd, his interpreter	Agilbert (French Bishop)
Some monks from Colman's monastery	Agatho, a friend of Agilbert
	James the deacon
	Romanus, the chaplain of the Queen
	Aldfrith
Oswy presided over the meeting	

The arguments [8]

Oswy opened the meeting with a plea for unity of observation among all Christians. Colmán was the first to speak and outline the Celtic position. Colman declared:

> "The method of keeping Easter that I observe, I received from my superiors who sent me here as a bishop; it was in this way that all our fathers, men beloved of God, are known to have celebrated it. Nor should this method seem contemptible and blameworthy seeing that the blessed evangelist John, the disciple whom the Lord specially loved, is said to have celebrated it thus, together with all the churches over which he presided."

Appeal to Celtic tradition and the Apostle John.

Agilbert was invited to present the reasons for the Roman method of dating Easter. He asked if Wilfrid, who was more fluent in the English tongue, could speak on his behalf. Wilfrid argued:

> "The Easter we keep is the same as we see universally celebrated in Rome, where the apostles St. Peter and St. Paul lived, taught, suffered and were buried. We also found it in use everywhere in

Appeal to universal practice.

Italy and Gaul when we travelled through those countries for the purpose of study and prayer. We learnt that it was observed at one and the same time in Africa, Asia, Egypt and Greece, and throughout the whole world, wherever the Church of Christ is scattered, amid various nations and languages. The only exceptions are these men and their compliances in obstinacy … in these two remotest islands of the ocean … [who] foolishly attempt to fight against the whole world."

Colmán responded:

"I wonder that you are willing to call our efforts foolish, seeing that we follow the example of that apostle who was reckoned worthy to recline on the breast of the Lord; for all the world acknowledges his great wisdom."

Wilfrid replied:

"Far be it from me to charge John with foolishness: he literally observed the decrees of the Mosaic law, when the church was still Jewish in many respects, at a time when the apostles were unable to bring a sudden end to the entire observance of that law which God ordained. … But in these days when the light of the Gospel is spreading throughout the world, it is not necessary, not even lawful for Jews to be circumcised. … So John, in accordance with the customs of the law, began the celebration of the Easter Day on the evening of the fourteenth day, regardless of whether it fell on the Sabbath or any other day.

But when Peter came to Rome … he realised Easter ought to be kept … on the Lord's Day, falling between the fifteenth and twenty first days of the moon. This [is] apostolic tradition. All the successors of

> Appeal to the authority of Peter.

John, since his death has followed this observance. … So Colman, you neither follow the example of John nor of Peter, whose tradition you knowingly contradict, you neither follow the law nor the Gospel. John took no heed of the Sunday; you celebrate Easter only on a Sunday."

Colmán argued:

"Did Anatolius, a man who was holy and highly spoken of, in the Church to which you appeal, judge contrary to the law and the Gospel when he wrote that Easter should be celebrated between the fourteenth and the twentieth day of the moon? Or must we believe that our most reverend father Columba and his successors, men beloved of God, who celebrated Easter in the same way, judged and acted contrary to the Holy Scripture, seeing that there were many of them to whose holiness the heavenly signs and miracles they performed bore witness? And as I have no doubt that they were saints, I shall never cease to follow their way of life, their customs and their teachings."

> Appeal to the tradition of the holy Colmcille.

Wilfrid retorted:

"It is true that Anatolius was a most holy and learned man. … He followed a correct rule in celebrating Easter, basing it on a cycle of nineteen years, of which you are either unaware of, or if you do know of it, you despise it, even though it is observed by the whole church of Christ. … So as far as your father Columba and his followers are concerned, whose holiness you claim to imitate and whose rule and precepts you claim to follow … I will not deny that those who in their rude simplicity loved God with pious intent, were indeed servants of God and beloved by Him. Nor do I think that this observance of Easter did much harm to them while no one had come to show them a more perfect rule to follow. … But once having heard the decrees of the apostolic see or rather of the universal Church, if you prefer to follow them, confirmed as they are by the Holy Scriptures, then without doubt, you are committing a sin.

Appeal to Papal Authority.

Wilfrid sees the dating of Easter as a matter of belief about which there can be no difference among Christians.

For though your fathers were holy men, do you think a handful of people in one corner of the remotest islands are to be preferred to the universal Church of Christ which is spread throughout the world? … that Columba of yours … is he to be preferred to the most blessed chief of the Apostles to whom the Lord said, 'Thou art Peter and upon this rock I will build my Church and the gates of Hell shall not prevail against it, and I will give unto thee the keys of the kingdom of heaven.'"

King Oswy intervened:

"Is it true, Colmán that the Lord said these words to Peter? … Have you anything to show that an equal authority was given to your Columba? Colmán answered 'Nothing.' … The king concluded 'Then I tell you, since he is the door keeper I will not contradict him; but I intend to obey his commands in everything to the best of my knowledge and ability, otherwise when I come to the gates of the kingdom of heaven there may be no one to open them, because the one who on your own showing holds the keys, has turned his back on me.'

When the king had spoken all who were seated there or standing by, both high and low, signified their assent, gave up their imperfect rules, and readily accepted in their place, those which they recognised to be better."

Other issues raised

Bede tells us that *"the question of Easter and of the tonsure and other ecclesiastical matters were raised"*.

- He states that there was *"no small dispute about the tonsure."* The tonsure is the haircut worn by monks. It came to symbolise on which side of the dispute individuals allied themselves as well as one's allegiance to the practices of the universal Church.

- There was a difference in tonsure between Celtic and Roman monks:

Roman clergy tended to wear the coronal tonsure, in the shape of a crown of thorns, in memory of the Passion of Jesus and also reportedly, the tonsure worn by Peter. At the time of the Paschal Controversy this was seen to be appropriate to the monastic life in which suffering and self-denial could be united with the suffering of Jesus. It also became a symbol of belonging to the universal Church. In the words of Coelfrith, *"a sign that you agree in your inmost heart with all that Peter stands for, if you also followed his known ways in your outward appearance."*	Celtic monks wore a frontal tonsure, from ear to ear. It was thought to be reminiscent of the tonsure of the druid Simon Magus who was the enemy of St Peter. It came to be thought of as a fashion unsuitable for Christians, although it was conceded that many who wore such a tonsure 'were holy men and worthy in the sight of God'.

- There is no consensus as to what the nature of Celtic baptism was. One suggestion is that when baptising in the name of the Trinity, the Celts immersed in water once instead of three times. Another theory suggests that the Celts omitted one of the 'anointings', perhaps the final anointing with the oil of chrism.

- Episcopal ordination also seems to have been an issue which concerned the Romani (Roman party). It would seem that the consecration of one bishop by just one other was practised out of necessity in the early days of the Celtic Church. It was probably introduced by Patrick and then became an established custom with the passage of time. In the wider Church, bishops could only be consecrated by three other bishops.

 TASK

Summarise the main events at the Synod of Whitby. Note the names of the people who attended. Show that you understand the significance of the exchanges and select some appropriate direct quotations from the narrative given above.

File your notes carefully and use them to complete the exam practice task later in the chapter.

The significance of the Synod of Whitby

The impact of Oswy's decision

Following the Synod, Oswy and Hilda conformed. Cedd too was convinced. A dejected Colmán, having difficulty accepting the ruling of the Synod, departed from Lindesfarne to Ireland, with thirty companions who shared his outlook, to the island of Inishbofin on the West coast of Ireland.

Standardisation

As a result of the Synod, the coronal tonsure was widely adopted and was the "outward expression of membership of a single unified Church" and was seen "by individuals on both sides of the dispute as a way of publishing their allegiance."[9] The Celtic practice of ordaining bishops was discontinued. Theodore, who arrived in England in 669, seems to have questioned the validity of the consecration of some Celtic bishops, whose consecration had been performed by those "who are not Catholic with respect to Easter and the tonsure".[10] Chad appears to have been re-consecrated, but this tendency was not widespread. Thus there was greater standardisation in the administration of the sacraments.[11]

Ireland

As Kathleen Hughes points out, "in England the effects of the dispute were immediate and obvious, in Ireland the effects were indirect and ill-defined, though of far-reaching importance."[12] The churches in the southern part of the country had already conformed approximately thirty years before Whitby.

The churches in the northern part of the country were not to conform until nearly thirty years after it, at the second Synod of Birr in 696–697. Unlike the English Church, the Church in Ireland had no central royal or other authority which could influence or speed up the process and so could only be converted to Roman practice "in segments and not without internal strife."[13]

Interestingly, as McNeill points out in the English Church, "the attitude and decisions of kings largely controlled the course of development for the church ... a precedent ... for much that would happen in the later history of England."

Iona

The Synod had a still less immediate response from the monastery of Iona. Despite the efforts of Adomnán to convince his own monks, they had still not conformed at the time of his death in 704. It remained "the last outpost of Irish resistance to the Romanizing reforms."[14] It was through the commitment of Egbert and 'political pressure' from the Pictish King Nechtan – who ordered Roman usages throughout his kingdom – rather than the decision taken at Whitby, that finally won round the Ionian community in 716. In 718 Nechtan ordered that those who still resisted reform should be expelled from his kingdom.

Kathleen Hughes points out that the organisation of the Celtic Church was not changed as a result of Whitby.[15] To some extent the arrival of the Norsemen had a bigger effect on the Celtic Church than the outcome of Whitby. She believes that despite the fact that they "lost the battle about the dating of Easter", they still succeeded in their main aim to "adjust their church to native law," rather than to "bring [it] into line with continental practice." The Celtic Church retained its monastic and abbatial character, so while the Romans "won the dispute on Easter and the tonsure, everywhere else the Irish party in the Church triumphed."[16]

The wider significance of Whitby

McNeill believes that the conclusion reached at Whitby was "a momentous decision for the course of English history."[17] It certainly marked the beginning of the Romanisation of the English Church.

The process was continued by Aldfrith, who was king of Northumbria from 685–704, by the use of quite moderate methods.

On the other hand, Cowdrey believes that Bede, our main source on the events of Whitby, "has invested the Synod with a larger and more entirely religious significance than it in reality possessed."[18]

Some argue that this was the 'beginning of the end of the Celtic Church'. While it was true that after the abbacy of Colman, Celtic usages were ended at Lindesfarne, it would be wrong to assume that the essence and character of Celtic institutions, such as Lindesfarne, were suddenly changed after Whitby; or that Celtic clergy ceased to hold prominent positions in the church in Britain. Meissner argues that the Celtic party remained strong and influential in Northumbria until "well into the late eighth century", as well as in Mercia and Wessex.[19] There was a succession of Celtic abbots at Lindesfarne after Colman, for example, Tuda, from the south of Ireland and a follower of Roman usages. Chad, brother of Cedd, was, after Whitby, made bishop of Lichfield in Lincolnshire.

McNeill notes that Celtic art "continued to be influential" in Northumbria, a product of which was the Lindesfarne Gospels. Celtic learning and education also continued to flourish and to influence, and is well testified by Bede.

The real battle: creating a unified Church

McNeill believes that the issues of the Synod of Whitby between the Roman and the Celtic Church had a very different underlying agenda than the arguments about Easter or the tonsure. It was really about the independence of the local Celtic Church, "against integration within the Roman ecclesiastical system. To some degree the participants were aware of this and understood what they were arguing about."[20]

In this sense, Whitby was essentially about creating a fully integrated unified and universal Church, rather than a family of local churches. Kathleen Hughes sums up the Roman position, "uniformity is essential: failure to conform imperils the soul."[21]

Whitby was concerned with bringing about the conformity of local churches to the practices of the Roman Church and as such it marked the official birth of the Roman catholic Church.

Establishing papal authority

The Synod also illustrated the different perceptions of authority within the Church. The Roman party felt that "persistent Celtic loyalty to their own traditions meant deliberate rejection of Roman authority and an indifference to the advances of conformity with the general body of Christians."[22] So in this sense, Whitby was also about establishing Papal authority in the wider Church. The introduction of the issue of Papal authority into the debate about the dating of Easter, to some extent, caught Colman and the Celtic party by surprise. It was because the Celts acknowledged the authority of Peter and therefore of the Papacy that they lost the argument about Easter.

> In the early Church the Pope was given primacy of honour, but the perception was that all bishops had been given the power to bind and lose. Each church had a certain degree of local autonomy. Ideas on the primacy of the Papacy were developed in the fifth century under Pope Leo. Kathleen Hughes emphasises that the local churches still remained independent. Papal authority over the practices of all local churches was a relatively new idea.

The political agenda

Smyth believes that the agenda at Whitby was more about the political concerns of Oswy who, as a result of his loyalty to Celtic practices, feared his power would be compromised in the kingdom of Deira which was controlled by his son. He believes that "the real issues at Whitby were primarily political." The other arguments "were no more than a smokescreen."[23] Indeed some see Oswy's changing sides at Whitby as politically very shrewd. Eddius, who wrote the *Life of Wilfrid*, tells us that Oswy gave his summing up, *"with a smile".*

Through the decision reached at Whitby, there was final resolution of the longstanding conflict within the Church concerning the dating of Easter.

Roman and Celtic Christianity – were there two types of Christianity?

Some commentators refer to a Celtic Church as distinct from a Roman Church. But is such a distinction a valid one?

There were a few differences between Roman and Celtic Christianity and the latter in many respects had many unique characteristics.

- The structure of the Celtic Church was monastic.
- The government of the Church was abbatial.
- They adhered to a different method of dating Easter.
- There were differences in the method of episcopal ordination.

- There were ceremonial differences in the administration of baptism.
- Diversity of practice was commonplace, with differing monastic rules and emphasis from monastery to monastery.
- The Celtic Church afforded a more prominent position to women, some of whom formed a kind of deaconate to the dismay of the bishops of Tours, who in turn wrote to complain of the practice.

 DISCUSS

Did these differences amount to a fundamentally different kind of Christianity?

Historians are divided on the extent to which the differences between the two Churches mean that there was a fundamental chasm between the Roman and the Celtic Church. Kathleen Hughes argues that the Celts were "doctrinally orthodox, they were exceptionally devout: no fault could be found in the early seventh century on these grounds."[24]

 DISCUSS

Did the Celtic Church differ from the wider Church in doctrine, or were the differences ones of liturgy and practice rather than belief?

Papal authority

The question of acceptance of the authority of the Papacy on the part of the Celts, raised at Whitby, has prompted some historians, such as Rees and Kerr,[25] to argue that the Celtic Church at the time "was distinctly separatist and independent and resolutely withdrew from the jurisdiction of the Pope."[26] Hardinge agrees that, in the perception of the representatives of the bishop of Rome, the Celts are considered to have fundamental differences with Roman Christianity.[27] Chadwick also suggests that "the fundamental and far-reaching nature of this great spiritual and intellectual contest between the Celtic Church and the adherents of Roman usage can hardly be overestimated."[28]

But did the Celts reject Papal authority?

We have to remember that at the time the very concept of Papal authority in the Church had not been clearly defined, and was still in a process of development. Even Cummian, an advocate of Celtic practices, referred to the decision of the Apostolic 'sees'. He was probably referring to the churches of Rome, Jerusalem, Antioch and Alexandria. But the situation had moved on in the two centuries since Christianity had been brought to Ireland and the Celts seemed unaware of the shift in thinking on Papal authority as well as other matters.

Gougaud challenges the idea that there was any rejection of Papal authority on the part of the Celts. He suggests a range of evidence to repudiate such claims[29]:

- Augustine would hardly have invited the Celts to assist him in his mission to the Anglo-Saxons had he been concerned about their orthodoxy. As Lloyd comments, "there was no insurmountable barrier between Augustine and the British Bishops."[30]

- Bede, although a loyal devotee of Roman practices and seriously concerned with the unity of the Church, is sure of the doctrinal purity of the Scots.[31]

- The third of the Dicta Patricii also evidences Celtic loyalty to the Church of Rome.

- Contemporary evidence is supplied by the action of the Christians of the southern Irish churches in sending a deputation to Rome, in 628–629, to seek clarification on the Easter Controversy.

- The writings of Columbanus, in particular his Letters to successive Popes, reflect the esteem in which the Papacy was held by the Celts. (Read again the excerpts from Columbanus' Letters to the popes of his time.)

Lloyd also believes that "No theological differences parted the Roman from the Celtic Church, for the notion that the latter was the home of some kind of primitive Protestantism is … without any historical foundation."[32]

Margaret Deanesly agrees that "there was no hostility, no suspicion of the See of Peter. … Rome was a place of pilgrimage, very holy, very distant."[33]

Differences in ritual but not belief

Gougaud feels certain that the "controversy turned solely on matters of pure discipline or liturgy."[34] The Celts seem to have regarded the dating of Easter as a matter of ritual, not belief. The difference between the two groups in this regard was one of perception. Lloyd agrees that "the British Church was orthodox and differed from Rome only in minor matters, of which the date of the celebration of Easter was chief." He continues that "Ecclesiastical arrogance on the one hand and national pride on the other, were the forces which brought about the schism, which nevertheless persisted for over one hundred and fifty years."[35]

 TASK

Do you agree that the controversy that erupted over the dating of Easter was purely a matter of liturgical difference? Give reasons for your answer.

Lang doesn't wholly agree that the differences were mere liturgical ones and facetiously points out, "with that singular fatality that dogged the Celtic races, their form of Christianity, however pure in doctrine, varied in certain ceremonial trifles of the most essential importance, from the Christianity of the Western Church."[36]

McNeill argues that while the issues central to the debate at the time were not perhaps in themselves of fundamental importance, that "[such] matters which in the abstract, may seem trifles, often assume central importance when they are bound up with the sacred traditions of a people or become symbols of certain ecclesiastical attachments."[37]

> Think about McNeill's statement in the context of symbols dear to the different communities in Northern Ireland or the importance of the right to wear religious dress for Muslims.

Cultural differences

Kathleen Hughes argues that the Celts were "accustomed to diversity in their religious practices, [and] felt no obligation in conscience to conform to the Easter advocated by the Romani."[38] This is most clearly illustrated in the words of Fintan at the Synod of Mag Ailbe, *"Therefore let each of us do as he believes and as seems to him right"*. This is certainly reflected in the plea of Columbanus to be *"left in peace to practice the traditions of our fathers."* Even though discussions were numerous about the points of difference between Roman and Celtic Christianity, "democratic freedom seems to have prevailed."[39] There was no one in the Celtic Church who could be the spokesman of all. In this sense, the difference between the two groups may have been cultural rather than doctrinal; therefore the Celtic Church could not be considered schismatic.

 TASK

> Think about and discuss the idea that there should be absolute uniformity of practice and outlook, if true unity is to be achieved in the Christian Church.

Certainly the attitude of some Christians at the time of the Paschal Controversy and the Synod of Whitby was that if the Christian Church as an institution was to survive and indeed thrive, then absolute uniformity was necessary. In fact, some believed that diversity or non-conformity of any kind was sinful. This belief appears to have influenced the argument of Wilfrid at the Synod itself and may have prompted some advocates of the Roman position to consider the Celts as schismatic.[40]

Whatever one's view, "the seventh and eighth centuries were a time of transition and conformity for the Celtic Church."[41]

PRACTICE ESSAY TITLE

Referring to some ideas in the box below and adding some of your own, try this evaluation task:

Critically assess the view that the central issues at the Synod of Whitby are still relevant in the Church today. (20)

Church Unity   Papal Authority   Tolerance
Diversity   Tradition   Conformity of all Christians

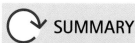 SUMMARY

The Paschal Controversy arose round the dating of Easter.

Many different Paschal Tables were in use in the Church in an attempt to accurately predict the date on which Easter might fall.

An 84-year-cycle may have been introduced into the Celtic Church by Palladius and Patrick.

Problems arose when the Celtic monks left Ireland to evangelise the Continent and Britain.

The dispute was bitter in some places. Some saw the real issues as being the independence of the Celts, the unity of the Church, and the authority of the Pope. Diversity in religious practice was unpopular.

The Celtic party perceived their practices as a matter of allegiance to their own tradition and that of their founding fathers. The two sides became entrenched.

Whitby was called to resolve the differences but political issues loomed in the background.

The underlying issues at Whitby were essentially about limiting the independence of local churches; conformity to practices of the Roman Church; uniformity of practice; standardisation of the administration of the sacraments and assertion of Papal authority.

The Celtic Church lost the battle at Whitby but did retain its unique characteristics.

Although the decision reached at Whitby was not implemented overnight, the process of the Romanisation of the Church had begun. "The Celtic church was absorbed into catholic Christianity piece by piece and the remnants which withstood, weakened and alone, finally disappeared."[42]

2. THE CLAIMS OF ARMAGH

Introduction

During the seventh century there was a flurry of activity to promote the claims of the church of Armagh to archiepiscopal authority over all the 'free churches and monasteries of Ireland.' There is no evidence to suggest that this claim to archiepiscopal supremacy was new in the seventh century, but it was certainly reinforced vigorously at this time.

One reason for this was probably the rise of monastic paruchiae. The Celtic Church had begun, from the second half of the sixth century, to take on a monastic character. This process seems to have been complete in the eighth century.[43]

We have seen that Kildare was making claims for itself, through the *Life of Brigit* by Cogitosus, to a huge monastic paruchiae, *"that extends through the whole island of Ireland."* Its claims were, however, a little "vaguer than those of Armagh."[44] Kildare and Glendalough both enjoyed patronage from the royal house of Leinster. Similarly, Clonmacnois enjoyed prestige because of its advantageous position on the borders of Meath and Connacht. Early on, Iona had support from the dynasty of the Uí Néill, which was rising to prominence. "Armagh entered the field very late for the race for ecclesiastical precedence."[45]

What was to become of the oldest of the episcopal churches in the face of such an advance by the monasteries? No doubt, this question concerned Armagh.

Interestingly, none of the sources we have from the sixth century mention Patrick or Armagh; it does not appear in the writings of Columbanus, Cogitosus, Jonas, Adomnán or even more strikingly, Bede. Sources from that period are scarce, but the absence of the name of Armagh might suggest that she was not a prominent church in the era of the great monastic churches.

It seems to have been the development of prominent and influential monastic *paruchiae* which spurred on the Armagh church and its lawyers to clarify its position.

The claims made by Armagh

The claims made are to be found in the *Book of the Angel*. It is a 'pseudo-Patrician' piece of literature of hagiographical character that "provides a statement of Armagh's claims and rights, put together by the Armagh lawyers from information collected there in the late seventh and early eighth century."[46] Kathleen Hughes assigns the work to the eighth century, although some of the sources on which it is based may have come from an earlier period.[47] Sharpe believes the authors were active in 640 or 650.[48]

In the *Book of the Angel*, an angel appears to Patrick and granted privileges to him and to his church at Armagh.

It opens with the grant of a *termonn*, an area over which the bishop of Armagh had direct government. The original boundary of the diocese of Armagh covered the Airgialla and part of the nearby kingdoms of Ulaid and Dál Riata. Yet the angel decrees that God has also given to Patrick, *"all the tribes of the Irish"*. Armagh was to be *summa* of all the churches and monasteries of Ireland. The boundaries of that church were thus extended and the abbot/bishop of Armagh was to have direct government of this extended territory. Patrick insists that even more advantages be given to his church and elicits from the angel the right to tax all the free churches of Ireland. It adds to these *"every place which is called domnach"* which, according to Binchy, is a very early, maybe pre-Patrician loan word for church.[49]

> *"... Every church everywhere that is called domnach, ought in accordance with the mercy of the kind and almighty Lord towards the holy teacher and with the word of the angel – to belong to the special societas of bishop Patrick and the heir of his see at Armagh, for as we have already said, God gave him the whole island."*

The total privileges granted by the Angel were:

1. That Armagh was the most important church/see in Ireland.

2. It had authority over all the free churches and monasteries in Ireland.

3. It had the right to tax these churches.

4. It was the highest Court of ecclesiastical appeal in Ireland, second only to Rome. All disputes which could not be resolved between churches themselves were to be referred to the bishop of Armagh as the coarb or heir of Patrick:

"Whatever difficult cause shall arise, one unknown to all the judges of the tribes of the Irish, it shall be rightly referred to the cathedral of the Irish archbishop i.e. Patrick and to the examination of that bishop."

Free churches were those not affiliated to any other church or monastic paruchiae and which were free from any current obligation to an overlord. For example, Armagh does not claim rights over Kildare.

The claims made by the church of Armagh were vast. However, there is a difference between making claims and gaining acceptance of them. Armagh set about engaging in a process of promoting her claims, employing all the tactics at her disposal.

How Armagh promoted her right to archiepiscopal authority

In the fifth century, Armagh lay in the territory of the Ulaid. But since then, the Ulaid had been displaced and was now considerably reduced in size. Armagh no longer lay within their territory. Politically, Armagh had lost importance during the contraction of the Ulaid. If Armagh were to survive as an important church it would need to recoup some ground. The Uí Néill dynasty was now the dominant power in Ireland and Armagh lay within its territory. Armagh needed the support of the most prominent political power and if possible the support of Rome.

The cynical may say that some seventh century developments were advantageous to Armagh's quest for recognition.

- The rise of the Uí Néill
- The Paschal Controversy
- The decline of the prestige of Iona

Evidence and propaganda

Armagh employed lawyers and hagiographers to supply the 'evidence' and propaganda for her claims.

Tírechán's *Brief Account* was useful. Tírechán's church had already affiliated itself to Armagh. He traces the geographical history of Patrick's mission. He gathers records of all the earliest places which were called *domnach*, identifying these as Patrician foundations. In his account, Patrick has either founded or blessed these churches while on a grand tour of Ireland. These churches then all owe their allegiance to Patrick's primary church at Armagh. The paruchiae is massive, with Tírechán "trying to establish a dossier of churches which he considers ought to belong to Armagh."[50] It incorporated the churches of Meath, Connacht, the Northern Uí Néill, as well as some in the Southern half of Ireland.

Small episcopal churches were isolated and vulnerable.[51] As Armagh became more powerful, affiliation to that church became more attractive.

Muirchú's *Life of Patrick* also served to promote the claims of Armagh. As we have seen, he wrote his *Life of Patrick* to associate Patrick with the Armagh church and to gain the support of the Uí Néill. The 'Tara story' was "designed to flatter the powerful"[52] and so gain their support. Similarly, the grant of Armagh by Dáire, and even the story of the death and burial of Patrick, all serve his purpose in illustrating the primacy of Armagh, attracting the support of the Uí Néill, and limiting the damage caused by the fact that Armagh did not possess the body of their saint.

Uí Néill and a rising church

The Uí Néill was the kin of Colmcille, but his paruchiae was losing prestige because of the strife and division caused by their position in the Paschal Controversy. Therefore the Uí Néill might well have been happy to associate themselves with a rising church. Armagh was in the territory of the Airthir, which was one of the nine petty kingdoms subordinate to the Uí Néill.

Recognition from Rome

Because Armagh's claims are being actively promoted during the time of the Paschal Controversy, some historians make a connection between the two. The Romani (Roman party) saw Patrick as one of their own; Cummian, for example, appeals to *"Noster Papa Patricius."* Some scholars argue that by adopting Roman usages in the Paschal controversy, Armagh could ensure that all churches in her paruchiae did likewise, hurrying the process of conformity in Ireland. Had Armagh not conformed, it would have been more difficult to assert her authority over the whole of Ireland. Hughes believes Armagh conformed to Roman usages before 688.[53] No doubt the influence of the church of Armagh was helpful to Rome and may in turn have gained Armagh the advantage of being recognised by Rome as a church of prominence in Ireland. In the view of Hughes, the adoption of *"Noster Patricius"* by the Roman party gave Armagh "an opportunity to reassert her claims to leadership",[54] possibly with support from Rome.

Developing a monastic system

Just as the monasteries were forming confederations and paruchiae of houses which all owed allegiance to one founder, so the church of Armagh employed a similar tactic. Ryan argues that the bishop of Armagh and the clerical community there had already adopted the monastic way of life before the end of the fifth century.[55] The leader of that church was also referred to as abbot and bishop of Armagh interchangeably. Hughes finds this adoption of the monastic life by the early episcopal sees a "most revolutionary change."[56] In this way the church of Armagh adopted a system of monastic *paruchiae*. She began to build up for herself a *paruchiae* of subject churches, which were not confined to the *tuath* in which Armagh was located.

Developing a system of over-lordship

While Armagh replicated monastic practices, she also mirrored the system of over-lordship used by the Uí Néill. The Uí Néill established themselves at Tara and claimed sovereignty over all Ireland. In reality they were dominant only in the northern part of Ireland. The stronghold of the Munster kings was at Cashel in Tipperary and they were in effect overlords of the southern part of the country. Nonetheless, Armagh tried to acquire a similar type of over-lordship.

- Just as over-kings in secular society claimed tribute from subordinate kings, so the coarb of Patrick had a right to tribute from the churches and monasteries in the paruchiae of Armagh.
- According to Brehon law, members of the upper classes could be accompanied by a retinue appropriate to their status. Brehon law also gives a bishop a higher honour price than a king. If a bishop visited another church on church business, he had the right to ask for hospitality for himself and a retinue of twelve men. The *Book of Armagh*, however, makes much greater claims to hospitality for the bishop of the church of Armagh. In one place the *Book of the Angel* tells us that:

  "the coarb of Patrick is to have a worthy and suitable hospitality for himself and his company to the number of fifty."

In another place the number entitled to hospitality is *"one hundred."*

This quite excessive claim to hospitality was made in order to emphasise the higher dignity and status of the bishop of Armagh. Should the hospitality be refused, a fine or seven years penance would be imposed.

In these ways the church of Armagh replicated the system of over-lordship that existed in secular society.

It is clear that the "Armagh lawyers were determined to extend the authority of their church, by using any arguments [or practices] which circumstances offered."[57] Therefore we can agree with Doherty that "the Armagh clergy were astute politicians."[58]

 PRACTICE ESSAY TITLE

Critically assess the view that the church of Armagh 'benefited from circumstances' in the seventh century. (20)

The strength of the claims of Armagh

It is very hard to imagine that at any time Armagh was given official authority over other churches. Tírechán seems to imply that Armagh did not always get the recognition she claimed. He laments that there were some *"who have taken away from Patrick what is his"*. There must have been some resistance to Armagh's claims over such a number of churches. In one instance Tírechán specifies that the paruchiae Colmcille and the church of Ardstraw were in competitive opposition to Armagh. Clonmacnois also encroached on the territory of Armagh. Nonetheless, by the eighth century, the ecclesiastical authority of Armagh was quite widely recognised. The interesting thing is that no other church made counter claims to authority on the grounds of Patrician association.

In the Additions to Tírechán's *Brief Account*, we see Aéd of Sletty accepting Ségéne of Armagh as his over-lord, and his successor, Conchad at Sletty, in turn accepting Flann Febla of Armagh as overlord. In the view of Hughes, "here at the end of the seventh century, there seems to have been a formal acknowledgement of over-lordship."[59]

The fifth century entries recorded in the *Annals of Ulster* refer to the bishops of Armagh listed there as the 'heirs' of Patrick. Carney and O'Rahilly both reject these as later interpolations.

Evidence supporting Armagh's claims

Tomás Ó Fiaich asserts that the strength of Armagh's claims lie in other supportive evidence.[60]

- Many early documents, for example the *Hymn of Secundinus*, refer to *"Noster Papa Patricius"* – Our Father Patrick, which, in the view of Ó Fiaich, suggests a kind of pre-eminence.

  Ó Fiaich also points to the appeal of Cummian in 632 to *Noster Papa Patricius* as the authority in support of Roman views. Cummian himself belonged to an entirely different confederation of churches. Ó Cróinín takes *Noster Papa Patricius* to mean 'our primate Patricius' and sees it as a "unique early witness to an honoured position for the saint north and south."[64] He does not, however, necessarily accept that the eminence given to Patrick was also to be given to Armagh.

- The Letter written by Pope John IV, concerning the Paschal Controversy in 640, places the name of Tomméne, bishop of Armagh, at the top of a list of eleven ecclesiastics. Ó Fiaich argues that "it bears witness to the fact that as early as 640, the letters or envoys to Rome accorded some kind of pre-eminence to Armagh ... the placing of his name [Tomméne] at the head of the list cannot be due to mere chance."[61] This may indicate some kind of recognition from Rome of Armagh's primacy, within a century and a half of Patrick.

Sharpe disputes this, arguing that Rome had been ill-informed about the hierarchy of the Irish Church and that the list merely reflects the order of signatories on the Letter received from Ireland, on which the "bishop of Armagh placed his own signature at the head of the list".[62]

Corish, however, is convinced that in the time of John IV, "The church of Armagh was accorded some kind of primacy which extended at least to the northern ecclesiastics to whom the letter was written."[63] It may have been that Armagh took the initiative among the northern churches to try to resolve the controversy over the dating of Easter.

- In addition, early canon law refers to the "bishop of bishops" and that matters of authority should be referred to "Rome or Patrick". No explicit mention of Armagh is made however. Nonetheless, when the church of Sletty was given over to Patrick, Aed goes to Armagh to do so.

- Armagh did possess the relics of Peter, Paul, Stephen and Laurence. These were apparently given by Rome in recognition of her position, perhaps when the Letter of John IV was delivered in 640. The relics were kept in the southern church in Armagh. Armagh did not, however, have the body of Patrick.

  The *Cain Patrick* (law of Patrick) shows the abbot of Armagh on visitation to other churches with the relics of Peter, Paul, Stephen and Laurence as an exercise of his authority over them and to exact the tax due to him.

- At the assembly of Birr, Flann, the abbot of Armagh (688–714), is placed at the top of a list of ecclesiastics there. Ó Fiaich indicates that this was at a time when Armagh was much overshadowed by the great monastic churches of Lismore, Clonmacnois and others. Yet still, the name of the bishop of Armagh appears before the names of these great abbots.[65]

- The *Hymn of Fiacc*, written around 800, speaks of Patrick's love for Armagh:

  "When Patrick was in sickness he desired to go to Armagh."

- The *Tripartite Life of Patrick* lists a number of place names around the area of Armagh, which show its connection to the saint.

Ó Fiaich concludes "that by the early seventh century, certainly by AD640, Armagh's pre-eminence was already recognised."[66]

While the list of supportive evidence suggested by the late Cardinal Tómás Ó Fiaich is impressive, all the evidence shares one common failing. Sharpe believes that although Ó Fiaich "has been rigorous in his criticism of them", the sources are only really indicative of the status of Armagh at the time in which they were written, that is, from the seventh to the ninth century. They do not tell us anything of her position from the fifth and sixth century.[67]

Ó Fiaich explains the lack of earlier evidence by suggesting that at this time the pre-eminent position of Armagh was taken for granted by all. There was no real need to restate her position. He also argues that there was no real opposition to Armagh's claims. The only dispute that we hear of is whether a particular church belonged to the paruchiae of Armagh or another church. Indeed, "None in the seventh century seems to suspect the Patrician origin of Armagh or its primacy."[67a]

However, it is clear that many of the sources on primacy of Armagh are a clear and unapologetic attempt to justify the claims of Armagh. There is no secular law tract that lends credence to the idea that Armagh was the highest court of ecclesiastical appeal. Furthermore, the order of signatures on the *Book of the Angel* is open to suspicion. The name of Patrick appears after that of Auxilius and the name of Benignus is with the name of Patrick, despite the fact that Patrick is several decades his senior. Nonetheless, although the origins of the claims of Armagh to primacy are "very obscure,"[68] "the main lines of the development do seem clear."[69]

 TASK

How valid are the claims made by Armagh? Make notes on the arguments and evidence you find most convincing both for and against the validity of the claims. Keep your notes for exam preparation.

Patrick and Armagh

The basis of the claims made by the Armagh church hinge on her association with Patrick, namely that Patrick founded his own church there and that church was his primary foundation.

Written evidence

The *Annals of Ulster* tell us that Patrick founded his church at Armagh in AD444. Patrick in his writings does not associate himself with any place in Ireland. The only place he names in Ireland is Silva Focluti. "If we had to depend solely on the saint's own writings, therefore, we should call him simply Patrick of Ireland, and nothing more."[70] However, Ó Fiaich argues that it would be wrong to think that Patrick was a wandering cleric with no fixed see, for such a practice would have been contravention of canon law.[71]

Archaeological evidence

We know that the church at Armagh was an early episcopal foundation. Archaeological work done in the Scotch Street area of the city has uncovered evidence

Saul has strong Patrician associations.

which might well support the references made in Muirchú to the Graveyard of the Martyrs. An underground spring was also discovered which might well be the one mentioned in the *Book of the Angel*, at which Patrick is reported to have baptised people. Although this evidence corresponds with the details of seventh and eighth century literature, it does not prove that Patrick himself was ever at Armagh.[72]

Downpatrick

Many scholars believe that "the evidence points to Downpatrick as the main focus of Patrick's activities."[73] Doherty, for example, believes that "the evidence linking Patrick with Armagh is slight ... evidence linking [Patrick] with anywhere is slight, but what evidence there is, points more in the direction of Saul and Downpatrick."[74] At least Downpatrick possessed the body of the saint. O'Rahilly argues that "we may dismiss the idea that Patrick was ever bishop of Armagh."[75] Carney agrees that "Patrick was never bishop of Armagh."[76]

Emhain Macha

A central argument in support of the tradition that Patrick founded Armagh is the proximity of Armagh to Emhain Macha. This was the capital of the kingdom of the Ulaid, among whom Patrick worked in the fifth century. As the capital of Ulster, it was a very important political centre. Binchy points out that, "it was the practice of all early missioners to set up their own headquarters as close as possible to the capital of the kingdom to which they were sent."[77] We do know from Patrick's own writings that he prioritised the conversion of nobility.

However, we cannot assume that Emhain Macha was still an important political centre at the time of Patrick.[78] This argument largely depends on the date of the destruction of Emhain Macha. Francis Byrne feels that Patrick did found the church of Armagh before the destruction of Emhain Macha, which may not have occurred until "as late as the mid fifth century".[79] Others argue that Emhain Macha was destroyed as early as 332, long before the mission of Patrick. It is unlikely that we will be able to conclusively prove the date of the destruction of Emhain Macha or that indeed Patrick did found his church close to it for politico-religious purposes.

Emhain Macha – the pagan sanctuary

Others argue that Armagh was not important for political reasons, but for religious ones. Anne Ross has claimed that Emhain Macha "is the only pagan Celtic sanctuary site, which we can identify with certainty."[80] Stancliffe believes Patrick's choice might have been a deliberate one in order to tackle paganism head on.[81] Sharpe believes that Armagh had long since forgotten its pagan past because another, earlier missionary had claimed it and the status of Emhain Macha as a religious cultic site had long since vanished.[82]

This view, however, does not gel with the evidence of Muirchú, which suggests that even in the seventh century, Armagh had not completely shaken free of its pagan past. In the Dáire story, there is a clear reference to the doe and its fawn which had taken up residence in the place on which Patrick wanted to build his church. Lambkin believes this to be a reference to a pagan cult of deer and the role of Dáire as guardian of a ritual site.[83] This reference, although rejected by Sharpe as fable, has a resonance of truth. It would not have been in the interests of Muirchú to acknowledge the still extant pagan culture around his saint's own church.

Place names and tradition

Ó Fiaich also points to the tradition of Patrick's Bell, Book and Crozier, which were preserved and handed on within the church of Armagh for over 700 years after Patrick's death.[84] In addition, he argues that the large number of place names in the locality of Armagh itself and throughout its archdiocese testify to Patrician association – such as Moneypatrick, Ardpatrick and Kilpatrick.

Emhain Macha outside Armagh city, was an important political and religious centre.

A sign at the entrance to Emhain Macha indicates its importance as a political site.

Ó Fiaich accepts that it is not possible to trace links between Patrick and Armagh back into the sixth century. As we have seen, no sixth century sources make mention of either Patrick or Armagh. However, as soon as Patrick is mentioned, "he appears as Patrick of Armagh." Ó Fiaich concludes that if "[Patrick] had been stolen by a church which had no right to him [it] shows either an amazing ingenuity in the Armagh clergy or an unsuspected gullibility in the whole Irish nation."[85] Binchy is clear "that St. Patrick, the British bishop, established his principal headquarters at Armagh seems to be as certain as anything can be in the confused history of the fifth century."[86]

In the final analysis, we must agree with Corish that "Armagh's ecclesiastical advance, is in its own right, a very complicated story indeed."[87]

 PRACTICE ESSAY TITLE

a) Appraise Armagh's claims to archiepiscopal authority. (30)

Your answer may include reference to the following:
- The *Book of the Angel*
- The rise of the Uí Néill
- The Paschal Controversy
- Strengths and weaknesses of the claim
- The views of scholars

b) Critically assess the view that it is difficult to separate the name of Patrick from Armagh. (20)

Your answer may include reference to the following:
- The evidence from the annals
- The importance of Emhain Macha
- Muirchú's *Life of Patrick*
- The views of scholars

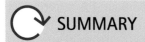

SUMMARY

During the seventh century, the church of Armagh began to promote the idea that she was a pre-eminent church with authority over other churches.

⬇

The claims she made are to be found in the *Book of the Angel*, presented as favours granted to Patrick by an angel.

⬇

The Armagh church employed hagiographers to bolster its claims and the reputation of its saint.

⬇

Armagh began to replicate the organisation of the monasteries and the system of overlordship used by the Uí Néill.

⬇

Armagh capitalised on circumstances of the day to further her own position, eg the ascendancy of the Uí Néill and the weakening of Iona. Armagh "flattered the powerful" to get their support.

⬇

A range of sources indicate a primacy of sorts for Armagh, but most of them are of a late date.

⬇

The claim to primacy is based on the church of Armagh's status as Patrick's own church.

⬇

Although Patrick makes no mention of it, Armagh's proximity to Emhain Macha could suggest that he chose it for political and religious reasons.

⬇

There can be no definitive proof that Patrick founded Armagh and it seems unlikely that the church there was given formal authority over other churches. But it is a tradition of long standing, and one without serious challenge or counter claim, which has persisted to the present day.

Endnotes

[1] Kenney, *The Sources for the Early History of Ireland, op cit*, p211

[2] Hughes, *The Celtic Church and the Papacy, op cit*, p10

[3] Colgrave & Mynors, *op cit*, p126

[4] McNeill, *The Celtic Churches, op cit*, p49

[5] Colgrave & Mynors (ed), *Bede's Ecclesiastical History of the English People*, Clarendon Press, Oxford, 1969

[5a] Cummian was abbot of Durrow.

[6] Some historians argue that 663 is a more accurate dating for the Synod of Whitby.

[7] Colgrave & Mynors (ed), *op cit*, xxxiv

[8] All quotations are taken from the above translation.

[9] James, E, *Bede and the Tonsure Question* in Peritia 3 1984, p13

[10] Cited in Colgrave & Mynors, *op cit*, 348

[11] Walsh & Bradley, *A History of the Irish Church 400-700 AD*, Columba Press, Dublin, 1991, p165

[12] Hughes, *The Church in Early Irish Society, op cit*, p110

[13] *ibid*, p 111

[14] McNeill, *Celtic Churches, op cit*, p117

[15] Hughes, *The Celtic Church and the Papacy*, p21

[16] Hughes, *Early Christian Ireland: an introduction to the Sources, op cit*, pp76–77

[17] McNeill, *Celtic Churches, op cit* p114

[18] Cowdrey, HEJ, *Popes, Monks and Crusaders* in Bede and the English People

[19] Gough Meissner JL, *The Celtic Church of England after the Synod of Whitby*, London, 1929, pp134–181

[20] McNeill, *Churches, op cit*, p109

[21] Hughes, *The Celtic Church and the Papacy*, p17

[22] Stenton, F, *Anglo-Saxon England*, Clarendon Press, Oxford, 1947, p114

[23] Smyth, AP, *op cit*, p137

[24] Hughes, *Church in Early Irish Society, op cit*, p103

[25] Rees, R, 'An Essay on the Welsh Saints', London 1836, pp289, 292; Kerr, WS, *The Independence of the Celtic Church in Ireland*, London, 1931

[26] Gougaud, *Christianity in Christian Lands, op cit*, p213

[27] Hardinge, *op cit*, p18

[28] Chadwick, N, *Studies in the Early British Church*, London, Cambridge University Press 1958, p14

[29] Gougaud, *Christianity in Christian Lands, op cit*, pp212–216

[30] Lloyd, JE, *A History of Wales*, Benn's Sixpenny Library, London, 1930, p 173

[31] Bede's *Ecclesiastical History, op cit*, Book 111, 25

[32] Lloyd, *op cit*, pp15–16

[33] Deanesly, M, *The Pre-Conquest Church in England*, London,1961, p83

[34] Gougaud, *op cit*, p210

[35] Lloyd, *op cit*, pp15–16

[36] Lang, A, *A History of Scotland Vol. 11*, Edinburgh 1890, p34

[37] McNeill, *Celtic Churches, op cit*, p109

[38] Hughes, *The Celtic Church and the Papacy, op cit*, p18

[39] Hardinge, *op cit*, p207

[40] Hardinge takes use of this word to indicate proof of his view that the Celtic Church at this time was indeed schismatic and heretical. (Hardinge, *op cit*, pp18–28)

[41] *ibid*, p201

[42] Hardinge, *op cit*, p207

[43] This is the view expressed by K Hughes in a number of her books.

[44] Hughes, *Introduction to A History of Medieval Ireland, op cit*, p 21

[45] Hughes, *The Church in Early Irish Society, op cit*, p89

[46] *ibid*, p20

[47] Hughes, *Early Christian Ireland: an introduction to the Sources, op cit*, p253

[48] Sharpe, R, *St. Patrick and the see of Armagh*, Cambridge Medieval Celtic Studies, 4, 1982, p35

[49] Binchy, *Patrick and His Biographers, op cit*, p166

[50] Doherty, C, 'The Cult of St Patrick and the cult of Armagh in the seventh century,' ed JM Picard, *Ireland and Northern France AD600–850*, Four

Courts Press, Dublin, 1991, p64

51 This was the period of the deadly plagues to which lone episcopal churches were especially vulnerable.

52 Doherty, 'The Cult of St Patrick and the cult of Armagh in the seventh century,' *op cit*, p86

53 Hughes, *The Church in Early Irish Society, op cit*, p116

54 *ibid*, p119

55 Ryan, *Irish Monasticism, op cit*, p101

56 Hughes, *The Church in Early Irish Society, op cit*, p83

57 Hughes, *The Church in Early Irish Society, op cit*, p119

58 Doherty, *op cit*, p68

59 Hughes, *Church in Early Irish Society, op cit*, p86

60 Ó Fiaich, T, *St. Patrick and Armagh* in Irish Ecclesiastical Record, 89, 1958, pp153–170

61 *ibid*, p161

62 Sharpe, *St Patrick and the see of Armagh, op cit*, p49

63 Corish, *The Christian Mission, op cit*, pp 25–26

64 Ó Cróinín, *op cit*, p161

65 *ibid*, p162

66 *ibid*, p169

67 Sharpe, *op cit*, pp33–59

67a Ó Fiaich, *op cit*, p164

68 Gougaud, *op cit*, p226

69 Corish, *The Christian Mission, op cit*, p30

70 Ó Fiaich, *op cit*, p15

71 St Patrick and Armagh, IER March 1958, pp153–154

72 Ó Cróinín, *op cit*, p155

73 *ibid*

74 Doherty, *op cit*, p72

75 O'Rahilly, *op cit*, p67

76 Carney, *The Problem of Patrick, op cit*, pxi

77 Binchy, *Patrick and His Biographers, op cit*, p148

78 Sharpe, *op cit*, p52

79 Byrne, F, *Irish Kings and High Kings*, London 1973

80 Ross, A, *Pagan Celtic Britain*, London 1967, pp151–152

81 Stancliffe, C, *Kings and Conversions: Some comparisons between the Roman mission to England and Patrick's mission to Ireland*, Frühmittelalterliche Studien, 14 1980, p64

82 Sharpe, *op cit*, p55

83 Lambkin, BK, *Patrick, Armagh and Emain Macha* in Emania No 2, 1987, p30

84 Binchy, D, 'The Background of early Irish Literature', in *Studia Hibernica* 1, Colaiste Phadraig, 1961, p19

85 *St Patrick and Armagh* IER, March 1958, p170

86 Binchy, *The Background of early Irish Literature, op cit*, pp15–16

87 Corish, *The Christian Mission, op cit*, p32

Glossary

Abbatial – where an abbot governs or leads the Church.

Abbot – the leader of a monastery.

Anamchara – a person to whom Celtic Christians confessed their sin. He was a spiritual advisor whose role was to walk beside the sinner on his/her Christian journey.

Anchoritical – a strict separation of oneself from secular society in order to pursue a religious life/practices.

Apostate – those who abandon their religion for unworthy reasons.

Apostolic – in the sense of Celtic monasticism, this means to engage in ministry and mission.

Archepiscopacy/Archepiscopal – to have leadership as an arch bishop over other bishops and diocese.

Arianism – a heresy in the early Church, named after the teaching of the fourth century presbyter Arius, which taught that the Son of God was neither fully God, nor eternal.

Asceticism – a lifestyle of self-denial, particularly of worldly pleasures such as alcohol or sexual relations, in order to attain spiritual/religious goals.

Austerity – severity of a way of life, extreme strictness, harsh discipline.

Baptism – a Christian sacrament which admits a person as a member of the Church. It is thought that in the Celtic Church the rite of Baptism differed in some way from that of the 'Roman Church'.

Barbarian – an uncivilised, uncultured person, or a nation with an inferior level of civilization.

Barbarous – cruel, warlike insensitive person/people whose behaviour is unacceptable in civilised society.

Bishop – church leader in charge of a diocese.

Cenobitical – monastic tradition which stressed community of life. It is usually regulated by a religious rule. It is commonly thought to have begun in Egypt in the fourth century.

Conservative – the favouring of traditional religious, cultural or national beliefs. It can also mean reluctance to change or to reform, or to want to achieve change slowly.

Contrary – used in the context of penance to mean opposite.

Controversy – argument, dispute or disagreement – for example, the Paschal Controversy arose out of a dispute or disagreement about the dating of Easter.

Conversion – the act of becoming a religious believer or becoming much more committed to the religious life/faith.

Crosfigil – the act of praying with arms outstretched for long periods of time as an act of mortification carried out by Celtic monks.

Dál Riata – an Irish/Celtic over kingdom on the western seaboard of Scotland. Some historians believe that it was an Irish colony in Scotland, others disagree. They also had some territory on the northern coast of Ireland. It reached its height under Aedán 574–608. The kingdom disappeared in the Viking Age.

Deacon – a role in the church associated with service. It was a religious office under or subordinate to that of priest.

Desert Fathers – Christian hermits and monks who lived mainly in the deserts of Egypt, in and around the beginning of the third century. The solitude of the desert attracted them and was a means of learning self-discipline. One example was St Pachomius.

Episcopal/Episcopacy – relating to bishops and the system of church government whereby the church was divided into dioceses which were overseen by a bishop.

Eremitical – the lifestyle of a hermit or person who lived in seclusion and/or isolation from society for religious and spiritual reasons. It comes from the Greek word *erémos* or desert. This form of monastic life was practised before the cenobitical form.

Eschatology – comes from the Greek, *Eschatos* meaning 'last' and *logy* meaning 'the study of'. It is a part of theology and philosophy concerned with the final events in the history of the world, commonly referred to as the end of the world.

Evangelism – the Christian practice of trying to make converts.

Excommunication – the act of expelling someone from membership of the Church.

Fasting – a means of asserting one's rights in Celtic society; a penance frequently prescribed by an *anamchara*; an ascetic practice performed within Celtic monasteries.

Fosterage – the practice of sending a child to another family to be educated, to work or to learn a trade, usually for one year. In Christian Ireland, children were often sent to monasteries under this custom.

Genre – a style or type of literature, for example, hagiography.

Grace – God's goodness to people.

Hagiography – writings about holy people. Comes from the Greek word (h)*agious* (holy) and *graphe* (writing). It was considered to be an important type of writing in the early Christian Church. It became increasingly popular in the seventh century Celtic Church.

Heathen – a term used by Patrick to describe the Irish, meaning they did not believe in God, but was also probably referring to the practices/beliefs of their pagan religion.

Heresy – comes from the Greek ρεσις, *hairesis* (from ρέομαι, *haireomai*, meaning 'choose'), which means either a *choice* of beliefs or a *faction* of believers. It means to deny an essential part of the truth of a religion, for example, in the case of the Arian heresy, the oneness of God and Jesus was denied.

Historical reliability – the notion of how trustworthy a source can be.

Historicity – historical reality and reliability.

Hospitality – the provision of food and shelter to visitors or travellers. The Celts were obliged by law to provide hospitality to people before asking their business. Monasteries also carried out this custom.

Idol – false god.

Idolatry – worshipping false gods.

Internal evidence – evidence found inside; for example, Patrick's writings or other texts attributed to him, usually in connection with the date or authorship of these.

Kingship – an institution/set of laws and customs in Celtic society relating to the position, role and succession of Irish kings.

Kinship – the laws and customs pertaining to the role of family in Celtic society.

Liberation theology – the theology of using sociology and economics to understand poverty; focuses on Jesus as the liberator of the oppressed.

Lough Derg – renowned in Irish Christian tradition since the time of St Patrick. It has been a place of pilgrimage continuously for well over 1000 years.

Miracle – an act of wonder which cannot be explained logically, eg a healing. A common feature of hagiographical writing.

Monasticism – derived from Greek *monos* meaning alone. It is the religious practice in which one renounces worldly pursuits in order to fully devote one's life to spiritual pursuits. It is governed by the vows of poverty, chastity and obedience.

Mortification – a simple expression of mortification would be, for example, denying oneself certain pleasures, such as abstaining from chocolate, meat, food (generally fasting). It can also be practised by choosing a simple or even impoverished lifestyle such as that lived by the Celtic monks. In some of its more severe forms, it can mean causing self-inflicted pain or discomfort. This too, was practised by some of the Celtic monks. It is believed that it was a means of bringing the body to obedience in order to achieve a more fulfilled spiritual state.

Narrative – an account or story, for example, the *Confessio* as the story of Patrick's spiritual life.

Neophyte – means beginner. It often refers to a newly-ordained priest, a person who recently took a monastic vow, or a new convert to the religion.

Panegyric – a speech or writing in high praise of a person. The intention may have been to inspire an audience to emulate the glorious deeds or qualities of the person. It is most commonly used to refer to Celtic hagiographical writing.

Pelagianism – is a theological theory named after Pelagius. It denies that humanity needs the grace of God in order to be saved. Humans are responsible for their own destiny.

Penance – traditionally, penance has been viewed as a punishment (the Latin *poena*, the root of pen(it)ance, means 'punishment'). Generally speaking, however, it describes the works of satisfaction imposed or recommended by the priest on or to the penitent. The Celtic monks perceived these to be a cure for the sickness of sin.

Penitential – is a book or set of church rules concerning the sacrament of Penance that was first developed by Celtic monks in the sixth century AD. They compiled lists of sins and corresponding remedies.

Peregrinatio – the pilgrimage for Christ undertaken by Celtic monks.

Presbyter – a church leader below the rank of bishop, also called an elder or priest.

Prologue – an introduction to a piece of work.

Purpose – the reason suggested for the writing of a book, or letter.

Relic – an object or a personal item of religious significance, carefully preserved with an air of veneration.

Repentance – expressing sorrow for sin.

Rite – a religious ceremony or observance.

Roman Empire – refers to the ancient Roman civilisation and a large expanse of territorial holdings in Europe and the Mediterranean. Ireland was not part of the Roman Empire.

Rustic – simple, countrified person, without sophistication. A term used by Patrick to refer to himself and/or his mission.

Schismatic – breaking away from the Church.

Solidi – a Roman coin referred to by Patrick which had gone out of circulation by the last part of the fifth century and used by some scholars as part of the body of internal evidence to date Patrick's mission.

Surety – a system of guarantee in Celtic society.

Synod – a council of bishops, other clergy and sometimes lay people.

Tonsure – is the practice of cutting the hair of clerics or holy people as a symbol of their renunciation of worldly fashion and esteem. The Celtic tonsure was an issue raised at the Synod of Whitby.

Tribute Paying – a gift or a payment made to recognise the authority and superiority of a leader.

Tuath – (plural *tuatha*) is often translated as 'people, tribe or nation'. *Tuath* referred to both the people who lived in a shared territory, and the territory they controlled. *Tuatha* have often been described as petty kingdoms or clans but could also have ranged to a much larger sovereign kingdom such as the Ulaid.

Uí Néill – Irish and Scottish dynasties descending from Niall of the Nine hostages. The term Uí Néill did not come into use until the reign of the grandsons and great grandsons of Niall. Dynasties descended from Niall held power in Ulster until 1603 and their defeat in the Nine Years War.

Ulaid – were a people of early north-eastern Ireland who gave their name to the modern province of Ulster. Their capital was traditionally at Navan Fort.

Vision – a spiritual experience or message believed to have come from God.

Index